Marital and Family Therapy

Marital and Family Therapy

Second Edition

Ira D. Glick, M.D.,
Professor of Psychiatry,
Cornell University Medical College;
Associate Medical Director for Inpatient Services,
Payne Whitney Clinic,
The New York Hospital—Cornell Medical Center,
New York, New York

David R. Kessler, M.D.,
Associate Clinical Professor of Psychiatry,
School of Medicine,
University of California, San Francisco;
Staff Psychiatrist,
Langley Porter Psychiatric Institute,
San Francisco, California

With a Foreword by **Theodore Lidz, M.D.**
Sterling Professor of Psychiatry Emeritus
Yale University School of Medicine
New Haven, Connecticut

27721

Grune & Stratton, Inc.
A Subsidiary of Harcourt Brace Jovanovich, Publishers
NEW YORK   LONDON   TORONTO   SYDNEY   SAN FRANCISCO

Library of Congress Cataloging in Publication Data

Glick, Ira D.   1935–

   Marital and family therapy.

   Includes bibliographical references and indexes.
   1. Family psychotherapy.   2.   Marital
psychotherapy.   I.   Kessler, David R., joint
author.   II.   Title.
RC488.5.G54   1980   616.89′156   80-12692
ISBN 0-8089-1232-1

   Grune & Stratton, Inc.
   111 Fifth Avenue
   New York, New York 10003

   Distributed in the United Kingdom by
   Academic Press, Inc. (London) Ltd.
   24/28 Oval Road, London NW 1

   Library of Congress Catalog Number 80-12692
   International Standard Book Number 0-8089-1232-1

   Printed in the United States of America

To Our Families

Contents

Tables and Figures

Acknowledgments

We wish to thank a variety of individuals and families who have helped to make this book possible.

First, our own families of origin, Bernard and Gertrude Glick and Benjamin and Thelma Kessler, who, in addition to steadfastly attempting to socialize us, provided us with our first major models of family structure and function. Second, our teachers, Theodore Lidz and Thomas Detre, at the Yale University Department of Psychiatry, Irwin Greenberg at Hillside Hospital, New York City, and Alan Leveton at the Mt. Zion Hospital, San Francisco, who, by their concern and enthusiasm, first helped to stir our interest in family study and treatment and provided us with a family model of understanding human functioning. Third, our colleagues in family therapy, especially Henry Lennard and Jay Haley, who, by their stimulating and provocative comments, tried their best to keep us honest. Fourth, our trainees, with whom we have been privileged to work on the teaching–learning process in family therapy. It is they who have had the courage to ask the critical questions about the field, and it was for them that much of the didactic material in this textbook was formulated and used in courses we have taught both here and at other institutions.

Finally, a special word of thanks to those of our students and colleagues who took the time to read and comment on what was then a fairly raw first draft, and who offered invaluable critical comments and suggestions for change. They include Dan Dinaburg, Leon Epstein, Stephen Fleck, Jay Haley, Jacob Katzow, Alan Leveton, Michael Peterson, Donald Ransom, and Carlos Sluzki. Of course, we take sole responsibility for the end results.

In addition, a number of people helped in preparing the manuscript. They include Judi Yabamoto, Barbara Lee, and Mary Hargreaves, for patiently typing the drafts of the manuscript; Jon Showstack for a variety of assistance; Margo Showstack for her help in preparing the index; and Mary Ann Esser for her valuable work in editing the manuscript.

Special thanks are also due to the United States Public Health Service for support of Dr. Glick from July 1971 to June 1973 when he was a career teacher of the National Institute of Mental Health, MH-12450, and spent part of that time working on this book.

For the preparation of this edition, we wish to thank Betty Scott for a superlative secretarial and editing job; John Patten and the residents of the Department of Psychiatry of the Cornell University Medical College for reviewing the manuscript; the members of our departments at Cornell and the University of California at San Francisco for extending help and cooperaticn; and both readers and reviewers of the first edition for their suggestions.

Most of all, we are indebted to the families whom we have treated. They have patently demonstrated the complexity of individual and family functioning and made it obvious that problems of families do not fit neatly into any one theoretical framework.

Foreword

Five years ago I had the privilege of writing the foreword to the first edition of this book and welcoming the first proper and much needed text in the relatively new field of family therapy. I recommended the book enthusiastically and predicted that it would enjoy a wide readership and many future editions as the field advanced. The book has not only been widely read but has become the standard introductory text for teaching family therapy. The field has advanced, and the new edition keeps pace with the latest developments and reflects the increased maturity of the field.

The preparation of a first text for a subject presents its authors with the formidable problems of assembling material and of organizing and selecting topics without the opportunity to lean upon earlier authors and to crib from them. Drs. Glick and Kessler managed the task superbly, writing clearly and concisely and with a deceptive simplicity that reflected their mastery of the topic and an awareness of what students need to know and what they can assimilate before they have extensive clinical experience. Although it is a criticism I rarely make as I cherish conciseness, the first edition seemed too brief. Now the authors have not simply added new sections but fleshed out their presentation with additional well-chosen clinical material. Other books about family and marital therapy have appeared in the past five years, including a few excellent works—Murray Bowen's *Family Therapy in Clinical Practice*, Minuchin's *Families and Family Therapy*, Napier and Whittaker's *The Family Crucible*, and Selvini's *Paradox and Counterparadox*—but these are works by innovators and are not always suited for the beginner. In *Marital and Family Therapy* we are offered a balanced and carefully planned approach. I found myself again admiring the authors' method of presentation, their selection of material, and their ability to remember that they were writing an introductory text and to forego the narcissistic gratifications of displaying their consummate knowledge of the field.

Some readers, probably more teachers than students, will consider the approach conservative. It does not promulgate innovative concepts or techniques; its creativity derives from the sorting out of diverse approaches introduced by persons of divergent training, ideologies, and personalities and from integrating them into a coherent presentation. The conservativism is not only appropriate in an introductory text but also needed in this therapeutic approach in which there has been a plethora of innovative techniques, some impractical, some unbridled, and some highly manipulative. Therapists have often impatiently sought shortcuts in promoting changes in personality functioning through changing family transactions without adequate appreciation of the strong forces that foster pattern maintenance in the family.

The authors properly do not consider methods and techniques alone but seek to establish an adequate foundation in family structure and dynamics for the future therapist. They recognize that the family not only forms a true small group in which the action of any member affects all, but that it has very special characteristics because of the prolonged and intense relationships between its members, because it is divided into two generations and two sexes, and because of the interrelated functions it serves for the couple who marry, for the children born into it, and for the society in which it exists. Although a marital or family therapist requires substantial knowledge of personality development and functioning on the one hand, and of larger social systems on the other, the authors confine themselves, as they must, to marriage and the family and assume that the student will have gained such knowledge elsewhere.

The authors take a broad view of marital and family therapy, rather than limiting themselves to the consideration of conjoint therapy. Taken in the broadest sense, family therapy can include any form of treatment that takes the import and impact of family transactions into account when considering the etiology and treatment of personality disorders. Only one person—the patient, a parent or a spouse—may be in actual treatment, but the focus is upon changing the family interaction; or the various members of the family may each be treated individually; or all members of the family may be seen together in a group together with members of other families. However, the focus of the book is, as it should be, primarily on conjoint family therapy. It requires careful judgment to know when it is preferable to work with the designated patient and his or her internalizations of family members, when with the family or marital partner conjointly, and when with multiple couples or families in a group. The authors offer judicious, nondogmatic opinions that provide guidance for reaching such decisions.

The authors review the more widely used and most widely promulgated of the many different types of family therapy that have emerged, but rather than giving lengthy descriptions of a variety of techniques or promoting one above the other, they sensibly seek to instruct the student in three basic therapeutic strategies: the facilitation of communication of thoughts and feelings between family members; the attempt to shift disturbed, inflexible roles and coalitions; and the therapist's use of himself of herself as a family role model, educator, and demythologizer. Family therapy is a difficult therapeutic technique that has all too often been undertaken by persons with little, if any, experience in working with individuals or with meaningful groups. Inexperienced therapists can inadvertently promote disorganization of an individual or of a family because of their countertransference to a family member, their transference of their own family problems into the situation, their exasperation with the rigidities or lack of empathy of family members, their shock at the cruelties that may go on within a family, their narcissistic needs, or simply lack of recognition of their own limitations, as well as in still other ways. The book recognizes that any form of therapy that can promote significant change in the individual or family can also misfire and cause harm. It provides the basic knowledge the future therapist needs before entering into supervised work with couples or families, and it emphasizes the importance of supervised clinical experience in addition to didactic instruction. The field as a whole, as well as those entering it and those teaching it, has greatly benefited from the first edition of this well-tempered work, and this new edition will consolidate the book's position as the major basic text for teaching family therapy.

Theodore Lidz, M.D.
Sterling Professor of Psychiatry Emeritus
Yale University of Medicine
New Haven, Connecticut

Preface

Since the publication of the first edition of this book we have been gratified by the response of both readers and reviewers, as well as by its adoption by some teachers as the standard introductory text. The original book has now gone through a number of printings. Because of the growth of the field, as well as suggestions received, we have decided that this is an opportune time to expand and amplify the text. In doing so, we believed that it would be best to use our previous framework, adding sections and at the same time substantially revising others.

In this book we have included a chapter on the past, present, and future of the family; and throughout this edition we focus on alternative family styles, such as single-parent families. We have enlarged the presentation of the family life cycle based on recent works published by several authors. The section on treatment has been broadened to include the approaches of some well-known family therapists. More detail has been provided with respect to the *basic* strategies and techniques of treatment, and a new chapter about supplementary strategies and techniques has been added. There are new topics in Chapter 12, "Family Treatment and Specific Psychiatric Disorders," which has been thoroughly revised based, in part, on a new edition of the American Psychiatric Association's *Diagnostic and Statistical Manual of Mental Disorders*. The reader will now find a chapter discussing the use of marital therapy in conjunction with sex therapy. New chapters have been added on brief family therapy and on the relationship of the family to other systems such as the legal and judicial system. The chapter "Results of Family Therapy" has been completely rewritten, and an entire chapter is now devoted to the transcript and comments of chronological excerpts from a family in therapy. We have also added considerably to the number of clinical vignettes and examples. In addition the references for each chapter have been updated.

Past readers have been very helpful and generous with their comments for revisions. We also invite the readers of this edition to write with their suggestions so that we can continue to make this book as helpful and practical as possible.

Preface to the First Edition

Marital and family therapy has evolved so rapidly from its inception 15 years ago that practitioners and teachers have "future shock." What seemed standard then seems questionable now. It seems appropriate, therefore, to summarize our knowledge of theory and techniques in the field at this time and to offer beginning students an introductory textbook that will provide some overall fundamentals on which to build. Our hope is: 1) to present some of the core concepts relevant to an understanding of families; 2) to offer a frame of reference for planning and carrying out family therapy strategies; and 3) to summarize some current research on family process and treatment.

We have found in teaching about marital and family therapy that certain questions are asked repeatedly, such as: How does family therapy compare with other psychotherapies in theory, technique, and results? What kinds of family situations do best with family therapy, and which present serious obstacles? And what kinds of change can be expected in individuals and in family systems as a result of family therapy? We think the reader of this book will develop some understandng of the issues raised by these questions.

This book is intended for beginning students in a variety of professional helping disciplines including psychiatry, medicine, psychology, social work, the ministry, law, corrections, and education. Marital and family problems are major aspects of the work in such fields, and some knowledge of and experience with the basic principles of dealing with them should help promote increased competence and confidence.

In this book we have tried to present some of the major principles of the field. To accomplish this, we have selectively distilled a few basic elements from a large and, at times, untidy pool of ideas. Although we have tried to focus on those concepts relating most specifically to a family systems framework, we have also included other models where they seem conceptually and practically useful.

Our intention is to educate rather than to advocate. Clearly the ideas presented here are those we feel will be most useful to a beginner in the field, but their inclusion, to the exclusion of others, should not be interpreted as a fixed, final, qualitative assessment. Rather we hope the family therapist will utilize the concepts presented herein as a point of departure and growth. Education is the process that helps the students to practice better family therapy and information is the tool to enable them to do so. Therapists will use their sense organs to detect the cries of distress and, in time, will arrive at the personal amalgam of concepts and techniques that seem most viable.*

We realize that a textbook alone will not suffice to give a complete picture of family therapy. There is, obviously, no substitute for observing and working with actual families in trouble. We hope that what we do offer here will equip the beginning family worker to feel more competent and comfortable in observing, understanding, and treating those families who need help.

Finally, a word of caution. Marital and family treatment uses relatively new techniques. This entire field is in its infancy. Therefore, despite the humanism, strong enthusiasm, and conviction of workers in the field, students should be scientifically skeptical regarding the diverse basic hypotheses of family therapy and evaluation of its methods and results.

We do not claim any blinding originality for this book. We have, indeed, unashamedly borrowed extensively from our teachers, our colleagues, and our students; but we take full responsibility for having organized and selected the materials presented.

*Ingelfinger F: Advertising: Informational but not educational. N Engl J Med 286:1319, 1972

A Guide for Using the Text

Since this book is intended to serve as an introductory textbook for individuals at different training levels and orientations, complex situations and their complex sequential management have been oversimplified and compressed. We realize this may be a disadvantage for the more advanced therapist and so have included up-to-date references, but the book probably will be most helpful when used with ongoing supervision or with an ongoing course, since case examples and interventions are written in bare-bone detail in order to make one or two teaching points at a time.

We recommend that the beginner read the text chronologically, although obviously the more experienced clinician initially may prefer to read particular sections or chapters only.

Contributors

Helen M. Blau, Ph.D.,
Assistant Professor,
Department of Pharmacology,
Stanford University School of Medicine,
Palo Alto, California

Carl S. Burak, M.D., J.D.,
Assistant Clinical Professor,
Department of Psychiatry,
School of Medicine,
University of California,
San Francisco, California

Suzanne Currie, O.T.R.,
Nedlands
Western, Australia

Edward Gould, Ph.D.,
Associate Clinical Professor,
Department of Psychiatry,
Langley Porter Psychiatric Institute,
University of California,
San Francisco, California

Contributors

Sheila H. Greenberg, R.N.,
Clinical Nurse III,
Department of Psychiatry,
Langley Porter Psychiatric Institute,
University of California,
San Francisco, California

Robert S. Hoffman, M.D.,
Assistant Clinical Professor,
Department of Psychiatry,
School of Medicine,
University of California,
San Francisco, California

George R. Johnson, M.S.W.,
Lecturer,
Department of Psychiatry,
Langley Porter Psychiatric Institute,
University of California,
San Francisco, California

Harvey S. Kaplan, M.D.,
Chief of Pediatrics,
Chope Community Hospital,
San Mateo, California;
Clinical Assistant Professor of Pediatrics,
Stanford University,
School of Medicine,
Palo Alto, California

Earl Pope,
Architect,
Professor of Environmental Design,
Hampshire College,
Amherst, Massachusetts

Gail J. Saliterman, Ph.D., J.D.,
Attorney,
Long and Levit,
San Francisco, California

Patricia R. Underwood, R.N., D.N.Sc.,
Clinical Nurse V,
Inpatient Treatment and Research Service,
Langley Porter Psychiatric Institute;
Associate Clinical Professor,
Department of Psychiatry,
Department of Mental Health and Community Nursing,
School of Nursing,
School of Medicine,
University of California,
San Francisco, California

Sanford R. Weimer, M.D., M.P.H.,
Director, Consultation/Liaison Service,
San Francisco General Hospital;
Assistant Professor,
University of California,
San Francisco, California

Susan Williams, M.A., O.T.R., A.T.R.,
Occupational Therapist and Director,
ISIS: A Creative Work Program,
San Francisco, California

Marital and Family Therapy

Portrait of a Man and His Wife, artist unknown, late 5th Dynasty circa 2500 B.C., Egypt. Courtesy of Honolulu Academy of Arts, purchase, 1937.

1

The Field of Marital and Family Therapy: Development and Definition

OBJECTIVES

- To understand the historical development of family therapy
- To define what family therapy is (and what it is not) and to compare it to individual and group therapy

INTRODUCTION

Although the fields of marital and family treatment are relatively young, there is nothing particularly new about the overall significance of marriage and the family.* It probably does not require any specific training or knowledge to perceive that these are important human systems and that they are different in several essential ways from other types of human groups and relationships.

Most people would likely agree that marriages and families perform vital tasks for the individuals involved, and for society at large. It has long been a commonsense view that we are all shaped in major ways by what we have experienced in our original families (see the reprinted example following this) and

*To avoid unnecessary duplication, the word "family" (as in "family therapy," "family system," and "family unit," etc.) will often be used instead of the more cumbersome terms of "marital and family." In those instances in which we wish to refer to marital issues specifically, only the word "marital" will be used. Similarly, the words "family therapy" and "family treatment" generally also refer to the field of "family counseling," since the distinctions between the fields are not well delineated and there seems to be considerable overlap.

that what occurs in our current marital or family system is, for most people, the prime element in our general sense of well being and functioning.

Father Sentenced to Dinners. (Topsfield, Mass.) Oct. 25 (UPI). The father of a 16-year-old accused shoplifter is serving a 30-day sentence—of dinners at home. A Salem district judge, Samuel E. Zoll, ordered the father of a Masconomet Regional High School student to be home between 5 and 7 P.M. every night. Judge Zoll said the father should "be at home for a meal where he could sit down and talk with the family."[1]

Clearly, individual family units are different from one another, and some seem to function better or are happier than others. Many helping professionals in the past two decades have begun to examine, using fresh approaches, the processes and circumstances that lead to family distress. They have attempted to devise techniques in order to alleviate distress and increase functioning. In the following chapters we will discuss some basic concepts and techniques associated with family therapy. At this point, however, we will offer a brief review of the emergence of this field, followed by a delineation of its scope.

DEVELOPMENT OF THE FAMILY THERAPY FIELD

Although exciting, innovative, and seemingly useful in helping families with problems in living, family therapy can be confusing at times. It may seem hard to understand the fundamentals of the field and to distinguish them from the personal styles of charismatic family therapists. Similarly, it may seem difficult to synthesize a coherent family theory from different fields, such as psychology, psychiatry, sociology, psychoanalysis, game theory, communication theory, Gestalt therapy, and the like. How did this state of affairs come about?

The significance attributed to the family's role in relation to the psychic and social distress of any of its members has waxed and waned over the centuries. The important role of the family in the development of individual problems was mentioned by Confucius in his writings, as well as by the Greeks in their myths. The early Hawaiians would meet as a family to discuss solutions to an individual's problem. For a long time in our own culture, however, what we now call mental illness and other forms of interpersonal distress were ascribed to magical, religious, physical, or exclusively intrapsychic factors. It was not until the turn of this century, however, that Freud delineated individual psychodynamics as determinants of human behavior. Although he stressed the major role of the family in the development of individual symptoms, he believed that the most effective technique for dealing with such individual psychopathology was treatment on a one-to-one basis.[2] At about this same time, others working with the mentally ill began to suggest that families with a sick member should be seen together and not "as individuals removed from family relationships."[3] Also psychiatric social workers in child guidance clinics, who often saw one or more parent individually or together, began to recognize the importance of dealing with the entire family unit.

In the 1930s a psychoanalyst reported his experience in treating a marital pair.[4] In the 1940s, Fromm-Reichmann postulated that a pathologic mother (called the "schizophrenogenic mother") could induce schizophrenia in a "vulnerable" child.[5] This speculation led other psychoanalysts, such as Lidz, to study the role of the father.[6] This work suggested that the father also plays an important role in the development of psychopathology. At the same time, Mittelman began to see a series of marital partners in simultaneous, but separate, psychoanalyses.[7] This approach was quite innovative because psychoanalysts previously believed that this method of treatment would hinder the therapist from helping the patient, since it was thought that neither spouse would trust the same therapist and consequently would withhold important material. Therefore, the other marital partner was usually referred to a colleague.

Outside the field of psychiatry proper, marital counselors, ministers, and others have been interviewing spouses together for some time. Apparently in the early 1950s the first consistent use of family therapy in modern psychotherapeutic practice in the United States was reported by several different workers.[7, 8] Ackerman began consistently utilizing family interviews in his work with children and adolescents,[9] and Lidz and associates,[10] as well as Bowen,[11] began an extensive series of investigations of family interactions and schizophrenia. Bateson and associates[12] and Wynne and associates[13] began an intensive study of family communication patterns in the families of schizophrenic patients and others.

It was not until the early 1960s, however, that these ideas were integrated into a general theory of family interrelationships and that the modern field of family therapy began to take shape.[9, 14] Various schools of thought developed and journals such as *Family Process* were established. Many people became interested in learning about family therapy and in utilizing its techniques. As a matter of fact, a recent poll taken of California psychologists who practiced psychotherapy showed that, as expected, 90 percent were using individual therapy, but more than 60 percent were now using family therapy; only 30 percent were doing group therapy.[15] These statistics well illustrate the rise in the growth of the family therapy field. During the 1970s the use of family therapy was expanded to include application of a "broad range of psychiatric problems with families differing widely in socioeconomic origin," but results were poor until crisis-oriented and short-term methods were developed to meet the needs of these families.[16]

Currently, family therapy is still a relatively new field compared to individual psychotherapy, group psychotherapy, or psychopharmacotherapy. Hypotheses and results, although enthusiastically proclaimed, are only beginning to be supported by data. Recently family researchers have begun more controlled studies on what actually transpires within families[17, 18] and on the outcome of family therapy.[19, 20] To some extent these same difficulties apply to most other psychosocial treatments in psychiatry (which do, however, have a greater volume of clinical experience and acceptance underlying them). Further discussion of research into family treatment outcome and family process will be found in Chapters 18 and 20, respectively.

For many mental health professionals, family therapy seems to be the "right" treatment at the "right" time. For example, a study carried out to determine the reasons people seek help for emotional problems reported that marital concerns ranked first, followed by other family problems.[21] Another survey revealed that 50 percent of the patients requesting psychotherapy did so mainly because of marital difficulties and that another 25 percent mentioned problems related to marriage. In 1979, a major national organization was formed called the American Family Therapy Association, and recently new training programs have been created and others expanded. In addition to these developments, a second journal exclusively devoted to family issues has emerged—*The International Journal of Family Therapy*.

DEFINITION OF MARITAL AND FAMILY THERAPY

Vonnegut has beautifully illustrated one interpretation of the family systems concept:

Your parents were fighting machines and self-pitying machines. Your mother was programmed to bawl out your father for being a defective money-making machine, and your father was programmed to bawl her out for being a defective housekeeping machine. They were programmed to bawl each other out for being defective loving machines. Then your father was programmed to stomp out of the house and slam the door. This automatically turned your mother into a weeping machine. And your father would go down to a tavern where he would get drunk with some other drinking machines. Then all the drinking machines would go to a whorehouse and rent fucking machines. And then your father would drag himself home to become an apologizing machine. And your mother would become a very slow forgiving machine.[22]

Marital and family treatment can be defined as a professionally organized attempt to produce beneficial changes in a disturbed marital or family unit by essentially interactional, nonpharmacological methods. Its aim is the establishment of more satisfying ways of living for the entire family and for individual family members.

Family therapy is distinguished from other psychotherapies by its conceptual focus on the family system as a whole. In this view, major emphasis is placed on understanding individual behavior patterns as arising from and inevitably feeding back into the complicated matrix of the general family system. Beneficial alterations in the larger marital and family unit will therefore have positive consequences for the individual members, as well as for the larger systems. The major emphasis is placed upon understanding and intervening in the family system's current patterns of interaction, with usually only a secondary interest in their origins and development.

In many families, the members may be "selected" as "symptom bearers." Such individuals will then be described in a variety of ways that will amount to their being labeled "bad," "sick," "stupid," or "crazy." Depending on what sort of label such individuals carry, they, together with their families, may be treated in any one of several types of helping facility—psychiatric, correctional, or medical.

On the other hand there may not always be an *identified patient*. Occasionally a marital or family unit presents itself as being in trouble without singling out any one member. A marital couple may realize that their marriage is in trouble and that the cause of their problems stems from interaction with each other and not from either partner individually.

There is a continuum between the intrapsychic system, the interactional family system, and the sociocultural system. Different conceptual frameworks are utilized when dealing with these systems. A therapist may choose to emphasize any of the points on this continuum, but the family therapist is especially sensitive to and trained in those aspects relating specifically to the family system—to both its individual characteristics and the larger social matrix.

Family therapy is not necessarily synonomous with *conjoint family therapy* (in which the entire family meets together consistently for therapy sessions). For example, instead of having regular sessions with the entire family, one of the clinical and theoretical pioneers in the family field has in recent years been experimenting with mainly the exclusive use of the healthiest member of the family system as the therapeutic agent for change in the family unit. This same therapist has also reported on his use of somewhat indirect means—such as provocative letters to family members—as an imaginative way to conduct family therapy, that is, to bring about change or movement in a family system.[23]

There are instances in which a family may be seen together, but the therapist's frame of reference is that of individual psychotherapy. Family members in such a setting may be treated as relatively isolated individual entities. In effect then such a therapist may be practicing conventional individual psychotherapy in a family therapy setting, without using the entire family system as a frame of reference.

Family therapy might broadly be thought of as any type of psychosocial intervention utilizing a conceptual framework that gives primary emphasis to the family system and, which in its therapeutic strategies, aims for an impact on the entire family structure. Thus any psychotherapeutic approach

that attempts to understand or to intervene in an organically viewed family system might fittingly be called "family therapy." This is a very broad definition and allows many differing points of view, both in theory and in therapy, to be placed under one heading.

Although many clinicians agree that there is faulty interaction in families containing an individual with gross disturbance, it is not always clear whether the faulty interaction is the cause or the effect of the disturbed individual. These two points of view were summarized by the Group for the Advancement of Psychiatry in 1970:

> Some practitioners continue to perceive and treat as the central issue . . . the disequilibrium in the intrapsychic apparatus of the individual, viewing the contextual social matrix of development and adaptation and most particularly the family as adding an important dimension to their conceptualization and treatment. Others see and treat as the central issue the disequilibrium in the family, viewing the altered balance of intrapsychic forces and counterforces in an individual to be of secondary to or even of inconsequential relevance to the task of the helping professional.[24]

For the present there is no reason to believe that both views may not be important. Pending further research and experience in this area, it seems prudent to evaluate each clinical situation carefully, attempting both to understand the phenomena and to select intervention strategies designed to achieve the desired ends.

DIFFERENTIATION OF FAMILY THERAPY FROM OTHER PSYCHOTHERAPIES

A family system viewpoint is especially useful in certain kinds of situations in which the family resists change (see Chapter 11). Family therapy is designed to deal with situations that are seen primarily as interfering either in the family system as a whole or in marital or parent-child relationships. On the other hand greater emphasis on the individual intrapsychic factors may be more practical in other kinds of families (see Chapter 12). Individual psychotherapy is, for example, designed to help an individual live better with himself. Other types of treatment may be appropriate under still other conditions; for example, group therapy may be particularly indicated for those who suffer from inadequate, nongratifying social relationships with peers (see Table 1-1). Guidelines for treatment are discussed in Chapter 19.

After understanding the nature of family therapy and its functions, the therapist must recognize how to distinguish it from and contrast it with the differing elements of individual and group psychotherapy.

Table 1-1

Family Therapy Compared with Other Types of Psychosocial Therapy

Type	Goals	Focus	Role of Therapist	Major Indications	Participants	Length and Frequency of Sessions	Overall Duration of Treatment
Family Therapy	Improved family functioning	Family communication; coalition and roles	Active, participant-observer	Marital and parent-child problems	1 family unit, 1–2 therapists	1½ hours, 1X/week	6 months– 2 years
Individual Psychotherapy Psychoanalysis	Personality restructuring	Past Unconscious Transference	Passive, nondirective	Unconscious conflicts in intact personality	1 patient 1 therapist	1 hour, 5X/week	2– 5 years

Psychoanalytically oriented psychotherapy	Personality modification	Present coping mechanisms	Active, participant-observer	Maladaptive pattern of defenses	1 patient¹ 1 therapist	1 hour, 1–2X/week	6 months– 2 years
Brief psychotherapy	Symptom removal	Restoration of functioning	Directive, suppressive	Disruption related to acute gross stress	1 patient 1 therapist	1 hour, 1X/week	1–10 weeks
Group Psychotherapy (e.g., analytic; encounter; marathon; psychodrama)	Improved social functioning	Group participation and feedback	Variable	Poor peer-group relationships	6–8 patients 1–2 therapists	1½ hours, 1X/week	6 months– 2 years
Milieu Therapy (e.g., "therapeutic communities"; day care centers)	Major modification of social behavior	Corrective social experience	Active, participant-observer	Pathogenic social environment	10–30 patients 10–30 staff	Residential (full or part-time)	3 months– 2 years

First, let us consider individual therapy. There are major differences in models (and assumptions) that underlie family therapy and individual therapy. The family model is based on the notion that personality development, symptom formation, and therapeutic change result from the family's function as an interdependent, transactional unit. The individual model is based on the view that these factors are largely determined by the dynamic, intrapsychic function of the individual.[25]* A more extreme view of this position is that of Schatzman who states in his critique of the "individual model" that, although this model is helpful, it is ultimately inadequate for understanding how people affect each other. He claims that:

Psychoanalytic theory cannot render intelligible someone's disturbed experience or behavior in terms of *disturbing* behavior by someone else on that person. In order to comprehend a relationship between two individuals—husband and wife, mother and child, or father and son—we must take into account that each individual experiences the world and originates behavior. Of course, psychoanalysts know that other persons' experiences act upon their patients and that certain persons who dealt with their patients as children influenced them greatly by their behavior. But in so far as psychoanalysts speak of object relations, their theory does not adequately account for this influence.[26]

Individual psychodynamic psychotherapy and family therapy seem at first to be vastly different. Family therapy or theory lacks the elegance, the elaborate language, and the general acceptance of technical terms of psychodynamic therapy. For example, "transference" is a word that has become highly valued and used in common parlance. To apply this word to a family therapy session would be to distort its true meaning and to use it incorrectly. Yet those trained in the use of both models of therapy might say that transference exists and is utilized in family therapy. A family therapist, however, may use the words "alliance," "rapport," and "communication congruency" to report the same phenomena.

Firm believers in either form of therapy would argue the differences. Yet the argument may be just an artifact of history, differing frames of reference and language similar to that of two people trying to converse with each other when one of them speaks only French and the other only Italian; they both end up talking in broken English.

It is evident that as early as the 1930s some analysts, such as Sullivan and Horney, shifted their beliefs from the intrapsychic to the interpersonal. Some believe that the two models are complementary, not mutually exclusive; whereas others believe that the family model cannot be grafted onto the individual model without seriously disturbing both. For example, in its broadest sense, family therapy seeks to understand communication patterns and to then change them if necessary. By influencing these current communication

*In this context "individual" refers to individual psychodynamic models.

behaviors, the therapist can provide for change in the future. Undoubtedly intrapsychic structures may be changed as a result of this, but the therapist does not assume that through this level of intervention structural change in the psychoanalytic sense will occur or is necessary for a successful family therapy outcome.

On one hand, goals and duration of family therapy may be more limited than that of intensive individual psychotherapy or psychoanalysis. On the other hand, if the therapist considers the subtleties and complexities of the complementary communication systems when treating several individuals at the same time, then the results of family work may be much more profound than individual work and may thus effect many more family members.

The question, "Do individuals in the family system change their personality structure as a result of family therapy?" is often asked. Without questioning whether or not individuals *can* change their personalities, family therapy attempts to change family interaction, structure, and function. As a result of such change, certain aspects of an individual's personality may change. Family therapy does not have a primary goal of changing underlying personality structure in isolation from its relationship to the family context.

Similarly, family therapy has to be differentiated from group therapy. Although in both therapies more than one patient is involved, the most obvious difference between the two lies in the presence or absence of a consanguineous relationship between the patients in treatment. As Parloff has pointed out, "family therapy is characteristically performed with members of the same family, while group therapy is conducted with persons who are not members of the same family." He further believes there is little difference in techniques between the two therapies, since ". . . the variability of therapist techniques and styles *within* the framework of family or group psychotherapy is probably fully as great as that *between* these approaches." According to him, the other distinction is in the difference between mediating and ultimate goals, since:

Mediating goals are those which reflect the clinician's assumptions regarding the necessary steps and stages through which a patient must progress if the treatment is to be effective. The ultimate goals of psychotherapy must, however, go beyond hypothesized mediating variables, inferences regarding the resolution of neurotic conflicts, growth, making the unconscious conscious, recall of the repressed, reciprocal inhibition, increasing function between family members, enhancing the communication systems, etc. Ultimate goals shared by all therapists are simply those of reducing discomfort and social ineffectiveness. These changes deal with reducing problems in the areas of thought, feeling, and behavior.[27]

Therefore, it can be said that family therapy changes the family unit, whereas group therapy changes individuals, who may or may not have a family.

REFERENCES

1. Father sentenced to dinners. New York Times, October 26, 1975
2. Sander FM: Marriage and the family in Freud's writing. J Am Acad Psychoanal 6:157–174, 1978
3. Smith ZE: Discussion on charity organizations. Proceedings of the National Conference on Charities and Correction, 1890, p 377
4. Oberndorf CP: Folie à deux. Int J Psychoanal 15:14–24, 1934
5. Fromm-Reichmann F: Notes on the development of schizophrenia by psychoanalytic psychotherapy. Psychiatry 11:267–277, 1948
6. Lidz R, Lidz T: The family environment of schizophrenic patients. Am J Psychiatry 106:322–345, 1949
7. Mittelman B: The concurrent analysis of married couples. Psychoanal Q 17:182–197, 1948
8. Bell JE: Family Group Therapy. Public Health Monograph No. 64 Washington, D.C., Department of Health, Education and Welfare, Public Health Service, 1961
9. Ackerman, NW: Treating the Troubled Family. New York, Basic Books, 1966
10. Lidz T, Cornelison A, Terry D, et al: Intrafamilial environment of the schizophrenic patient. VI. The transmission of irrationality. Arch Neurol and Psychiatry 79:305–316, 1958
11. Bowen M: A family concept of schizophrenia, in Jackson DD (ed): The Etiology of Schizophrenia. New York, Basic Books, 1960, pp 346–372
12. Bateson G, Jackson DD, Haley J, et al: Towards a theory of schizophrenia. Behav Sci 1:251–264, 1956
13. Wynne L, Ryckoff I, Day J, et al: Pseudo-mutuality in the family relations of schizophrenics. Psychiatry 21:205–220, 1958
14. Satir VM: Conjoint Family Therapy: A Guide to Theory and Technique. Palo Alto, California, Science and Behavior Books, 1964
15. Zimet CN: NIMH backs up on its forward plan and the National Register survey of licensed/certified psychologists. Psychother Bull 10:1–3, 1977
16. Zuk GH: The three crises in family therapy (editor's introduction). Int J Fam Ther 1:3–8, 1979
17. Reiss D: Individual thinking and family interaction, III. An experimental study of categorization performance in families of normals, those with character disorders, and schizophrenics. J Nerv Ment Dis 146:384–404, 1968
18. Reiss D: Individual thinking and family interaction. IV. A study of information exchange in families of normals, those with character disorders, and schizophrenics. J Nerv Ment Dis 149:473–490, 1969
19. Gurman AS, Kniskern DP: Research on marital and family therapy: Progress, perspective and prospect, in Garfield SL, Bergin AE (eds): Handbook of Psychotherapy and Behavior Change: An Empirical Analysis, 2nd ed. New York, Wiley, 1978
20. Wells RA, Dezen AE: The results of family therapy revisited: The nonbehavioral methods. Fam Process 17:251–274, 1978
21. Gurin G, Veroff J, Feld S: Americans view their mental health: A nationwide interview survey in Joint Commission on Mental Illness and Health, Monograph Series 4. New York, Basic Books, 1960

22. Vonnegut K, Jr: Breakfast of Champions. New York, Dell, 1973, pp 256–257
23. Towards the differentiation of a self in one's own family, in Framo JL (ed): Family Interaction: A Dialogue Between Family Researchers and Family Therapists. New York, Springer, 1972, pp 111–166
24. The Field of Family Therapy, Report No. 78. New York, Group for the Advancement of Psychiatry, 1970, p 534
25. Robinson LR: Basic concepts in family therapy: A differential comparison with individual treatment. Am J Psychiatry 132:1045–1048, 1975
26. Schatzman M: The Schreber case. Fam Process 14:594–598, 1975
27. Parloff MB: Discussion: The narcissism of small differences—and some big ones. Int J Group Psychother 26:311–319, 1976

Family in Tenement by Lewis Hine, New York City, 1910. Courtesy of the International Museum of Photography, in the George Eastman House, Rochester, New York.

2

The Past, Present, and Future of the Family

OBJECTIVES

- To understand the history of the American family in order to increase awareness of the development of present-day family structure and function
- To understand recent changes in the family
- To share speculations about the future of the family

INTRODUCTION

The family therapist is often confronted with individuals or families who are concerned that their family structure or function is not "proper," depending on their own conception of the nature and function of a family. This issue is related to the attitudes of a particular culture about what a family should be at that particular time. Because of the attitudinal changes in the concept of the family unit, it is necessary to present a brief review of the history of the American family, as well as selected recent changes in the family model and in its trends for the future, in order to place these issues in a broader perspective and context for the beginning family therapist.

PAST CHANGES IN STRUCTURE AND FUNCTION OF THE AMERICAN FAMILY

Throughout history, the structure of the family has altered to conform to the social mores of the times. The particular roles and tasks of individual members of the family have also varied from one time period to another. For example, during colonial days the family was a self-sufficient economic unit which produced more of its daily sustenance than did that of the family in later periods. During this time there was a greater emphasis on the economic basis of marriage than there was on romance. Traditional roles for husbands and wives were fixed and accepted with little possibility of role and task rearrangement. There was little recognition given to the separate needs of children and adolescents. Family members who were as young as seven years old were treated as junior-sized adults and were expected to work. Throughout most of history, children (and women) were seen as chattels, producing income or salable merchandise, and existing solely to help fulfill a parental (or family) need. Only recently have most families been concerned with providing for the creative and developing needs of their children.

Over the years there has been a decline in infant mortality as well as in birthrate, thereby enabling women to have more time and freedom. Parents are now able to give more attention to each individual child, and the family itself is moving toward developing the maximum potential of each of its members as it begins to decrease the rigidity of gender roles and increase overall sexual freedom.

Lasch believes that there has been a gradual erosion of the private life of the family ever since the eighteenth century when the family was a self-contained unit providing for the emotional, financial, and daily needs of each of its members,[1] and Davis suggests that, "the preindustrial family performed a variety of economic, religious, educational, and welfare functions that have since been assumed, for good or ill, by other institutions."[2] Later in the nineteenth century the focus of work moved from the home to the factories and the family was suddenly no longer providing for all of its needs. In the twentieth century the family has been invaded by outsiders who now fulfill its needs—including teachers, social workers, doctors, and other professionals.

THE CHANGING MODEL OF THE FAMILY

The current state of the family is well described in the following editorial concerning the changing family.

The family is the basic unit in all societies regardless of cultural diversities. Families everywhere consist of men, women, and children united by ties of kinship and mutual obligations. Within its capacity, the family is expected to meet the basic needs of its members for food, shelter, and clothing, and to provide the intangible needs for affection and a sense of belonging. It helps to transmit from one generation to the next the traditions and the cultural, moral, and spiritual values unique to each society. Inevitably, in each era there are changes, large or small, gradual or abrupt, which may alter or transform family patterns. Foremost among the forces influencing family life today is the rapid pace and nature of social change. First, the effect of national development is to change the economic, social, and physical environment, possibly to open up new horizons and opportunities, certainly to pose challenges for the family, if not to impose additional burdens on it. Second, development almost invariably involves adjustment within the family itself, in the roles and responsibilities of family members, and in relationships among the generations. Because of their complete dependence on adults, children are the first to suffer or benefit from changes affecting the family. Throughout the developing world, the past few decades have witnessed dramatic changes. The gradual awakening of women to their rights and dignities, the rapid rate of urbanization, population pressures, increasing education, and technology are factors that are affecting the family in countless ways. Change is a continuing and inescapable reality in today's world.[3]

Heated discussion continues concerning the extent to which the family is changing and whether or not the family is dying altogether. The traditional model of the "average" family—one which is made up of husband-breadwinner, wife-homemaker, and two children—has been questioned,* but there are other models of living together in a continuing intimate relationship whereby adults are involved in "family" functions. Also, some writers think of a much broader definition of the system which Pattison and associates call the "kinship model."[4] By kinship they mean the variety of individuals, extended families, the community, and the neighborhood who are seen as "the family." Sociologists call this new version of the family unit "the modern nuclear family," in contrast to the "traditional, extended family" in which several generations of a family all lived under the same roof. The "old" nuclear family had two parents and several children and relied on relatives for economical and emotional support, as well as for childrearing. Until recently the modern nuclear family was considered an undesirable adaptation to the increased mobility of family members, thereby making the modern family more vulnerable to instability, isolation, and stagnation.

Although an extended family may have been adaptive to the life-styles of the past, it did, however, have its disadvantages. Roles were rigid and the restrictions on individuals and individuation were greater. Intergenerational conflicts were more intense. On the other hand, the ideal modern version of the nuclear family does allow for freedom from some of these constraints with the hope of finding a mutually satisfying balance between restraint and permissiveness.

Because there are many possible and workable types of family organization, family therapists need to be careful not to project, knowingly or unknowingly, their own, and perhaps inappropriate, ideals of family structure and function when they are treating their patients. From the initial contact with a family, the therapist should pay special attention to the actual structure of that family: its goals, resources, and potentialities. Only after understanding the specifics of a particular family can the therapist begin to think about treatment.

---

*The model has been challenged for not representing the statistical mode and for its stereotyped role allocations.

THE PRESENT AMERICAN FAMILY—CIRCA 1980

Recent data strikingly demonstrate that the "typical" family has changed markedly from the past.*[5]

Marriage and Divorce

It is not well known that in recent years the United States has had one of the world's highest marriage rates (at its peak, 11 per 1,000 people in 1972) among the world's industrialized countries. This rate has declined each year since 1972. Marriage rates appear to correlate with a country's economic stability—the countries with rising economies have rising marriage rates. At the same time the divorce rate has also been high. Americans have been getting both married and divorced at a higher rate than they have in the past (Figure 2-1).

Rates of first marriage, divorce, and remarriage for U.S. women, 1921-1977

Fig. 2-1. Courtesy of the Population Reference Bureau, Washington, D.C., from Glick PC, Norton AJ: Marrying, Divorcing, and Living Together in the U.S. Today. Popul Bull, Vol 32, No. 5, p 5.

*Unless otherwise cited, all data are based on P.C. Glick and A.J Norton, reference 5.

In the last decades, after a postwar peak, first the divorce and marriage rates fell in unison, but then in the late 1960s they began to take divergent paths with marriage rates going down and divorce rates rising. Now more than at any other time in history young people are deciding not to get married at all, and there is a greater proportion of adults than ever before who never marry during their lifetime.

In many cases marriages are delayed. This is probably due to the increasing number of young single women who choose higher education and career experience instead of an early marriage. According to Glick and Norton:

> Young adults have been entering first marriages later and shortening the intervals, not only between marriage and divorce, but also between remarriage and divorce. Thus the marital state is being compressed into a shorter span of years, a trend referred to as the "marital squeeze."[5]

There is also a strong relationship between socioeconomic status and marital stability; for example, higher socioeconomic class marriages have a lower rate of separations than do those of a lower socioeconomic level. Among highly educated women, however, there is a greater risk of divorce then among less-educated women.

The United States divorce rate has constantly far exceeded that of any other country . . . "but the gap (due to an upsurge in rates in other countries) has been narrowing."[5] There has been a rise in the U.S. divorce rate that has been coincident with a variety of other social changes, including an increase in the number of women working, in the use of birth control, and in the availability of greater options for both men and women. The divorce rates show that early and late marriages are less stable than others; for example, teenage marriages are twice as likely to end in divorce as those that occur when people are in their twenties (Figure 2-2). Women who marry for the first time after the age of thirty also tend to have less stable marriages than those who marry in their twenties. Upward mobility is associated to some extent with marital stability as is downward mobility related to instability. Remarriage among this group tends to occur relatively soon after divorce, if at all.

Family Life Cycle Events

Although there have been markedly changing trends in marriage, divorce, childbearing, and mortality, most Americans "still play out their lives in some version of the traditional family life cycle."[5] The most significant variation of this is a longer period between the marriage of the last child and that of the death of one's spouse due to the increasing longevity of the parents (Figure 2-3).

Unmarried women are accountable for more than half of all births. Never-

Percent of women divorced
within 3 to 5 and 6 to 10 years after
first marriage. U.S., 1970

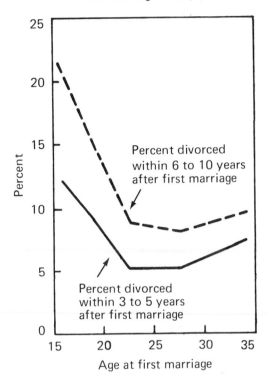

Fig. 2-2.   Courtesy of the Population Reference Bureau, Inc., Washington, D.C., from Glick PC, Norton AJ: Marrying, Divorcing, and Living Together in the U.S. Today. Popul Bull, Vol 32, No. 5, p 16.

theless, the U.S. birth rate continues to decline. The annual number of births declined 30 percent within a span of less than 20 years. This is due, of course, in large part to the effect of oral contraceptives," as well as to the many more legal than illegal abortions in the last 10 years. The control of pregnancy has dramatically restructured our society and is related to massive changes in birthrates, sexual mores, employment patterns, gender roles, and relationship styles.

Another factor that has dramatically restructured our society is that of a growing trend among wives to seek employment. In more than half of the nation's husband-wife families, both spouses work. In these cases the wives contribute to one-fourth of the average family income, although there is an increasing number of homes in which the wife either makes more money than her husband or is the sole wage earner.

Median age of typical mothers
at selected points in the family life cycle

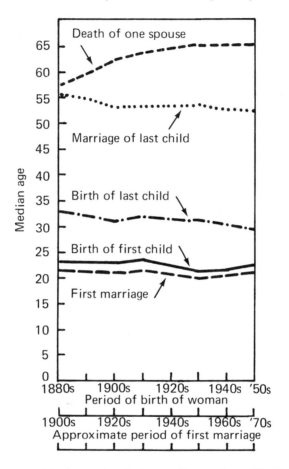

Fig. 2-3.   Courtesy of the Population Reference Bureau, Inc., Washington, D.C., from Glick PC, Norton AJ: Marrying, Divorcing, and Living Together in the U.S. Today. Popul Bull, Vol 32, No 5, p 21.

Living in Groups and Living Alone

Traditional family patterns have undergone important changes. A family as defined by the Census Bureau is "two or more persons, related to each other by blood, marriage, or adoption, who live together." Statistics show that over 80 percent of all families (one or two generations) in the United States in 1975 were traditional husband and wife (or married couple) families; but this number is now decreasing. Woman-headed households run about 13 percent, and man-headed households run about 2 to 3 percent. The "typical American family" with bread-winner-husband, homemaker-wife, and two children now make up only 7 percent of the nation's families. Currently the most "typical" family is the childless couple with both spouses working.[6, 7]

In 1976, 50 percent of the 7.5 million female heads of household were either divorced or separated. Almost 4 out of 10 working Americans today are women, and the ratio is increasing; 40 percent of Americans under the age of 18 have working mothers; 3 out of every 5 working women are married.

Black families are more likely than white families to include young children among their members, "to be maintained by younger and less educated persons, and to have considerably smaller family incomes."[5]

Eighty percent of children under 18 live under one roof with two parents (not necessarily both of which are their natural parents); but this proportion has been declining in recent years. Among black children, the proportion is only 50 percent. About 45 percent of the children born in 1978 will spend at least several months in a one-parent household. There has also been a threefold increase in the proportion of young, school-age children who are living with a divorced father.

All but 9 percent of adults with their own households are married couples or persons living alone. American households are becoming smaller, having declined from 5.8 people in 1790 to 4.8 by 1900 and to about 2.8 by 1980. This decline is due to a smaller number of children in the home, as well as to single-parent households. There has also been a recent upturn in the proportion of adults living alone and a marked increase in the single, young persons (especially women) setting up their own households. Many men and women are living together without being married and this proportion is increasing. Such informal unions of men and women tend to be relatively brief.

In summarizing these data, a number of trends can be noted. People now marry later in life. The divorce rate is rising. Nearly 40 percent of all marriages involving young adults are likely to end in divorce. More wives are working outside of the home. A growing proportion of divorced men and women are not remarrying. The data indicate that:

1.   Of each 100 first marriages, 38 will end in divorce
2.   Of the 38 divorcees, 29 will remarry
3.   Of the 29 who remarry, 13 will become redivorced

In commenting on recent changes in family life, Professor I. Zwerling has noted that family functions have decreased historically and now consist mainly of "mutual emotional support."[8] The family has increasingly turned over its functions to other societal agencies. There has been a rise in family isolation, which relates to the increase in mobility, in the number of women out of the home, and in the rate of divorce. Signs associated with family change include: decreased birth rate; increased absence of parents due to work; increased reliance on technology (TV, etc.); increased use of day care centers; increased use of contraception; increased mate swapping and extramarital sex; increased separation of the place of work from the place of residence; and decreased belief in religion. There has been such a rapid rate of change that some parents feel early in their lives that they have little to offer their children. More women now abandon their children than they do their husbands, and there are cases now on record of neither parent wanting to take custody of children in divorce actions. All of these issues will be discussed in greater detail with a focus on clinical issues in Chapters 3 and 4.

THE FUTURE OF THE FAMILY

A recent editorial in *Science*[9] and a 1977 conference entitled "The Family: Dying or Developing"[10] were both concerned with the future of the family. The writers noted that the percentage of married households (out of total households) has declined so drastically that it is questionable whether or not we will have any married households left within a generation or so from now.

Family form has changed remarkably toward a kinship model. Students of the family predict even more changes in life-style, peer and power relationships, social and intellectual competence, health patterns, and family values. There will be an increase in dual-career and single-parent families in the future, and, although there will be a leveling off of single-parent families, there will be more female-headed families.

With all these shifts within the structure of the family, it is only natural to ask: Is the family, as an institution, disintegrating or is it only changing? What happens to the children of divorce? What should roles be for males and females and how should these roles differ in single-parent homes and dual-career marriages? What do lasting or satisfying marriages have in common? How do public policy, societal attitudes, and educational efforts influence these attributes?[9]

We prefer to view the family as evolving and developing rather than as dying. In contrast with the past, there are increasing numbers of options for women, men, and children. Individuals are no longer forced to work at an early age and can thus develop their creative potential. Society now allows men to take a "supportive" as well as a "constrictive" role. They can become involved in the nuturing of younger children and not merely in "limit setting." The family itself has more options. Because we have moved to an extended kinship model (father, mother, grandparents, relatives, housekeepers, ex-spouses), each individual may provide support in various ways for the other members.

It is not at all clear that being in a one-parent family, as an alternative style, is necessarily detrimental.[11] There may be advantages in terms of certain options that allow individual growth for both the child and the adult that two-parent families are unable to foster.

Eisenberg believes that, "in a full human society, the goal of social institutions should be to maximize the possibilities of personal choices for women and men."[12] Rather than a rigidly prescribed distribution of roles, individual differences in family units should be the determining factor in deciding who fulfills what role.

Finally, Sussman has made a number of predictions of trends for the future.[13]

1. The divorce rate will continue to rise with a corresponding drop in the marriage rate. Between one-third and one-half of all marriages in 1977 are likely to end in divorce, the majority occurring during the first 3 years of marriage.
2. A continuous rise in singlehood is expected. This is a consequence of increasing decisions not to marry; increased rates of cohabitation—basically a nonlegal marriage form; and a longer postponement of remarriage among the divorced.
3. There will be a continuous increase in the incidence of child-free marriages with major efforts to sanction this union as a socially approved form. The costs of having and supporting children, increasing emphasis on equitable dyadic relationships and the importance of the marital health of couples, and the increasing incidence of sterilization—which, incidentally, is the preferred form of contraception in the United States and world-wide—are reasons for the rising number of childless marriages.
4. Political and legislative efforts will be made to "stabilize" the family of the future. The planned "White House Conference on the Family" will be one such beginning effort. The actions to date are too preliminary to forecast the ideological caste of the Conference. Will family pluralism be used as its conceptual base or will there be efforts to reestablish a nuclear family with a traditional role structure?
5. Increasingly, the "everyday" family or focal family will become the significant primary group for the individual, perhaps even eclipsing the legal family, both psychologically and socially. This is the group of individuals who may or may not be related by blood or marriage and who provide intimacy, emotional support, companionship, role models for children, and help when in need. These are the persons one can count on, with whom one has free and easy access, and with whom one likes to spend free time.

Others have suggested other trends:

1. Offspring will increasingly rely on peers and the media (especially TV) for role models, with decreasing reliance on parental models.
2. There will be an increasing sense of dislocation, alienation, and confusion of marital partners and parents as to their appropriate roles and functions, with increasing numbers turning for help and guidance to outside sources.
3. On the horizon lie such possibilities as increased availability and utilization of abortion, pregnancy for single individuals by use of artificial insemination and other "laboratory" means, and changes from passage and implementation of statutes similar to the Equal Rights Amendment.

Based on these trends, Sussman also suggests the following:[13]

1.   An organized policy and program for childbearing
2.   Divorce insurance
3.   Utilizing the extended "everyday" family as caretakers
4.   Training people to deal with bureaucracy
5.   A qualifying test for marriage

RELEVANCE FOR THE FAMILY THERAPIST

The family has maintained itself as an institution throughout history and through all recognized cultures. In various subtle and major ways it has also changed with respect to specific ways of carrying out its functions. The family therapist needs to examine the particular family to see to what degree it has carried out its functions and to what extent other intrafamilial people and institutions are available to help the family to continue to do so.

Now that we have examined the family in its historical context, we can more profitably discuss how families function.

REFERENCES

1.   Lasch C: Haven in a Heartless World. New York, Basic Books, 1977
2.   Davis D: The American family and boundaries in historical perspective, in Reiss D and Hoffman HA (eds): The American Family: Dying or Developing. New York, Plenum Press, 1979, pp 13–33
3.   Editorial. Coping with change. UNICEF News 89:3, 1976
4.   Pattison EM, DeFrancisco D, Wood P, et al: A psychosocial kinship model for family therapy. Am J Psychiatry 132:1246–1251, 1975
5.   Glick PC, Norton AJ: Marrying, Divorcing, and Living Together in the U.S. Today. Popul Bull, Vol 32 No. 5 (Population Reference Bureau, Inc., Washington, D.C., 1977)
6.   Unmarried couples multiplying fast. San Francisco Chronicle, February 9, 1977, p 2
7.   The new "typical" family. San Francisco Chronicle, March 8, 1977, p 1 (back page)
8.   Zwerling I: Family Structure and Function. Presented at a Seminar entitled, "Issues in Family Therapy" at the California Psychiatric Association Conference, Palm Springs, California, November, 1975
9.   Etzioni A: Science and the future of the family. Science 196:487, 1977
10. The Family: Dying or Developing. Conference sponsored jointly by the Department of Psychiatry and Behavioral Sciences of the George Washington University School of Medicine and the Center for Continuing Education in Mental Health of the Psychiatric Institute Foundation, Washington, D.C., June, 1977

11. Schulman GL: The changing American family: For better or worse. Int J Fam Ther 1:9–21, 1979

12. Eisenberg L: Changes in family life have medical implications. JAMA 230:1241–1247, 1974

13. Sussman MB: Actions and services for the new family, in Reiss D and Hoffman HA (eds): The American Family: Dying or Developing. New York, Plenum Press, 1979, pp 213–237

Spirit of Life by Robert Russin. Courtesy of Robert Russin and the Palm Springs Desert Museum.

3

Understanding the Functional Family

OBJECTIVES

- To understand the concept of the family as a system
- To list and characterize the phases of the family life cycle
- To understand the family qualities important in the development of healthy individuals
- To list and understand primary family tasks
- To understand the similarities and differences in the functional single-parent family compared to those in the functional two-parent family

INTRODUCTION

There is probably little need to stress the general importance of marriage and the family. These institutions have existed throughout recorded history in all places and at all times. Even now in late twentieth-century America—despite the talk in some quarters about the death of the family—family and marital relationships, although changing, are clearly very much with us and undoubtedly will continue to be so in the foreseeable future. Well over 90 percent of all people in the United States still live in families and, except for early adulthood, human beings live in families most of their lives.[1]

It is also certainly true, however, that marriage and the family have carried different assignments and expectations at various places and times. This variability appears when we compare the traditional American family with the radical modifications of this pattern. The current lack of a generally accepted pattern for marriage and the family is a cause for uncertainty, instability, and distress for many people. On the other hand, this flexibility can also provide for a multiplicity and richness of solutions for both individual and societal situations that a more rigid, unchanging pattern could not. Birdwhistell has suggested that the "average American family" is organized around idealized, nonachievable goals (for example, romantic love).[2] Failure to live up to such family myths is a cause of conflict and distress for all family members (see Chapter 4). As we pointed out in Chapter 2, there is a great diversity of family types and styles related to a variety of demographic and psychological variables. All families have conflicts: their feelings toward each other are mixed, their love is not always constant, and so forth. Furthermore, the completely well-functioning, growing, long-term marriage is a rarity.

The frame of reference provided in this chapter for understanding the family is not intended to be exhaustive or complete. In our present stage of knowledge, no such final statement about the family can be made. Instead, our model is intended to be supplemented by those frames of references that apply to individual and sociocultural models. Exclusion is not meant to imply that the other models are not important, only that they are not in keeping with the general tenor of this book—that of presenting ideas of particular interest to the family therapist. Undoubtedly the richness, complexity, and variety of marriages and families will not be completely described or explained by our categories, nor will all of the categories fit precisely into every specific family system. It is hoped, however, that this material will offer a useful structure for thinking about all families, including those members in distress who present themselves in one way or another to professionals for help.

The model for examining families will be presented in three perspectives: *the family as a system; the family life cycle;* and *the family tasks.* Each topic will be related to both the two-parent family and to the single-parent family.

THE FAMILY AS A SYSTEM

Marriage and the family are important human institutions that are different from other human groups in many ways including duration, intensity, and type of function. For human beings, the family constitutes the most important group in relation to the individual psychological development, emotional interaction, and maintenance of self-esteem. For many of us the family is a group in which we experience our strongest loves and our strongest hates, and in which we enjoy our deepest satisfaction and suffer our most painful disappointments.

The characteristics of the family (or of marriage) as a unit are different from the mere sum of its components. Knowing the attributes of all the individuals in the family is not the same as understanding the family system as an entity. The family has a history and function of its own, the specifics of which differ from those of its individual members.

Marriages and families need to be thought of as interactive milieus in which transactions between component parts are continually taking place. Thus the action of one member will affect the entire family. A ripple set off anywhere internally or externally that impinges on the family will reverberate throughout. There is a basic, underlying consistent homeostasis in every family that is used to maintain each member's identity,[3] defined as the sum of the individual's internal and external patterns of adjustment to life.[4] The family is a system in dynamic equilibrium. Stresses and strains of family existence inevitably affect each family member. At times, these reactions may be of such a nature as to cause them to be labeled as symptoms. For example, when a father and mother stop communicating (a change in homeostasis), the father may begin to drink (a symptom) or the mother may become depressed (a symptom).

The family is usually bound together by intense and long-lasting ties of past experiences, social roles, mutual support, and expectations. These are factors constantly at work, more or less successfully, to keep the family system in equilibrium and to keep it from undergoing a too severe or rapid change. This, too, has been referred to as family homeostasis. These equilibrating mechanisms often have to do with maintaining a continuing system of symmetrical and complementary relationships.

Family homeostasis refers most generally to the concept of the family as a feedback system designed to maintain a relatively stable state so that when the whole system or any part of it is subjected to a disequilibrating force, the system will operate to restore the preexisting equilibrium. Family therapists have noted that changes in one member of the family often bring about changes in other members. For instance, the onset of illness in the family member identified as the patient (for example, a child becoming schizophrenic) can cause another member to decompensate (become depressed). As the child improves, the other member may improve, and, concurrently, the marriage may deteriorate.

Families can be thought of as having personalities or styles analogous to those of individuals, for example, "isolated" families or "musical" families or "tragedy-prone" families. A generally accepted system of family typologies is not available (although badly needed), but there is a general recognition of differences in family patterns of thinking, feeling, interacting, and of the types of coping mechanisms used to deal with stress, as well as the kinds of "myths" or "scripts" that families seem to act out (see Chapter 4). All marriages and families are subject to stress, disequilibrium, and crisis, and they all develop habitual techniques to deal more or less successfully with these situations.

Although stability and homeostasis are important elements of marital and family systems, inevitably there are also other forces that are continually changing the family, pushing it in the direction of development and differentiation. Some of these forces constitute the growth pattern known as *the family life cycle*. This can be thought of as the expectable events that most families go through in a fairly standard sequence. Other stresses can be thought of as traumatic or unexpectable in that they are extraordinary; they are not necessarily experienced by most families or they occur outside of the normal sequence. Thus each family finds its own balance between those forces that tend to keep it stable and those that encourage change.

Given that life is a series of "ups and downs" for all people and all families, the family unit has to continually cope with the unavoidable changes that time inevitably brings. This notion is contrary to the popular romanticized version of life and of marriage.

Early childhood trauma, deprivation, or difficulties may not necessarily result in later inability to function adaptively.[5] Researchers following 200 children over a 30-year period found that those with the most traumatic childhoods often developed into successful and happy adults. Predictions of future adaptation based on the beliefs that children from unfortunate home situations would be troubled adults and that those with idyllic childhoods would be successful were wrong in two-thirds of the cases. Such early-life difficulties would seem, therefore, to have potential for either successful or unsuccessful later-life functioning. Those individuals who came from troubled families but were able to go outside their troubled family system for other supports and models had better outcomes than did those who remained immersed in an unchanging, dysfunctional family system.[6]

THE FAMILY LIFE CYCLE

The longitudinal view of the family's development has been referred to as its life cycle (Fig. 3-1) and is analogous to the individual's life cycle. Also various authors have studied the specific tasks for each phase in an individual's and in a family's life,[7-12] and in Table 3-1 we have juxtaposed psychosocial models of adult development with family stages.[13, 14]

As in individual development, the family evolves through *expectable* phases. These phases include: the beginning family (engagement, marriage, and honeymoon); the childbearing family (birth of the first child); the family with school children; the family with teenagers; the family as a launching center (the offspring's marriage and separation from home); the family in its middle years (one or both spouse's retirement); and the aging family (eventual death of a spouse).

There are also the *unexpected* or traumatic stresses on the family. Sometimes these consist of one of the normal phases coming out of turn, such as the death of a spouse or parent at an early age. Other such stresses are the illness or incapacitation of a family member and financial reverses. These traumatic changes involve either someone's entering or leaving the family (actually or imminently) or a threatened or actual role change for a family member (such as a job change or loss).

Table 3-1

Comparison of Psychosocial Models of Adult Family Development*

		Author of Model		
Age	Erikson	Gould	Levinson and Associates	Duvall
18-20		Getting away from parents	Leaving the family	— Beginning Family
20-25	Intimacy versus isolation			— Childbearing Family
25-		Working on the business of living	Getting into the adult world	— Families with Preschool Children
30-		Questioning what life is all about	"Should I make a change?" (unstable period)	— Families with School Children
35-	Generativity versus ego stagnation		Settling down	— Families with Teenagers

34

40-	Awareness of time squeeze—turning toward family	Becoming one's own man	— Families as Launching Centers
	Growing satisfaction with marriage and friends	Disparity between what I've got and want (unstable period)	
50-	Ego integrity versus despair	Restabilization period outcome of mid-life transition	— Families in the Middle Years
55-	Mellowing and reviewing what life is all about		
60-			— Aging Families

* Adapted with permission from the publishers and Stein, SP, et al.[13] and Duvall, E.[14]

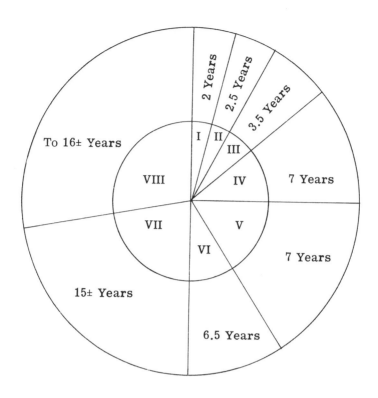

Fig. 3-1. The Family Life Cycle

Phase	Family phase	Family description
I	Beginning family	Married couple without children
II	Childbearing family	Oldest child, up to 30 months
III	Families of preschool children	Oldest child, 30 months to 6 years
IV	Families with school children	Oldest child, 6-13 years
V	Families with teenagers	Oldest child, 13-20 years
VI	Families as launching centers	First child gone to last child leaving home
VII	Families in the middle years	Empty nest to retirement
VIII	Aging families	Retirement to death of both spouses

The family's ability to pass successfully from one specific developmental phase to another will depend to a considerable extent on how prior stages have been mastered. There are various phase-specific psychosocial tasks that need to be worked out at each stage. The extent to which this is accomplished will depend on the flexibility and functionality of the family as a whole and as individuals. [15] One research group describes this process as follows:

> A competent family self-destructs; children grow up, leave the nest; parents grow old, and having failing function, die. Adaptation to these stark realities is successful only to the degree that individuation is complete. In such evolved people, a sense of capability does not depend on unchanging relationships. There is an ability to accept the future, to acknowledge and adapt to the great changes brought about by growth and development, aging, and death. A family member can then operate with respect for his own dignity and that of others. He can have joy in encountering a loved one, even though that very encounter brings awareness of the implications of loss and passage of time. When individuation is incomplete, separation is resisted and family pain and functional difficulty increase. [16]

In this section on the family life cycle, we will first discuss tasks involved in the beginning family and then those concerning the adult life cycle as they relate to the family. Finally, we will discuss an alternative cycle—serial relationships, marital separations, divorce, and remarriage.

Marriage

THE ENGAGEMENT PHASE

Rapoport states that there are three tasks involved in the *intrapersonal* preparation for marriage. [17, 18] They are: (1) making oneself ready to take over the role of husband or wife; (2) disengaging (or altering the form of engagement) of oneself from especially close relationships that compete or interfere with commitment to the new marital relationship; and (3) accommodating patterns of gratifications of premarital life to patterns of the newly formed couple (marital) relationship. Rapoport also states that completion of these tasks leads to consideration of the second major group of engagement tasks, namely those involved in the couple's *interpersonal* preparation for marriage. [17]

1. Establishing a couple identity
2. Developing a mutually satisfactory sexual adjustment for the engagement period
3. Developing a mutually satisfactory system of communication between the pair
4. Establishing a mutually satisfactory pattern with regard to relatives
5. Developing a mutually satisfactory pattern with regard to friends
6. Developing a mutually satisfactory pattern with regard to work
7. Developing mutually satisfactory patterns of decision making
8. Planning specifically for the wedding, honeymoon, and the early months of marriage that lie ahead

THE HONEYMOON PHASE

In the honeymoon phase, the work seems to involve the following:[14]

Intrapersonal Task I: Developing competence to participate in an appropriate sexual relationship with one's marital partner

Intrapersonal Task II: Developing competence to live in close association with the marital partner

Interpersonal Task I: Developing the basis for a mutually satisfying sexual relationship

Interpersonal Task II: Having a mutually satisfactory shared experience as a basis for developing a later husband-wife relationship

AGE 18 THROUGH 22

Marriage in this age group often represents a search for a substitute parent in the spouse. This is because the partners usually have not yet been able to effectively separate themselves, physically or emotionally, from their parents to define themselves as competent individuals. These early marriages may actually interfere with the further individuation of the partners.

Before the recent rise of women in the labor force, it was more difficult for women to master the task of individuation, for they were unable to accessibly gain the vocational competency that is often necessary to help individuals to define themselves as worthwhile and autonomous. For many women, a job role, other than that of being a wife and mother, has not been as readily acceptable as it has been for men. Thus many women have felt prematurely arrested in their potential, both by general cultural patterns and by an early marriage.

THE MID-TWENTIES

The accepted myth is that people in their mid-twenties marry for love. A closer examination reveals, however, that first marriages are often a matter of: conforming to social expectations; regularizing sexual outlets; wanting to be dependent on a parent substitute; getting away from home; or that of filling some psychological void. Marital satisfaction is greatest in the first year and soon begins to decline, reaching a low point in the late thirties before starting to ascend again. The seventh year of marriage is often a critical one with many divorces occurring at that time.

AGE 28 THROUGH 34

Many men go through their twenties and thirties feeling that success in their careers is their main task. These are the men who may become workaholics and locked into their jobs with the often unexamined idea that vocational achievement will offer a continuing sense of security. For this end they may sacrifice other aspects of their lives, most noticeably their wives and families. There are other men who drift through their twenties without firm commitment, which for them may not come until the thirties or, rarely, later.

For women during the same period, the feeling is that a dependent role as wife will make them a whole person. As some women become increasingly disillusioned with this role, they may become more passive, angry, and depressed. Husbands may begin to look outside the marriage for their satisfaction and indicate that they want their wives to become more assertive, as long as the wives do not overdo it and disrupt the marital equilibrium. Divorce may be seen as the way to eliminate the problems for either the husband or the wife or for both.

THE MID-THIRTIES

For women with other goals, it may nevertheless not be until age 30 or 35 that they are able to work out a satisfactory amalgam of career and family responsibilities.

Most women, up until very recently, have taken on the role of care-givers, marrying by their early twenties and seeking their major satisfaction via their husbands and families.

By the mid-thirties the average mother has sent her last child off to school and has reentered the labor market. It is the most common time in which the wife runs away and the divorced woman remarries, since in both cases the woman feels free to try a new life-style.

THE FORTIES

Individuals in their forties are subject to important reevaluations of their basic attitudes with the realization that their remaining years are limited. For the man this may involve his coming more in touch with his own tender and care-giving qualities which have been relatively neglected over the preceding years. His wife may often become more self-assertive and self-concerned, his children more independent, and his work more routinized and stultified. The wife may be feeling freer at the time her husband may be feeling more entrapped. As they examine themselves and their partners, couples often sense the need for a reevaluation of their marital contract. This process is often accompanied by communication difficulties and marital separations on the basis that the partner no longer "fits."

According to Gould, if this period goes well then, "marital happiness and contentment with the spouse continues to increase, along with renewed interest in friends and social activities . . ." although, ". . . friends and social activities are not substitutes for concern with one's own children, which continue at a very high level."[11]

THE FIFTIES AND BEYOND

Marriage in this age group has not yet been well studied. In general, parents may be seen by children more realistically and as less blameworthy for their own problems. Levinson feels that: "In the fifties, the data indicate that one begins to feel less responsible for one's children and begins to look for the children's approval, as a meaningful concern to be ranked as co-equal with self-approval and the spouse's approval. The concern with health increases during the fifties. There is a certainty that time is running out."[7] Having an orientation toward the future is helpful in maintaining not only physical health but also mental health.

When a loss (through death, separation, or relocation) occurs in the family, healthy families are able to cope with the mixed feelings about the lost member. One remembers the good and the not so good. In dysfunctional families the occasion is used to even old scores.

The R family consisted of Mr. and Mrs. R, two older sons in their thirties and a daughter age 20. There was a 70-year-old grandmother who committed suicide. The family reaction was that the mother became severely depressed; she cried incessantly and was unable to work. The father drank continuously from the time he got home until the time he went to sleep; and the two older boys accused their mother of "killing grandmother." The mother used the occasion to berate the boys for not achieving all that she and her husband had expected of them.

Serial Relationships

So far in this chapter, we have discussed the family system and its life cycle. The notion that at the age of 20 one will have selected his or her partner for the next 60 years seems a bit unrealistic. Some individuals choose marriage and then never divorce; others marry and then divorce and choose a series of relationships (i.e., serial relationships); and others choose never to marry at all, preferring only serial relationships. People may need different types of partners at different stages of their lives, and this has sometimes been referred to as the "7-year switch." Statistics indicate the increasing rate of marital separation, divorce, and remarriage. These data have been used to forecast the "death" of the family, but they can be seen as indicators of an alternative cycle to the traditional pattern.

MARITAL SEPARATION[19]

Separation is a relatively common crisis of marital life. Although it is emotionally traumatic for the individuals involved, it can serve as a time for reassessment of the marital contract and of individual goals. Depending on what phase of the marriage is involved, different precipitants will have brought about the separation and therefore different issues may need to be addressed.

Separation in the early stages of a marriage may be caused by the partners coming down from their infatuation "high," with subsequent disillusionment and eagerness to flee from the task of working things out. For those who got married under the gun of pregnancy, later recriminations or second feelings about the reasons for the marriage may bring about a stormy period.

Some people get married to get away from their parents' home or in desperation about their inability to ever attract anyone else who will be seriously interested in them. When these underlying motives lose their force, the foundation of the marriage may be undermined.

Spouses whose children are grown and have left home may not easily become accustomed to living along together as a marital couple. With the parental role diminished or absent, there may be little emotional or functional viability left in the marriage.

Although it is natural to think of marital separation as an unfortunate event, the tendency to do so must be avoided in order to view it as symptomatic of the marital-system problems needing attention. In this sense, separation and its subsequent resolution can be considered as offering the potential for growth.

Trial separations can be useful to provide a "cooling-off" period for couples whose difficulties seem insurmountable. It offers them the opportunity to examine more objectively their relationship. At the same time the individuals can test their ability to adapt to living alone. This separation, together with new life experiences of various sorts (which may not have taken place had the couple stayed together) will often enable the husband and wife to change their behavior and feelings toward each other by the time they attempt a reconciliation.

Often enough, however, one spouse may use a separation as an attempt to manipulate the other spouse or to have that spouse experience defeat and humiliation. In such cases little or no objectivity or growth occurs. An individual may become fixed in an angry or depressive posture, either of which positions, if adhered to rigidly, will prove self-defeating.

A recent study found that there are notable differences between men and women that are precisely the opposite of the traditional stereotypes.[20] For instance, a woman's love appeared to predict better than that of a man's the direction in which the relationship would continue. Either as a prelude or a consequence, women fell out of love more quickly and easily than did men. Usually the partner least involved in the relationship was more likely to intitiate the break up. A woman who was more committed but felt less reciprocity in the relationship was the partner who was more likely to break up the relationship. Men less commonly withdrew unilaterally from their relationship when they were over-committed and involved. Overall, women seemed more realistic than men in appraising the future of their relationships. Predictably, the rejected partner was more distressed than the partner who introduced separation, and men were generally more distressed by the ending of their relationship than were women. Even the women who were the more involved partners had greater equanimity after the break up than did men in comparable situations. The stereotype of women being more socially sensitive and more in touch with their feelings seemed to be true.

DIVORCE

As was indicated in Chapter 2, the divorce rate in most developing countries is rapidly rising. Weiss states that, "divorce is an essential adaptation to the conflict between the value we place on commitment to a mate versus the value we place on self-realization."[19] If the relationship has been long standing, divorce is one of the most painful experiences in anyone's life. The ambivalence that ex-spouses feel about each other is probably more extreme than that in any other human relationship.

Usually the rejected party feels enormously wounded and hurt, while the rejector often reacts with guilt. Later reactions may include playing out earlier parental conflicts with both partners with the intent of "getting even." Postmarital fighting is often predicated on realistic issues (such as those of custody and money and on what went wrong in the marriage), and sometimes offers a way of staying in contact with the other spouse. Each spouse tends to develop a version of what went wrong in the marriage. This serves the function of reestablishing their intrapsychic equilibrium, since the social network of marital partners is often disrupted with one partner usually retaining most of the friends. The process of reestablishing a social and sexual network usually takes from one to three years. Regardless of how bad the marriage was for both spouses, many divorced people find that the transition to living alone is excruciatingly painful.

What about children of divorce? Contrary to popular belief, most children of divorce do not appear to be permanently damaged. As with any other crisis, divorce can offer a potential for growth. Children in this situation may be forced to cope with separation, issues of self-reliance, and change. Over 90 percent of divorced children live with their mothers, and, if the father remains involved, empathic, and warm, the adjustment of the children is thought to be better than if the father showed no interest at all.

REMARRIAGE

Concurrent with the rise in divorce rate (nearly one million people get divorced every year) is the increase in the number of people remarrying (four out of five divorced people remarry). Marital and family therapists are confronted with a set of problems not seen previously.

The old assumption in the psychiatric and sociological literature was that people tended to recreate the same patterns they had in their first marriages. With further study, this assumption appears not to be always true. The reasons for first marriages (true love, getting away from parents) appear to be quite different from the reasons for second marriages. The first marriage is seen as a training school for the second. Following breakups of first marriages, both partners are usually quite "depressed and devastated." New relationships seem to produce a "rebirth." However, there is a complex intermixing of past families and present families. These create problematic situations for both spouses, children, old and new families.[22]

These individuals find that the second marriage is more egalitarian and happier than the first. Remarried people usually marry a different kind of person with a different personality structure. They find that they value friendship and companionship more than they did when they first married. And yet, 59 percent of second marriages, but only 37 percent of first marriages, end in divorce. The meaning of these statistics awaits clarification.

FAMILY TASKS

Provision of Basic Physical Needs: Food, Shelter, Clothing

The essential life-maintaining tasks of the family group may at times be overlooked by middle-class therapists treating middle-class families. Those who have come into contact with family systems for which these basics have not been provided become much more aware that there is a fundamental biological requirement for all families. All of the more complex functions of the family will be affected in one way or another and become distorted or deficient, depending upon the extent to which these needs are adequately met or dealt with in an idiosyncratic fashion. A therapist must pay attention to the basic reality factors and, where indicated, the major, or at least the initial effort, may have to be to help the family deal more adequately with its basic needs. A family system already overwhelmed by gross deficiencies in basic needs will not usually be motivated or sensitive to more sophisticated or symbolic considerations.

Development of a Marital Coalition

The core of the family is the marital coalition. This term implies that the spouses have been able to loosen their ties appropriately from their families of origin and have been able to develop a sense of their own individuality and self-worth. Marriage is not merely a joining together of two individuals; it is also a distillation of their families of origin, each with its own experiences, history, life style, and attitudes. One marries not only an individual, but also the family context in which the individual lives.[23] Actual members of these original families often play important roles in the new family. Some individuals may come to a marriage hoping to gain families they never had, such as the child who spent many years in foster homes.[24]

If grandparents are alive, they may be involved very clearly and specifically in the daily operations of nuclear families. They may take sides, comment on childrearing practices, or live next door. In healthy families, in-laws can provide a good deal of cohesion and financial and emotional support to make a new family function more efficiently. In-laws can also be a destructive force, however. This can happen, for example, when the mother-in-law tries to reform or control her daughter-in-law, or when the husband reacts unrealistically towards his mother-in-law, unthinkingly seeing her as a carbon copy of his own mother.

Even when the extended family is not physically present, however, the patterns experienced by the spouses in their original families inevitably influence their current marital and family interactions. In its extreme the "three-generation hypothesis" refers to the notion that influences may be passed down from grandparents to grandchildren.[25,26] Therefore a therapist must constantly bear in mind the presence of these third parties.[27]

The couple must be able to work together toward common goals and to establish both complementary and symmetrical relationships that are mutually functional and satisfactory. A *complementary relationship* occurs when two people exchange different sorts of behavior (for example, giving and receiving). A *symmetrical relationship* occurs when two people exchange the same behavior (for example, passivity). When a couple is unable to form either of these relationships, the marriage in that context may be restricted.[23]

The process of working out a satisfactory marital relationship involves shared agreements, largely undiscussed, between the two people involved. These agreements may consist of explicit rules, implied rules (which the couple would agree to if they were aware of them), and rules that an observer would note but that the couple itself probably would deny. Seen this way, conflicts in marriage are brought about when there are disagreements about the rules of living together, about who is to set those rules, and about who is to attempt to enforce those rules that are mutually incompatible. For example, there may be disagreements as to whether the husband or wife should wash the dishes, but there may be further disagreements as to who should make this decision. More complex still is the situation in which one spouse forces the other to agree "voluntarily" to wash the dishes.

Another convenient and useful way of understanding marital or dyadic (two person) relationships involves three critical dimensions:[28]

1. *Power:* Who is in charge? There are some subtleties in this category, for example, an apparently "weaker" or "sicker" member may conquer by means of this very "weakness" or "sickness." Also, leadership need not be all or none—the father can be leader in deciding which car to buy and the mother can be leader in deciding what food to serve.
2. *Intimacy:* Partners struggle with their need for and fear of closeness.
3. *Inclusion and Exclusion:* Who else is considered to be part of the marital system? This question applies not only to actual relatives and other persons but also to time allocations for career, recreational interests, and so on.

The ways in which these dimensions will be handled will depend on the intrapsychic characteristics of the individuals, the marital and family styles that have evolved, and the phases of the marriage at the time in question. Dysfunctional couples tend to be less flexible and more static and rigid. One of the core issues of marital therapy and marriage is the meshing of individual needs with the needs of the relationship.

Berman and Lief indicate that, "issues that appear to be purely individual or purely dyadic are often actually a result of a complicated interaction between marital and individual crisis points (especially at ages 30 and 40)."[28]

At this point it may be worthwhile to review and elaborate on the concepts discussed thus far. Table 3-2 compares the stages of development for individuals and for marital systems including phases, specific tasks and conflicts, and how these dimensions of marital relationships emerge during the marital life cycle. (The reader is also referred to the earlier, more basic discussion of some of these issues, centered around Fig. 3-1 and Table 3-1).

Table 3-2 should be carefully studied, since no attempt will be made to repeat in narrative form all the details contained therein. As an example of how the information may be helpful, however, we can consider the case of a marital couple coming for treatment, both partners of whom are in their late thirties. Referring to Table 3-2, under Stage 4, the therapist can, at a glance, focus on what the expectable individual and marital tasks and challenges of this period are likely to be, and guide the evaluation and treatment accordingly. By shifting to earlier and later stages, one can get a sense of how adequately previous periods have been handled, and of the capacity of the marital dyad for dealing with the future.

The extent to which these issues—involving family rules, roles, and coalitions —are satisfactorily clarified and developed and the manner in which the process occurs are related to the couple's style of communicating thoughts, feelings, and attitudes. Partners who are experienced in expressing themselves (and are permitted to do so) about relevant, meaningful, interpersonal issues will stand a better chance of coping competently with the challenges of family living. If the marriage is one in which the members are not free or accustomed to indicate their concerns and needs, then the members will be hampered in dealing productively with the inevitable stresses that will befall the marriage. Each of these two styles may be self-reinforcing, so that "virtuous" and "vicious" cycles, respectively, may be set up.

For the spouses the marriage will present an opportunity for them to deal with their sexual needs. It may offer, in part, a relationship of friends in which there is mutual sharing of feelings, interests, activities, availability, and emotional support. Historically marriages were based to a large extent on ecomonic considerations. This continues to be the case today, but for the most part not as prominently so. Marriage offers a fairly practical and acceptable way to conceive and raise children. Marriage seems to offer a sense of stability, continuity, and meaningful direction into the future. For some, marriage is a response to a variety of social pressures that sanction and reinforce it as an institution. For any two individuals, marriage may afford the opportunity for the meshing of particular psychological traits and needs.

The marital coalition over the entire course of the family cycle is marked by changing circumstances. Usually the spouses have a period of time alone together as husband and wife before the arrival of offspring. Later they must accommodate to being a father or mother as part of a *parental dyad,* in addition to being either husband or wife as part of a *marital dyad.* With the passage of time the

Table 3-2
Individual and Marital Stages of Development[28]

Item	Stage 1 (18-21 years)	Stage 2 (22-28 years)	Stage 3 (29-31 years)	Stage 4 (32-39 years)	Stage 5 (40-42 years)	Stage 6 (43-59 years)	Stage 7 (60 years and over)
Individual stage*	Pulling up roots	Provisional adulthood	Transition at age 30	Settling down	Mid-life transition†	Middle adulthood	Older age
Individual task	Developing autonomy	Developing intimacy and occupational identification: "getting into the adult world"	Deciding about commitment to work and marriage	Deepening commitments: pursuing more long-range goals	Searching for "fit" between aspirations and environment	Restabilizing and reordering priorities	Dealing effectively with aging, illness and death while retaining zest for life
Marital task	Shift from family of origin to new commitment	Provisional marital commitment	Commitment crises; restlessness	Productivity: children, work, friends, and marriage	Summing up: success and failure are evaluated and future goals sought	Resolving conflicts and stabilizing the marriage for the long haul	Supporting and enhancing each other's struggle for productivity and fulfillment in face of the threats of aging

Marital conflict	Original family ties conflict with adaptation	Uncertainty about choice of marital partner; stress over parenthood	Doubts about choice come into sharp conflict; rates of growth may diverge if spouse has not successfully negotiated stage 2 because of parental obligations	Husband and wife have different and conflicting ways of achieving productivity	Husband and wife perceive "success" differently; conflict between individual success and remaining in the marriage	Conflicting rates and directions of emotional growth; concerns about losing youthfulness may lead to depression and/or acting out	Conflicts are generated by rekindled fears of desertion, loneliness, and sexual failure
Intimacy	Fragile intimacy	Deepening but ambivalent intimacy	Increasing distance while partners make up their minds about each other	Marked increase in intimacy in "good" marriages; gradual distancing in "bad" marriages	Tenuous intimacy as fantasies about others increase	Intimacy is threatened by aging and by boredom vis-à-vis a secure and stable relationship; departure of children may increase or decrease intimacy	Struggle to maintain intimacy in the face of eventual separation; in most marriages this dimension achieves a stable plateau

Table 3-2 (continued)

Item	Stage 1 (18-21 years)	Stage 2 (22-28 years)	Stage 3 (29-31 years)	Stage 4 (32-39 years)	Stage 5 (40-42 years)	Stage 6 (43-59 years)	Stage 7 (60 years and over)
Power	Testing of power	Establishment of patterns of conflict resolution	Sharp vying for power and dominance	Establishment of definite patterns of decision making and dominance	Power in outside world is tested vis-à-vis power in the marriage	Conflicts often increase when children leave, and security appears threatened	Survival fears stir up needs for control and dominance
Marital boundaries	Conflicts over in-laws	Friends and potential lovers; work versus family	Temporary disruptions including extramarital sex or reactive "fortress building"	Nuclear family closes boundaries	Disruption due to reevaluation; drive versus restabilization	Boundaries are usually fixed except in crises such as illness, death, job change, and sudden shift in role relationships	Loss of family and friends leads to closing in of boundaries; physical environment is crucial in maintaining ties with the outside world

(Reprinted with permission from the authors and the American Journal of Psychiatry)

*From Levinson and associates[9]

†For some individuals, this stage may run throughout their forties.

parental role decreases in functional significance and the marital partnership becomes the primary, perhaps almost the exclusive, dyad once again.

If the marital interaction has atrophied while the children were being parented, it will be difficult to let the children go. A major readjustment will be necessary when the two partners find themselves alone in an empty house after the children have grown, since they will have to renew their roles of husband and wife. Figure 3-1 makes clear that the average family life cycle will find the marital partners alone together for about half the total lifetime of the family after the children have left home. For about half of this latter period the breadwinner often is no longer working (thereby losing another important role function and self-esteem support) and the two marital partners are physically together more than they were in previous years.

Individual roles and views of the relationship may contribute to the couple's problem.[29] With the shift in marital expectations, increasing attention must be paid to individual developmental goals. Even the individuals of a well-functioning couple can grow apart or distinct from each other. As goals, values, and expectations change, marital interaction may cease to be gratifying or rewarding. The individual adaptive changes, which disturb the balance of the relationship itself, may cease to be functional if complementary shifts are not possible or if they are not strongly desired by the other partner.

Marital conflict arises from many sources including differences in information, beliefs, interests, desires, and values, as well as competition between the partners. One can distinguish between productive and destructive conflicts. Productive conflicts may be characterized by mutual recognition of different interests, open and honest communication, and trusting attitudes that allow both partners the possibility of finding creative solutions. Destructive conflicts may be characterized by tendencies to rely on strategies of power and on tactics of threat, coercion, and deception—all of which lead to mutual suspicion and lack of communication. With a dysfunctional marriage the therapist must elucidate the patterns that have resulted in the predominance of destructive conflicts in the marital interaction.

A recent author explores the factors that make marriages successful.[30] Not surprisingly, there are no simple answers. Some positive relationships consist of a matching of individuals with complementary styles, while others are of a pairing of individuals with symmetrical styles. The one finding that seems constant is that of "interest in each other as companions." These people are "not boring and they are not bored within their marriages." Are the two people capable of being friends, in addition to being compatible with respect to sex, money, social class background, and the like?

Computer matching of potential couples tends to use the variables of socioeconomic class, which usually amounts to education and income, religious, ethnic, and racial backgrounds, political and social attitudes and values, avocational interests, and others, with the notion that the closer the two individuals are on these parameters the greater the chance for a successful match. Dissimilarity or complementarity of personality styles may actually enhance a partnership, as might other subsidiary interests. Two people matched with this set of variables would also be capable of being friends, as well as marital partners.

A couple may start out as friends but, as in other relationships, differential growth rates or patterns between the two of them may lead to a realization that they have relatively little in common. Life stresses can cause irreparable divisions between partners—for example, an unwanted pregnancy; loss of income (which forces one partner to work with resultant resentment from the other); illness or invalidism in one spouse. Life-stress events can be more potent than the intensity of the friendship, and negative feelings about the stress event may outweigh the positive feelings of mutuality.

An increasingly common variant of the typical American marriage is the so called *dual-career family*. By dual-career families, we mean families "in which the husband and wife engage in careers involving a high degree of emotional commitment and time involvement while they are rearing young children."[31] When these families are successful, they are distinctive in their flexibility and role interchangeability. "They gave evidence of some degree of jointly solving problems that arose in the areas of childcare and scheduling of domestic responsibilities."[31] There are simultaneously significant role strains which revolve around two areas. The first is the strain the wife feels in fulfilling her role as wife and mother. The second is the husband's feeling that he is not getting enough emotional support from his wife.

A number of techniques exist for modifying role strain including: (1) assigning priority to domestic roles; (2) using rationalization, "It's the quality of the time I spend with the children rather than the amount"; (3) translating into family patterns the objective of maximizing family time—for example, skiing, camping trips, dinners with the whole family together; (4) raising children to be independent and giving them values involving sensitivity, compassion, receptivity, and extroversion. These techniques can be contrasted to those of working-class mothers who give high priority to behavior performance, obedience, and respect (see Chapter 13).

Dual-career families work best when they can afford domestic help or when the extended family can fill the gaps. The success or failure of a dual-career family can revolve around the relationship with or the availability of a grandparent. Coping with the stresses of dual careers can enhance personal growth and lead to a more rewarding marital relationship.[32]

Personality Development

Families are thought of as crucial in socializing offspring in relation to a particular culture. The degree to which parents are physically responsible for determining the outcome of the nature of their children varies from one culture to another, as well as from one family and one offspring to another. Our own present-day American culture seems to offer a variety of norms for families in this respect, and enculturation is also strongly influenced by peer groups, schools, and TV.

UTILIZATION OF AGE-APPROPRIATE
CHILDREARING TECHNIQUES

Both parents should have at their disposal the techniques for childrearing and the emotional capacity for relating appropriately to the offspring at each phase of development. Given the qualifications mentioned earlier, early experiences are critical in intellectual and emotional development. It has been shown that differential rearing can even affect the actual structure and chemistry of brain tissue.

Progress is now being made toward ascertaining the specific effects of rearing conditions on brain and behavior, properties of the environment that contribute to these effects, and developmental periods in which brain tissue is most sensitive to environmental modification.[33]

Each stage of childrearing provides opportunities as well as pitfalls. The decision to have a child; the period of pregnancy, birth, and the immediate neonatal period; the varying and insistent demands of the infant and the growing child; and then the demands of the school years, adolescence, and further independence; the culminating period in which offsprings leave home and form their own families; and then the relationship to offsprings as coadults—all constitute a process that is amazingly complex and challenging.

It is not surprising that families experience many difficulties along the way. For many individuals, parenthood will be one of the most fulfilling roles in their lives, but for others it will seem painful and unrewarding. Marital partners may be relatively unsophisticated and ignorant with respect to appropriate techniques and cultural expectations relating to various developmental phases. They may have particular difficulty in some specific phase, perhaps because of what they experienced in their own families of origin. They may find it difficult to move from one stage to another, and may find themselves "hanging on" inappropriately to a phase that is past. For example, some couples seem to be particularly comfortable with infants and children, and do a good job in raising them, but have a stormy and troublesome time with adolescents.

Mr. and Mrs. Z were in their late thirties and had considerable experience in raising puppies and violets. Only after several years of marriage did they decide to have a child. They had done quite well when their son was an infant, enjoying diapering, feeding, and so forth; but as soon as he became autonomous and had desires of his own, they found that he upset the routine they had worked out over many years, and they began increasingly to fight with one another. Patterns that had been set for the past 13 years suddenly were no longer available.

Families may become so rigid that they are unable to move successfully from one phase to another. For example, it is the job of the family, among other tasks, to make sure that during late adolescence the children are appropriately emancipated from the family. This will be a difficult task for families in which the spouses do not have a gratifying marital relationship to fill the void created when the children leave the family. Such parents may refuse to let the adolescents out of the house to date or to spend time with their own peers.

MAINTENANCE OF THE PARENTAL COALITION

The arrival of children signals the need for the marital partners to broaden their roles to include those of being parents. The task is to form an appropriate *parental* coalition with respect to childrearing practices. It is beneficial to have parental agreement and consistency in these areas, with a sharing of responsibility and mutual support. Children may become confused if they do not know what is expected of them, or if they receive continually conflicting messages from each of the parents. Clearly, parents cannot agree on everything, and there may be danger in attempting to present a facade of agreements that is in fact only pseudoagreements. On basic important matters, however, it is preferable that parents have some sort of mutual, consistent childrearing guidelines, rather than not being able to form a working coalition.

Mr. and Mrs. L were only children who married in their late twenties. They both had been favorite children in their respective extended families. They found in the early years of their marriage that whenever a decision had to be made (as it did some 30 to 40 times a day), decision making was accomplished by one partner "winning" and the other "losing." When they had children, this pattern continued and was accentuated by the children's own desires. The children quickly found that they could get what they wanted by aligning themselves with one parent or the other. The couple sought treatment at the point where they were unable to communicate and agree about anything, because discussion exploded into throwing pots and pans with the children "cheering them on."

Are two parents required? It is believed that the parent of the same sex as the offspring serves as a role model for identification, while the parent of the opposite sex provides the basic love object. In a family in which the parents do not form a workable coalition, the child may have difficulty in development.

In a family with one parent absent (through death or divorce, for example), personality defects of various types may be formed at certain periods in the child's development, unless the remaining parent or parent-surrogate is able to fill the role of the absent one.[34] A critical factor in this situation seems to be the quality of the parental relationship prior to the loss of the parent. If the parents got along well, then the loss of one of them may be much less significant for the child than if they did not get along well. The remaining spouse is able to encourage positive, rather than negative, identification with the lost parent.

The relationship that existed between the lost parent and the child is also of crucial importance to the child's adjustment following "parental deprivation." The term "parental deprivation" is popularly used to connote the belief that loss or deprivation is etiological in a child's deficiencies. This view is not always justified by the data. If parent and child got along well before the separation, then there is a much greater likelihood of the child's continuing to do well after the separation. In one case, a father often took his 7-year-old son fishing, put him to bed every evening, and participated in most childrearing decisions. After the loss of his father, the son showed no decline in functioning.

Parents may be able to maintain a reasonable coalition with their children and be relatively good parents, even though in other areas there may be considerable marital disharmony. This is sometimes seen in the extreme case in which the spouses have been divorced but are able to maintain positive parental functioning. In other families the opposite can also be seen, for even though the marital relationship functions fairly adequately, the two spouses seem unwilling or unable to devote the requisite amount of time, energy, and interest to the parental role. They are good marital partners, but relatively poor parents. This is sometimes the case with immature, selfish, or narcissistic parents.

In a family in which there are children who are seriously disturbed, the parents, instead of forming a workable coalition, may (1) deprecate each other in a hostile manner; (2) become rivals for the child; (3) equate the child's loyalty to the other parent with rejection of themselves; (4) indicate to the child that growing up to be like the other parent is unacceptable; or (5) promote unhealthy parent-child dyads. The child may respond by (1) trying to bridge the gap between parents; (2) feeling responsible for the parents' problems (the scapegoat role); or by (3) supporting the parent who the child feels the need to cater to the most.

Often the child who is considered disturbed is the bond that holds the marriage together, for the parents in many ways can become dependent on the child's problems to keep the focus off their own relationship. Improvement in the child may then be expected to cause disruption in the parental relationship.

MAINTENANCE OF GENERATION BOUNDARIES

Broadly speaking, parents must act like parents and children like children. The nature of the generation boundary changes at various stages of the family life cycle. The nurturing role of parents in relation to their children is different when the child is 1 week old from when the child is 40 years old. Parents should not be emotionally dependent on their immature children but, rather, should look to one another for support and reinforcement.

The R family consisted of father, mother, older daughter, and two sons. Mr R was barely able to hold a half-time job while Mrs. R stayed at home, alternately complaining of various bodily ailments and crying hysterically. In this family the daughter planned and cooked the meals, the two sons both worked to supplement the family income, and the three children together did the planning of family activities each week. When major decisions had to be made, the older son would call the family together; the parents would be brought in to the room and would then sit passively while the three children made the decisions, such as how to finance a family house.

In the B family, the father had been killed in an automobile accident soon after the third daughter was born. Mrs. B found herself overwhelmed by having to raise her daughters and had turned over this job to the eldest daughter. This daughter had become overly rigid in enforcing limits, not allowing either of her two younger sisters to date. Consequently, the two younger sisters were at war with her. The eldest sister, at the age of 19, felt deprived of her own chance to have fun.

In the P family, both father and mother were brilliant physicians. The couple was thought to have an ideal marriage and both seemed to be functioning successfully. They had three children. The mother suffered a severe automobile accident in which she was brain damaged. The father's reaction to this was to spend less and less time with the family. He turned the responsibility of running the family over to the older son. The older son was told that he was responsible for the mother because he was the man of the house. The older son actually did assume responsibility; for example, he paid the bills, did the shopping, and took care of younger siblings. The father spent less and less time at home and the older son spent most of his hours with the mother. Eventually he began to have several fights with the younger siblings and the mother's condition took a turn for the worse. The father accused him of killing the mother because she had become upset over the fighting. The older son's solution was to get out of the house (that is, to go *away* to college), but he had many misgivings and much guilt over his decision to do so.

The maintenance of generation boundaries tends to lessen role conflicts that follow the blurring of roles and the ambiguity this fosters. A totally "democratic" family in which all members, regardless of age, responsibility, and experience have an equal voice in all decisions seems wholly unrealistic. Far from being something to be decried, a "generation gap" between parents and children is an absolute necessity, if we mean by the term a difference in responsibility, role, maturity, and often of attitude. It should not, however, consist of a deficiency in communication. Recognition must be given to the different affectional relationships that need to exist between parents and between parent and child. Emotional room must be left for the child to learn, for the child to interact with peer groups, and for the child to develop an identity.

In a seriously disturbed family, parents may exist in a childlike dependency on one another; may be rivals for the child's affection; or may be jealous of the child. Incestuous feelings may become pronounced, and parents may leave the task of decision making to the child rather than appropriately assuming that responsibility themselves.[35] Other parents may be dissatisfied with their own lives and become jealous of their offspring and thus compete with them. Parents in a disturbed family may also feel inadequate in their parental role (perhaps because of unfortunate experiences in their own family of origin) and may be inappropriately and unrealistically permissive, abdicating many of the duties and responsibilities that revolve around the role of the parent. In some instances, because of economic or other realistic pressures, an older child may be called on to fulfill a parental role for the younger siblings and thus may never have the opportunity to experience and master the developmental tasks of childhood or adolescence.

Unlike the unrealistically permissive parents, overly dictatorial parents at least offer their offspring a clear model (if only one to revolt against), although they often may be using the child to attempt to master some of their own unresolved issues. Often such parents find it extremely difficult to let go of their offspring in the realization that they have become autonomous after a certain stage in their development. The parents should recognize that they have done the best they could and need no longer feel responsibility for their children; instead they should deal with them as fellow adults.

Special problems exist in a society such as our own which is extremely youth oriented and in which the rate of change is constantly accelerating. In such a society, it is hard for parents and children to feel that what the parents have to offer is relevant. Children are bombarded by the outside influences from the communications media (notably TV). The age-peer group may prematurely come to be a dominating influence. Parents (and their children) may become confused, and as a consequence some may throw up their hands in permissiveness, whereas others put their foot down in authoritarianism.

ADHERENCE TO APPROPRIATE SEX-LINKED ROLES

The sexual identity of the offspring is an important factor in personality formation. Appropriate sex-linked role attributes do not develop merely by the accident of biologically male or female birth; they are acquired by role allocations starting in infancy and continuing with role assumptions and identification as the child grows older. The crucial factor in determining one's basic *sexual identity* (that is, whether one regards oneself as basically a male or female) is that of how our parents deal with us in this respect. This factor will be dominant even if it contradicts every known biological gender indicator. Even clearer are the environmental influences in *gender role* (how masculine or feminine we consider ourselves to be and what the components of this identity are).

Lidz has written that clear-cut reversals with respect to gender role functioning and task divisions lead to important distortions in the child's development.[15] This traditional view holds that the female should be the expressive-affectional gender and the male should be the instrumental-adaptive gender. Furthermore, a cold, nonaffectionate mother would be relatively more harmful to the offspring, especially to female offspring, than would a cold, nonaffectionate father. A weak, ineffective father on the other hand would tend to be more damaging to the offspring, especially the male offspring, than would a weak, ineffective mother.

These traditional, idealized gender roles have been increasingly challenged in recent years, viz through changes in sex-appropriate grooming and dress and in the emergence of changing attitudes of women. Children raised by a lesbian parent are psychologically healthy and do not become homosexual when evaluated in their teens.[36] An increasing number of people are becoming more free to explore whatever potentialities exist within themselves without being constrained by the gender stereotypes imposed by society. Many men are more comfortable being "expressive and empathic," and many women are feeling less threatened by being "capable and logical." The negative aspect of this development lies in the fostering of greater sexual and gender role confusion.

One of the current areas of conflict in families is that of role assignments. Women have been assigned to roles and tasks that place them in a submissive position to the husband and give them little gratification. Men, as fathers, have been found to be as significant in a child's development as women are as mothers.[37] There is a gradual changing of role assignment, and a more egalitarian sharing of tasks. Clinicians have noted that changes in role disrupt families in which a dominant-submissive pattern exists.[38] Vital family tasks need to be performed, although who should perform them might best be decided on the basis of mutual accommodation, rather than cultural gender stereotypes.

ENCULTURATION OF THE OFFSPRING

It is one of the tasks of parents to teach the younger generation the basic adaptive techniques of their culture. It is necessary for them to transmit instrumentally valid ways of thinking, feeling, and acting.

Communication skills are basic for any type of successful and gratifying social interaction and personality growth. Parents usually play the major role in the children's proper development of these skills. They themselves are models for the children in behavior and in the appropriate and effective methods of expressing thoughts and feelings. Children need to be given the proper labels and comments with respect to what and how they feel and think. A child who is clearly angry needs to have this feeling recognized and labeled, rather than having a parent consistently deny, overlook, or misinterpret such feelings. The children need to be given leeway to experience their own feelings as valid and not be restricted to those of their parents.

We learn basic rules of how and what to think, feel, and do, primarily as a result of early family experiences. General styles of interacting and fundamental attitudes toward ourselves and the environment—as well as what thoughts, feelings, and actions are acceptable and how and under what circumstances they may be expressed—are all laid down for us by our early and repeated transactions with our parents.

In pathological families, various difficulties in these areas of psychological development may be noted. Members of dysfunctional families may show particularly intrusive, projective, tangential, concrete, or bizarre thinking. There may be considerable ambiguity and vagueness with a prevailing feeling of meaninglessness. Some investigators have noted these difficulties especially in families of schizophrenic patients (see Chapter 12). In some families the children's emotions may be distorted because the children are consistently denied, contradicted, ignored, or punished. For example, in some families sadness or disappointment cannot be expressed by the child because it "upsets" the parents.

Certain families seem to have difficulty teaching their children socially acceptable techniques of behavior, and these children seem to grow up with either a deficient or a distorted repertory of social-behavioral skills. Both overly authoritarian and overly permissive attitudes in the parents may lead to inflexible, maladaptive patterns in the children.

How are childrearing tasks dealt with by different socioeconomic classes?* There are certain practices that do seem "typical" for each class. The higher the parents' social class position, the more likely they are to value characteristics indicative of self-direction and the less likely they are to value those of conformity to external authority. Working-class parents are consistently more likely to employ physical punishment and to live in the present and in terms of an action orientation and early gratification of impulses. Middle-class families rely more on "constrictive" practices, such as reasoning, isolation, and appeals of guilt (and other methods involving the threat of loss of love); they are future oriented; deal more with words (and often symbolic process); and repress and delay gratification. When some families move up the socioeconomic ladder thay adopt the parental practices of their new class; others, however, still raise their children the way they themselves were raised.[39]

CHARACTERISTICS OF THE FUNCTIONAL FAMILY

The previous discussion on family function has been based largely on the work of Lidz and his coworkers.[15] Other views on adaptive family qualities have been provided by recent studies in which white middle-class urban families were evaluated and placed on a continuum from "healthy" to "severely disturbed."[16, 40] Characteristics found in the well-functioning families included:

1. A flexible power structure with shared authority and a clear family rule system, a strong parental coalition, intact generation boundaries, and an "affiliative" (rather than "oppositional") style
2. Individuation of family members which included both separateness and

*By socioeconomic classes we mean the classification of families according to a given educational and occupational status.

closeness, comfort with disagreement and uncertainty, freedom and spontaneity in communication, respect for and sensitivity to the differentness and subjective world of others, and relatively little scapegoating or blaming

3. Strong marital and community relationships, and ability to deal with separation and loss realistically
4. Family myths closely attuned to reality
5. Humor, tenderness, caring, and hopefulness, with conflicts out in the open, and an absence of chronic resentments

This empiric study appears to validate and overlap in many ways the other formulations presented in this chapter. Therefore it lends support to the belief that the qualities noted may indeed be crucial ones for healthy family functioning. (The reader is referred to Chapter 4 for further discussion of how less adaptive families were evaluated along these same parameters. Table 4-1 summarizes all these findings. See pp. 71-73)

The Functional Single-Parent Family

One of the most dramatic social statistics of the decade is the increase in single-parent families (see Chapter 2) in which there is only one parent at home by reason of death, divorce, separation, or births outside of marriage. About 10 percent of all families are now one-parent families. About 90 percent of these families are headed by females. The single-parent family can be viewed as an alternative form of family life. When the role of the absent parent is taken by the remaining parent or by someone else, the homeostatic forces may operate essentially as they do for a two-parent family. With the exception of the marital coalition phases, the family life cycle may be the same as for the two-parent families.

Most of the interesting differences between one-parent and two-parent families exist in the area of family tasks. Many single parents find themselves much closer to their children than they were when the other parent was also present. They consciously compensate for the absent parent. In other cases the single parents may spend less time with the children than they did previously because of a need to work and support the family, and also because they are involved in dating and social activities outside the home.

Being the only parent creates family issues that may include:[21]

1. Social isolation and loneliness
2. Possible awkwardness in dating and jealousy from the children
3. Demand by small children for the continuous physical presence of the one parent
4. Children fending for themselves and carrying a greater share of the domestic responsibilities because the sole parent is working

5. Children feeling different from other children because they are a member of a single-parent family
6. Less opportunity to discuss pros and cons of decisions and to get support and feedback when decisions are made
7. Crises and shifts caused by the introduction of a potential new mate or lover or companion, or a combination of these

Evaluation of the impact of an absent spouse on the rest of the family unit must take into account the phase of family development in which the absence occurred and the total length of the absence, the feelings of the remaining family members about the nonpresent member, and the mechanisms the family has utilized in coping with its different constellation. For example, for the remaining spouse, the absence of a partner can lead to loneliness and to the increased burden of not being able to share in marital and parental role complementarity. The remaining spouse may have to be both mother and father to the children. At first all of this may seem overwhelming. After a time, however, the family unit may have reorganized itself and may have reached a new equilibrium utilizing the potentialities that were not readily apparent earlier. Single-parent families in which the father is the head of the household appear to do just as well as those in which the mother is the main figure. The effectiveness of parenting depends not on the sex-stereotypic role but on the qualities of the specific parent. Despite this reassuring fact, however, one report concludes that it is still preferable to have a two-parent family.

In those families without one parent, or those who have had a child die, the incidence of childrearing failure increases. A whole family is generally better than part of a family. Identity formations seem more difficult without family role models and opportunities to observe adults of both sexes functioning intimately within a framework of mutual commitment.[16]

MOTHER-HEADED, SINGLE-PARENT FAMILIES

Some of the stresses of mother-headed families include task overload, financial stress, social isolation and loneliness, and a need for "time out." These stresses may be greater for mothers than for fathers, if the mother has custody. They are greater for divorced women than for women who are widowed.

In such families potential problems for developing children may include defects in cognitive performance. Children growing up in mother-headed families may show deficits in such abilities, especially in cases in which children lost their fathers at an early stage of their development. The effects of such a loss on children may be cumulative and may not appear until they reach grade school. A father with low participation or low warmth in his relationship with the family may be just as detrimental to his child's intellectual growth as one who is totally absent. Therefore the mere presence of a father is not the important variable, rather it is the type of participation that a caring father can provide. A warm father may substitute successfully, as will an achievement-oriented mother.

A second problem area can be in the social and emotional development of the offspring. Recent research seems to indicate, contrary to popular thinking, that in terms of sex-role typing the presence of a father can be more important than the presence of the mother—not only for development of the boys but also for girls.[21] In mother-headed families boys, but not girls, demonstrated some difficulties in sex-role typing when the separation from the father occurred before the age of five. Other areas of potential risk for the child exist in the development of heterosexual relationships and in self-control.

In general, the developmental disruptions that do occur "seem to be attributable mainly to father absence, but also from stresses and lack of support systems that result in changed family functioning for the single mother and her children."[21] When the mother is able to handle her role effectively, such disruptive patterns need not occur.

The study by Kellam and associates on the risk of social maladaptation and psychological ill-health in children of Chicago black ghetto families suggests that (1) mother-alone families entail the highest risk; (2) the presence of certain second adults has an important ameliorative function—mother-grandmother families being nearly as effective as mother-father families, with mother-stepfather families similar to mother-alone families with regard to risk; and (3) the absence of the father was less crucial than the aloneness of the mother in relation to risk.[42]

FATHER-HEADED, SINGLE-PARENT FAMILIES

Father-headed families consist of only about 10 percent of single families, but this statistic is climbing since more divorced men are demanding the right to have custody of their children. "Close to 900,000 American children under the age of 18 (nearly 50,000 of them preschool age) now live with their male parents and the numbers are going up."[43] With many more men taking over important instrumental roles in parenting, fathers are arguing that they are just as capable and as indispensable to a child's development as are mothers. Usually fathers get custody when mothers prefer to pursue their own careers or other relationships.

Men of father-headed families have problems and concerns that are different from women of mother-headed families. In general, most fathers are much less comfortable in assuming custody of children than are mothers. This is due to the fact that up until the last decade, childrearing and domestic roles have been parceled out to mothers. After the initial period of apprehension, however, fathers seem capable of assuming the nurturing role with equal effectiveness as the mother. They do it in their own style and in their own way, with their own set of values, which may be different from those of the mother. The father needs to develop not only a set of childrearing and domestic skills, but also a method of coping with the mother's feelings about his role. To the extent that he can achieve this, the adjustment of the children will be positive.

JOINT CUSTODY, SINGLE-PARENT FAMILIES

A good and functional arrangement for custody appears to be when both parents can spend a great deal of time with their children. Although in psychiatric literature there is some bias against joint custody, more couples are electing this route.

There are many ways to set up joint custody, such as, when geographically feasible, to have the children alternate the weeks or the days in which they can visit either parent. Despite the usual objection that such an arrangement will confuse and upset the children, it appears easier for children to adapt to a new life style than it is for adults. The most important issue for the children may be to have ongoing regular contact with each of their parents; this advantage may outweigh the disadvantages of their having two homes.

Women are thought to be more capable of being nurturing figures for their children than are men, and therefore they are usually awarded custody. This belief may have been true in the past and is probably still true in the traditional family setting; but this belief certainly does not pertain to all men and women, nor to family systems and role allocations of contemporary college graduate families. Within these systems there appears to be more flexibility. Women are permitted to be career oriented and men to be relatively more nurturing and "maternal" with children. Therefore, in these cases, the factors to be considered when awarding custody should include the personal qualities of each parent, as well as the age, sex, and particular needs of the offspring. Probably more careful evaluation by judges, lawyers, and other professionals would be beneficial.

The family therapist, by virtue of interest and expertise in the family system, brings a new viewpoint to the evaluation and outcome of custody and other childrearing issues. In critically assessing the parents, the family therapist should not be guided by societal biases and prejudices against granting custody to one parent and not the other merely on the basis of sexual preference, especially in the cases in which both parents are involved in childrearing and the family therefore has suitable, adaptable, and workable options. The family therapist brings new and relevant viewpoints and techniques to increase the function and happiness of single-parent families.

REFERENCES

1. Family life in America (editorial). N Eng J Med 274:1209, 1966
2. Birdwhistell R: The idealized model of the American Family. Social Casework 5:195–198, 1970

3. Ackerman N: Family therapy, in Arieti S (ed): American Handbook of Psychiatry, Vol III. New York, Basic Books, 1966, pp 201–212
4. American Psychiatric Association. A Psychiatric Glossary. New York, The Association, 1967
5. Pines M: Superkids. Psychology Today, January, 1979, pp 53–63
6. Clausen JA, Huffine CL: The impact of parental mental illness on children, in Simmons R (ed): Research in Community and Mental Health. Greenwich, Connecticut, JAI Press (in press)
7. Levinson DJ: The mid-life transition: A period in adult psychosocial development. Psychiatry 40:99–112, 1977
8. Levinson DJ: Eras: Anatomy of the life cycle. Psychiatric Opinion, September, 1978, pp 10–48
9. Levinson DJ (with Darrow CN, Kelin EB, Levinson MH, McKee B): The Seasons of a Man's Life. New York, Knopf, 1978
10. Lowenthal MF, Thurnher M, Chiriboga D: Four Stages of Life: A Comparative Study of Women and Men Facing Transitions. San Francisco, Jossey-Bass, 1975
11. Gould R: The phases of adult life: A study in developmental psychology. Am J Psychiatry 129:33–43, 1977
12. Sheehy G: Passages. Predictable Crises of Adult Life. New York, Dutton, 1974
13. Stein SP, Holzman, S, Karasu TB, et al: Mid-adult development and psychopathology. Am J Psychiatry 135:676–681, 1978
14. Duvall E: Family Development. Philadelphia, Lippincott, 1967, pp 44–46
15. Lidz T: The Family and Human Adaptation. New York, International Universities Press, 1963
16. Lewis JM, Beavers WR, Gossett JT: No Single Thread: Psychological Health in the Family System. New York, Brunner/Mazel, 1976
17. Rapoport R: Normal crises, family structure and mental health. Fam Process 2:68–80, 1963, pp 76–77
18. Rapoport R, Rapoport RN: New light on the honeymoon. Human Relations 17:33–56, 1964
19. Weiss RS: Marital Separation. New York, Basic Books, 1975
20. McDonald MC: On the matter of love. Psychiatric News, April 15, 1977, pp 41–42
21. Hetherington EM, Cox M, Cox R: The development of children in mother-headed families, in Reiss D, Hoffman HA (eds): The American Family: Dying or Developing. New York, Plenum Press, 1979, pp 117–156
22. Westoff L: Two-time winners. New York Times, Magazine Section, August 10, 1975, p 10
23. Haley J: Marriage therapy. Arch Gen Psychiatry 8:213–234, 1963
24. Leader AL: The place of in-laws in marital relationships. Social Casework 56:486–491, 1975
25. Mendell D, Cleveland S: A three-generation view of a school phobia. Voices 3:16–19, 1967
26. Mendell D, Cleveland S, Fisher S: A five-generation family theme. Fam Process 7:126–132, 1968
27. Zuk G: Triadic-based family therapy. Int J Psychiatry 8:539–569, 1969
28. Berman EM, Lief HI: Marital therapy from a psychiatric perspective: An overview. Am J Psychiatry 132:583–592, 1975

29. Nadelson CC, et al: Evaluation procedures for conjoint marital therapy. Social Casework 56:91–96, 1975
30. O'Brien P: Marriages That Work. New York, Random House, 1977
31. Johnson CL, Johnson FA: Attitudes toward parenting in dual-career families. Am J Psychiatry 134:391–394, 1977
32. Nadelson T, Eisenberg L: The successful professional woman: On being married to one. Am J Psychiatry 134:1071–1076, 1977
33. Wallace P: Complex environments: Effects on brain development. Science 185:1035–1037, 1974
34. Block J: Lives Through Time. Berkeley, California, Bancroft, 1971
35. Coe WC, Curry AE, Kessler DR: Family interactions of psychiatric patients. Fam Process 8:119–130, 1969
36. Green R: Sexual identity of 37 children raised by homosexual or transsexual parents. Am J Psychiatry 135:692–697, 1978
37. Block J: Lives Through Time. Berkeley, California, Bancroft, 1971
38. Silverman J: The women's liberation movement: Its impact on marriage. Hosp & Comm Psychiatry 26:39–40, 1975
39. Kohn M: The effects of social class on parental values and practices, in Reiss D, Hoffman HA (eds): The American Family: Dying or Developing. New York, Plenum Press, 1979, pp 45–72
40. Lewis JM, et al: Family systems and individual functioning: Healthy families. Presented at the American Psychiatric Association, Annual Meeting, Anaheim, California, May, 1975
41. Finer M: Report of the committee on one-parent families. London, England, Her Majesty's Stationery Office, 1974
42. Kellam SG, Ensminger ME, Turner RJ: Family structure and mental health of children. Arch Gen Psychiatry 34:1012–1022, 1977
43. Molinoff DD: Life with father. New York Times, Magazine Section, May 22, 1977, pp 12–17

The Interrupted Marriage by Rigaud Benoit, 1972. Courtesy of Selden Rodman, from *The Miracle of Haitian Art* by Selden Rodman.

4

Understanding the Dysfunctional Family

OBJECTIVES

- To understand the relationship between dysfunctional families and disturbances in the family system, family life cycle, family tasks, and family myths
- To understand the theories of how one individual family member becomes the identified patient

INTRODUCTION

In the preceding chapter, we described the organization and course of the functional family. We discussed the concept of the family as a system with its own life cycle, as well as the relation of family tasks to functional family units. In this chapter we will focus on the disturbances in these same areas and the ways in which families are dysfunctional. We will discuss the family life cycle, the inability of the family to accomplish family tasks, dysfunctional family myths, types of disturbances manifested by the dysfunctional family systems and the particular family member manifesting those disturbances.

THE DYSFUNCTIONAL FAMILY SYSTEM

Members of dysfunctional families appear to lack a healthy sense of involvement and interaction in a developing and differentiating group. In many such families, members have only the most tentative minimal contact with each other. They may be physically separated from one another in a variety of ways and for a variety of reasons. They may scarcely speak with one another or when they do, their topics of conversation will rarely deal with important family issues.[1-3] Their emotional involvement with one another may be flimsy, and, instead of feeling close to one another, they may be cold and distant. Such families are likely to develop a sense of noncohesiveness, pervading meaninglessness, and noncommitment.[4,5]

The husband in the M family was a 40-year-old Baptist of strong religious persuasion. The wife was a 25-year-old atheist. The father worked on the night shift as a factory worker, the mother as a secretary. They saw each other for 5 minutes in the morning before she went to work and for 5 minutes at night before he went to work. They came into treatment as they began to be more and more suspicious of each other, coincident to the gradually decreasing communication that had evolved over a period of 2 years.

At the other extreme are those families that appear to be relatively non-individualized masses with little or no differentiation of members.[4] It is difficult for people in such families to be separate human beings, for there may be a considerable blurring of boundaries between one's own thoughts, feelings, attitudes, and roles, and those of others in the family. The family may appear to be cohesive but is more accurately described as being agglutinated. There is a pseudocloseness and a pseudomutuality not based on true empathy or on individual needs, feelings, and stages. Under the surface, the same weakness may emerge in this type of family as in the type with minimal contact.

Families with such defects will have serious problems coping with the challenges and developments of family life, for they cannot satisfactorily communicate with each other and have not defined themselves as individuals. Such failures in not being able to communicate satisfactorily lead to further deterioration of already gravely inadequate problem-solving abilities.

The R family consisted of a father in his late forties, a mother in her early forties, and a son, Sam, in his early twenties. Sam was the identified patient. The parents, although seemingly close, had given up sexual relations and attending social functions together. Sam had dropped out of school and was staying in the house playing his guitar and watching television. The mother was perfunctory in her housework, eventually intending to clean up her closet and to study gardening. The father managed his work as a salesman by routinely following the same pattern he had for many years and was barely eking out a living. The family never seemed to disagree with one another on anything. Individual members seemed unable to allocate separate time for themselves but always did everything "together." They were afraid to deal with differentness. There was a pervading sense of emptiness; the mother spent much of her time in bed, the father complained of not getting satisfaction from his work or his family, and the son felt hopeless.

THE LIFE CYCLE OF THE DYSFUNCTIONAL FAMILY

Although some families will be plagued by minor generalized problems throughout their existence, others will have trouble at specific periods. Most episodic family difficulties may be related to an inability to cope adequately with either the tasks of the current family phase or the need to move on to a new family phase or the stress of traumatic, excessive, and out-of-order events in the family developmental cycle or all three problems.

The stresses and difficulties may be those attendant on the normal, expectable family life crises. The marriage or family may be unable to cope adequately with the current phase in its life cycle and any particular phase of the family cycle may be affected, depending on a variety of factors relating to the adequacy and availability of the family members' resources for accomplishing the tasks inherent in their current stage.

For example, as indicated in Chapter 3, two people optimally need to have reached a certain stage in their own personal development, as well as in their relationships with their own families of origin, before being ready as two independent individuals to consider marriage. To the extent that this and other prior stages have not been successfully mastered, the individuals and the marital unit will be hampered in dealing with current challenges. This concept applies to each of the family phases.

Everyone is familiar with the young married couple who find it difficult to break away from their own families to establish a successful independent unit.

On their wedding night, Mr. and Mrs. W. found that they were unable to have intercourse because of Mrs. W's nausea and vomiting. Mr. W became so depressed that the couple had to return from the honeymoon after one night. Soon after this, both husband and wife found themselves spending so much time with their own parents after work that they had very little time for each other, and "sex just never seemed to get off the ground." Each partner developed a feeling of anger and resentment toward the other and their communication became markedly decreased. At the same time, their social life became more restricted and they were unable to plan any events together. They came to therapy at the point where they were considering divorce.

A couple may feel compelled to get married because the woman has become pregnant ("the shotgun marriage"). The two people become instant marital partners and parents, perhaps involuntarily. In this situation, various developmental phases are skipped altogether or are drastically condensed.

Mrs. V, age 18, came for treatment following a suicide attempt. She had married a boy, age 19, whom she had known for four months, after discovering that she was pregnant. Although she did not really care for him, she married in order not to disgrace the family. Week nights were spent with her mother who prepared supper for the couple. On weekends Mrs. V went shopping with her mother while Mr. V played ball with his friends. He preferred not to waste time around the house since his in-laws also lived there, and since he had never gotten to know (or like) his new father-in-law. Soon after the wedding sexual relations ceased and screaming fights eventually culminated in Mrs. V's suicide attempt.

Families may find it extremely stressful to move into the next appropriate phase of marital development. Marriages and families may have chronic difficulty attempting to deal with the requirements of a particular phase; they may appear to cope quite successfully until a threatened transition plunges them into distress and dysfunction. Change is difficult, and the need to modify or abandon old familiar roles and patterns of interaction and to take on strange new ways is not easy. The "empty-nest syndrome" refers to one such difficult phase.

The J family had four teenage children, the youngest was 16 and the oldest 20. All of the children lived with their parents and were forbidden to date. On the occasions when the family did go out, they went together to "noncontroversial" movies. The family was referred by the juvenile court for treatment after the oldest child had run away several times. Inquiry revealed that both parents, although insisting that they wanted their children to grow up and be on their own, were quite frightened about the prospect of being together in the house without the children. They thought that they had probably lost interest in each other, having focused their relationship on taking care of the children.

Unusual or unexpected events in the family life cycle may overwhelm the coping capacities of family systems to handle developmental changes. Common examples of such event are those of separation, illness, accident, violent crime, or death in the family.

The Q family consisted of the father, an engineer, the mother, a housewife, and an infant daughter, age 3. The father suddenly was sent to work in Alaska, 3,000 miles from home. The mother felt lost and abandoned. She found great difficulty in taking care of the house and her daughter. The daughter was the identified patient, referred by the pediatrician because she was setting fires. It became clear that the mother was so depressed that she would go to bed early, leaving the daughter to play by herself for a couple of hours. During this time, the daughter managed to climb up to the stove and ignite a piece of paper. The father was brought home to be with his family. The mother got out of bed and the fire setting stopped.

COPING WITH TASKS IN THE DYSFUNCTIONAL FAMILY

Various deficiencies in carrying out the family's functions will lead to strains and distortions in family life. The major family tasks, as discussed earlier are:

1. To provide for the basic physical requirements
2. To develop a working marital coalition
3. To rear the offspring

In the dysfunctional family these tasks are handled differently and less adaptively than in healthy families. In Chapter 3 some of these processes and outcomes are detailed for both the functional and dysfunctional family.

Family qualities found to be important in rearing healthy children were listed in Chapter 3 (p. 57-58). In that same empiric study, families who were labeled "severely disturbed" (e.g., tending to produce psychotic offspring) were strikingly dissimilar:[6]

1. There was chaotic power structure with no parental coalition, poorly defined generation boundaries, and an "oppositional" style.
2. Individuation of family members was incompatible with acceptance by the family; instead, there was an "undifferentiated family ego mass," "group thinking," unclear communication, failure to take responsibility for one's own feelings, intrusiveness, and unresponsiveness to others.
3. There was use of fantasy and denial to defend against loss.
4. Family myths were incongruous with reality, and these families had a sense of timelessness.
5. The prevailing family affect was one of hostility or depression.

Adequate mid-range families (those tending to produce neurotic or behavior-disordered offspring) could be differentiated from both functional extremes, utilizing the same basic parameters. For details regarding this group, as well as a more complete summary of the overall findings, the reader is referred to Table 4-1.

DEVELOPMENT OF FAMILY DYSFUNCTION

Marital and family systems, like individuals, have characteristic patterns of coping with stress. The family's first line of defense is usually to evoke, strengthen, and emphasize characteristic adaptive patterns that the family unit has used in the past. If these are inappropriate or maladaptive, the type of disturbance resulting therefrom may be similar to the rigid inflexible character of an individual with a personality disorder.

If such characteristic adaptive mechanisms are not available or fail to deal adequately with the situation, however, one or another family member may develop overt symptoms. These symptoms in the family member may cause the individual to be labeled "bad," or "sick." The appropriate social helping institutions may become involved with that individual in an attempt to deal with the particular symptomatic expression. The individual then takes on the role of the

Table 4-1
Family Qualities Important in the Development of Healthy Individuals*
(Derived from Studies of White, Urban, Intact Middle-Class Families)

	Severely Disturbed Families	Adequate (Mid-range) Families	Healthy Families
I. Power Structure	Chaotic	Rigid	Flexible; shared power, with benign and generous leaders; clear, flexible family rule system
A. *Parental Coalition*	Absent; father has little power	Weak; one member dominant	Strong; father as leader; high degree of marital complementarity
B. *Generation Boundaries*	Broken; frequent overt mother-son coalition	Blurred; occasional covert parent-child coalition	Intact; children share in decisions
C. *Affiliative vs. Oppositional Style*	Behave as if encounters will be oppositional (dominant or submissive)	Intense conflict: 1. overt (producing competitive, explosive behavior disorders) 2. covert (producing depressive, compulsive, or neurotic characters)	Behave as if encounters will be affiliative
II. Degree of Family Individuation	Individuation incompatible with acceptance by others; "group think," "undifferentiated ego mass" (Bowen); "pseudomutuality," "rubber fence" (Wynne); "double-bind" (Bateson); "mystification" (Laing)	Coherent individuation but with rigidity and guilt	Separateness with closeness

71

Table 4-1 (continued)

	Severely Disturbed Families	Adequate (Mid-range) Families	Healthy Families
A. *Autonomy (ability to express and take responsibility for separateness)*	Failure to take responsibility for own feelings, actions, goals; unclear communication; indirect use of power—control of interaction without clear statement of own feelings, thoughts, or responsibilities, via: 1. asking questions 2. evasions or shift of meaning 3. diffuse attacks on others' positions 4. hostility, sarcasm, ridicule	Commonly statements relate to others' behavior or are negative statements about one's self; difficulty with ambivalence	Autonomous interaction, relatively conflict-free; comfortable with uncertainty, ambivalence, and disagreement; trial and error without loss of self-esteem; freedom in communication, spontaneity, permission to think and feel freely
B. *Respect for another's Differentness*	Invasiveness; "mind-reading"	Attempts to control others' thoughts and feelings as well as actions; frequent criticism; scapegoating inside or outside of family; many "shoulds" or blaming of others	Respect and sensitivity to subjective world of others; tolerance of uniqueness; infrequent scapegoating, projection, blaming, or denial
C. *Ability to be Responsive and Open to Others*	Impermeability; lack of acknowledgment; no negotiations	Members talk in turn, but children often ignored by parents, or several people talk at once	Open, receptive; acknowledging; skill in negotiations, agreements result from inventive compromise ("respectful negotiation")

III. Acceptance of Separation and Loss	Fantasy and denial as defenses against loss	Offspring still in conflicted relationships with parents, or unable to grieve a dead parent successfully; recreate old relationships with parents in current relationships	Able to accept separation and loss of loved ones; strong marital and wider community relationships; transcendant value system extends identity beyond family
IV. Perception of Reality			
A. *Family Mythology*	Incongruous, shared family myths maintained by denial and obliviousness	Distorted, most evident in area of feelings	Myths flexible, closely related to reality
B. *Time Binding*	Sense of timelessness	Passage of time distorted, but not obliterated	Real sense of time's passage
V. Affect (Prevailing Mood, Degree of Expressiveness, Quality of Empathy)	Hostility or depression	Unpleasant, constricted world view: humans basically evil	Humor, tenderness, warmth, hopeful, caring; conflicts open without lingering chronic resentments

*Adapted from Chapter 3 of Beavers WR: A theoretical basis for family evaluation, in Lewis JM, Beavers WR, Gossett JT, et al: No Single Thread: Psychological Health in Family Systems. New York, Brunner/Mazel, 1976. pp 46-82.[6]

"identified patient." More often than not, the family context from which the individual's symptoms emanate will be overlooked entirely, deemphasized, or inadequately attended to. The "bad," "sick," "stupid," or "crazy" individual family member will be treated and either will be found intractable or "improved." If "improved," he will soon become symptomatic again when returned to the family context or may cause another family member to become symptomatic. The underlying family disturbance will have to be dealt with.

A major tenet of family therapists, therefore, is that the symptomatic family member is often thought of as being indicative of widespread disturbance in the entire family system.[7-11] For a therapist to overlook or deal inadequately with the more general family disturbance would cause at least one family member to continue to be symptomatic.

In the X family, Mr. and Mrs. X found that over the course of 12 years of marriage their sexual relationship had become more and more unsatisfactory. They contemplated divorce. At about the same time, their son began to do poorly in school and they sought help for this problem. Concurrently, they felt less concerned about the unsatisfactory nature of the marriage. As the boy's school work improved, the marital problem returned to the fore.

Dr. B brought Mrs. B for help because she had "headaches again." Her headaches always followed problems he had with his patients. Dr. B was a hardworking, but rigid person who firmly believed in male superiority. Things had gone well for them in the early years of their marriage until Mrs. B became dissatisfied with the role of "number two" in the marriage and pressed for equality. At that point Dr. B intensified the authoritarian approach and rather than fighting back, Mrs. B became depressed.

The focus of understanding, evaluation, and help must be broadened to include not only the individual but also the marital and family system of which that individual is a part. It should be noted here that, although this is an important frame of reference for family therapists, it is not the only one that may be relevant in the treatment of various types of problems (see Chapter 12).

The patterns of interaction within a family cannot always be clearly related to any specific dysfunction. The reasons why a specific type of disturbance is manifested in a family system or family member are not understood clearly at the present time, but certain innate tendencies and life circumstances probably favor the development of one or another symptomatic expression in a particular instance.

Similarly, the reasons why one family member rather than another becomes symptomatic have not been definitively settled. A number of reasons, however, have been described to account for this phenomenon. They are as follows:

1. Individual susceptibility, that is, genetic predisposition. For example, an individual who was born brain damaged and is under family stress is likely to

become symptomatic. Genetic temperamental differences may contribute.[12] Chess and associates, who have studied activity levels of infants, have suggested that the more phlegmatic babies have a greater tendency toward developing schizophrenia, whereas active, awake, exploring babies have a greater tendency to become delinquent.[13]

2. The situation in the family at the time of birth. For example, a parent whose own parent died around the time of the birth of a child might use the newborn infant to work out his feelings about his own dead parent.

3. Physical illness of the child. A child who is chronically ill may have family problems projected on him whenever he has an acute episode.

4. Precipitant in the external family. Accidents or a death that relates somehow to one child more than another (an eldest daughter who was with her grandmother the day the grandmother had a heart attack) may make one family member the focus for family problems.

5. Sex of a child may correspond to a particular difficulty of the parent. For example, if a father feels particularly inadequate with other males, his son may become symptomatic.

6. Birth order of siblings. The eldest child may get the major "parental loading," whereas the youngest child is often "babied" and kept dependent.

7. Family myth attached to a specific individual. Certain people in families are known as the "stupid" one, the "smart" one, the "lazy" one, the "good-looking" one, the "ugly" one. First names of children and nicknames may reveal these myths. Children are sometimes named after godparents or other people significant in the parents' past and, in turn, carry along a myth attached to that person. Girls are sometimes given names of somewhat ambiguous gender; for example, Lee, Dale, Marion, Frances, Glenette, Alberta, Carol, as though to indicate parental displeasure at having a girl. This is also true for males. Sometimes assigned names are grossly inappropriate for the gender of the child.

It has been suggested that:

In less than optimal families, the mother is the first to suffer from the system's inadequacy. She is most often the first to become dissatisfied, distressed, or symptomatic. At increased levels of family system dysfunctioning, a child may also begin to experience distress and become symptomatic. Frequently, he will then become an identified patient. The father, with more in the way of outside sources of esteem, is often the last family member to become symptomatic.[6]

The symptomatic family member may be the family scapegoat and may have family difficulties displaced on him or may be psychologically or constitutionally the weakest, the youngest, or the most sensitive family member, unable to cope with the generalized family disturbance. The identified patient may be the family member most interested or involved in the process of changing the family. For example, there are teenagers who want to "save" their parents because they are not getting along with each other. One hypothesis about family functioning is that these children may begin to steal in order to get caught, so that the entire family can be referred for help.

Robinson has summarized the literature on the family theory of the development of family dysfunction:[18]

Family theory views symptoms as connected with the conflict located at the transactional interface between the natural developmental strivings of an emerging individual and the distorted relational objectives of the dysfunctional family system. A dysfunctional family is one whose organizational peculiarities cause it to mismanage those aspects of family interaction associated with individuation, distance, and closeness in such a way that the social maturation of family members is impaired or arrested. This impairment is caused by . . . forces that seek to maintain the parent-child relational axis as the principal determinant of family organization. Symptoms are an expression of the conflict between the inherent strivings of the individual to establish himself as an adequate member of his own generation and the opposing pressures generated by a dysfunctional family motivated to maintain the status quo. For example, if the marital relationship is underdeveloped as the center of parental need satisfaction, the chances that the parent-child relationship will become overdeveloped are increased. In such families the child is inclined to develop a preoccupation with his role and the problems of his parents. He may be emotionally trapped by the dynamics of the family whether he accepts or rejects the roles designated for him by the family system. Acceptance . . . means that the child attempting to leave the family is inadequately prepared for separation and faces a concealed but active opposition. He is therefore likely to experience high levels of anxiety and guilt and to collapse in his efforts toward independent living. Rejection of the roles and values of the dysfunctional family may result in a premature breaking away from the protective functions of the family and the child being forced to sustain himself in the outside world. The parents in these families are therefore participants in the conflicts underlying individual symptom formation because they suppress individuation and separation in order to protect the family's triangular bigenerational base.

FAMILY MYTHS

Individuals and families have systems of belief that determine their feelings and behavior. These attitudes, largely unexpressed directly, run below the surface of the family's interactions and help to shape its general outline and specific features. These subterranean structures have been referred to as "family myths." They are often found to be important roots of family difficulty, and family therapists must be aware of them if they are to understand family behavior that might otherwise seem inexplicable.

Ferreira defines family myths as "a series of fairly well-integrated beliefs shared by all family members, concerning each other and their mutual position in the family, which go unchallenged by everyone involved, in spite of the reality distortions which they may conspicuously imply."[14] The implications of Ferreira's definition involve very personalized and specific myths for each family in which individual family members are singled out for particular slots, roles, or self-fulfilling prophecies, such as "mother is the emotional one in the family" or "our son misbehaves continually."

Although we discuss these types of specific family myths in various parts of this book, at this point, however, we will turn instead to generalized myths having to do with a family's overall view of itself as a system with its own "philosophy" of life. In discussing some of the important and frequent myths that seem to cause difficulty, we will attempt to include those that seem most prominent in the experience of family therapists.[14-16] Not everyone will agree with the value judgments about the myths that are expressed here. Each therapist must work out his or her own values with respect to these issues. The therapist must be sensitive to, and deal appropriately with, those attitudes and beliefs that seem to be deleterious to a family's functioning and, conversely, must understand that some myths aid functioning.

If life has not worked out well for you as an individual, getting married will make everything better. No matter how unfortunate one's life experience has been in terms of relationship with parents, peers, career choice; or how satisfactorily one is living alone; or how dissatisfied one is with one's genetic endowment, social and economic situations—getting married will make things much better.

This myth is often shared not only by the individual who had the myth but, more surprisingly, by the spouse. If the marriage does last, each spouse bears the resentment that the other feels for not making it a happy one and for not overcoming all the obstacles that existed prior to the marriage. What happens is that many of these same problems get played out between the spouses.

Marital and family life should be totally happy, and each individual therein should expect either all or most gratifications to come from the family system. This romantic myth dies hard in some quarters. Many of life's satisfactions are found outside the family setting. There is a whole range of gratifications that families need to work out to fit their own particular components.

The "togetherness" myth. To what extent will merely remaining in close proximity or jointly carrying out all activities lead to satisfactory family life and individual gratification? Again, there will probably be great variation from one family to another, but surely this cannot be an ideal pattern for all families under all conditions. One should be able to be separate and autonomous; otherwise any relationship will be potentially distorted.

Marital partners should be totally honest with one another at all times. In its modern guise, this idea may be derived from experience with "encounter groups" in which people are encouraged to express their feelings freely (especially negative ones, it seems) and also from the concept that what is suppressed will of necessity damage us eventually. In fact, full and open frankness in feeling, action, and thought may cause at least as much harm as good. Also, "honesty" can be enlisted in the service of hostility or it can be a constructive, problem-solving approach. Many people feel that a degree of interpersonal sensitivity will often mitigate this concept of "total honesty" and that many hurtful statements, especially regarding factors that cannot be changed, are perhaps best left unspoken.

A happy marriage is one in which there are no disagreements, and when family members fight with one another it means that they hate each other. It seems inevitable that family members will have differences with one another and that these will often lead to overt disagreements. These arguments, in turn, may lead to "fights" or arguments. If they are dealt with constructively, clarification and resolution can be found without anyone suffering loss of self-esteem. Many families, however, seem afraid to disagree and therefore cover up differences by pseudoagreement. On the other hand, there are families that fight all the time about almost every issue but seemingly are unable to resolve any disagreements; instead, they seem to resort to personal attacks on each other's motives and veracity.

The marital partners should see eye to eye on every issue and should work toward being as identical in outlook as possible. The first part of this statement is just about impossible to achieve, and the second part is of questionable benefit. Open recognition of the inevitable differences may be helpful and constructive. Many married couples seem either unwilling to accept or incapable of recognizing their inevitable differences with respect to past experience, basic attitudes, and personality styles. Instead, there often seems to be a marked projection of one's personality attributes, both positive and negative, onto the partner with relatively little ability to see the partner realistically.

Marital partners should be as unselfish as possible and give up thinking about their own individual needs. Most successful marriages seem able to reconcile the needs of the separate individuals with those of the needs of the family unit. Some individuals, however, unsuccessfully pretend that they do not have personal needs and satisfactions, but are rather merely satellites or undifferentiated masses attached to the larger family system. For example, a mother may live only for the sake of the family. Successful family units recognize the differential allocations and satisfactions to be derived from one's role as an individual human being, as a marital partner, and as a parent.

When something goes wrong in the family, one should look around to see who is at fault. At times of stress, many people react almost reflexively by blaming themselves or others. This is often not a useful response; instead, it may be more productive for them to look toward other frames of reference. When things go wrong in nongratifying family interactions, it may be in relation to the interactional properties of the entire system, which can be examined with a problem-solving approach in a relatively nonpersonalized, nonblaming manner. Each family member can be encouraged to assess his or her own role in the situation and in the solving of the problem. When two pieces of a jigsaw puzzle do not seem to fit well together, which of the two pieces is to blame?

When things are not going well, it will often be of help to spend a major part of the time digging up past as well as present hurts. Arguments that involve endless recriminations about past disappointments and difficulties may serve to give temporary relief by allowing the parties to air their resentments. This can often lead to futile escalation of the argument with a sort of "Can you top this?" discussion. Besides usually making things worse rather than better, this detracts from any constructive attempts at problem-solving. Often one of the first jobs of the family therapist is to act as a kind of "traffic cop" in stopping these non-productive family maneuvers. Nothing can be done to change what has happened in the past. "Crying over spilt milk" rarely, by itself, does much good unless it leads to increased understanding and modification of present patterns.

In a marital argument one partner is right and the other is wrong, and the goal of such fights should be for the partners to see who can score the most "points." Obviously this is not the case. When one marital partner wins a fight, it is usually the marriage as a whole that loses. Competitiveness in the marital relationship is not usually preferable to a cooperative working together in which neither marital partner necessarily scores points, but in which the outcome is such that the individuals and the marriage itself stand to gain.

A good sexual relationship will inevitably lead to a good marriage. Everyone has seen examples of individuals who married when they were physically infatuated with one another, but who woke up after the honeymoon to discover that in respects other than physical, they were relatively poorly suited to one another. A good sexual relationship is an important component of a satisfactory marriage, but does not necessarily preclude the presence of difficulties in other areas.

If the marriage is satisfactory in other respects, sex will more or less take care of itself. The sexual relationship in a marriage may need specific attention. It cannot automatically be taken for granted that a good marriage and good sex go together. Difficulties in the sexual sphere do seem to lead to difficulties in the rest of the marital relationship. Specific sex therapy for the couple may be indicated, following which other basically secondary difficulties may diminish.[17]

Marital partners increasingly understand each other's verbal and nonverbal communications, so there is little or no need to check things with one another. This may certainly be the case in functional, nonproblem families, but it is often strikingly untrue for families in trouble. Marital partners and other family members may assume that what they have said or done was clearly understood. They may also believe that they are able to read someone else's mind or know what someone else really means. When they are encouraged in therapy to specifically check some of these assumptions with one another, they are often shocked at their own misperceptions and misinterpretations.

Positive feedback is not as necessary in marital systems as is negative feed-

back. Many marital couples have gotten out of the habit of reflecting back to their partner when he or she has done something pleasing. However, there is often less hesitancy in commenting on something that has caused hurt or disappointment. Positive reinforcement of desired behavior usually serves to increase its occurrence and is usually a much more effective behavior-shaping technique than is negative feedback or punishment.

"And then they lived happily ever after." A good marriage should just happen spontaneously and should not need to involve any work on the part of the participants. This is perhaps another carry-over of the romantic idea of marriage as some type of blissful, dreamlike state. The sad but realistic truth, however, is that marriage involves day-to-day and minute-by-minute interaction of the people involved, as well as constant negotiation, communication, and solving of problems. Members of dysfunctional families may spend only a few minutes a week talking with one another about anything meaningful.

Any spouse can (and should) be reformed and remodeled into the shape desired by the partner. In many marriages an inordinate amount of time and energy is spent in the often mutual effort to mold the spouse to a desired image. This is commonly done with little or no recognition of the fact that basic personality patterns, once established, are not easily modified. Attempts to do so lead mainly to frustration, anger, and disillusionment, although certain characteristics may be moderated or even rechanneled, and partners can be made to be more sensitive to each other's reactions. But even though the "reform movement" marriage may work out satisfactorily as long as both partners consent to play the requisite roles involved, it may still lead to futile arguments about personal qualities and lack of cooperation. Therefore, it would be better for a spouse to look inward in order to assess which personal characteristics should be modified to best profit the marriage.

A stable marriage is one in which things do not change and in which there are no problems. To be alive is to face continual change. Those systems that attempt to remain fixed in some unchanging mold will sooner or later come to be out of phase with current needs. Systems do have a tendency toward a dynamic equilibrium in which certain patterns and interactions repeat themselves, giving a sense of continuity and stability. At the same time the entire system is moving inevitably onward.

Everyone knows what a husband should be like and what a wife should be like. This statement may have been truer in the past than it is now. There is increasingly less agreement on this subject with a constant flood of conflicting messages. The lack of a preconceived or defined notion of marital roles presents a possibility of greater confusion, but it also offers an opportunity for much greater development of each partner's and the marriage's actual potential.

If a marriage is not working properly, having children will rescue it. Although the arrival of children may often temporarily make the spouses feel somewhat more worthwhile and give them a new role (that of being parents), children are not the cement that will hold poor marriages together. What often happens instead is that children become the victims of marital disharmony.

No matter how bad the marriage, it should be kept together for the sake of the children. It is not necessarily true that children thrive better in an unhappy marriage than they do living with a relatively satisfied divorced parent. If the marriage partners stay together, the children may bear the brunt of the resentment that the partners feel for one another with the parents feeling they have martyred themselves for their children's sake.

If the marriage does not work, an extramarital affair or a new marriage will cure the situation. Although on certain occasions this is true, what may often happen is that the new partner is uncannily similar to the rejected one, and the same nongratifying patterns begin all over again; only the names of the players have been changed.

Separation and divorce represent a failure of the marriage and of the individuals involved. This almost always has been the traditional view of marital partners, family members, friends, and professional counselors. Individuals in a marital union, however, may grow apart or be poorly matched at the outset. At different phases of one's family life cycle different partners may be desirable. Separation or divorce (or both) may represent a creative and positive step rather than a failure for the family members.

A dysfunctional family seldom has the internal resources to change due to the unwritten rules by which it operates. If it were to have these resources, then it could change and the family would therefore not be dysfunctional. A member of the family may ask for external help for himself or another family member or may try to harm himself or someone or something and thus come to the attention of an external agency. To take the "identified patient," at face value and to deal only with that person, without seeing the rest of the family, would represent a very distorted and limited perspective of the dysfunction inherent in the family.

SUMMARY

Although techniques for measurement of family dysfunction are not yet sensitive enough to clearly demarcate the differences between functional and dysfunctional families, clinicians have observed that in healthy families there is a sense of ongoing cooperation, communication, and togetherness that can best be described by using the following analogy.

A functional family is like an orchestra playing a beautiful symphony; each of its members plays a different instrument, but together they add up to an overall configuration of harmony that is effective and fulfilling. Conversely, in a dysfunctional family there is a lack of this congruence, as well as a pervasive negative mood of unrelatedness.

A dysfunctional family is like a poker game in which each player holds certain cards, yet no one will put them on the table. Therefore, the same old game keeps being played. No one will risk losing (or winning) by playing a *new* card, so in effect no one wins and no one loses and the game becomes a pointless exercise; or one player may win the same hollow victory repeatedly and another may indeed always be identified as the loser.

REFERENCES

1. Rabkin R: Uncoordinated communication between marriage partners. Fam Process 6:10– 15, 1967
2. Stachowiak J: Decision making and conflict resolution in the family group, in Larson C, Dance F (eds): Perspectives on Communication. Milwaukee, Wisconsin, University of Wisconsin Speech Communication Center, 1968 pp 113– 124
3. Westley W, Epstein N: Patterns of intra-familial communication, in Cameron DE, Greenblatt M (Eds): Recent advances in neuro-physiological research. Psychiatric Research Report No. 11. New York, American Psychiatric Association 1959, pp 1– 9
4. Wynne LC, Ryckoff IM, Day J, et al: Pseudomutuality in the family relations of schizophrenics. Psychiatry 21:205– 220, 1958
5. Wynne LC, Singer MT: Thought disorder and family relations of schizophrenics. I. A research strategy. II. A classification of forms of thinking. Arch Gen Psychiatry 9:191– 206, 1963
6. Lewis JM, Beavers WR, Gossett JT, et al: No Single Thread: Psychological Health in Family Systems. New York Brunner/Mazel, 1976, p 225
7. Ackerman NW: Psychodynamics of Family Life, Diagnosis and Treatment in Family Relationships. New York, Basic Books, 1958
8. Bell JE: Family group therapy. Public Health Monograph No. 64. Washington, D.C., Department of Health, Education and Welfare, Public Health Service, 1961
9. Carroll EJ: Treatment of the family as a unit. Pennsylvania Medicine 63:57– 62, 1960
10. Bateson G, Jackson DD, Haley J, et al: Towards a theory of schizophrenia. Behav Sci 1:251– 264, 1956
11. Counts R: Family crisis and the impulsive adolescent. Arch Gen Psychiatry 17:74, 1967
12. Thomas A, Chess S: Temperament and Development. New York, Brunner/Mazel, 1977, p 270
13. Chess S, Thomas A, Birch H: Your Child is a Person. New York, Viking, 1965
14. Ferreira AJ: Family myths and homeostasis. Arch Gen Psychiatry 9:457– 463, 1963
15. Lederer WJ, Jackson DD: Mirages of Marriage. New York, Norton, 1968
16. Ferreira AJ: Family myths: The covert rules of the relationship. Confin Psychiatry 8:15– 20, 1965
17. Masters W, Johnson V: Human Sexual Response. Boston, Little, Brown, 1966
18. Robinson LR: Basic concepts in family therapy: A differential comparison with individual treatment. Am J Psychiatry 132:1045– 1048, 1975

Andean Family by Hector Poleo. Courtesy of the Museum of Modern Art of Latin America (OAS), Washington, D.C.

5
Evaluating the Family

OBJECTIVES

- To illustrate the different techniques for gathering of data
- To formulate important problem areas in preparation for planning and choosing the therapeutic approach
- To show when and how to use special evaluation techniques such as structured interviews, psychological testing, and home visits

OVERVIEW AND THE PROCESS OF GATHERING DATA

Evaluation of a marital couple or family should be understood as a continuing process, begun at the first contact but not necessarily completed at any particular point. Some initial formulation is useful to the therapist to help with the marshaling of data and forming of hypotheses, but in a larger sense, the evaluation is often an inextricable part of the therapy itself.

As data are gathered, the therapist forms hypotheses based on one or another conceptual frame of reference. The therapist attempts to assign priorities and weight to the variety of contributory variables and then sets up an overall stategy with particular intervention tactics designed to lead to certain desired goals. (This strategy and its tactics will be described in subsequent chapters on family therapy techniques.) In this process further data are obtained that serve to confirm, modify, or negate the original hypotheses, strategies, and tactics. These later formulations are then tested in the matrix of the family sessions as further data are obtained.

There are several points of view regarding the type and quantity of the evaluative data to be gathered. Some family therapists begin with a specific and detailed longitudinal history of the family unit and its constituent members, which may perhaps span three or more generations. (A complete and detailed outline for family history and functioning will be found in Appendix B.) This procedure has the advantage of permitting the family and the therapist to go over together the complex background of the present situation. The therapist will begin to understand unresolved past and present issues, will usually gain a sense of rapport and identification with the family and its members, and may then feel more comfortable in defining problem areas and in planning strategy. The family, for its part, may benefit by reviewing together the source and evolution of its current condition, which may prove to be a clarifying, empathy-building process for the entire family. The good and the bad are brought into focus, and the immediate distress is placed in a broader perspective. Sometimes a family in crisis is too impatient to tolerate exhaustive history gathering and therefore, in acute situations, lengthy data gathering must be curtailed.

Other therapists do not appear to rely heavily on the longitudinal approach, attempting instead to delineate the situation that has led the family to seek treatment at the time and to obtain a cross-sectional view of its present functioning. This procedure has the advantage of starting with the problems about which the family is most concerned, and is not as potentially time-consuming nor as seemingly remote from the present realities as the preceding method. The therapist, however, may not emerge with as sharp a focus on important family patterns, since much of the discussion may be negatively tinged because of a preoccupation by the famly with its current difficulty.

More experienced (and often more courageous) therapists may severely curtail past history gathering and may also minimize formalized discussions of the family's current situation. They may begin, instead, by dealing from the onset with the family's important characteristic patterns of interaction as they are manifested in the interview setting. They may tend to utilize primarily, or exclusively, the immediate "here and now" observable family transactions, understanding these to be charcteristic of the family. They may clarify and comment on these, intervening in a variety of ways. This approach has the advantage of initiating treatment immediately, without the usual delay of history gathering. There is often a heightened sense of emotional involvement, which may cause more rapid changes to occur. Sometimes families are overhwelmed by such an approach, however, feeling threatened and defensive. Also, when specific information and patterns are allowed to emerge in this random fashion, the therapist does not always have the same degree of certainty as to whether the emerging family patterns are indeed relevant and important. (Such a procedure is not usually recommended for beginning therapists.)

To a considerable extent these differences in technique may mirror differences in the therapists' training, theoretical beliefs, and temperaments. Most therapists, however, probably use combinations of these approaches as the situation warrants, for there is no evidence of one technique being superior to the others.

OUTLINE FOR FAMILY EVALUATION

We have indicated that there is more than one potentially useful way to evaluate a family, depending on the situation. The procedure offered in the evaluation outline below combines useful aspects of the first two approaches discussed previously. It offers a practical alternative to gathering an exhaustive history or to plunging into the middle of the family interaction. In addition, the reader is provided with several outlines for famly evaluation, ways of observing a family interaction, and a variety of other evaluative techniques. These approaches combine both verbal and nonverbal techniques for obtaining information. (The process of gathering information is discussed in greater detail in Chapter 10.) Although far from exhaustive in scope, this outline does provide

Table 5-1
Outline for Family Evaluation*

I. Current Phase of Family Life Cycle
II. Explicit Interview Data
    A.   What is the current family problem?
    B.   Why does the family come for treatment at this time?
    C.   What is the background of the family problem?
        1.   Composition and characteristics of nuclear and extended family, e.g., age, sex, occupation, financial status, medical problems, etc.
        2.   Developmental history and patterns of each family member
        3.   Developmental history and patterns of the nuclear family unit
        4.   Current family interactional patterns (internal and external)
    D.   What is the history of past treatment attempts or other attempts at problem solving in the family?
    E.   What are the family's goals and expectations of the treatment? What are their motivations and resistances?
III. Formulating the Family Problem Areas
    A.   Family patterns of communicating thoughts and feelings
    B.   Family roles and coalitions
    C.   Operative family myths
    D.   Family style or typology
IV. Planning the Therapeutic Approach and Establishing the Treatment Contract

*In developing this outline, we have adapted material from two major sources: Gill M, Newman R, Redlich F: The Initial Interview in Psychiatric Practice. New York, International Universities Press, 1954;[1] and The case history method in the study of family process, Report No. 76,Group for the Advancement of Psychiatry, New York, Group for the Advancement of Psychiatry, 1970[2]

some anchoring points for initial understanding and planning. It is not meant to be inflexible or unchangeable, and it certainly can be expanded or contracted as the situation warrants. Each topic of the outline will be discussed in greater detail later in this chapter.

CURRENT PHASE OF FAMILY LIFE CYCLE

Identifying the current phase of the family life cycle can readily be accomplished by ascertaining the ages and relationships of those family members living under one roof. Knowing which stage the family has reached in its developmental cycle is an important criterion for a basic understanding of the family's structure and functioning, in both the actual and optimal sense. (This has been discussed at greater length in Chapters 3 and 4.) Each stage of the family life cycle has unique stresses, challenges, opportunities, and pitfalls. By being alert to these, the therapist is in a position to observe and explore those particular tasks, roles, and relationships that are phase-specific for the family. The therapist can also ascertain to what extent the family members clearly recognize and are attempting to cope with actual issues relevant to the family's current stage of development. For many marriages and families, the basic difficulty underlying the need for professional help can be related to their inability to cope satisfactorily with their current developmental phase.

The J family, mentioned in Chapter 4 (p. 69), is a good example of the type of problem arising in a later stage of marriage—the "empty-nest" syndrome—in which the parents could not cope with the separation of their children from the home because of their fear of being alone as husband and wife.

EXPLICIT INTERVIEW DATA

What is the current family problem? The interviewer asks this question of each family member, in turn, with all family members present. The interviewer attempts to maintain the focus on the *current family problem,* rather than on one or another individual, or on past difficulties. Each family member receives an equal opportunity to be heard, without interruption, and to feel that his or her opinions and views are worthwhile, important, and acknowledged. The interviewer will begin to note what frames of reference are delineated by the family members in discussing their difficulties. It will be determined whether there exists a family or an individual problem, which individuals seem to be bearing the brunt of the blame, how the identified patients deal with their role, what are the alliances in the family, who seems to get interrupted by whom, who speaks for whom, who seems fearful or troubled about expressing an opinion, who sits next to whom, and so forth. (These issues and others are discussed more fully in Appendix A.)

The nonverbal communication of families is a gold mine of information. Because nonverbal communication is not dependent on words, a family evaluator must train himself to observe other signals. Videotaping a family interaction is one way to closely observe nonverbal communication, which may be expressed by a child who twiddles his thumbs in the same way as his mother, a father whose facial expression and bodily movement indicate the opposite of what he is actually saying, or a parent who stares off into space when his adolescent son yells. All of these observations are of as much or more value than some of the verbal comments that the family may make to the interviewer.

Why does the family come for treatment at the present time? The answer to this question helps to move the focus of difficulty even closer to the current situation and also provides an opportunity for further specifying the kinds of factors that lead to family distress. The kinds of "last-straw" situations usually present the important patterns of family interaction in a microcosm.

In the L family, a son, Tom, age 25, had symptoms of paranoid schizophrenia for many years. The parents "allowed" Tom to sleep in their bedroom at night. On the day after he moved out, Mr. and Mrs. L began to blame each other for the son's behavior and sought attention because their son was "out on the streets where anything could happen." The son had maintained an uneasy balance between the parents by staying in the parental bedroom at night, thus obviating their need for intimacy or sex. It was only when he moved out that the parents' problem came into sharp focus.

The answer to the above question also helps alert the therapist to any acute crisis situation that may need either the therapist's or the family's immediate intervention. The answer will be relevant, too, in assessing the goals the family has in mind for the therapy and the degree to which it is motivated for help. Until recently it was usually the wife who requested psychotherapy. This may have reflected the wife's greater involvement in the family, rather than her having a greater degree of intrapsychic disturbance.

What is the background of the family problem?

1. Composition and characteristics of the nuclear and expanded family, including age, sex, occupation, financial status, medical problems, and so on.
2. Developmental history and patterns of each family member. Individual family member's life histories are evaluated in terms of patterns of adaptation, including an impression of how the individual manages affects, frustration and disappointment, self-image, personal values and goals, and role and identity outside the family. The evaluator should not underestimate the importance of individual styles of adaptation, the use of defenses and resistances, tolerance of stress and ego strengths, signs and symptoms of any mental disorder, and the capacity of each person to be supportive and empathic to his or her partner.
3. Developmental history and patterns of the nuclear family unit. The longitudinal course of the family unit is explored with reference to the role of the spouses' individual expectations, values, goals, and conflicts in their rela-

tionship; the effect of each partner's adaptive patterns on the other partner; the need for control by one partner or the other, including how control is obtained and maintained; the existence of mutual trust and ability to share; the importance of individual and mutual dependence issues; and the family's ability to deal effectively with its earlier life phases.

4. Current family interactional patterns (internal and external).[2] Is the power structure flexible, rigid, or chaotic? Are the generation boundaries intact, blurred, or broken? Is there an affiliative or oppositional style? What degree of individuation is noted? Is there: clarity of communcation; tolerance for ambivalence and disagreement; respect for others' differentness versus attempts at control or intrusiveness; responsiveness to others; ability to deal realistically with separation and loss? Are the family myths close to reality or are they gross distortions? What is the overall family affect: that of warmth, humor, caring, hope, tenderness, and the ability to tolerate open conflicts, or that of constricted, unpleasant, hostile and depressive or resentful behavior?

This part of the evaluation—the background of the family problem—lends itself to expansion or contraction depending on the circumstances. For example, an intensive examination of a particular sector of the family's current functioning or past history might be thought relevant in a particular instance. In another situation only a relatively brief amount of background data might be gathered initially, with the feeling that more would come out as the treatment sessions proceeded. In any event, the therapist would always want to recognize the important participants in the family's current interactions, the quality of the relationships, and the developmental patterns of the family unit over a period of time. (For those interested in obtaining a more detailed family history and process data, a more extensive outline is provided in Appendix B.)

What is the history of past treatment attempts or other attempts at problem solving in the family? It usually is illuminating to understand the circumstances that have led a marital couple or family to seek assistance in the past, from what sort of helpers this assistance was elicited, and the outcome of the expectations, experiences, and results of this assistance. Experience in previous help-seeking efforts serves to illuminate more clearly both the family processes and the possible therapist traps and often delineates useful strategies. Past help-seeking patterns are often useful predictors of what the present experience will be in both family therapy as well as in other therapies.

The B family came into treatment presenting the complaint that they could not get along with each other and were contemplating divorce. They gave a history of being in family therapy several years before. They had had some 20 sessions, which "of course led to nothing." In discussion with the couple and with the former therapist, it was discovered that the couple had spent most of the sessions blaming each other and attempting to change each other, rather than making any change in their relationship or in themselves. In addition, Mr. B, who was quite authoritarian, had persuaded the therapist to line up on his side and say that his wife was quite unreasonable. This treatment had been unsuccessful. The strategy in this case was to go over, in detail, the past problems in treatment, suggest that the present therapist would not be a judge, and that the focus was to be on the couple's relationship rather than on what the other partner would *have* to do.

Often one spouse has been in intensive individual psychotherapy or psychoanalysis and has been seeking help with the marital relationship. When this has proven unsuccessful, both therapist and patient may blame the failure on the spouse not in treatment. This may exacerbate the difficulty and lead to separation or divorce.

Mrs. P came into treatment because she felt her husband was inadequate. Her own life had been replete with difficulties, starting from the time she had lost both her parents in an automobile accident when she was 2. She had lived in various orphanages, had had two marriages by the time she was 22, and had periodic bouts of alcoholism and depression. She felt that her present marriage of 5 years was "okay" until she had children. She felt that although she had some difficulty in raising the children, the real problem was in her husband. She went into individual psychotherapy three times a week and in the course of this began to "see quite clearly what a loser he was." Although her therapist at first struggled valiantly to point out her own difficulties, he, too, began to see the difficulties in the husband. The husband himself was never called into therapy and after 2 years of treatment, the couple was still experiencing the same problems and they were contemplating divorce. A consultant suggested marital therapy.

What are the family's goals and expectations of the treatment? What are their motivations and resistances? Some families come to treatment for short-term goals, such as making final an already fairly well decided separation between husband and wife. Others come for more long-term goals, such as making a basic change in how the family functions. Other families come because of "mother's depression" (an individual-oriented goal), whereas still others come because "the family isn't functioning right" (a family goal). In a case in which the goals are individual-oriented, the therapist's task is to translate for the family the relationship between the symptoms and the family process. Goals are, at times, unclear or unrealistic. In such instances the therapist and the family must work out from the beginning an appropriate and clear set of goals (see Chapter 6).

The marital couple and family presumably will have certain types of positive hopes and motivations for seeking help, but at the same time will have some hesitations, doubts, and fears about this very same help. One of the therapist's jobs is to explore and reinforce the positive motivations, to clarify them and to keep them readily available throughout the process of therapy, which at times may be temporarily stormy and stressful. In marital therapy the motivation of each partner for conjoint therapy should be evaluated, and the evaluation should include stated commitment to the marriage, the evaluator's opinion of their commitment to therapy, the reality of their treatment expectations, and the secondary gain for each spouse that the marital distress may represent.

It is the positive expectations, goals, and motivations that keep the family members in treatment, and every effort should be made to insure that each family member will benefit from the family therapy sessions as individuals, and also as concerned members of the family. It has been found helpful to work out these expectations explicitly, so that both the family members and the therapist understand them in order to avoid the situation wherein one of the family members has the feeling that he or she is not attending the sessions as an individual, but only to help some other member of the family.

Ideally it would be desirable for each involved family member to know clearly what positive reasons there are for his own participation, as well as to understand what the more general family system goals may be. At the same time the therapist must be aware of individual and family resistance to treatment and, where appropriate, try to make explicit these obstacles and negative feelings before they undermine either the successful utilization of treatment or its actual continuance. Clinical judgment will suggest when such fears and resistances need immediate attention and when they need only to be kept in mind as potentially major obstacles.

Such resistances may be of various sorts. Although some may be specific to particular families, many are commonly seen. Among these is the feeling that the situation may be made worse by treatment; that some member of the family will become guilty, depressed, angry, or fearful as a result of the treatment; that a family member may go crazy; that the family may split up; that perhaps there is no hope for change and it is already too late for help; that shameful or damaging "family secrets" may have to be revealed; or that perhaps it would be better to stick to familiar patterns of family interaction, no matter how unsatisfying they may be, rather than attempt to change them in what may be unknown and hence frightening directions. (Chapter 11 is devoted to a more detailed review of resistance to treatment.)

In the newlywed Q family, the wife felt that to continue in marital treatment after her recovery from an acute psychotic episode might mean that she would go crazy again. She believed that she would have to explore with her husband their unsatisfactory marriage and that this might lead to separation or divorce. She also felt that she would have to be strong and powerful to prevent her husband's committing suicide in the same way that his own father had committed suicide, presumably in relation to having a weak, nonsupportive wife. The husband, for his part, had a very obsessional personality structure with little interpersonal sensitivity or emotional awareness. He felt angry at psychiatrists and was insecure and threatened by the therapist as a male role model.

FORMULATING THE FAMILY PROBLEM AREAS

Meeting with the family, the therapist experiences its patterns of interaction and uses the data obtained in order to begin formulating a concept of the family problem.[3] Data for these formulations may come from historical material, but just as important will be what the therapist has observed in personal contact with the family. This will help to form a basis for hypotheses and therapeutic strategies. The data gathered from the outline provided should permit the family therapist to pinpoint particular areas or aspects of the family that may require attention. In addition, the data assist in laying out a priority system, so that the therapist can decide which areas of the family problem should be dealt with first. The data also make possible greater clarity about therapeutic strategy and the tactics indicated for the particular phases and goals of treatment. (The following four topics are discussed in greater detail in Chapter 8 from the point of view of treatment strategies.)

Family patterns of communicating thoughts and feelings. The areas of communication to be assessed include expressions of affection, empathy, and mutual support; areas of sexual satisfaction and dissatisfaction; daily interaction, including the sharing of activities; flexibility of roles, rivalry and competition, and the balance of power; and major conflicts in the marital relationship, including development intensity and means of resolving conflict; and relationships to family, including children and friends. To what extent does the family group engage in meaningful and goal-directed negotiations, rather than being engulfed in incoherent, aimless talk?

Other factors include the general feeling tone of the family and of individual members, dyads, and triads, together with appropriateness, degree of variability, intensity, and flexibility. To what extent does the family appear to be emotionally "dead" rather than expressive, empathic, and spontaneous? What is the level of enjoyment, energy, and humor? To what extent does there appear to be an emotional divorce between the marital partners? To what extent does the predominant family mood pattern seem to be one of depression, suspicion, envy, jealousy, withdrawal, anger, irritation, and frustration? To what extent is the family system skewed around the particular mood state or reaction pattern of one of its members? (For example, in the X family, whenever the son begins to hallucinate, the mother becomes angry, or the father begins to withdraw, or both.) These questions will be important in determining the extent of affective difficulty in the family system. (The variety of dysfunctional communication patterns and suggestions for changing them are presented in greater detail in Chapter 8.)

Family roles and coalitions. To what extent does the family seem fragmented and disjointed, as though made up of isolated individuals? Or does it rather appear to be one relatively undifferentiated "ego mass"? To what extent are there role differentiations within individuals, as well as between one individual and another? To what extent is the marital coalition the most functional and successful one in the family system? To what extent are there cross-generational dyadic coalitions that are stronger than the marital dyad? How successfully are power and leadership issues resolved? To what extent is this a schismatic family in which there are two or more alliances seemingly in conflict with one another? (These and similar issues are discussed further in Chapter 8.)

Operative family myths. Some individuals in families are "selected" to be "bad, sick, stupid, crazy," and often these roles constitute a kind of self-fulfilling prophecy. Families as well as individuals function with a set of largely unexamined fundamental attitudes that have been termed "myths." These markedly influence the family's manner of looking at and coping with itself and the world. (These have been discussed in greater detail in Chapter 4.)

Family style or typology. There is no one way of classifying the complexity of marital and family life styles that is universally applicable. Some of the characterizations presented below may be found helpful, depending on the circumstances.[4]

Classification 1: Based on rules for defining power
  1. The symmetrical relationship
  2. The complementary relationship
  3. The parallel relationship

In *symmetrical relationships,* both people exhibit the same types of behavior (which minimize the differences between them), role definitions are similar, and problems tend to stem from competition.

In *complementary relationships,* the two people exhibit different types of behavior, and this is found most often in the so-called traditional marriage. This form maximizes differences and tends to be less competitive and often highly workable. Unless role definitions are agreed on, however, serious problems can result.

In *parallel relationships,* the spouses alternate between symmetrical and complementary relationships in response to changing situations.

Classification 2: By Parental Stage
  The move from the dyadic marital configuration to the larger, more complex one involving children tends inevitably to bring with it the potential for increased activities. Possible subcategories under this classification are as follows:

  1. Before childrearing
  2. Early childhood
  3. Latency and adolescent children
  4. After the children have left home (empty-nest syndrome)

Classification 3: By Level of Intimacy[5]

  1. The *conflict-habituated marriage* is characterized by severe conflicts, but unpleasant as it is, the partners are held together by fear of alternatives.
  2. The *devitalized marriage* has less overt expressions of dissatisfaction, with the marital partners conducting separate lives in many areas. This interaction is

characterized by numbness and apathy and seems to be held together principally by legal and moral bonds and by the children.

3. The *passive-congenial marriage* is "pleasant" and there is sharing of interests without any great intensity of interaction. The partners' level of expectation from the relationship is not very high, and they derive some genuine satisfaction from it.
4. The *vital marriage* is intensely satisfying to the spouses in at least one major area, and the partners are able to work together.
5. The *total marriage,* which is very rare in the investigators' findings, is characterized by similarity to the vital marriage except that the former is more intense and satisfying in the whole range of marital activities.

Classification 4: By Personality Style*

1. *The obsessive–compulsive husband and the hysterical wife.* Conflicts of intimacy often become of major importance.
2. *The passive–dependent husband and the dominant wife.* Power is the central theme of this system.
3. *The paranoid husband and the depression-prone wife.*
4. *The depression-prone huband and the paranoid wife.*
5. *The neurotic wife and the omnipotent husband.* Power is the primary conflict area. The wife's resentment is expressed through depression and a variety of other symptoms.

These marital styles often work very satisfactorily if the needs of the two partners are met and if they are not overly inflexible in their application. Problems arise only when the cost of keeping the system going is too high—when one spouse changes, thereby upsetting the system, or when one partner indicates the desire to change the "rules."

Classification 5: By Descriptions of Families in Treatment[6]

No overall concept or model underlies the following six clusters; they are descriptive in nature. Because they were derived from families referred for treatment, the clusters imply a generally maladaptive tendency.

1. *Constricted.* Characterized by excessive restriction of a major aspect of family emotional life, such as expression of anger, negative affect, or ambivalence. These emotions become internalized into anxiety, depression, and somatic complaints. The presenting patient is often a passive, depressed child, or young adult.
2. *Internalized ("enmeshed").* Characterized by a fearful, pessimistic, hostile, threatening view of the world, leading to a constant state of vigilance. Such a family has a well-defined role structure, high family loyalty, and a pseudo-mutual bond between parents.
3. *Object-focused.* Characterized by overemphasis on the children *("child centered"),* the outside community, or the self *("narcissistic").* Motivation for treatment depends on the willingness of the marital couple to form an effective coalition.

*See Chapter 12, page 182, under "Personality Disorder."

4. *Impulsive*. Characterized by an adolescent or young adult acting out anger toward a parent onto the community or expressing his or her parents' difficulties in a socially unacceptable way.
5. *Childlike*. Characterized by spouses who have remained dependent on their own families or on the community, based on either inadequacy or immaturity.
6. *Chaotic*. Characterized by disintegration, lack of structure, chronic psychosis and delinquency, and low commitment to the family unit.

PLANNING THE THERAPEUTIC APPROACH AND
ESTABLISHING THE TREATMENT CONTRACT

After the evaluation data have been gathered and formulated into hypotheses and goals regarding important problem areas, the therapist is ready to consider what therapeutic strategies will be appropriate. (This subject is discussed in Chapters 6 through 15.)

At this point, a definite, clearly defined contract with regard to goals and treatment should be established. This should include who is to be present; the location, times, estimated length, and frequency of meetings; the fee and contingency planning with respect to absent members and missed appointments. For some families, treatment will be very brief and crisis oriented, lasting only one or two sessions, whereas for other families treatment may continue for years.

At this point, the therapist should make a concise, explicit statement of the family problem(s) using language the family can understand. Such a statement can be used as a springboard for discussing the treatment plan. For example, the therapist might say, "I think your drinking has to do with some of the feelings you and your wife have about each other. Perhaps it has to do with your feeling that she is trying to limit your 'fun.' From her point of view, she feels that you do not understand how hard she has to work. I think we should meet together to see how we can change things in the family and explore what has happened."

Case Example Illustrating the Outline

The following case example will illustrate the use of the outline for family evaluation.

I. CURRENT PHASE OF THE FAMILY LIFE CYCLE

The therapist notes that the identified patient is Mrs. R, a 44-year-old white female. Her husband, Mr. R, is 55, and there are three children ranging in age from 17 to 22 years. This family is approaching the empty-nest phase, in which the parents will have to face being alone together. The therapist begins to wonder and to ask to what extent the couple has emphasized the parental role, rather than the marital relationship, and to what extent they have encouraged the development of the children's ability to move out of the house and complete their maturation and separation from their parents.

II. EXPLICIT INTERVIEW DATA

A. *What is the current family problem?* The oldest son said that the family problem was his mother, because she had recently stopped using barbiturates on the advice of her doctor and subsequently began having ideas that people in the family were trying to harm her. The father added that his wife had always been "the problem." He was joined in these sentiments by the daughter, age 17, and by the younger son, age 20. The mother, however, said that the problem was that nobody would help her and that she could not get any cooperation from the family members around the house.

The therapist then asked the family to think in terms of what the current *family* (not individual) problem was. The younger son said he thought that maybe the problem was not the mother, but the fact that nobody in the family was communicating or was happy.

The oldest son had been living in a room by himself in some other part of the house. Seven days prior to the first therapy session, he had indicated that he was moving out to live with his girl friend.

B. *Why does the family come for treatment at this time?* The family reported that about the time the older son announced that he was going to move out, the parents' quarreling intensified. The mother went to a family doctor for a tranquilizer. The doctor said that she appeared confused and suggested she stop taking the barbiturates she had been using. She then became even more suspicious and had a fight with her husband in which they both threw pots at each other. At this point, everybody felt that she should see her family physician, who recommended admission to an inpatient psychiatric unit.

C. *What is the background of the family problem?*

1. Composition and characteristics of nuclear and extended family: The identified patient was a 44-year-old white housewife. Her husband was a 55-year-old white male who was a manual laborer in a shipyard. The older son was 22 and worked part-time in a record store; the younger son was 20 and a part-time student at college; there was a 17-year-old daughter.

2. Developmental history and patterns of each family member: Mrs. R's father was manager of a cemetary, and she described her mother as being sick all the time. Her parents' relationship revolved around the father's taking care of the mother through much of the marriage, because of her sickness. Mr. R's father was well liked but his mother was "an overprotective bitch," and the father essentially catered to his wife.

   Mrs. R gave a history of being chronically sick. She had been born prematurely and developed sinusitis and asthma at an early age. She was the younger of two siblings, having an older brother.

Mr. R was the oldest of four and took care of two younger siblings who were always sick. He also had physical problems. He never quite lived up to his parents' expectations. He quit college, did not want to move out of the house, and dated very little.

3. Developmental history and patterns of the nuclear family unit: The wife and husband were introduced by relatives. Most of their courtship was involved with family social events, and there was very little intimacy during the courtship period. Mrs. R described the marriage as somewhat disappointing. She indicated that she had married for stability, whereas he had said that he thought she would provide some of the spark that he lacked. Both partners stated that they had no knowledge of contraception, and a child was born early in the first year of the marriage. They had very little experience being alone together as husband and wife. After they had the other two children, Mr. R began spending more and more time at work. Mrs. R found herself becoming more sick with various respiratory and other ailments. They both had to turn to their own mothers, his for financial support, hers for help in raising the children and taking care of Mr. R.

4. Current interactional patterns: At the time of the referral the situation had progressively worsened during the past two years. Husband and wife found themselves drifting farther apart and spending less time together, barely talking to each other. Mr. R was working much more, which made Mrs. R suspicious that he was chasing around. Mrs. R continued to complain of physical symptoms, to take more medications, and to become less able to perform childrearing or housekeeping tasks. The older son began to experiment with the use of psychedelic drugs, the younger son had difficulty with his grades, and the daughter attended school less frequently and did poorly when in class. The two mothers-in-law fought over who was helping the family more, each placing the blame for the family problems on the other's child.

D. *What is the history of past treatment attempts or other attempts at problem solving in the family?* The mother had been seeing the same internist over the past 15 or 20 years. The doctor had frequently suggested psychiatric treatment, but she had refused. She went for individual psychotherapy over a 3-month period but quit, saying "It didn't make my husband better." They also consulted their local family clergyman on several occasions, and he counseled tolerance and patience. Both Mrs. R and the family had not found past treatment helpful since it did not get to the heart of the problems in the family and because she seemed to be developing all kinds of "phony insights."

E. *What are the family's goals and expectations of the treatment? What are their resistances?* The family's expectations at first were to help the mother so she could get better. During this evaluation interview, when the therapist opened up some channels of communication that were not previously available, it became apparent that the father had abdicated his role as a parent and a spouse. The marital coalition was almost nonexistent; instead the daughter and father were on one side and younger son and mother on the other. The older son had in many ways withdrawn from the battle by using drugs to blot it all out of his mind.

The primary resistances that existed during this evaluation interview were the family members' scapegoating of the mother and a reluctance to change themselves, the latter quite evident in the father's saying he could not get to treatment sessions because of his job, no matter what time was suggested for the meeting.

Although it was less apparent than the resistance, each person in the family did seem to recognize that there was something wrong with the overall functioning of the family and with its individual members and that this problem could be worked on.

III. FORMULATING THE FAMILY PROBLEM AREAS

A. *Family patterns of communicating thoughts and feelings.* The therapist noted that the general emotional tone of the family was one of anger and frustration. The family had difficulty agreeing on anything, even the making of a laundry list. The topic of the laundry list led to various arguments involving many members of the family. There was little or no spontaneous interaction or communication between husband and wife. The children seemed somewhat at odds but were united, however, in a struggle to prevent their parents from taking power. Even when the therapist tried to get them to talk to each other, it was impossible, as the wife felt that the husband never listened to her, and the husband felt his wife was always complaining and could not do anything. There was very little communication follow-up from one to the other.

The family seemed to be five unrelated people, each pulling in a different direction from the others. There did not seem to be any continuity of communication or closure. The parental coalition was mainly nonverbal. It consisted of the mother's clutching her stomach, grabbing her heart, and rolling her head back, as though she were about to have a stroke or a heart attack, at which point the father would move his chair farther away from everyone in the family.

B. *Family roles and coalitions.* Mrs. R, who was currently a daughter, wife, and mother, had been unable to move out of her family of origin to her present family. She seemed almost childlike in her presentation and her functioning. She seemed to be overly involved as a daughter and less involved as a wife and mother. The husband was likewise very involved with his family of origin. He had essentially given up his role as husband and turned over the role of father to the older son, who had been managing the family finances, bringing in extra money, and making the kinds of family decisions that Mr. R used to make.

There had been a reversal of generation roles with the daughter running the household and doing the cleaning and cooking. The daughter also fulfilled part of a spouse's role, in that father and daughter frequently went to the movies together, whereas the identified patient stayed home with her headaches. The strongest coalition in the family appeared to be a father-daughter instead of the more usual husband-wife.

The main alignments and communication patterns pitted the father and daughter against the younger son and mother, with the older son being a neutral mediator. In his role as mediator, the son was the center of all communication. All fights seemed to be resolved in "his court." This seemed to be taking a toll on him as he "had not found himself" and was having great difficulty in making a job decision or career choice. It became clear that this son's leaving home would be a grave crisis for the family.

C. Operative family myths. In this family it appeared that the mother was "sick" and the father was "helpless"; the daughter was a "pest," the older son a "mediator," and the younger son "noninvolved."

The family operated under the myth that a happy marriage is one in which there are no disagreements. Mrs. R lived under the fantasy that everything should be rosy and that any flaws or problems were to be avoided and not to be discussed. Mrs. R also felt that both marital partners should be as unselfish as possible and that she had sacrificed her life for her children and husband.

On the other hand, Mr. R felt that he had worked himself to the bone to bring home the money to keep the family going, sacrificing everything for everyone else. Both parents were bitterly resentful of the nonresponse of the rest of the family to their sacrifices.

Mrs. R was the scapegoat in the family. Whenever anything went wrong, everyone turned on her. If what she had done did not seem to be an adequate explanation of the problem, an explanation was found taking into account her past transgressions.

Positive feedback had been virtually abandoned in this family for years. Most importantly, Mrs. R had felt all along that things would work out if she could just remake her husband into a handsome Prince Charming instead of the small, rotund, shy, withdrawn man that he was.

D. Family style or typology

Classification 1 Based on rules for defining power: this is a dysfunctional complementary relationship.

Classification 2 By parental stage: this is a family in the empty-nest stage.

Classification 3 By level of intimacy: this is a conflict-habituated marriage.

Classification 4 By personality style: this is a dependent husband and a hysteroid-dysphoric wife.

Classification 5   By description of families in treatment: this family can be described as childlike.

IV. PLANNING THE THERAPEUTIC APPROACH AND ESTABLISHING THE TREATMENT CONTRACT

The first decision was to approach this family's problem from a family standpoint rather than by treating Mrs. R, the identified patient, as an individual, isolated from her family.

The family seemed to be in a crisis, facing the imminent departure of the older son, the family mediator. The parents seemed unable to handle this separation, that is, they could not cope with the empty-nest phase. The father seemed to be chronically weak and ineffective, and both parents' relationship with their own families of origin was still a dependent one. The basic strategy was to strengthen the marital coalition by increasing interaction between the marital dyad, by attempting to decrease the inappropriate interaction between these two people and their families of origin, and by attempting to decrease the cross-generational ties between these two people and their children.

The therapist treated the family as a unit, and he also met with only the marital dyad together for many of the sessions; for a time, the children were consulted alone without the parents. The considered decision was made to exclude the parents' in-laws from treatment and to encourage the marital dyad to take over the parental role that they had abrogated not only to the older son, but also to their own parents. In those sessions in which just the marital dyad participated, positive attention was given to reinforcing communication patterns between husband and wife. They were taught to pick up emotional cues and to respond to each other, rather than to withdraw or to somatize.

The mother was encouraged to reassume the maternal role and the father was encouraged to start making some decisions after discussing them first with his wife. The older son was steered toward his girl friend and a career choice, letting his father make the decisions the son had once made. The daughter was encouraged to improve her failing schoolwork and to stop doing the housekeeping and the cooking.

OTHER EVALUATION TECHNIQUES

Often the family is not verbally facile or may use words as a smokescreen. The family therapist, therefore, may want to use a variety of techniques to gain information other than those used in traditional interviewing. What families say and what they actually feel and do may often be quite different. Verbal techniques rely on both a family's ability to give information and the therapist's ability to elicit it. There may be great variance from interview to interview.

Observing Family Mealtimes

Family members interact around the task of preparing meals, and this is thought to be a good representation of family functioning. The family mealtime is a microcosm of the family in sociological and dynamic terms.[7] Direct observations of family mealtime planning, preparation, and consumption can be made. Alternatively the family therapist can ask the family to draw a diagram of the seating at a typical family meal. Sometimes family members will not eat together. Children rather than parents may prepare the meals. An adolescent who is angry with his parents will often take his meals alone—if the parents allow this. One particular child might be used as a mediator between the parents and be asked to sit between them, whereas the other siblings are not so involved in the parental drama. In a situation in which one parent cannot function (for example, a drinking father), that parent may take meals in the bedroom. Such observations are often helpful in determining the family patterns.

Structured Inverviews

Structured interviews are useful in both office and research situations. (An extended discussion of the procedure will be found in Appendix A.) Watzlawick found:

. . . family interaction testing, that is, asking the family (or marital couple) to approach a task (without the clinician present), to be a particularly useful initial evaluation procedure [since] often it appeared that the clinician interfered with the family's characteristic processes. Both his presence and his activity can become the focus of family attention.[8]

The therapist, where appropriate, can observe the interaction by monitoring it both visually, through a one-way vision screen, and audibly, through the use of microphones.

Psychological Testing

Psychological examinations of the family are of two types: those that are individually oriented and those that are interpersonally, system oriented. The first type has the advantage of affording greater standardization and validity; however, it may not measure crucial family variables. There are as yet no data available from functional families.

A few investigators have adapted the Thematic Apperception test[9, 10] and the Rorschach test[11] (originally designed for individual use) for family evaluation. The entire family, meeting together, is, for example, asked to look at a Rorschach card, discuss their percepts with one another, and try to arrive at a common story or interpretation. As in individual testing, the *process* by which the family arrives at its interpretation is as carefully noted as the *content* of the interpretation itself.

Notable success has been reported in being able to predict the nature of the identified patient's clinical psychiatric symptomatology from an examination of the psychological test protocols of the patient's parents, tested jointly, with the patient absent.[12]

It is the experience of most clinicians that routine psychological testing of the family has not been of major clinical usefulness in family therapy. At the present time these procedures are too costly and time-consuming and offer only a limited amount of additional information beyond that gained from a diagnostic interview. (Psychological tests are further discussed in Chapter 20.)

Medical Examinations

In order to rule out physical problems as the cause of family dysfunctions, medical examinations need to be done for each family member when indicated.

Mr. G, who was a successful musician in his late forties, was noted to become progressively paranoid and quarrelsome. His family therapist felt that his paranoia was related to his wife's love of dancing (sometimes with his friends), her younger age, and to the reality of the children's leaving home. Even with excellent family therapy over three or four months, however, Mr. G began complaining of headaches and double vision. A neighbor suggested that he consult a physician, who, after a medical workup, discovered a brain tumor. When the tumor was removed, Mr. G's paranoia decreased dramatically, and so did the problems between him and his wife.

Major psychiatric illness should be evaluated using traditional history-taking and mental-status examinations.

Home Visits[13-15]

Many family therapists visit the family in its own home, with as many family members present as possible. Sometimes this is done only once during the evaluation period. Some family researchers, however, have lived with a family for a period of several weeks, much as an anthropologist might do in an unfamiliar culture. Home visits can be considered at any time when the therapist senses a gross discrepancy between the interactions observed in the office sessions and the reports of what is taking place at home. The timing of the visit can vary depending on its purpose, but it should always be discussed with the family and agreed to in advance.

Home visits enable the therapist to see the family on its own turf and may lead to a better understanding of its interactional patterns. The family may feel more comfortable being seen in their own home. Some families have the feeling that the therapist is more interested when he is willing to make a home visit. The family, however, may see the visit as an intrusion or may try to convert the therapy into a purely social situation. In such cases, the time consumed may be uneconomical.

Family Games

"Games" refer to techniques utilizing the entire family in a structured task. For example, the family plans a picnic together or furnishes a room together, using hypothetical furniture and a fixed amount of money. Such techniques give the family therapist useful ways of evaluating families in which verbal interventions are not the common communication method. In such situations, games are a most useful way of obtaining information.

The Interpersonal Behavior Game Test as devised by Ravich is based on interpersonal dynamics that have been used in clinical practice for evaluative purposes.[16] This test is set up with a toy train engine and one set of tracks used to complete 20 "trips" for imaginary money. There are two players, usually marital partners. Neither can see the other's manipulation of the train, but they can see each other and communicate if they wish. Points are scored based on what the couple decide to do and how they communicate. There can be a profit or loss for both, or a gain for one and a loss for the other. The situation is set up in such a way as to make it impossible for either side to win unless both parties communicate and cooperate. This is meant to simulate the reality of actual married life. The nature of the couple's interaction, particularly the degree of their competitiveness compared to their cooperativeness can be observed, and numerical scores can be assigned to these two qualities.

REFERENCES

1. Gill M, Newman R, Redlich F: The Initial Interview in Psychiatric Practice. New York, International Universities Press, 1954
2. Group for the Advancement of Psychiatry. The case history in the study of family process. Report No. 76. New York, Group for the Advancement of Psychiatry, 1970
3. Mandelbaum A: Diagnosis in family treatment. Bull of the Menninger Clinic 40: 497–504, 1976
4. Berman EM, Lief HI: Marital therapy from a psychiatric perspective: An overview. Am J Psychiatry 132:583–592, 1975
5. Cuber JF, Harroff PB: Sex and the Significant Americans. Baltimore, Penguin Books, 1966 pp 43–65
6. Fisher L: On the classification of families: A progress report. Arch Gen Psychiatry 34:424–433, 1977
7. White SL: Family dinner time: A focus for life space diagrams. J Clin Social Work 4:93–101, 1976
8. Watzlawick P: A structured family interview. Fam Process 5:256–271, 1966
9. Winter WD, Ferreira AJ, Olson JL: Hostility themes in the family TAT. J Projective Techniques and Personality Assessment 30:270–275, 1966
10. Winter WD, Ferreira AJ, Olson JL: Story sequence analysis of family TATs. J Projective Techniques and Personality Assessment 29:392–397, 1965

11. Willi J: Joint Rorschach testing of partner relationships. Fam Process 8:64–78, 1969
12. Jackson DD, Riskin J, Satir V: A method of analysis of a family interview. Arch Gen Psychiatry 5:321–339, 1961
13. Fisch R: Home visits in a private psychiatric practice. Fam Process 3:114–126, 1964
14. Friedman AS: Family therapy as conducted in the home. Fam Process 1:132–140, 1962
15. Henry J: The study of families by naturalistic observation, in Cohen IM (ed): Family structure, dynamics and therapy. Psychiatric Research Report No. 20. New York, American Psychiatric Association, 1966, pp 95–104
16. Ravich R: Game-testing in conjoint marital psychotherapy. Am J Psychother 23: 217–229, 1969

A Ride for Liberty by Eastman Johnson. Courtesy of The Brooklyn Museum.

6
Goals of Family Treatment

OBJECTIVES

- To detail the process of setting goals of treatment
- To conceptualize the different types of general goals of family therapy
- To apply these general goals of family treatment to specific families

INTRODUCTION

The therapist forms a concept of the family's difficulties based on the evaluation of the family's history and interaction (see Chapter 5). The treatment often begins with the issues that seem to be most crucial to the family; the treatment at the outset helps the family to deal with an immediate crisis situation. Only after some stability and rapport have been achieved is it possible for the therapist to begin to help the family in areas that will also be beneficial. The work is often slow and gradual; sudden or miraculous major shifts in long-standing family patterns are not likely to occur. When such rapid changes occur, they may prove to be mirages, as well as harbingers of later difficulty.

In setting goals it is helpful to think not only of the family as a whole and of the various interpersonal dyads and triads, but also of the individuals who make up the system. Each individual will have a history, a personality, and set of coping mechanisms. A thorough knowledge of individual personality theory and psychopathology is essential for knowing what to expect from the individual atoms as well as from the family molecule.

At times it will be necessary to provide specific treatment for, or to direct specific attention to, the needs of an individual family member (for example, when one family member is floridly psychotic) with individual sessions, somatic treatment, and sometimes hospitalization (see Chapter 16).

Even under ordinary circumstances, however, a thorough understanding of the strengths and weaknesses of each family member (basic personality patterns, reactions to stress, and so on) will help to determine the goals and techniques of the family therapy.

The goals of family treatment must be in some way congruent with what the family members seem to desire and what they are realistically capable of achieving at any particular point. The therapist's views of the appropriate therapeutic possibilities, however, may differ from those the family members initially envision. Overall goals encompass the entire family system as well as its individual members. Ideally, the entire family should function more satisfactorily as a result of family therapy, and each family member should derive personal benefit from the experience and results of the therapy. The family therapist, for example, should not be in the position of taking the focus off a scapegoated member (saying, for instance, It's not Dad's drinking that is the problem) only to consistently refocus on one or another family member (It's Mom's yelling) as the cause of the family's difficulties.

Families traditionally enter therapy because of gross symptomatic difficulty. This is often related to one family member. A marital partner may blame the spouse for causing his or her distress or may feel guilty because the children are not behaving properly. A child may be singled out as the only problem in the family. One member, therefore, may have already been labeled "the identified patient."

Less commonly, family members talk about system difficulties as "marital troubles" or "family unhappiness." One family member may have instigated the seeking of help, or, even less frequently, the family as a whole may have discussed the difficulties and may have agreed to seek professional assistance. Families may come into treatment on their own with varying levels of motivation and expectations or they may be referred by other agencies or individuals.

Some families today are seeking professional help, not for these more traditional reasons, however, but rather for clarification of family roles and as a growth-enhancing experience. In such cases, a problem-solving model seems less appropriate than a growth-development model.

The goals of treatment will be related to what has been learned during the initial evaluation period, as well as to whatever develops as the therapy progresses. All specific goals need not be clearly spelled out at the onset of treatment; sometimes goals are left somewhat vague, with details being clarified only later or perhaps never being discussed explicitly. The particular areas to be dealt with, as well as a determination as to the priority in dealing with them, must be carefully considered. Some family therapists are relatively comfortable with allowing goals to develop as the therapy proceeds. Such treatment sometimes appears as a sequence of short-term problem resolutions. Other therapists attempt to delineate major goals early in the course of treatment or to get the family to cope better with problems that cannot be reversed, such as the death of a family member.

Some trainees feel uneasy setting goals for family therapy since they fear they are being too authoritarian by taking away from the family members their right to set their own life goals. Indeed, families should be encouraged to set their own goals to the greatest extent possible. It is in disorganized families that the therapist will need to be more active.

One convenient way to conceptualize the categories of marital and family therapy goals is indicated below. It is based on some of the material presented in the preceding five chapters. These are relatively broad areas that allow for considerable flexibility according to the specifics of each particular marital or family unit, and they are not mutually exclusive but are often intermixed. These broad categories are of use because they help clarify the therapist's own idea of what is to be achieved, and they suggest potential treatment techniques and end results. When successful, these strategies will have the general effect of reducing the quarreling and conflict within the family, symptomatically improving one or more family members, increasing agreement about roles taken by family members, and enabling the family unit to continue to develop and grow.[1] These general goals are

1. *To facilitate communication of thoughts and feelings.* The therapist's skills are utilized to aid the family members in the process of open, direct, gratifying, and meaningful communication. The therapist clarifies blurred or ambiguous thoughts and he is also involved in fostering improved empathy between family members, in diminishing the atmosphere of "emotional divorce," and in bringing to the surface those buried feelings that are obstructing a more functional family interaction.
2. *To shift disturbed, inflexible roles and coalitions.* This may include helping to improve the autonomy and individualization of family members, to facilitate the more flexible assumption of leadership by any particular family member as circumstances require, and to facilitate general task performance by one or more members.
3. *To increase options and demythologize.* By example and by what he says, the therapist helps to change family patterns. The therapist may, where indicated, temporarily serve as a more benign model of a parent, and may in such cases, by his own attributes as well as by his exposing of myths, lead the family to a more appropriate view of its potential.

The relative importance of the treatment *process* as compared with its *content* is an issue sometimes raised by family therapists. The more traditional view tends to favor substantive content issues, whereas the newer holistic view looks more closely at the characteristic patterning in an interpersonal network, with less emphasis on the subject matter. In some ways this may be an artificial dichotomy. For example, the communication process may become the most important subject matter of the therapy. Any attempt to deal with a specific content issue inevitably brings process issues to the surface.

The C family requested help because their 19-year-old son, T, was very angry at his mother, and the parents were having difficulty in controlling him. The trouble started when he became engaged a year prior to treatment. In sessions T would talk angrily all the time and the mother would complain about him whenever he did stop talking. It was clear after seeing this pattern repeatedly that an initial goal was to facilitate a wider range of communication possibilities between them. All the family members agreed to this goal. The content of what the mother and T talked about was irrelevant and emotionally charged; the context and pattern of the communication was the key.

The therapeutic interventions were to stop T from talking all the time, to get T to listen to his mother, to stop the mother from complaining, and to get the mother to express her feelings toward T. A younger brother was used as a spokesman for T to answer the mother in a way T might have. Thus, all family members had a chance to observe and interact in a new way.

Sometimes major emphasis is placed on a particular process technique and goal, such as clarifying a family's communication patterns,[2] or helping family members deal with their feelings.[3] Family therapists may see such process goals as being primary, either on ideological grounds or because of the appropriateness to a particular family, with the family being encouraged to deal with content issues as they arise now that the family has the general process tools to do so. Other family therapists, perhaps because of differing conceptual bases applicable to different types of family goals, will tend to work in the other direction—that is, from the more specific content issues toward the more general process issues.

Many family therapists have adapted some of the techniques of individual and group psychotherapy, social case work, and individual counseling to their work with families. Although the family therapy field represents a different way of looking at and conceptualizing what transpires between people, in many ways some of the specific therapeutic practices of more traditional interpersonal helping procedures are useful in treating families. For example, the aforementioned three general strategies—psychotherapy, case work, and counseling—would not be altogether unfamiliar to the person engaged in treating individuals. The family therapist, however, utilizes them in particular ways and in a particular setting.

Each of these strategies entails the use of a repertory of intervention tactics designed to produce the desired goal. These strategies are not based on any generally agreed upon theory of family structure, function, and therapy but represent ad hoc attempts by clinicians to deal with the kinds of problems with which they are presented. Some family therapists believe strongly in one or another of these strategies and their underlying concepts and utilize the same basic strategy with every family. Others feel that one strategy may be particularly well suited to one type of family, whereas a different strategy is more appropriate for another sort of family. Still other therapists move flexibly from one to another of these strategies as the situation in any one family at any one time seems to require.

The family therapist has as the overall goal the improvement of functioning of the entire family system. This includes enabling the family to deal more appropriately and productively with its current life phase, helping each of its members to grow and differentiate appropriately, and helping the various constituents of the family system to achieve the goals they have outlined for themselves. At any particular moment in the therapy, the family therapist may find himself allied with one or another subgroup of the family system, but these temporary tactics need to be viewed against the overall background of a strategy which is directed toward producing benefit for the entire family system.[4]

There are short-term goals (see Chapter 15) and long-term goals. The beginning therapist, however, is cautioned against trying to produce instantaneous behavioral change that may only prove to be evanescent. The chronicle of nonconventional therapies is replete with claims of being able to change behavior in the short term. In contrast, family therapists should aim for a more permanent, long-term change in family structure and function.

These differences in outlook and practice can be bewildering to the inexperienced therapist who is not aware of the underlying rationales and guidelines. Given the current state of the field, with no unifying theory of family pathology, nomenclature, or even of treatment, each new situation represents an "experiment" in which the therapist is required to clarify and test hypotheses.

Examples of goals can be found in the case of the R family presented in Chapter 5; how to obtain family-therapist congruence and agreement regarding goals is discussed in Chapter 10; examples of process and content are discussed in Chapter 22; and goals with different types of families are discussed in Chapter 12.

REFERENCES

1. Sluzki C: A strategy for research in family therapy. Paper presented at the Langley Porter Neuropsychiatric Institute Noon Conference, December 13, 1972
2. Satir V: Conjoint Family Therapy: A Guide to Theory and Technique. Palo Alto, California, Science and Behavior Books, 1964, pp 162–167, 175–176
3. Paul NL: The role of mourning and empathy in conjoint marital therapy, in Zuk GH, Boszormenyi-Nagy I (eds): Family Therapy and Disturbed Families. Palo Alto, California, Science and Behavior Books, 1967, pp 186–205
4. Group for the Advancement of Psychiatry. The field of family therapy. Report No. 78. New York, Group for the Advancement of Psychiatry, 1970, pp 581–593

Gypsy Family. Photograph by Jack Reed Royce, 1973.

7

Family Treatment: General Considerations

OBJECTIVES

- To be able to decide which family participants to include in treatment and to be aware of the guidelines for including children, adolescents, grandparents, and others
- To know the advantages and disadvantages of various therapist combinations
- To be aware of the variety of settings in which family therapy has been used
- To be able to manage the complexities of combining family treatment with other therapies

INTRODUCTION

By this time the reader should have some understanding of how families function and how their difficulties may be conceptualized. In addition, material has been presented relative to evaluating troubled families and to setting appropriate treatment goals. The following discussion considers more general features of marital and family treatment, namely, the participants, the setting, the scheduling of treatment, and the use of family therapy in combination with other treatment methods and helping agencies.

FAMILY PARTICIPANTS

In practice it is often preferable to begin treatment by seeing the entire family together. The family can broadly be defined to include all persons living under the same roof; all those persons closely related to one another, even though they do not live together; or even more broadly, all persons significant to the family, even though not related to them (friends, "caretakers," or "social network").[1, 2]

Sometimes family therapy is carried out with the same therapist meeting with the whole family and with each family member individually. This is termed *concurrent family therapy*. At other times two therapists who maintain some contact with each other, but who do not work jointly, may each see separately one or more members of a family in what is known as *collaborative family therapy*. *Conjoint family therapy* has been defined as family therapy in which the participants include at least two generations of a family, such as parents and children, plus the therapist, all meeting together. *Conjoint marital therapy* is limited to the two spouses plus the therapist meeting together.[3]

Although it often seems desirable to meet with all family members present, in actual practice this may be impossible or even contraindicated. For example, it would usually seem more appropriate when discussing the sexual adjustment of the parents that the children not be present. Often, too, the therapist will be involved with incomplete families, either because the family itself has experienced divorce or death, or because one or more family members temporarily or permanently refuse to participate. In the latter case a decision will have to be made either at the outset of treatment or following the evaluation as to whether it is worthwhile and possible to continue working with the incomplete family.

At times individuals will feel uncomfortable talking about certain topics in front of the other family members. In such instances the family therapist will have to use his or her judgment as to when individual interviewing might be indicated. This might be done, for example, with the goal of eventually bringing the material from the individual session to the entire family group. It must be recognized that there may be family secrets that cannot be productively shared with other family members and that should be kept private between an individual family member and the therapist. (This issue is discussed more fully in Chapter 11.) On this issue no rigid guidelines can be established.

An example of an unshared family secret comes from a family in which a 20-year-old girl was the identified patient.* The patient's mother had had a postpartum psychosis following the patient's birth, during which she had jumped in front of a train, resulting in bilateral amputation below the knees. The patient's grandmother had also had a postpartum psychosis after the birth of the mother. The patient had not known about these secrets. The story was revealed by the father in a family session that did not involve the identified patient. The patient was never informed of her mother's psychosis based on the judgment of all concerned that she was not psychologically capable of dealing with this material at that time.

The family concept can be extended to cover nonrelated people who have an impact on the individuals in treatment. These might be friends, neighbors, pro-

*We are indebted to Pamela Ingber, M.D., for this example.

fessional helpers, or custodians. Such people often do not have the same kind of emotional impact and influence that the natural family unit has, but at any one particular time, these groups of "significant others" may be quite important.

Many experienced family therapists hold to the view that the probability of improvement increases as the number of nuclear family members involved in treatment increases.

Adolescents

Adolescents will be crucially involved in the family unit's concerns and interactions and often represent the "identified patient." They should be included in the sessions so that intergenerational conflicts and inadequate communication can be dealt with. One of the primary tasks of the late adolescent, however, is to achieve increasing psychosocial autonomy from his family of origin. If such adolescents are consistently included in all family sessions, there is a structural reinforcement of their being involved in all of the family's interactions. In addition, there may be little recognition of those specific interactions of the husband–wife pair, which do not, and should not, involve their children. Thus it may be useful to have some sessions with only the husband and wife. Other sessions may be devoted to seeing an adolescent alone for the special purpose of reinforcing or increasing autonomy. Conjoint sessions, however, may also be successfully used to explore issues of differentness and separation.

When a marital relationship has ruptured to the extent that treatment cannot be accomplished without the inclusion of the adolescent children, the children may serve as buffers, neutralizers, or reality testers until such time as the couple is able to resume functioning as a dyad.

Careful recognition must be given to the readiness and ability of both the adolescent and his or her family to separate. Although individual autonomous functioning is seen as a desirable goal, there will be situations in which the therapist must be realistic with respect to the family's ability to tolerate an abrupt separation, as well as to the autonomous potential of adolescents suffering from brain damage, chronic schizophrenia, or severe characterological difficulties.

Infants and Young Children

Many therapists prefer to involve everyone in the household, including infants (and perhaps even pets), during the evaluation period in order to observe how family members relate to one another. Helpful observations may be gathered, such as how one parent holds an infant and what the role of the other parent is. After the initial evaluation is completed, the therapist must decide whether the continued inclusion of an infant or relatively nonverbal child tends to aid or disrupt the work of therapy.

Most family therapists would probably agree that infants and children should be included at least once for diagnostic purposes. Certainly much can be gained from having children present for many of the sessions, if for no other reason than that they often tend to be more open and direct than adults and will say what they think.

When young children are present, the parents are expected to exert appropriate behavioral control over them. If not, the therapist helps the parent to accomplish the task. The therapist explains the "rules of the house," including behavioral limits and freedom of communication. The therapist must decide who should handle requests to go to the toilet and water fountain. The therapist may wish to provide material for play, such as toys, paper, and crayons.

Bell, writing about the general process of therapy, has offered some pertinent guidelines concerning children in therapy sessions.[4] He first meets with parents, alone in order to explain the basis of family therapy. Then he meets with children and parents together for orientation. He explains that the children have a voice in what is said and that the parents are expected to listen and not to talk while the children are talking. He calls this the "parent-child phase." He then moves into the parent phase, during which the problems of the parents are explored. During this time, the children, as they gain trust in the therapist, are usually more active. In the next phase, the identified patient is more active in the family in a more constructive way. Most so-called "forbidden" topics usually have already been heard by the children, and, in this, Bell's experience with children in therapy concurs with ours.

Extended Family and Significant Others

Family therapists include grandparents or in-laws as participants when they seem to significantly influence the family difficulties (see Chapter 3).*

Grandparents and other extended family members play vital roles in many families. For some they may provide important help financially and functionally in carrying out the family's tasks. They may be a repository of emotional support and warmth, available in times of crisis and need. Their contributions and participation may at times be viewed as interference or infantilization. They may create or demand obligations in return for their involvement.

The grandparents may provide money with strings attached, which may be in the form of rules and regulations concerning the rearing of their grand-

*An excellent example of a family in which a child may feel much closer to a grandparent than to his father or mother is provided in the 1976 movie, *Lies My Father Told Me*. In this film, a 7-year-old boy is being raised by a mother who is totally devoted to a rather insensitive, chronically inadequate spouse. The boy spends most of his time with his grandfather, who acts as a father substitute.

children; such aid may also imply an obligation that the family visit the grandparents on a prescribed schedule.

The question of whether or not a friend, fiancé(e), boyfriend, or girl friend should participate in a therapy session is occasionally raised. Such individuals should be included if their involvement is judged to be important to the progress of the therapy. Such outsiders are less motivated to change than are family members, however, and are hence more likely to drop out of family therapy.

Caretakers

Caretakers (e.g., baby-sitters or housekeepers) are playing an increasingly important role in the function of families, especially those in which both parents work. They are often usefully included in treatment.

In the G family Mr. and Mrs. G were separated. Mrs. G had great difficulty functioning as a person and mother. Mr. G, therefore, had custody of the children. Care of the children, ages 14, 12, and 10, was left to a baby-sitter who was the 21-year-old sister of Mr. G's current girl friend. Feeling despondent, Mrs. G made a suicide attempt. It was at this point that attempts at family therapy were initiated, but Mr. G refused to attend because he was angry with his wife. At the onset of family therapy, Mrs. G complained that she was unable to get the children to attend. They were on Mr. G's side. The children refused to attend when the therapist called them, saying the baby-sitter would not let them travel to the sessions. The baby-sitter was, of course, on the father's side. Furthermore, once the children began to attend therapy, the sitter would, after each session, belittle the mother to the children. They would then in turn berate their mother, who would again become suicidal. It was only after both the husband and the baby-sitter were included in family therapy that this sequence of interactions could be understood and modified.

Pets

Pets often serve important functions in the family:[5]

1. As safe, faithful, intimate, noncompetitive, nonjudgmental love objects and friends
2. As substitute children for childless couples or for those whose children have left home; couples planning to have children may find that practicing their parental skills first on pets is desirable
3. As ways of compensating for personal deficiencies by identification with the pet's strength, courage, assertiveness, attractiveness, size, playfulness, directness, animality, dependence, or independence
4. As scapegoats or allies in intrafamily conflicts
5. As a means for children to learn responsibility and compassion

Ms. P was from a family based on dyads (mother–father, older sister–younger sister). The "confidant" for this person during her emotional crisis was her dog. When she left home to attend school, the dog developed a rash and lost his hair. He manifested the symptoms during the beginning of his empty-nest syndrome. There was also a family crisis that revolved around who should take care of the dog.

In the G family, Mr. G was unable to express any affection to his wife, son, or daughter, but he spent long hours caressing, talking to, and grooming his five dogs.

Veterinarians have observed the relationship between the neurotic behaviors of pets and those of their owners. One veterinarian has recently taken a family approach, stating that "you can't change a dog's behavior without changing the dog owner in terms of how he relates to the dog."[6]

The family therapist may want, at least temporarily, to include a pet as part of the therapy to observe and discuss the role of the pet in the family system. A pet may be used as a more neutral way of getting into the family's dynamics, because it may be easier to talk about the pet than to talk about the problems involving the human beings in the family.

THERAPIST COMBINATIONS

Most family therapists work alone. A number of therapists, however, prefer to work with a *cotherapist* to help monitor the complexity of the transactions and as a check-balance on the other therapist. For training purposes, a student therapist can work with either a more seasoned veteran or with a student of another discipline. Cotherapists can present an experiential model of a two-person inter-action that is similar to a marital dyad by openly dealing with their own differ-ences and by providing models for healthy communication. If, on the other hand, the cotherapists feel that they need to present a united front or that they need to be identical in their attitudes and interactions with the family members they are jointly treating, the family will then be provided with a very unrealistic model.

Cotherapists are usually of the opposite sex. This gives each family member someone of the same sex with whom to identify and to use as a model. Often cotherapists are or become personally intimate.

Cotherapists may come to be seen as parents or as husband and wife by the family and may therefore be the recipients of the typical patterns, feelings, and attitudes that the family has toward people in these roles. The cotherapists may find themselves in danger of being split and having to take sides between one family member and another, in a manner very similar to what takes place in the actual treatment family. The cotherapy team must avoid falling consistently into this trap. A solution is for one cotherapist to be sensitive to a family member who is in distress and who may need support, while the other therapist focuses on someone else. A cotherapist may either complement or synergize with the other therapist.

It is necessary to consider whether or not a therapist can work effectively with a cotherapist and if cotherapy is the best use of each therapist's time. A recent study suggests that therapist satisfaction with a cotherapist decreases as experience in family therapy increases.[7] Furthermore some authors have found that a cotherapist causes problems that can impede family progress. For example, if the male cotherapist has had significant problems with his mother and is in the process of treating a family that has a "difficult" mother, he might have difficulty working effectively with a female therapist. Another obvious reason for the more common use of a single therapist is that it costs less.

In order to make cotherapy a successful experience, the cotherapists should know and like each other. They should have worked together, so that they are able to appreciate each other's therapy style and attitude. They should have time to discuss together what has been going on in their therapy sessions and to have a chance to work out their mutual roles with respect to the family and each other. Ideally cotherapists should meet together prior to each session in order to review their objectives and ideas. Cotherapists should meet after each session for a review of what went on and to plan for the next session.

Another technique of family therapy is to use more than two therapists—one for each individual family member and one for the whole family together. This method has been used as part of multiple impact therapy (MIT).[8]

An innovative approach is the use of cotherapists from different disciplines, which, as stated, is a desirable approach for beginning therapists. This technique has the advantage that each therapist may complement the other, since each discipline has different training and may bring its own areas of expertise. This method requires the use of extra staff time, however, and to justify it, one would have to prove its differential effectiveness over family therapy as it is usually practiced.

One report has noted the use of the *therapist and his family* to treat the identified patient and his family.[9] This method must be considered experimental at this time.

SETTING

Family therapy has been carried out in settings such as child-guidance clinics, psychiatric hospitals, emergency rooms (walk-in or crisis clinics), outpatient clinics, juvenile probation offices, domestic relations courts, private offices, schools,[10] social welfare services,[11] and many other places. There have been cases in which entire families have been hospitalized for treatment[12] and for research purposes.[13] Other therapists have carried out treatment in the family's own home. (Advantages and disadvantages of home visits have been discussed in Chapter 5.)

SCHEDULING

Most family therapists will see a family once a week for a duration of 50 to 90 minutes. A minority of therapists sees a family more than once a week. In inpatient settings, family sessions may be scheduled more frequently. There is nothing sacred about once-a-week scheduling. In fact, since the frequency of sessions is somewhat arbitrary (once a week is the commonest), meeting less frequently may be strategically better for some families. Palazzoli meets with a given family in treatment once a month. She mails the family a "prescription" between sessions.[26]

In multiple impact therapy, families are seen on an intensive basis and in different combinations—marital couple, mother and son, whole family, individuals, and so on—over a two- or three-day period by various members of a therapy team, consisting of psychiatrist, psychologist, social worker, and vocational counselor. Techniques focus on bringing about rapid change in the family during this time period, because its members have come for therapy from distant locations. A variant of this technique is the one employed by Masters and Johnson[14] in their sex therapy, which consists of a two-week treatment course of multiple daily sessions with one male and one female cotherapist.

The decision as to the overall duration of treatment would, in part, depend on the goals of treatment (see Chapter 6). On the average, family therapy is a short-term method compared to individual or group psychotherapy or psychoanalysis.

FAMILY THERAPY IN COMBINATION WITH OTHER PSYCHOSOCIAL THERAPIES

At present the differential effectiveness of family therapy alone as compared with its use in combination with other therapies is unknown (see Chapter 18). Therefore each therapist must "play it by ear." During the 1970s use of family therapy in combination with somatic, individual, and group therapy has increased.

A minority of family therapists uses *conjoint* family therapy alone. All contacts are kept strictly within the joint family setting, and the therapist will not communicate even by telephone with individual family members. No other treatment is used, including individual therapy. This is done to avoid any type of coalition derived from material shared by the therapist and any part of the family system.

It is becoming more usual for the therapist to employ individual psychotherapy and family therapy.[15] The therapist here has the advantage of knowing both the individual and the family. This combination, however, changes the nature of the therapy as follows: (1) the patient in individual therapy feels that what he reveals in the one-to-one situation may in some way (either overtly or covertly) be communicated to the family by the therapist; (2) family members may be reluctant to deal with sensitive issues in the conjoint sessions, preferring to reveal them in individual sessions; and (3) transference in individual sessions does not develop as fully, because the patient can directly express his feelings about his family in the family therapy. This may present an insurmountable obstacle to the individual therapy. Inexperienced therapists may tend to identify with the individual patient, thus seeing the family from the patient's point of view. The therapist may see all problems as resulting from "this cold, passive, authoritarian father and smoldering, double-binding, rejecting mother" and from what they have done to the "poor patient." This may make it extremely difficult to work conjointly with the whole family.

In addition to conjoint family treatment, individual therapy has simultaneously been carried out with only one parent, or with both parents in separate sessions.

In the C family the identified patient was the son, Henry, who had chronic schizophrenia. He was 20 when he was brought for treatment because he had not gone out of his room for a year. The mother and father were bringing him his meals in bed, and he had stopped attending school. History revealed that there were two older sisters who were functioning well. Mother and father had met 25 years before. The father was shy and withdrawn. The mother was overbearing, domineering, and brought in most of the money. She worked as a cashier. Life for them had been good up until the birth of the youngest child—the identified patient—at which point mother and father stopped having sexual relations (the previous frequency had been about two times per week). The mother said that she was "uninformed" about contraceptive methods and that since she did not want any more children, the only way she could think of was to stop having sex. Since the father was a noncommunicative person, this had not been discussed for 19 years, up until the time that the patient returned to the hospital.

Treatment intervention was initiated with somatic therapy for the identified patient's schizophrenia. Once his symptoms (negativism and autistic thinking) began to clear, treatment was directed toward his rehabilitation. In order to do this, and to place the patient in a work setting, the parents had to let him "out of the nest." Family meetings were held with the mother, father, sisters, and the identified patient. Mother and father were also seen separately, to help them rebuild their marital relationship. A series of progressive behavioral exercises markedly improved their sexual relations, which resumed with a satisfactory frequency. Once all this had occurred, the parents helped to find a halfway house for the son.

Individual treatment as a supplement to conjoint family therapy has also been carried out with mother and/or child. Individual sessions supplemented by conjoint sessions for all family members is an approach employed commonly in child psychiatric practice (see Chapter 19).

Family therapy has been prescribed in combination with group therapy[16, 17] and with behavioral therapy.[18, 19] It has been used in conjunction with hospitalization for one member (usually the identified patient) or for all members of the family in both inpatient[13, 20] and day hospital[21] settings; in conjunction with psychiatric medications[22] and electric-shock therapy, which are used to control the identified patient's acute symptoms. One of us (IDG) has found that family therapy was possible and effective only after both marital partners had been treated for their depressions (which predated the marriage) with antidepressants.

Family therapy has been prescribed as an adjunct to individual therapy[23] and psychoanalysis. In these situations it may be useful for diagnostic purposes to correct distorted perceptions and to shorten treatment.[24] (See Chapter 1 for indications for and comparisons of several types of psychosocial treatments; see Chapter 19 for guidelines in prescribing the desired treatment.)

FAMILY THERAPY IN COMBINATION WITH OTHER HELPING AGENCIES

The family therapist often finds himself in the situation of using family therapy at the same time that other helping agencies are also exerting influences on the family. This may create unwanted complications.

Commonly, families have multiple problems that involve a wide variety of agencies: welfare, probation, school, housing, and so on. These agencies may be pulling the family in different directions. The need is often to open up communication among the various agencies and to allocate areas of responsibility. It then becomes necessary to coordinate the work of the various agencies in the service of the family's goals, thus avoiding much duplication and wasteful contradictory efforts.

In some families there is simultaneous treatment by the therapist and physician of one or more members of the family, and this may exert a significant influence.[25] For example, one family member may be receiving cortisone for rheumatoid arthritis, which may make that person euphoric. He or she may be difficult for the family to live with. The family therapist will have to be in continuing contact with the family physician to coordinate treatment in such cases.

Family members may play one agency against the other in the service of their needs. For example, the family members may need to have the identified patient remain dysfunctional so that they can get welfare or disability payments; but they simultaneously experience the distortions in the family system that this may produce. In another case a spouse who is not getting along with her husband may suggest to the probation worker that the husband has been violating his parole and should go back to jail, whereas she tells the family therapist that she is trying to work out their problems in order that they may stay together.

REFERENCES

1. Speck RV, Rueveni U: Network therapy: A developing concept. Fam Process 8: 182–191, 1969
2. Speck RV, Attneave C: Network therapy, in Haley J (ed): Changing Families. New York, Grune & Stratton, 1971, pp 312–332
3. Cutter AV, Hallowitz D: Diagnosis and treatment of the family unit with respect to the character-disordered youngster. J Am Acad Child Psychiatry 1:605–618, 1962
4. Bell JE: Family group therapy. Public Health Monograph No. 64. Washington, D.C., Department of Health, Education and Welfare, Public Health Service, 1961

5. Feldman B: Pets soothe their owners' hang-ups. San Francisco Examiner, November 20, 1977
6. Campbell W: Owners cause dogs' mental problems. San Francisco Chronicle, October 29, 1975, p 45
7. Rice D, Fey W, Kepecs J: Therapist experience and "style" as factors in co-therapy. Fam Process 11:227–238, 1972
8. MacGregor R, Ritchie AM, Serrano AC, et al: Multiple Impact Therapy with Families. New York, McGraw-Hill, 1964
9. Landes J, Winter W: A new strategy for treating disintegrating families. Fam Process 5:1–20, 1966
10. Moss S: School experiences as family crisis. J of the International Association of Pupil Personnel Workers 15:115–121, 1970
11. Morris R: Welfare reform 1973: The social services dimension. Science 181:515–522, 1973
12. Abrams G, Fellner C, Whitaker C: The family enters the hospital. Am J Psychiatry 127:1363–1370, 1971
13. Bowen M: Family psychotherapy. Am J Orthopsychiatry 31:40–60, 1961
14. Masters W, Johnson V: Human Sexual Response. Boston, Little, Brown, 1966
15. Greene BL (ed): The Psychotherapies of Marital Disharmony. New York, Free Press, 1965
16. Leichter E, Shulman G: The family interview as an integrative device in group therapy with families. Int J Group Psychother 13:335–345, 1963
17. MacGregor R: Group and family therapy: Moving into the present and letting go of the past. Int J Group Psychother 20:495–515, 1970
18. Fine S: Family therapy and behavioral approach to childhood obsessive-compulsive neurosis. Arch Gen Psychiatry 28:695–697, 1973
19. Coe W: Behavioral approach to disrupted family interactions. Psychother: Theory, Research and Practice 9:80–85, 1972
20. Fleck S: Some general and specific indications for family therapy. Confin Psychiatry 8:27–36, 1965
21. Zwerling I, Mendelsohn M: Initial family reactions to day hospitalization. Fam Process 4:50–63, 1965
22. Cohen M, Freedman N, Engelhardt D, et al: Family interaction patterns, drug treatment, and change in social aggression. Arch Gen Psychiatry 19:1950–1956, 1968
23. Szalita A: The combined use of family interviews and individual therapy in schizophrenia. Am J Psychother 22:419–430, 1968
24. Szalita A: The relevance of the family interview for psychoanalysis. Contemporary Psychoanal 8:31–44, 1971
25. Anthony E: The impact of mental and physical illness on family life. Am J Psychiatry 127:138–146, 1970
26. Selvini Palazzoli M, Cecchin G, Prata G, et al: Paradox and Counterparadox: A New Model in the Therapy of the Family Schizophrenic Transaction. New York, Aronson, 1978

Birth of a Notion by Susan Kay Williams, private collection.

8
Family Treatment: Specific Strategies

OBJECTIVES

- To understand the general elements of psychotherapy as they apply to family treatment
- To become familiar with three broad family treatment strategies and their applications in various specific situations
- To become aware of other approaches and their principal proponents

GENERAL ELEMENTS OF PSYCHOTHERAPY AND THEIR RELATIONSHIP TO FAMILY THERAPY

There appear to be at least eight elements that most kinds of psychotherapy have in common:[1]

1. A good patient–therapist relationship
2. Release of emotional tension
3. Cognitive learning
4. Operant reconditioning of the patient toward more adaptive behavior patterns by explicit or implicit approval–disapproval cues and by a corrective emotional relationship with the therapist
5. Suggestion and persuasion
6. Identification with the therapist
7. Repeated reality testing or practicing of new adaptive techniques in the context of implicit or explicit emotional therapeutic support

Family therapy, too, may use all eight of these elements but will do so with the goal of improving the overall functioning of the entire family. The particular mix of the elements will vary with the specific needs of the family. There is hardly any specific technique of individual or group therapy that could not in some way or other be adapted for use in family therapy.

ELEMENTS OF FAMILY PSYCHOTHERAPY

Currently there are various strategies for treating families. Each may emphasize different assumptions and types of interventions. Some therapists prefer to operate with one strategy in most cases, whereas others intermix these strategies depending on the type of case and the phase of treatment. At times the type of strategy used is made explicit by the therapist, whereas in other instances it remains covert; but irrespective of whether a therapist specializes in one or another approach or is eclectic, some hypotheses will be formed about the nature of the family's difficulty and the preferable approach to adopt.

Various schools of family therapy may differ on where they place their emphasis on the following major treatment dimensions:[2]

1. Past versus present orientation
2. Verbal interpretations versus action
3. Growth model versus problem model
4. General method versus specific plan for each problem
5. Therapeutic focus on one individual versus focus on two or more individuals
6. Equality versus hierarchy in therapeutic relationship
7. Analogical versus digital thinking (Digital thinking concentrates on individual "bits" of behavior; the analogical view is more concerned with multiple levels and contexts of behavior)

Some therapists emphasize reconstruction of past events, whereas others choose to deal only with current behavior as manifested during the therapy session. Some therapists favor verbal exploration and interpretation, whereas others are more in favor of utilizing an action or experiential mode of treatment, either in the session itself or by requiring new behavior outside the interview. Some therapists think in terms of problems and symptoms and attempt to decode or understand possible symbolic meanings of symptomatology, whereas other therapists focus on the potentials for growth and differentiation that are not being fulfilled. Some therapists utilize one or a very limited number of methods in dealing with a whole range of "problems," but others are more eclectic and attempt to tailor the treatment techniques to what they consider the specific requirements of the situation.

With the therapeutic focus on one person, the emphasis is often on the individual's perceptions, reactions, and feelings, and also on the equality of status between the individual and the therapist; when two people are the operative system, attention is directed to interactions and relationships. Therapists who think in terms of a unit of three people look at coalitions, structures, and hierarchies of status and power. The number of people actually involved in the interviews may not be as important as *how many people are involved in the therapist's way of thinking about the problem*.

Table 8–1 presents a comparison of different approaches to family therapy according to which of the major treatment dimensions they emphasize.

Some family therapists have adapted treatment techniques from traditional, psychodynamically oriented individual and group therapies for use with family systems. They have been referred to as the psychodynamic school. They deal with such issues as unconscious motivations, the importance of individual past experience, repressed feelings, and transference. For example, Nathan Ackerman, who pioneered in the use of family therapy, was trained in a psychoanalytic frame of reference. His therapeutic approach tended to be eclectic, and he mixed "deep" interpretations with behavioral directives and tended to view "emotional divorce" of the parents as one of the core problems in treatment families.[3] Ivan Boszormenyi-Nagy also uses many of the concepts of the psychoanalytic approach, but in a family setting.[4] Norman Paul has stressed in his writings the therapeutic efficacy of emotional catharsis of past and present feelings, especially when depression is a prominent symptom.[5]

Other family therapists avoid the traditional techniques of individual therapy. They do not concentrate on eliciting historical material, are not particularly interested in fostering increased awareness or expression of buried feelings, and do not engage in interpreting psychodynamics. They do not consider understanding and insight to be important or essential in producing change. Instead, this group of family therapists manipulates variables such as the participants and rules of therapy by active suggestion and direction. They may utilize paradoxical commands and clearly attempt to alter the arrangement and intensity of family coalitions.[6]

The experiential school stresses the present and the open expression of thoughts and feelings as being therapeutically beneficial. The *extended families systems school* combines the various strategies in a context involving all the significant people in the person's life. The *behaviorists* focus is on changing the behavior involved in the presented problem by devising a specific, directive strategy. The *structural school* manipulates communication to bring about structural changes in the family, and those who utilize *strategic therapy* channel communication into directives to solve the presented problem.

In summary, all the schools can be condensed into three approaches:[7]

1. With the insight–awareness approach, observation, clarification, and interpretations are used to foster understanding (and presumably change)
2. In the structural–behavioral approach, manipulations are devised to alter family structures and conduct

Table 8-1

Comparison of Different Approaches to Family Therapy According to Various Dimensions[2]

Dimensions	Psycho-dynamic	Experiential	Extended Family	Behavioral	Structural	Strategic
					Communication	
Past	x	x				
Unit 1 person	x	x		x		
Interpret (past)	x	x				
Interpret (present)	x	x	x		x	
Method	x	x	x			
Growth	x	x	x		x	
Analogical	x	x	x		x	x
Present		x	x	x	x	x
New experience		x		x	x	x
Directives			x	x	x	x
Plan for therapy				x	x	x
Unit 2 people			x	x	x	x
Unit 3 people			x		x	x
Hierarchy			x		x	x
Presenting problem				x		x
Digital				x		x

Reprinted with permission of the authors and publisher, from Madanes C, Haley J: Dimensions of family therapy in the Journal of Nervous and Mental Disease, Vol. 165, p 92, 1977.

3.   In the experiential approach, emotional experience is designed to change the way family members see (and presumably) react to one another

THREE BASIC STRATEGIES OF FAMILY THERAPY

Three major therapeutic strategies have been singled out for discussion here and follow from the material presented in the chapters on evaluation and goals (Chapters 5 and 6). They are:

1.   Those that facilitate communication of thoughts and feelings
2.   Those that shift disturbed, inflexible roles and coalitions
3.   Those that aid family role-assumption, education, and demythologizing

These three strategies are not necessarily mutually exclusive and in part overlap considerably. To some extent they represent different frames of reference for understanding and dealing with the same family phenomena. Nevertheless, each strategy seems to offer something unique in its concepts and techniques. In a clinical situation the therapist will be hard put to remain a purist. A therapist's efforts to clarify communication may produce shifts in family coalitions or initiate an exploration of family myths that may lead to a considerable outpouring of previously concealed affect.

Although some specific therapeutic strategies are listed, there is no one magical phrase or technique that will "cure" the family. Interventions are instead a series of repetitive maneuvers designed to change feelings, attitudes, and behavior. If the overall goals and strategy are kept in mind, specific interventions will suggest themselves and be modified by the particular circumstances and the therapist's own style.

What is unique in family therapy is not so much the specific technique utilized but rather the overall focus and strategy that aims to evaluate and produce a beneficial change in the entire family system.

Strategies to Facilitate Communication of Thoughts and Feelings

The therapist is an expert in communication and thus can help the family members express their thoughts and feelings more clearly to one another. The therapist tries to promote open and clear communication, emotional empathy, and positive rapport between family members, being aware that disturbed families often have major problems in this regard.[8, 9] For example, although it is impossible *not* to communicate in a family, nevertheless in many troubled families, members spend very little time talking meaningfully with one another. Not only thoughts but feelings, too, are distorted, hidden, negated, or blurred.

The therapist supplies an arena for family discussion, being cognizant of the different levels of meaning in messages and how these influence and sometimes contradict each other; and being sensitive to "double binds,"[10, 11] the therapist can discourage one family member's "reading" another's mind. The therapist does not allow anyone to monopolize a session or to speak for someone else. At the same time the therapist attempts to encourage interpersonal sensitivity and empathy and tries to help each person become more aware of his or her own thoughts and feelings.

The therapist encourages family members to be specific, to state who did what to whom (for example, "Dad hit me with a stick," rather than "He did it"). The therapist stresses that individuals are held accountable for their actions. He fills in gaps in communication, points out discrepancies, and deals with nonverbal communication.[12] The therapist points out nonproductive verbal and nonverbal family communication patterns and tries to identify the implicit, unstated patterns or attitudes that may be causing trouble. Through his efforts, the covert is made overt; the implicit is made explicit. Blocked channels of communication and feeling are opened up.[13] The therapist counsels that good communication includes listening. Often three or four family members are heard talking at exactly the same time during a session, presumably to avoid hearing thoughts and feelings other than their own. The therapist, in such a situation, may function as a communications traffic cop or referee.

The therapist keeps the emphasis on the present and future, rather than on the past. This does not mean that the past may not be usefully explored in order to deal more appropriately with the present and future. Geraldine Spark[14] has described what she calls *intergenerational family therapy*. She believes that conflict in families is an ingredient to growth, rather than being an obstacle. She attempts to rebind family loyalties and relationships between generations. Exclusive, obsessive concentration on a family's "spilled milk," however, usually does not lead to constructive change.

The therapist may use a number of techniques common to all forms of psychotherapy, such as confrontation or pointing out patterns to the family—"I notice that whenever your son steals a car, you beat up your wife"; support—"I can understand how hard you have tried to be good parents"; and interpretation or pointing out the whys of behavior—"I notice that whenever you beat up your wife, it is as if you are beating up your mother." A unique advantage of family therapy is this, that when an intervention does not work because of one or more family member's feelings about the therapist, the therapist can allow or even encourage another family member to say the same thing, which may then prove more acceptable.

The N family consisted of father, mother, two adolescent boys, and a seven-year-old girl. In this family the father spoke to his wife as though he were running his plant. He expected her to listen because he was "the boss." He would say to her, "You take out the garbage, prepare the supper, and get things ready for the weekend." She would sit looking out the window, and when he really yelled at her she would begin to cry. The children, meanwhile, would laugh while this was going on. The therapist questioned whether either of them was aware of what the other was feeling or thinking. Neither of them was able to state with any assurance that they did.

The therapist's intervention was to have each parent say what he or she expected, or wanted to do, and how he or she would do it. The attempt was to get both partners to work out a modus operandi. Several times the therapist commented that the father seemed to be reacting to the mother as though she were an employee at his plant. He seemed totally unable to comprehend this until the seven-year-old girl said to him, "Daddy, Mommy doesn't work for you." He then appeared surprised. Subsequently he became more aware of the effect of his authoritarian manner on his wife and changed his behavior toward her.

The therapist decreases the need for defensiveness by bringing both positive and negative feelings into the open. The therapist will try to decrease the atmosphere of "emotional divorce," meaninglessness, nonproductive conflict and arguing, endless recriminations and blaming, and pseudoagreement. To do this, he may find it necessary to bring to the surface long-buried feelings, which often are the primary cause of the family's current dysfunction.[5]

Emotionally charged material may need to be handled carefully and in a step-wise manner. A variety of techniques may be used to help the family feel safe with emotionally charged material, including the use of support and humor (Chapter 9). When necessary this can be done by switching subjects, generalizing, and changing the temporal focus until the family is ready to deal with a particular issue.

The therapist may try to bring out into the open both the interpersonal and individual conflicts that are causing family problems. A husband who hates his own mother may set up situations in which he is in continuous conflict with his wife and other female members of the family.

Don Jackson and others of the Palo Alto group focused much of their attention on pathologic communication. Together with Gregory Bateson, they wrote about the "double bind" playing a prominent part in family difficulties.[15] Jay Haley,[16] originally a member of the same group, has recently become more interested in the paradoxical intervention approach of Milton Erickson.[17] Virginia Satir, long interested in the communication frame of reference, has recently moved into the area of family growth enhancement.[18] A current member of the Palo Alto group, Paul Watzlawick, believes in "illogical," unreasonable action as producing desired change.[8] He borrows from the concepts of (1) communications, (2) double bind, and (3) action-oriented techniques of problem resolution.

Strategies to Shift Disturbed, Inflexible Roles and Coalitions

A graphic representation of some family coalitions is provided in Figure 8-1. A "typical" four-member family is taken as the unit, with the squares representing the males and the circles the females. The larger symbols stand for

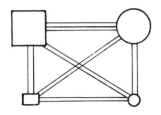

A. Functional

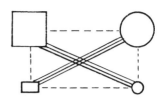

B. Schismatic

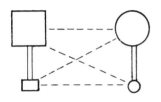

C. Schismatic

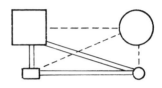

D. Skewed

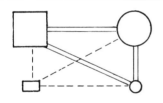

E. Skewed

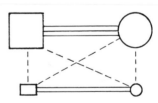

F. Generation gap

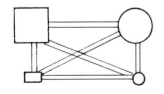

G. Pseudodemocratic

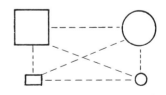

H. Disengaged

Fig. 8-1. Types of Family Coalitions

spouse/parent, and the smaller symbols represent the offspring/siblings. The solid straight lines joining these symbols are intended to represent positive communicational, emotional, and activity bonds between the individuals involved, in a semiquantitative fashion according to the number of straight lines utilized. Dotted lines, on the other hand, are used to represent the relative absence or negative quality of the interactions.

In Example A, the *functional family,* the marital coalition is the strongest dyad in the family, the generation boundary is intact, and all other channels are open and about equal to one another in importance. In contrast to this are the various types of dysfunctional families that follow.

In Example B the marital coalition is relatively weak or absent, and instead there are strong alliances across the generations and sexes—between father and son and mother and daughter—with a relative absence of other effective channels. In Example C there are cross-generational alliances between same-sexed parent and child. Examples B and C can be thought of as representing types of the *schismatic family* (see Chapter 3).

Examples D and E depict *skewed families* in which one family member is relatively isolated from the other three, who form a fairly cohesive unit. Example F represents the *generation gap family,* in which the marital unit and the offspring each form a fairly cohesive duo, with little or no interaction across the generational lines. Example G represents the *pseudodemocratic family* in which all channels seem to be of about equal importance, with the marital coalition and the parental role not being particularly well differentiated. Example H, the *disengaged family,* offers the representation of an extreme case in which each family member is pretty much cut off from every other member, and in which one would expect very little sense of positive interaction, feeling, or belonging to a family unit.

Clearly these representations are highly oversimplified and are pictured only for a two-generation, four-member family. Infinite variations could be added to the list. Such representations enable the therapist to conceptualize more clearly the nature of the coalitions in a particular family and to begin planning a strategy to bring those coalitions into a better functional alignment, presumably more closely approximating Example A. In Example B, for instance, the therapist might give attention to activating the marital coalition, the coalitions between parent and offspring of the same sex, and those between the offsprings themselves. Also an attempt might be made to attenuate the force of the existing cross-generational, cross-sexed interactions.

The tactics and goals of family therapy, viewed in this light, might include making changes in the marital coalition (very commonly the case), as well as in the parent–child dyads. Although triads are not considered to any great extent in this discussion, an isolated family member, such as the one in Example D, might be brought into interaction with the rest of the family unit. Looking outside of the nuclear family for a moment, it is important to consider the appropriateness of encouraging extrafamilial contacts with outside peers, both for the parents about to face the "empty nest," as well as for children and adolescents. At times, when such outside interactions, especially those with in-laws, seem maladaptive, modifications might have to be considered. Temporary triads, incorporating the therapist, are often purposely formed in order to produce structural change.

The therapist constantly tries to keep the major focus on the family system and off its individuals. Guilt and blame are reduced by pointing out that there are reasons why family members do what they do. The family therapist usually tries to deemphasize scapegoating, "sickness," and "problems." Clarification is often needed to enhance mutual understanding, and there is the need to point out that everyone in the family has been doing his best, and for valid reasons—although the results are not always fortunate. The therapist supports the healthy aspects of family functioning and counteracts those that are "sick" or maladaptive.

The therapist attempts to shift the balance of relationships in the family in a more positive direction.

In the S family, Mr. and Mrs. S had been married for 20 years. There was a son, 17, and a daughter, 15. Mr. S was a smooth-talking salesman who had sold his wife on how "sick" she was. His wife was a product of a family in which her mother made her feel extremely guilty because the mother's own marriage was not working. The "patient" grew up extremely masochistic, became a nurse, and had made multiple suicide attempts. In this family the father and the two children were aligned against Mrs. S. This alignment seemed to function to cover up the father's areas of deficiency—he was not able to make a living, nor was he able to set limits for the children. Therapeutic interventions helped to shift the balance of forces in the family by getting more support for Mrs. S in her attempt to resolve some of the problems that had brought the family into treatment.

The therapist may first need to define and encourage the expression of those issues about which the family disagrees. The family's efforts to cover up conflict must be resisted and recent or current issues involving available family members must preferably be dealt with rather than old themes concerning absent members.[19]

The therapist may intervene as a mediator, emphasizing that certain conflicts are particularly important. The therapist should generally be in control of the process, although at times someone else may be allowed or selected to act as the mediator. In this role the therapist may be active, intrusive, and confronting, or inactive and passive. Overt conflict between two family members may be pointed out, or the therapist may remain in control by refusing to take sides in a continuing dispute. An alternative viewpoint in a disagreement may be offered, or the therapist may attack two family members in hopes of bringing conflict to the surface.

The therapist may then side with or against any one family member, or the entire family unit, in a particular conflict. It is impossible in most disputes not to take sides, and the therapist will always be seen by the family as doing so. The real problem for the therapist is deciding under what circumstances he should take sides and with whom, as well as discovering with whom the family thinks he is siding. Judicious siding can tip the balance in favor of more productive therapy; at the very least, it will disrupt a chronic pattern of pathogenic relating.[20]

Families may attempt to resist this process of change by denying the validity or importance of the conflictual issues the therapist has emphasized, by trying to preempt the therapist's position as mediator, and by forcing the therapist into an inflexible mediation position that can be called "unfair" (see Chapter 11).

The therapist must maintain rapport with the whole family, however, and must consider the family as a unit. Alignment must not consistently be made with one or another family member, and the therapist must be ready to shift support from one member or coalition to another, depending on the circumstances. Also, the therapist must know and respect each family member and accent the positive rewards for the whole family and for each family member.[3] At the same time the marital coalition must continually be evaluated against the criterion that it be the strongest one in a healthy family.

Murray Bowen, a family therapy pioneer, concerned himself with ideas about the lack of differentiation of various family subsystems and, on the other hand, with the extreme disengagement of many individuals in families—individuals who hardly seemed to participate meaningfully in their family.[21] He has used a variety of techniques over the years, including seeing in therapy only the healthiest family member and using that person as the agent, or model, of family change. He has used letters written from one family member to another as an indirect method for stirring up change in family systems.

Strategies to Aid Family Role-Assumption, Education, and Demythologization

The therapist serves as a *reality tester* for the family, distinguishing between what is actually going on and what is fantasy. This may be in relation to behavior, attitudes, or emotions. Such reality testing is not confined to grossly psychotic family members. For example, one rural family was referred for treatment when the parents refused to allow their children to go to school for six months because of the possibility of an earthquake.

The therapist avoids any claim to omnipotence. As much as the case allows, the family is helped to do the work of changing. The intent is ultimately to enable the family to solve its own problems. The more the family can do—without the therapist—the more autonomy it will develop.

The therapist serves as a *model for identification* and can provide an education in family living, roles, clear communication, emotional honesty, problem solving, and the realities of married life. The family learns from the therapist's speech and conduct. If the therapist role plays a more empathic spouse to a defensive wife, the family may see the possibility for an alternative set of transactions. If the therapist can focus on sexual issues in an open, direct, and mature manner, a sexually guilt-ridden, fearful family may be helped to come to terms with these issues. The therapist should be cautious about trying to remake the family in his or her own image, however.[22]

The family therapist may make use of advice and direction by trying first to identify and then to change maladaptive methods of coping. Therapists often indicate the importance of limit setting as a method to encourage change—for example, "I think your son should begin attending school *within two weeks.*"

Carl Whitaker believes in the technique of paradoxical intention and manipulates the family members into believing the therapist has to overpower them, as if in a battle.[23] He believes that the therapist has to deprogram himself and advance his own growing edge in order to conduct effective family therapy. Whitaker in many ways appears to see family sessions in experiential terms with a good deal of emphasis on "feeling states" during the session and during immediate feedback.

Well-functioning families have been found to have particular attributes that are lacking in dysfunctional families. A family therapist can apply this knowledge in his work as follows:[24]

1. *The therapist works as collaborator,* implying respect for the other's subjective world view. He demonstrates with the treatment family an affiliative rather than an oppositional attitude, and a commitment to negotiation as the basis for treatment.

2. *The therapist conveys a belief in complex motivations,* especially with respect to the reciprocal nature of human interactions, paying special attention to (and including himself as being involved in) the interactions that occur in the family-treatment setting.

3. *The therapist needs to be a model of clarity, spontaneity, nonintrusiveness, and permissiveness with respect to the expression of all types of affects,* frequently expressing empathic comments, acknowledging other people's views, and demonstrating a caring attitude.

    An authoritarian style of treatment, in which the therapist sets himself up as the all-knowing and all-powerful manipulator of the family's interactions and goals, may at times prove to be helpful, even though it contradicts the model outlined in the preceding sentence. People in some socio-cultural settings are accustomed to a directive style and may be left confused or unconvinced by an invitation to share authority and responsibility. This directive style may be needed at times with the most dysfunctional families, aiding them in becoming less chaotic and enabling them to move to an intermediate "adequate" stage.

Several authors have stressed the desirability of having family therapists clarify their own values and concepts regarding family life. Among these is the idea of the family as a system, with both homeostatic and developmental models. The marital relationship is seen as the core of the family, and the identified patient as a signal of family distress. Family therapists usually feel that marital partners have difficulty with respect to such issues as separateness, differentness, open communication, the realities of married life, the changing phases and roles in the marriage, and the expression of healthy self-assertion. Most therapists also favor a problem-solving approach, rather than one emphasizing blame or guilt. Family therapists should clarify their own positions on such issues as gender roles, maturity, marital roles, career, money, sex, and parental relationships to children. To the extent that they are sure of their own positions, they stand less chance of unwittingly imposing their own values and conflicts on the family during the therapy.

Therapists often will find themselves called on to function as demythologizers, or philosophers of family life. This usually involves helping the family to experience and to make explicit covert family myths (for example, "Father can't work," or "Neil is the stupid one in the family"), rather than giving direct advice to the lovelorn or loveworn. The myths by which people live can serve as gratifying anchoring points for stable relationships, but some myths may be mutually incompatible to certain other extreme or relatively unrealistic ones or to those that are not accepted by all the members of the family. In such instances these beliefs may cause disappointment and pain, and it will be part of a family therapist's job to recognize the disruptive role that they may be playing. (These myths are discussed in greater detail in Chapter 4.)

CLINICAL APPLICATION OF THE THREE BASIC STRATEGIES

A case of a "folie à deux" will illustrate the clinical application of three basic strategies as they might be applied to the same case. The relevant system involves a psychotic mother and her teenage daughter, who share a set of paranoid delusional beliefs. Utilizing the three general therapeutic strategies outlined in this chapter and applying them to this particular case, the following illustrations of specific technical maneuvers can be made.

In the communicational frame of reference, mother and daughter should be discouraged from speaking directly to each other and encouraged to speak only to or through the therapist. The therapist should make explicit to the mother and daughter that they each have opinions, thoughts, and feelings of their own, and should encourage each of them to demonstrate this with reinforcement during the sessions. The therapist should discourage "mind reading" and speaking for the other person.

Utilizing the coalitional strategy, we assume that mother and daughter constitute the extent of the currently available family, the father being absent. The therapist might form new coalitions separately with the mother and the daughter, and, by attempting to interfere, interrupt, or attenuate the existing intimate coalition between mother and daughter, the therapist might encourage outside, independent coalitions of each of the two family members by trying to connect the mother with other relatives or neighbors, while at the same time encouraging the daughter to become involved in peer-group relations outside the home.

Through the therapist's role as demythologizer and educator, the mother and daughter could be encouraged to join a group that includes less pathological mother–daughter pairs. Disbelief could be expressed that any two individuals could hold either identical opinions or the specific types of beliefs that these two individuals demonstrate. An attempt could be made to clarify the underlying "myths" in this dyad, which might include the feeling that they are "two people against the world" or that they are actually fused together as one.

REFERENCES

1. Marmor J: Marmor lecture. Psychiatric News, November 5, 1975, pp 1, 15
2. Madanes C, Haley J: Dimensions of family therapy. J Nerv Ment Dis 165:88–98, 1977
3. Ackerman NW: Psychodynamics of Family Life: Diagnosis and Treatment in Family Relationships. New York, Basic Books, 1958
4. Boszormenyi-Nagy I, Framo JL (eds): Intensive Family Therapy: Theoretical and Practical Aspects. New York, Harper & Row, 1965
5. Paul NL: The role of mourning and empathy in conjoint marital therapy, in Zuk GH, Boszormenyi-Nagy I (eds): Family Therapy and Disturbed Families. Palo Alto, California, Science and Behavior Books, 1967, pp 186–205
6. Camp H: Structured family therapy: An outsider's perspective. Fam Process 12: 269–277, 1973
7. Grunebaum H, Chasin R: Thinking like a family therapist. Paper presented at the Downstate Medical Center's Symposium on Family Therapy, Training of Child Psychiatrists, New York, December, 1978
8. Watzlawick PJ, Beavin H, Jackson DD: Pragmatics of Human Communication. A Study of Interactional Patterns, Pathologies, and Paradoxes. New York, Norton, 1967
9. Satir V: Conjoint Family Therapy: A Guide to Theory and Technique (2nd ed). Palo Alto, California, Science and Behavior Books, 1967
10. Bateson G, Jackson DD, Haley J et al: Towards a theory of schizophrenia. Behav Sci 1:251–264, 1956
11. Watzlawick PJ: A review of the double bind theory. Fam Process 2:132–153, 1963
12. Scheflen AE: Stream and structure of communicational behavior. Behavioral Series Monograph No. 1. Philadelphia, Eastern Pennsylvania Psychiatric Institute, 1965

13. Ackerman NW: Treating the Troubled Family. New York, Basic Books, 1966
14. Boszormenyi-Nagy I, Spark G: Invisible Loyalties. New York, Harper & Row, 1973
15. Bateson G, Jackson DD, Haley J, et al: Towards a theory of schizophrenia. Behav Sci: 1:251–264, 1956
16. Haley J, Hoffman L: Techniques of Family Therapy. New York, Basic Books, 1967
17. Haley J: Uncommon Therapy: The Psychiatric Techniques of Milton H. Erickson, M.D. New York, Norton, 1973
18. Satir V: Peoplemaking. Palo Alto, California, Science and Behavior Books, 1972
19. Zuk G: Family Therapy: A Triadic Based Approach. New York, Behavioral Publications, 1971
20. Zuk G: When the family therapist takes sides: A case report. Psychother 5:24–28, 1968
21. Bowen M: Family Therapy in Clinical Practice/Murray Bowen. New York, Aronson, 1978
22. Lefer J: Countertransference in family therapy. J of the Hillside Hospital 15:205–210, 1966
23. Napier AY, Whitaker CA: The Family Crucible. New York, Harper & Row, 1978
24. Lewis JM, Beavers WR, Gossett JT, et al: No Single Thread: Psychological Health in Family Systems. New York, Brunner/Mazel, 1976

Encounter by Naomi Gerstein, private collection.

9
Family Treatment: Some Specific Techniques

OBJECTIVE

- To become familiar with some specific techniques of family therapy and their use in fostering family change

INTRODUCTION

Many specific techniques (in addition to those three that have already been described) can be employed during the course of treatment. Most of the techniques mentioned here have more recently been developed and may not yet be in general use; therefore, they have not been evaluated as to effectiveness.

In family therapy, just as in other types of psychotherapy, it is advisable to be familiar with a set of treatment strategies and techniques, rather than to be limited to only one or two. These can then be combined in skillful ways according to the needs of the situation. One should not, however, become a slave to techniques and should guard against using them rigidly or mechanically.

A skillful therapist, like an accomplished artist, devotes years of practice to acquiring techniques. Once acquired they are invisible.[1]

FAMILY TASKS

Family therapy focuses on behavioral change. Accordingly many family therapists routinely prescribe various tasks for the family to perform during the session and, more commonly, between sessions. The rationale for this is to have the family work out and repeat behavior patterns outside the session. The therapist (rather than the family) takes control of the symptom or problem and helps realign coalitions. For example, family members that have not had any recreactional activity together in several years may be asked to take a vacation together, or a husband and wife may be instructed to discuss a family secret (see Appendix A).

Special techniques have been devised for helping lower socioeconomic class families, ghetto families, and highly disorganized families. The work of Minuchin[2] and others[3, 4] indicates that it is both necessary and possible to help these families deal with some of their basic needs by using indigenous populations as family advocates with social agencies; by mobilizing the most constructive forces in the family system; and by providing training in basic task performance.

Such tasks might involve getting the family registered with a housing agency. This serves to train and strengthen the family unit's ability to handle its problems in concrete terms and helps to solidify the often shaky and inadequate manner in which the family provides for its elemental needs. In this way such a family can gain the experience of accomplishing something meaningful for itself during its daily struggle for existence and stability. This may be more useful than would be the more symbolic, attitudinal, psychological techniques appropriate for middle- and upper-class families.

PRESCRIBING THE SYMPTOMS*

Jackson, Weakland, and Haley have written about a therapeutic technique in which the therapist "prescribes the symptoms."[5, 6] After the therapist "orders" the family members (or individual) to intensify the occurrence of the symptoms, the symptoms begin to lose their autonomy, mystery, and power. Whereas they previously seemed to have been out of control, they now appear to come under the therapist's control. The participants in the behavior become more conscious of them, and often the disruptive behavior lessens or disappears. A marital couple that has engaged in nonproductive arguing now finds that the therapist has asked them to continue fighting and even to increase it; the couple is told to fight about the menu before dinner, so that they can enjoy the food. This injunction jars the continuing process, and they may rebel against the outsider's orders (which is often a necessary step to change).

The therapist is obligated to follow through to make sure that the directions have been followed in the way that was intended. The therapist does this by seeing the family in his office on an ongoing basis, by asking more than one family member what changes have taken place, or by visiting the family at home.

*Also called paradoxical prescription or intention, symptom scheduling, negative practice, or reverse psychology.

Other therapists write a family prescription after the initial session, telling the members they will receive a message about what the therapist thinks is wrong with the family and what needs to change.[7] This gives the therapist time that is not available in the heat of the session and creates an opportunity for a more accurate formulation of the family's problems. The prescription is a type-written letter sent separately to each family member. It may describe just what the family is doing and ask each member to continue doing it.

For example, the therapist agrees with Joe (the identified patient) that he should not move out of the house at present. His parents, however, should continue to vacillate in alternately supporting his moving out and undermining it. This prescription was sent to a family with a 32-year-old son who kept "messing up" each time he left home and then had to return to the family. The prescription had the effect of making Joe angry, of shifting him out of the house, and of identifying what his parents were doing. For some families there is something quite powerful about a well-thought out message that is "official" and to the point.

FAMILY RECONSTRUCTION

An in-depth exploration of family background is believed to improve the therapeutic outcome. All family participants explore their own life histories, learning about themselves and one another in the process. Such techniques as *role play* and *psychodrama* can be used to bring out significant past events in the lives of families. A "family map" or genogram is used to diagram the family of origin.

HUMOR AND BANTER

With the technique of humor and banter, the therapist intentionally makes humorous comments in order to ease a tense moment or to make changes in the family. The therapist exaggerates aspects of an individual's or a family's behavior. Prerequisites include, but are not limited to, the family and the therapist having a sense of humor and maintaining a good rapport.

INCLUDING THE FAMILY OF ORIGIN

Framo believes that involvement of the family of origin is one of the most effective techniques in family therapy.[8] It is based on the noncontroversial ration-ale that current family problems are based in part on reenactments of previous problems that the husband and wife have had with their own families of origin.

The therapist routinely has at least one session with each marriage partner, together with that partner's own family of origin. There is usually a great deal of resistance to this technique. The individual's spouse and children are not present. This enables the therapist to discuss here-and-now "corrections" with the aim of increasing present relatedness to the spouse's current family. (This issue is also discussed in Chapter 7.)

COACHING[9-11]

With the coaching technique, the therapist acts like a coach in helping the family member make changes. For example, the therapist may explain concepts and theories, give examples, draw diagrams, ask questions, make predictions, or suggest alternatives. The therapist can get up from a chair and stand behind family members whispering instructions or a supervisor can phone instructions into a specially equipped room.

MOURNING AND EMPATHY[12]

With the technique of mourning and empathy, the therapist elicits unresolved grief in a family or family member for a parent, child, or relative in order to effect change. This technique is in part borrowed from Gestalt therapy, in which there is an attempt to release long-hidden feelings, expectations, and emotions.

VISITS

With the voyages technique—modeled on the home-visit techniques mentioned in Chapter 5—the therapist travels wherever necessary to bring leverage to the family problem. For instance, he may go to schools, homes, housing projects, churches, clinics, bars, hospitals, and so forth. He meets with individuals or agencies that influence the family (e.g., the principal of a school).

SELF-DISCLOSURE

In individual psychotherapy the therapist does not usually reveal much information about himself. The therapy is focused on the patient's problem, feelings, and behavior rather than those of the therapist. Some family therapists prefer, however, to use themselves as a major instrument in changing the family by revealing material about themselves, their nuclear and extended families, job philosophy, conflicts, goals, and plans.

This technique has not been accepted for most training programs because of the belief that it may create more problems than it solves.

GUIDED FANTASY[1]

With the technique of guided fantasy, the therapist helps the individual share his internal system of fantasies and thoughts with other family members. The rationale is that "daydreaming" can provide people with a powerful tool for their growth and problem solving. It is important to have each member share his or her inner thoughts with the rest of the family, so that they can be empathic in helping the individual grow.

FAMILY SCULPTURE[13]

Family sculpture is a technique in which the therapist asks one or all of the members of the family to create a physical representation of their relationships at one point in time by arranging their bodies in space. Alliances and estrangements can be concretized by such an exercise. The technique can be used as part of the diagnostic workup to generate hypotheses or to represent a concept being worked on concretely during the course of therapy. Both the content of the "sculpture" and the way the "sculptor" (i.e., family member) uses mass and form are examined. It is an excellent technique for nonverbal families.

MULTIPLE-FAMILY GROUP THERAPY[14-18]

The technique of multiple-family group therapy brings together several family units into a group just as traditional group therapy brings together individuals. These groups may meet on a regular basis. The size of such groups has varied from three to eight families at any one time. Groups sometimes have included infants to those old enough to be living independently, as well as including significant others such as grandparents, in-laws, and fiancé(e)s. The duration of the treatment on an outpatient basis has been from three months to one year, whereas on an inpatient basis, the family has participated in treatment usually only as long as the identified patient remains hospitalized.

This technique seems to work best when there is a good balance between the families who have been in the group previously (i.e., more experienced families) and those that have not. A balance between interfamily and intrafamily interaction is also desirable.

As part of the process, there is a great deal of mutual disclosure and sharing, as well as peer review and evaluation of what has gone on. Socializing between these families outside of the formal group sessions has been used but with uncertain results.

Gould has summarized the process of such groups as follows:[19]

1. They are sharing and interactional rather than analytical
2. They are fast moving, experiential, often hectic, and very much in the here and now
3. There is a great deal of crucial interfamily contact that makes it possible for families to learn from one another

It has been reported that multiple-family therapy groups, in contrast to individual family treatment sessions, have very few dropouts. They are thought to be especially useful when the family expresses a great deal of denial.

NETWORK THERAPY[20-22]

Speck and his associates have described a novel approach to help the identified patient. Members of the kinship system, friends of the family, and significant others are brought together to work on the problem. This includes all persons who bear on the problem, and adds healthier voices to the mix. These groups meet for 3 to 6 biweekly sessions lasting about 4 hours that are held usually in the identified patient's home with 30 to 45 people involved.

PSYCHODRAMA AND ROLE PLAYING

Psychodrama and role playing techniques have also been used to help families enact family problems and work out new patterns. They are especially useful in nonverbal families.[23] In role playing or reverse role playing, one partner either plays himself in a hypothetical situation or takes on the role of his partner, often switching roles back and forth and commenting on the observations, feelings, and behavior elicited. Role reversal is believed to be useful for developing empathy in family members.

GESTALT THERAPY[24]

In adapting Gestalt therapy to family problems, the therapist stresses that the only real time is the present, and he does not rehash the past. He stresses that each individual is responsible for his or her own behavior (countering the familiar resistance, "I did it only because he or she made me do it"), and that symptoms and conflicts are the here-and-now expressions of unfinished situations of childhood that can be finished in treatment. Significant attention is paid to nonverbal behavior.

WEEKEND FAMILY MARATHONS[25]

Weekend family marathons have been reported in which one or several entire family units get together for extended periods (anywhere from 8 to 12 hours or longer) with leaders, or "facilitators," for a variety of intensive types of encounters, usually including affect catharsis and nonverbal experience.

BEHAVIORAL APPROACHES

Behavioral approaches deal with the means by which certain behaviors can be learned, reinforced, or extinguished, irrespective of the original causes for such behavior. Even relatively minor changes in the behavior of one family member, or in a dyad, may bring about a significant alteration in the behavior and feelings of other family members. External behavioral change may precede internal attitudinal change.

Techniques of behavioral therapy include assertiveness training, operant conditioning, relaxation and desensitization, contingency reinforcement, and cognitive behavior modifications. Family members can be utilized as cotherapists in various behavior modification exercises that are rehearsed initially in the therapist's office and are assigned for practice at home.

SEX THERAPY

For a discussion of sex therapy, see Chapter 14.

VIDEOTAPE

The ready availability of video equipment has made possible its increasing use. Therapists often find it beneficial to review their sessions and to have a record of an entire course of therapy. Immediate playback of a videotape helps families attain some psychological distance, makes them increasingly self-aware, helps to correct distortions or conflicts about communication, and is invaluable in revealing the important nonverbal aspects of interactions that might otherwise be lost.[26] Families often comment constructively on their own videotaped interactions in a way that they might not readily accept from a therapist.

AUDIOTAPE[27]

Audiotape has also been used as an adjunct to family therapy. A tape of a session can be made and the family can take it home and listen to it, or a tape can be made at home and then played at the session.

ONE-WAY MIRROR[2]

The family meets in a room equipped with a one-way mirror. The therapist can leave the family alone and observe its members through the one-way mirror or have one or more selected members, including an estranged member observe the interactions. The family member comes out of the "heat of the battle" and is presumably then able both to distance himself from what is going on and to change the unwanted behavior in the family system.

Some cotherapists find it useful for one therapist of the team to be in the room with the family while the other therapist observes (alone or with selected family members). The therapy can be interrupted at any time, so that the cotherapists can confer and plan. Having one therapist as an observer can be helpful and can add objectivity.

REFERENCES

1. Friedman PH: Outline (alphabet) of 26 techniques of family and marital therapy: A through Z. Psychother: Theory, Research and Practice 11:259–264, 1974
2. Minuchin S, Montalvo B, Guerney BG, et al: Families of the Slums: An Exploration of Their Structure and Treatment. New York, Basic Books, 1967
3. Sager C, Brayboy T, Waxenberg B: Black Ghetto Family in Therapy: A Laboratory Experience. New York, Grove Press, 1970
4. McKinney J: Adapting family therapy to multideficit families. Social Casework 51:327–333, 1970
5. Jackson D and Weakland J: Conjoint family therapy: Some considerations on theory, technique and results, in Haley J (ed): Changing Families. New York, Grune & Stratton, 1971, pp 13–35
6. Haley J: Strategies of Psychotherapy. New York, Grune & Stratton, 1963
7. Selvini Palazzoli M, Cecchin G, Prata G, et al: Paradox and Counterparadox. A New Model in the Therapy of the Family Schizophrenic Transaction. New York, Aronson, 1978
8. Framo JL: Personal reflections of a family therapist. J Married Family Counsel 1:15–28, 1975
9. Leveton E: Psychodrama for the Timid Clinician. New York, Springer, 1977
10. Bach GR, Wyden P: Intimate Enemy: How to Fight Fair in Love and Marriage. New York, Morrow, 1969

11. Haley J, Hoffman L: Techniques of Family Therapy. New York, Basic Books, 1967

12. Paul NL: The role of mourning and empathy in conjoint marital therapy, in Zuk GH, Boszormenyi-Nagy I (eds): Family Therapy and Disturbed Families. Palo Alto, California, Science and Behavior Books, 1967, pp 186–205

13. Simon R: Sculpting the family. Fam Process 11:49–58, 1972

14. Laqueur HP: Multiple family therapy and general systems theory, in Ackerman NW (ed): Family Therapy in Transition. Boston, Little, Brown, 1970, pp 82–93

15. Curry A: Therapeutic management of a multiple family group. Int J Group Psychother 15:90–96, 1965

16. Laqueur P, Wells C, Agresti M: Multiple-family therapy in a state hospital. Hosp & Comm Psychiatry 20:13–20, 1969

17. Blinder M, Colman A, Curry A, Kessler, DR: "MCFT" Simultaneous treatment of several families. Am J Psychother 19:559–569, 1965

18. Chazan R: A group family therapy approach to schizophrenia. Israel Annals Psychiatry 12:177–193, 1974

19. Gould E: Self-help aspects of multifamily group therapy. Unpublished paper

20. Speck RV, Rueveni U: Network therapy: A developing concept. Fam Process 8:182–191, 1969

21. Speck RV, Attneave C: Network therapy, in Haley J (ed): Changing Families. New York, Grune & Stratton, 1971, pp 312–332

22. Speck RV, Attneave CL: Family Networks. New York, Pantheon Books, 1973

23. McKinney J: Adapting family therapy to multideficit families. Social Casework 51:327–333, 1970

24. Leveton A: Elizabeth is frightened. Voices 8:4–13, 1972

25. Landes J, Winter W: A new strategy for treating disintegrating families. Fam Process 5:1–20, 1966

26. Silk S: The use of videotape in brief joint marital therapy. Am J Psychother 26:417–424, 1972

27. David A: Using audiotape as an adjunct to family therapy: Three case reports. Psychother 7:28–32, 1970

Supper by J. F. Willumsen (1918). Courtesy of J. F. Willumsens Museum, Denmark.

10

The Course of Family Treatment

OBJECTIVES

- To acquire techniques for gathering history
- To become familiar with some of the processes of each stage of family treatment and the various opportunities and interventions appropriate to each stage

HISTORY GATHERING IN THE EARLY STAGES OF TREATMENT

For clarity of presentation we have separated family evaluation and family treatment. In practice this rarely happens and is not particularly desirable. A process of continual evaluation and hypothesis testing takes place throughout the course of therapy, with the therapist constantly checking his perceptions. At the same time every session should have some beneficial outcome. The more skillful and experienced the therapist, the less rigid the approach and the more total the blend of evaluative and therapeutic aspects and the more extensive the use of improvised variations, condensations, and extensions on some of the themes.

Mr. and Mrs. G, a young couple in their early twenties, came for treatment because their marriage was in trouble. An evaluation was done (using the format described in Chapter 5). At the onset of the session the following week, the therapist asked the couple what had happened since the evaluation. Mr. G said he realized that they were not communicating, although they had made it a point to increase communication during the week. Mrs. G said that she thought the session had not done anything, but she *had recognized* for the first time that there was a communication problem.

If one is engaged in short-term crisis intervention, 30 minutes may be all the time that is avaliable for evaluation. In a training setting, with no fixed time limit for treatment, one may be able to allot more time for thorough evaluation. Some clinicians take the time at an initial phone contact to gather detailed biographical and historical information. This leaves the evaluator much freer in the initial interview to ask selective questions, to stay more in the here-and-now, and to conduct the session in a more dynamic way.

Presented here are some of the important topics that can be evaluated by the therapist in a manner and order appropriate to a particular family. The intention is to increase the range of the therapist's repertory, rather than to impose any preconceived, arbitrary framework.

A beginning therapist may want to obtain a fairly extensive history, perhaps mainly in the opening sessions, whereas a more experienced practitioner may rely on only a few bits of historical data, working more with what happens in the session and gathering longitudinal data only as needed during the course of the meetings. The inexperienced therapist, however, should guard against rushing into shortcut techniques before having had the benefit of understanding in detail many different family patterns and the more standard family therapy techniques.

The therapist may decide to hear from each family member in turn on certain important issues or may let the verbal interaction take its own course. A decision may be made to call on one parent first, then the other, and then the children in descending chronological order, or it may appear more advantageous to call on the more easily intimidated, weaker, or passive parent (or spouse) first.

The therapist may decide to use first names for all family members to help put everyone on an equal footing, or he may prefer to be more formal in addressing the parents in order to strengthen relatively weak generational boundaries and parental functioning.

Some therapists may encourage the family members to talk with one another, whereas others may focus the conversation largely on themselves, at least during the first sessions or at times of stress or chaos. (For a fuller discussion of some of these issues, see Appendix A—The Structured Family Interview.)

At the outset, family therapists usually introduce themselves and ask for the names of all family members. They then ask how they can be of help to the whole family. Usually a statement from one of the parents about the presenting problem will follow. As a rule this statement is focused on the identified patient and is often accusatory in tone. Most therapists try to get as many points of view as possible by asking other members what they think, especially those that have been silent during much of the session.

The assumption is made that the family's behavior in the office and at home is similar, although perhaps modified in some ways in the office by the presence of the therapist. At this point the therapist is somewhat the outsider, whose main function may be to allow everyone to be heard, including the weakest members of the family. Some family members will often be on the attack, whereas others will be defensive during the initial period. An identified patient who is an adolescent will often demand changes at home, because those in this age group are frequently the ones most interested in change. An angry, frustrated spouse will demand that the marital partner change.

Some therapists may point out that they will not be decision makers for the family but will try to help the family members clarify their problems and help them with their decision-making processes. Such therapists may act as referees or traffic cops when necessary, making sure that one person speaks at a time, that no one person is overwhelmed by attacks during the sessions, and that nongratifying family patterns are not allowed to continue unchallenged during the therapy sessions. They create an atmosphere that encourages the verbal expression of feelings toward constructive ends.

Therapists indicate that in an unhappy family everyone hurts and therefore everyone wants to get something positive out of the sessions. A therapist conveys the feeling that all the family members are doing the best they can and that one needs to understand the motives of oneself and of others. The family therapist explains that well-intentioned attitudes and actions are nevertheless sometimes less than totally positive in their outcomes.

Families vary considerably in their readiness to move from a discussion of the current crisis situation to an exploration of their patterns and histories. Therapists will follow the family's lead in these respects. For example, a therapist may be willing to start the sessions even though the father is absent and may sense that the family members need some time to talk about the "badness" of one of the offspring.

It is important that a therapist gets an idea of what the family's mode of operations is in order to convey a sense of respect for and understanding of the family's initial point of view. At the same time the therapist will need to guard against being so passive and accepting that nothing new will be added to the equation. The family's experience in the therapy hour should not be merely a repetition of the nongratifying interactional patterns for which they originally sought help. It may be helpful to indicate to the family that individual problems often are related to family problems and that they all need to find out more about the family as a whole, in order to enable each member, and the family as an entity, to benefit from the treatment.

It may be desirable to move on to a longitudinal, chronological narrative of the family's history (perhaps through three generations) or instead to begin with a cross-sectional inventory of how the family currently functions. Which of these areas will be elucidated first depends on the therapist's predilections, the family's distress, and the nature of the difficulty. The major longitudinal data to be gathered will refer to the parents' period of courtship, engagement, marriage, honeymoon, early years of marriage prior to the arrival of children, and the changes in the family as a result of the first child and each subsequent child and so on through the family cycle.

One may start with the courtship period (which is, in part, predictive of marital patterns), move on to the marriage, and then work backward, with each partner going back to his or her original family. For each partner one can discuss the life history prior to the marriage, including any previous marriages. In going back to the parents' families of origin, one gets a picture of the functioning of those previous families that serves as a foundation for understanding the present family and its problems. Careful attention must be given not only to recollections of the past and to expressions regarding attitudes and values, but also to overt behavior. For example, gross difficulties in sexual adjustment should be carefully delineated by taking a thorough and complete sexual history. It is the authors' experience that this is something still done all too rarely in the field of family therapy, as though sexual problems were regarded as only secondary to other interpersonal difficulties.

Primary difficulties in sexual adjustment, however, will often sour the rest of the marital relationship. Sometimes sexual difficulties are the major area of difficulty for the married couple and perhaps the one most difficult for them to deal with. There are couples who appear to need and who will benefit from specific therapy directed toward improving their sexual adjustment. To the extent that this can be done satisfactorily, other areas of marital and family interaction may then markedly improve. The sexual adjustment of the marital pair should be evaluated as carefully as other areas of marital and family interaction. It is not safe to assume that any sexual problems are secondary and will resolve themselves more or less spontaneously when other areas of family difficulty have been overcome.[1]

Another area often overlooked or slighted in the evaluation phase is that of the family's dealings with money. The authors have found this to be an important issue in marital and family friction. As with sexuality, this is not always merely secondary to other marital problems. Some marital couples have never been able to work out a satisfactory way of managing money as a marital pair. Any other marital problem may be reflected in fights about money, just as they may be reflected in sexual maladjustment.

The amount and type of data to be assembled will be strongly influenced by the current phase of the family life cycle. It is appropriate to concentrate on material relevant to issues pertaining to that particular phase of family life. The relative emphasis, as well as some of the specific content of the history to be gathered, would be quite different if one were dealing with a couple in the first year of marriage or a family whose last offspring is preparing to leave home.

Should the family present the history or should the therapist structure the history with an outline? Most therapists seem to combine both approaches. It is often helpful to let the family members talk until they run "dry." On the other hand, the therapist presumably has expertise in helping families with problems and can help them in structuring a history. What is excluded by the structuring usually will emerge as time goes on, but what is missed by not structuring (for example, not taking a sexual history) may never be revealed.

History gathering requires complex skills. Excellent references on methodology for getting a family history include works by Satir,[2] Bell,[3] and the Group for the Advancement of Psychiatry.[4] There are also training films on family therapy, parts of which demonstrate history taking.[5-8]

HOW TO GET THE WHOLE FAMILY
INTO TREATMENT

What can be done if one member of the family will not come to treatment? Often the resistance is not just from the member who will not come, but from the other members of the family who covertly (or overtly) encourage such an absence. They may be unaware of their collusion, however, and often ask for help to get the reluctant member to participate.

The therapist may help the family try to understand why the person is not coming in. In a previous family experience, the absent member may have ended up being blamed and may believe that it was some other member's difficulty. There may be something in the past that is embarrassing, and shame will prevent a person from coming. Commonly, a partner such as the husband, does not want to come because he believes that if marital problems are discussed, the marriage will break up: "It's bad now, but it will only get worse by talking about it." When faced with such resistance, the therapist may try to find an intervention technique that would deal with the resistance. The family members who are attending may be asked to change some of their behavior in a way that will effect a change in the homeostasis of the family unit, and this might then bring the noninvolved member into treatment; or they may be asked to attempt to reinforce consequences for the absent member. (See Chapter 11, under the heading, "Absent Member.")

In the F family Mr. F was the identified patient with a long history of unipolar depression. Once his depressive episodes had been regulated with medication, he told the therapist that his wife was unhappy with their relationship. The therapist suggested marital therapy. He stated that this was his cross to bear because she would not come in for therapy. The therapist suggested that he again try talking to her about this. Mrs. F surprisingly appeared for the next session and stated that she was unhappy with the relationship but had never been asked to come in for therapy. Mr. F stated that he had asked her but admitted he might have "mumbled the invitation."

It should be remembered that it is usually difficult for a therapist to accurately predict the personality or behavior of the other spouse solely from the partner's report.

EARLY, MIDDLE, AND END STAGES OF TREATMENT

We have arbitrarily divided the course of treatment into early, middle, and end stages.

Early Stage

Some of the primary concerns of the early stage include the following:

1. Detailing the primary problems and nonproductive family patterns.
2. Clarifying the goals for treatment.
3. Solidifying the therapeutic contract.
4. Strengthening the therapeutic relationship.
5. Shifting the focus from the identified patient to the entire family system. In the early stages, the therapist may give directives designed to reorganize alignments of structures in the family that quite often serve to take the focus off the identified patient. As soon as this is accomplished, the relationship between the marital partners may become the core of the treatment and in the middle stage most of the work may be devoted to seeing only the marital couple together, often with the identified patient.[9] If there are offspring, they are seen little, if at all.
6. Decreasing guilt and blame.
7. Increasing the ability of family members to empathize with one another.

During the early phase, the therapist comes to a better understanding of the life of the family, making contact and promoting empathy and communication. Some major nonproductive patterns are spotlighted and scapegoating is neutralized. The painful shift begins to move away from the identified patient and attention is directed to the entire family system.

A crisis often develops when the problems that have been hidden away or have been too painful to face are brought to the conscious awareness of the family members.

In the T family the identified patient was Mr. T, who had chronic schizophrenia. Mrs. T was a long-suffering housewife. There were two young children. Mrs. T had been doing most of the childrearing. The couple socialized very little. When the family was brought together, Mr. T talked about his wife's chronic hostility to him. She responded by saying, "Look what I put up with." This gradually accelerated until they were talking about divorce. This crisis was used to change the patterns of childrearing on the part of both parents. Mr. T shared some of the family tasks, such as getting the kids to school on time and helping them do their homework. Mrs. T had more time for herself. She returned to work as a biochemist. Feeling better about herself, she suggested to her husband that they go out to movies and concerts.

In this stage, the situation may appear to worsen, rather than improve. Symptomatology may accelerate, new symptoms may arise, and families may talk about quitting treatment. This upheaval usually is related to the family's barely perceived awareness that for things to get better, some member will have to change. Rather than change, a family member may accentuate or exaggerate symptoms. Family therapy changes have to be made sequentially. A family can not let go of an offspring until the marital couple has found increased satisfaction in their own lives and in their relationship.

Middle Stage

The middle stage is often considered to be the one in which the major work of change takes place. (Chapters 7, 8, and 9 are devoted to these specific issues.) Because of this only brief mention will be made here regarding this stage. What the therapist does during the middle stage will vary, depending on the goals that have been singled out as being of primary importance. Commonly examples of persistent, nongratifying interpersonal patterns and attitudes, preferably drawn from recent or here-and-now interactions, are discussed repeatedly. Old nonfunctional coalitions, rules, myths, and role models are challenged, and the possibility of alternative modes is presented. New habits of thinking, feeling, and interacting take time to develop, and much repetition is often required. At the same time resistance to change comes to the fore, and must be dealt with accordingly (see Chapter 11).

The initial focus may be on the identified patient, but the focus then moves to the family. Often the identified patient may improve before the family does.

End Stage

In the closing phase the therapist reviews with the family which goals have been achieved and which have not. It is often useful to review the entire course of therapy, including the original problems and goals. Videotape playback may be helpful at this time, so that the family can see what it looked like at the start of treatment, compared to its present state.[7] It is important to acknowledge that some behavior cannot be altered and that life will continue to change and therefore be filled with problems. The family should be provided with the skills for solving future conflicts and challenges.

What are the criteria for suggesting termination of therapy? If the original goals have been achieved, the therapist may consider stopping. Even if the goals have not been achieved but have been worked out to the best capabilities of therapist and family, therapy can stop. When the treatment has been successful, new coping patterns and an enhanced empathy by family members for one another will have been established. There will come recognition that the family itself seems capable of dealing satisfactorily with new situations as they arise. There may be little to talk about during the sessions and little sense of urgency. Nonproductive quarreling and conflict having been reduced, the family will be freer to disagree openly and have methods of living with and working out its differences and separateness. The family will seem less inflexible in its rules and organization and appear more able to grow and develop. Individual family members will be symptomatically improved and positive channels of interaction will be available between all family members. There will be improved agreement about family roles and functions.

Families often cannot or do not recognize changes that have occurred during therapy. A therapist should carefully check for any change and amplify it, giving positive reinforcement. If a family can produce a small change, then this may be an indication that bigger changes are possible. With some families no change may occur until the therapy is completed.

During this end phase there may be an exacerbation of presenting symptoms. A son may begin hallucinating again because the father has stopped communicating with the mother. These eruptions are usually short lived and may represent a temporary response to the anxiety of terminating treatment, rather than being a sign of treatment failure. It is thus part of the separation process, which is always a key issue to be worked on in termination and which in some theoretical orientations may represent the major theme of the entire therapy.

KEEPING A RECORD OF THE COURSE OF TREATMENT

Opinions differ as to the value of keeping written notes on the course of family treatment. Such a record may be useful both in monitoring goals and also in recording changes. The problem-oriented record modified for families provides a concise overall picture of the identified patient and the family and outlines problems, goals, and strategies.[10] Ongoing progress notes record significant family developments, enable goal achievement to be measured, and provide a record of treatment modalities used for achieving these goals. Referrals to other agencies are also noted. Such a system has a definite advantage over the traditional practice of keeping a separate record for each family member.

Many therapists focus on the process rather than the content of the sessions and therefore believe that there is no need to write down the "facts" of what goes on. Records are often more helpful for training purposes. Many family therapists prefer not to keep any records of treatment to protect themselves against the possibility of their being subpoenaed. (This issue is discussed in Chapter 17.)

REFERENCES

1. Masters W, Johnson V: Human Sexual Response. Boston, Little, Brown, 1966
2. Satir V: Conjoint Family Therapy: A Guide to Theory and Technique (2nd ed). Palo Alto, California, Science and Behavior Books, 1967
3. Bell JE: Family group therapy. Public Health Monograph No. 64. Washington, D.C., Department of Health, Education and Welfare, Public Health Service, 1961
4. Group for the advancement of psychiatry. The case history method in the study of family process. Report No. 76. New York, Group for the Advancement of Psychiatry, 1970
5. The enemy and myself. 16mm black and white sound film 50 min., by Nathan Ackerman, M.D. (The Family Institute, New York)
6. Family in crisis. 16mm color sound film 48 min., by David R. Kessler, M.D. (Langley Porter Neuropsychiatric Institute, University of California, San Francisco Medical Center, San Francisco, California)
7. Family therapy: An introduction. 16mm black and white sound film 43 min., by Ira D. Glick, M.D., and George J. Marshall, Sr. (Cornell University Medical College, Payne Whitney Clinic, New York)
8. In and out of psychosis: A family study. 16mm black and white sound film 120 min., by Nathan Ackerman, M.D. (The Family Institute, New York)
9. Berman EM, Lief HI: Marital therapy from a psychiatric perspective: An overview. Am J Psychiatry 132:583–592, 1975
10. Deming B, Kimble JJ: Adapting the individual problem-oriented record for use with families. Hosp & Comm Psychiatry 26:334–335, 1975

Recondiliation of the Family by Jean-Baptist Greuze. Courtesy of the Collection of the Phoenix Art Museum.

11

Family Treatment: Resistance to Change

OBJECTIVES

- To be aware of and understand resistances to change in the family
- To consider a few of the strategies to counteract these resistances and promote change in the family
- To understand those therapist reactions to the family that interfere with progress in treatment

DEFINITION

In family therapy the primary focus is on change. Patterns and transactions that prevent change can be thought of as possible resistances. There may be multiple reasons underlying specific resistance maneuvers. The family members will fear change but at the same time want relief from their problems. The family is often reluctant to change because, even if the present family system is working poorly, it is at least familiar—change involves giving up old patterns. As bad as they are, these known patterns may be better than anything else the family can envision.[1]

Families may anticipate that getting involved in therapy may not improve their situation and that no real change can be expected. They may even fear that therapy will make their lot worse through exposure of repressed or suppressed feelings, with resulting guilt, anger, and recriminations. They often feel that it may be better to "let sleeping dogs lie." Too much exploration might ultimately lead to the breakup of the marital or family unit or to another individual's decompensation—an outcome that the family symptoms may in some way have been attempting to prevent.

Hidden resistance can account for lack of improvement in a family that otherwise seems to have good overt motivation. The patient himself is not wholly a "victim." He, too, controls by means of his own resistances. Resistance shifts from one member to another, and its intensity may vary with the content. A mother, for example, may want to talk about the father's drinking but may balk at discussing her own inability to clean the house or go to work. A father may stay away from therapy, leaving the mother and identified patient together.

There is often a massive resistance in the middle phase of treatment, (manifested by the patients' quitting treatment, threatening divorce, etc.), because the immediate crisis of the identified patient is past and the family members are no longer hurting as much as when they began treatment.

One traditional method for handling such issues is to call attention to the phenomenon, clarify the unspoken communication involved, and explore the degree of appropriateness to the present situation. The historical development of such resistances can be elucidated, and their specific correlations with other current happenings in the family situation and in the therapy brought out. Resistances may represent core interpersonal issues in microcosm and can be utilized by experienced therapists to produce change.

TYPES OF FAMILY RESISTANCE

Solomon has compiled an extensive list of family resistances. He enumerates them as follows:[2]*

RESISTANCES TO THERAPY

1. Using silence, passivity, superficial discussion, or intellectualization to avoid emotional involvement
2. Demanding practical advice or counseling to avoid dealing with conflict
3. Denying of the therapist's clarifications, confrontations, or interpretations
4. Denying previously expressed awareness or insight
5. Denying the therapist's ability to understand the problem on the basis of ethnic, linguistic, or other cultural differences
6. Expressing a fatalistic attitude in which one accepts blame and indicates inability to change
7. Denying of ability to pay for treatment
8. Revealing a miraculous loss of symptoms or, conversely, aggravation of symptoms used as a ploy to terminate therapy
9. Coming to sessions late or avoiding of sessions, or both
10. Dropping out and unilaterally terminating therapy

*Reprinted with permission, from Solomon M: Family therapy dropouts: Resistance to change. The Canadian Psychiatric Association Journal, 14:21–29, 1969, pp 22–23.

RESISTANCES TO INTERACTION

1. Refusing to bring up new or meaningful material while exhorting the others to do so
2. Asking other family members questions to avoid self-involvement in meaningful interaction
3. Changing an emotionally charged subject through diversion, distraction, interruption, or other means
4. Refusing to communicate in front of other family member(s)
5. Using a second language to exclude another member from the interaction
6. Talking about an absent member to avoid dealing with current interaction

FAMILY-SPECIFIC RESISTANCES

1. Employing varied maneuvers to avoid dealing with the marital conflict
2. Insisting that the presenting patient is the main or only family problem (scapegoating); offering oneself as a scapegoat to avoid anxiety-laden interaction
3. Predicting persistence of the presenting symptoms or of the impossibility of change
4. Denying evident change in role behavior or in improvement in the presenting patient
5. Denying evident affect expressed by another family member
6. Protecting or defending another member so that he or she will persist in maintaining his or her behavior and resist change
7. Withholding certain meaningful information from the therapist (family secrets)
8. Giving injunctions against family disloyalty to prevent the uncovering of conflict
9. Threatening to desert the family as change approaches
10. Threatening to abandon a family member who effects change
11. Using other family members as an excuse to avoid therapy

Some of the common types of resistances will now be discussed in greater detail.

Family Secrets

Individuals in the family often have "secrets" that, in most cases, are known but not acknowledged by other family members. They may involve overt behaviors, such as marital infidelity, that one marital partner feels he has been able to conceal from the other, or they may involve thoughts, feelings, and attitudes that family members believe others are not aware of. For example, parents may not realize (or may deny) that children pick up the general emotional tone existing between mother and father. They may act as if marital discord is hidden from their children and may want to keep that discord "secret."

Secrets can also be kept hidden from the therapist by the family.

The X family consisted of a hospitalized adolescent, the parents, and two older siblings. For ten weeks, the family therapy seemed to be bogged down. The family stopped treatment. Two months later the family therapist discovered a secret that the entire family already knew—that is, the identified patient was having sexual relations with a ward nurse. The patient had told his siblings, who told the parents, who then signed the patient out of the hospital. The secret served the purpose of denigrating the hospital staff (including the family therapist) and effectively halting the family therapy.

Helping the family bring these pseudosecrets into the open usually results in a clearing of the air and eventually leads to a sense of relief and greater mutual understanding. Interestingly, it is commonly the children who talk openly in the family sessions about what was thought by others to be a secret. The therapist should, however, be prepared to deal with acute shock waves at the time the secret first emerges. When an individual in a family requests an individual session for the purpose of revealing a secret, the therapist may listen and try to explore the consequences of discussing the issue within the family setting. If, for example, one of the spouses has an incurable illness and the other spouse does not know about it, the reasons for the secrecy would be examined and the spouse would be encouraged to share the information with the whole family. If the secret does not seem crucial, the therapist might take a more neutral stance. The therapist must guard against being trapped into becoming a repository of secrets. At times a family member may insist on total honesty, either because of emotional insensitivity or as an active way of hurting another family member. For example, a parent might report to a child every negative feeling that crosses his or her mind in the guise of honesty.

Absent Member

When all the family members attend the therapy sessions, the therapy has the best chance of being successful. Absence of family members may occur from the outset or intermittently during the course of treatment. Such absences, especially if consistent or patterned, may offer important clues as to family organization and coping styles.

Such continued absences may be due to a covert agreement on the part of the family that a particular member not attend. The other family members play a role in encouraging the absent member to stay away.

The therapist should try to ensure that each family member personally sees the positive value to be derived from attending the sessions. This may either be personal growth and comfort or the overall improvement in the family's ability to live together, which will have secondary positive consequences for each family member. Sometimes, in order to ensure that all family members attend, the therapist may find it necessary to start the treatment with the focus remaining on the identified patient. A move can be made to a more family-focused view as soon as the family feels comfortable doing so.

When a family member is absent, the first approach may be to explicitly note this fact at the session. Often this proves effective in helping the family to look productively at the issues that relate to the family member's absence. The therapist may help the family to see that the absence of an individual is an important family problem that they all need to understand and overcome. The therapist will often help the family broaden its view beyond just focusing on the absent person to ways in which the family's structure and patterns of interaction may actually be designed to ensure that one member will not attend. Dealing with these issues can also help realign a dysfunctional family structure, such as a weak marital coalition.

One parent may seek family therapy for issues having to do with a behavior problem with an adolescent child. In the first meeting mother and father may be present and indicate to the therapist that the adolescent identified patient refused to attend the session. The experienced family therapist will not be surprised to learn that the parents have been chronically unable to agree or be mutually supportive with respect to dealing with this adolescent. Their inability to ensure the adolescent's attendance is merely an example of their lack of a united front with their offspring and more generally of their inability to deal effectively with many differences between them as a marital couple.

As some of these issues become defined, the parents may be asked to work out some procedure that will result in the adolescent's coming to the sessions. They may find techniques that have proven effective on past occasions. If the parents concur that it is important for the adolescent to attend, an agreement may be reached that will make it mandatory for them to establish and maintain a united front on this issue. For example, the father, who has heretofore been the daughter's ally, will be required to tell her that she must come to the sessions. The mother, who had been battling with the daughter about this in the past, will be asked to support her husband's position.

The therapist may want to contact the absent family member directly and clarify the reasons for nonattendance. This will ensure that the family member has received the message that this person is needed in the therapy sessions. The therapist will be able to explore with that person the possible reasons for a reluctance to attend. The therapist's message will often be perceived as more positive in tone than one that has been conveyed by another family member. Sometimes the person has decided to stay away because of a previous therapy experience with which blame and guilt are associated. This person may not feel very involved in the family or may indicate that there is something embarrassing that preferably should not be talked about in a family setting; or he may fear that attendance at family therapy sessions will make a family or marital problem even worse.

Some therapists have found that conducting family therapy sessions in the home is an effective way of involving the whole family. This may be especially useful for resistant fathers (or adolescents) or for families who may not feel comfortable coming to the therapist's office.

Ultimately it may be necessary and desirable to discuss the limitations of what can be accomplished if only the incomplete family is seen in treatment. A decision will have to be arrived at as to whether to continue therapy under this circumstance. In some cases one member will absolutely refuse treatment, and the therapist's seeing the rest of the family may be preferable to not seeing the family at all.

The Family Friend

A person who is not part of the family (such as a friend, professional advisor, or neighbor) may significantly influence the family in directions contrary to those of therapy. Exploring this person's influence in detail (even in his absence) and how it is being used by the family sometimes proves fruitful. When possible this person should be brought into the family sessions. This course must be weighed against the disadvantages of nonfamily participation discussed in Chapter 7, but as a short-term technique, it is often helpful.

Sexual Material

Family members may be reluctant to discuss sexual material in the presence of their children. Children usually are sensitive to the emotional climate existing between their parents. In conjoint therapy, sexual material can often be alluded to in terms of closeness between parents. Separate sessions for the parents to discuss more specific intimate subject matter can follow, as indicated.

FAMILY REACTIONS TO THE THERAPIST

The therapist will be the recipient of a combination of feelings, attitudes, and behaviors from each of the family members. These can be both positive and negative in tone. They may or may not be appropriate and productive to the therapy situation. They may be based on a carry-over from problematic important past relationships. The therapist must be alert to such phenomena and will need to deal especially with those very strongly positive or negative relationship factors in the treatment that appear to be getting in the way.

The following are some common types of reactions to the therapist. The therapist might be viewed as a judge—"You decide who is right and who is wrong"; as a focus of all anger—"If it weren't for you we'd be okay"; or as a curing figure—"You fix us up, doctor; we don't have to discuss our problems." Another common reaction is the attempt by members of a single-parent family to force the therapist to become a parent substitute—"You tell Henry to do his homework instead of watching television."

THERAPIST REACTIONS TO THE FAMILY

The therapist, too, may develop unrealistic and inappropriate reactions, and these likewise may be of such intensity and nature as to present difficulties in treatment. For example, the therapist may behave toward the patient and family as though they were the therapist's own family, either past or present. When this occurs the therapist must recognize and deal with the situation.

In individual therapy there is a one-to-one therapist-to-patient relationship. In the family setting, the relationship is quite different. The therapist can act out feelings with any member of the family but must bear in mind that intense affect and interaction is often activated in families and in therapists during the session. The family's feelings about the therapist and the therapist's feelings about the family may be intensified, rather than diluted. Keeping distance and avoiding being drawn into dysfunctional interactions and special alliances may be difficult for the beginning therapist.

In the early phase of treatment, the therapist may have the tendency to try totally to overhaul the family. There may be much blaming. In the middle phase of treatment, the therapist may become overly identified with various family members. In the late phases the therapist may have difficulty in separating from those members.[3]

Certain psychiatric syndromes lend themselves to particular inappropriate reactions by the therapist. For example, in families with a member who has schizophrenia, the mother (by her apparent overindulgence) may be the therapist's target, whereas in families with a delinquent member, the target may be the father (by his absence).

In family therapy, contrasted to individual therapy, the presence of additional people helps to keep a better check on the therapist's reactions. Families may not hesitate to point out to the therapist that he is reacting inappropriately to a family member. Another such corrective factor can be the presence of a cotherapist.

An important issue in the treatment of families and the training of family therapists is the problem of blaming the family. Appleton has pointed out a number of crucial areas in which therapists inappropriatly blame parents for the pathology of children.[4] The notion of more than one causal influence on psychopathology is difficult for the neophyte therapist who may still be hoping for simple answers. Patterns of blame have been related to traditional notions of sex roles and sex-role stereotypes. It is assumed that the father is responsible for psychopathology relating to stereotyped masculine behavior. Where there is no clear-cut, sex-role stereotype, the mother is usually blamed. Many theories of psychopathology place major emphasis on the commonsense but untested notion that the crucial family relationship is the one between mother and child.[5]

As in individual therapy the therapist must avoid being drawn into a role that confirms the reality of the patient's misconceptions. The therapist's attitudes to such matters as family, marriage, and money, for example, must be open to introspection and worked through so as not to interfere with the therapy.

Many therapists find that in working with families, unresolved personal issues are stimulated to the degree that they affect the therapist's own personal relationships.[6] Having personally undergone therapy may be of help, and this includes both individual psychotherapy and, especially, family therapy. The ability of family therapists to work with difficult families may be directly in proportion to their ability to know their own family. It is beneficial for beginning therapists to have supervision during their work with families.

The question is often raised about a match between the family's stage of development and the therapist's own stage. Although the accepted dogma is that such a match counts for little in the ultimate outcome, clinical experience in family therapy has led us to at least question this assumption. Common sense indicates that the more the therapist has in common with the family, the better the likelihood of a positive relationship; for example, both being of the same class, race, or sexual orientation would appear to have implications for a greater chance of working together successfully. In the course of family therapy training, the therapist should be helped to recognize the implications his own particular life stage and family experience has on therapeutic work. For example, there might be serious therapeutic blind spots when a newly wedded 25-year-old therapist begins working with a couple who have been married for 25 years and are undecided about whether to stay married.

REFERENCES

1. Greenberg IM, Glick ID, Match S, et al: Family therapy: Indications and rationale. Arch Gen Psychiatry 10:7–25, 1964
2. Solomon M: Family therapy dropouts: Resistance to change. Can Psychiatric Assoc J, 14:21–29, 1969, pp 22–23
3. Whitaker C, Felder RE, Warkentin J: Countertransference in the family treatment of schizophrenia, in Boszormenyi-Nagy I, Framo JL (eds): Intensive Family Therapy. New York, Harper & Row, 1965, pp 323–342
4. Appleton WS: Mistreatment of patients' families by psychiatrists. Am J Psychiatry 131:655–657, 1974
5. Kellerman J: Sex-role stereotypes and attitudes toward parental blame for the psychological problems of children. J. Consult Clin Psychol 42:153–154, 1974
6. Kramer C: Personal communication. 1978

Quarrels between Mr. and Mrs. Latimer, and Brutal Violence between Them, Were the Natural Consequences of the Too Frequent Use of the Bottle, from ''The Bottle'' by George Cruikshank, 1847. Courtesy of the Quarterly Journal of Studies on Alcohol.

12

Family Treatment and Specific Psychiatric Disorders

OBJECTIVES

- To be aware of some of the family interactional patterns associated with specific psychiatric disorders
- To be able to use family therapy in combination with other treatment methods in specific psychiatric disorders

INTRODUCTION

The purpose here is not to discuss in any great detail each of the diagnostic entities. (This information is available in standard textbooks of psychiatry.) Rather the authors will indicate those specific issues that are of particular interest to the family therapist in relation to a few selected psychiatric disorders. For each psychiatric condition discussed in this chapter, guidelines for family intervention are suggested, and their relative effectiveness assessed.

At times the treatment will be largely dependent on the psychiatric diagnosis of the identified patient (as in manic-depressive psychosis) or on the personality types and behavior of each family member (as in alcohol abuse). When the identified patient has a specific major psychiatric diagnosis, treatment of the individual may be relatively conventional. For example, antipsychotic medications will probably be used to treat schizophrenia.

In many instances it will be necessary to treat both the specific psychiatric condition of the individual family member and the family problems that are concomitant to these conditions. Some of the family problems may be related to the etiology of individual illness, some may be secondary to it, and others may not be clearly connected. For example, if schizophrenia has developed in a spouse early in the marriage, the therapist's attention must be directed to treatment of the mental illness as well as to the nature of the marital interaction, including its possible role in producing the illness. If there is a major psychiatric disorder in one of the family members, attention must be paid to the manifestations of the disorder that may be symptomatic of, or interfering with, the attempts to deal with the family's problems in living.

WHY LABELS?

Labeling is used by all people in all lines of work as a kind of shorthand for more complex ideas. In medicine, psychiatry, and related fields, the traditional focus of healing has been on *disease* (meaning structural change) and *disorder* (meaning functional change). The focus of this book has been on a systems concept of viewing the identified patient in the context of the family and the family within the greater context of society. Even so, in the family field, labels can be used to focus our thinking and to communicate.

For some family therapists any kind of labeling of the individual is anathema. Psychiatric labeling, however, does exist and is still commonly used. Many people practicing family therapy continue to utilize an individual model (which eschews most labeling) at certain times for certain patients, while also thinking about the family system involved.

DIAGNOSTIC AND STATISTICAL MANUAL OF MENTAL DISORDERS

In this chapter we discuss a few syndromes described in the American Psychiatric Association's *Diagnostic and Statistical Manual of Mental Disorders* (DSM–III, Draft 3).[1]

Some of the innovative features of the DSM-III include not only the course, age and onset, essential clinical features, degree of incapacity, differential diagnosis, and predisposing factors of each disorder, but also the sex ratio and *familial pattern*. It is planned that the system be multiaxial as follows:

Axis I   Clinical psychiatric syndrome(s) and other conditions
Axis II   Personality disorders (adults) and specific developmental disorders (children and adolescents)
Axis III   Physical disorders
Axis IV   Severity of psychosocial stresses
Axis V   Highest level of adaptive functioning past year

It is in Axis IV that the family therapist will be able to classify predisposing factors—for example, death of a family member, parental neglect, and so forth.

The disorders of greatest interest to the family therapist are subsumed under the rubric of "Conditions Not Attributable to a Mental Disorder That Are a Focus of Attention or Treatment."

This category includes codes for conditions that are a focus of attention or treatment but are not attributable to any of the mental disorders noted previously. In some instances, one of these conditions will be noted because, following a thorough evaluation, no mental disorder is found to be present. In other instances, the scope of the diagnostic evaluation was not such as to adequately determine the presence or absence of a mental disorder, but there is a need to note the reason for contact with the mental health-care system. (With further information, the presence of a mental disorder may become apparent.) Finally, an individual may have a mental disorder, but the focus of attention or treatment is for a condition that is not due to the mental disorder. For example, an individual with bipolar affective disorder may have marital problems that are not directly related to the manifestations of the affective disorder but are the principal focus of treatment.[2]

The subcategories of "Conditions Not Attributable to a Mental Disorder . . ." include (but are not limited) to the following:[2]

1. *Marital Problem*
   This category may be used when a focus of attention or treatment is a marital problem that is apparently not due to a mental disorder.
2. *Parent–Child Problem*
   This category may be used when a focus of attention or treatment is a parent–child problem that is apparently not due to a mental disorder of the individual (parent or child) who is being evaluated.
3. *Other Interpersonal Problems*
   This category may be used when a focus of attention or treatment is an interpersonal problem (other than marital or parent–child) that is apparently not due to a mental disorder of the individual who is being evaluated. Examples may include difficulties with coworkers or with romantic partners.

These categories have the qualification that they are not diseases. It was decided *not* to include a set of family diagnostic categories among the psychosocial stresses because of a lack of consensus among family researchers and clinicians.

FAMILY RESPONSES TO MENTAL ILLNESS OF A RELATIVE

The Acute Stages

Families have been shown to experience a patterned sequence of responses to the occurrence of mental illness in an identified patient.[3] These stages are as follows:

1. *Beginning uneasiness:* The family does not know what to expect.
2. *Need for reassurance:* The family hopes that everything will be all right.
3. *Denial and minimizing:* The family denies that anything is wrong and minimizes the patient's difficulties.
4. *Anger and blame:* The family begins to see the extent of the problem and each member lays blame on the others or on the hospital staff
5. *Guilt, shame, and grief:* Each member perceives his or her role and feels guilt and shame.
6. *Confusion in the changed family:* The family adopts new roles with resultant confusion.
7. *Acceptance of reality:* The family adapts to a new homeostasis.

In treating families in which an identified patient has a psychiatric illness, the therapist needs to be aware of these stages in order to make effective treatment plans. For example, to ensure that the identified patient with a manic–depressive illness takes his lithium medication as regularly as an individual with diabetes mellitus takes insulin, one needs to know how the family feels about the illness and its treatment.

The Chronic Stages

Thirty percent of the patients discharged from mental hospitals are rehospitalized during the first year following discharge. Sixty percent of all admissions to state hospitals are readmissions. For many patients rehospitalization occurs more than once and, indeed, becomes a way of life. One implication of these facts is that for many patients, the family has become more involved in their long-term outcome. Families often tend to overlook grossly inappropriate functioning and may tend to become adjusted to the pattern of the individual's illness. Interestingly, wives may be more tolerant of psychiatrically ill husbands than husbands are of psychiatrically ill wives.

SCHIZOPHRENIC DISORDERS

Classical Family Studies of Etiology

The schizophrenic syndrome has been the psychiatric disorder most extensively studied by family therapists. An early, uncontrolled study of 16 families of schizophrenics by a group at Yale found the following characteristics: failure to form a nuclear family; family schism and skew; blurring of generational lines; pervasion of the entire atmosphere with irrational, usually paranoid ideation; persistence of unconscious incestuous preoccupation; and sociocultural isolation.[4]

The group described two types of family conflict patterns. In the *schismatic* family, the parents fill complementary roles, undercut each other, and compete for the children. The family is in two camps, and the identified patient cannot use one parent as a model for identification or as a love object without losing the support of the other parent. In the *skewed* family the psychopathology is dominant in one parent. One parent is strong and the other is weak. The psychopathology is accepted or shared by the mate without any attempt to change it.

Most reports show a high incidence of serious pathology in the parents when there is schizophrenia in a child.[5] Lidz's data suggest that one or both parents of schizophrenic patients have had serious emotional problems.[6] Wynne and associates have described what they call *pseudomutuality* in families with a schizophrenic member.[7] This is a type of relatedness in which there is a preoccupation by family members about fitting into formed roles at the expense of individual identity. Such families lose their ability to test reality; rather than see the world as it is, they strive for an agreed-on interpretation. No divergence is allowed. Others have suggested that some of the symptoms of schizophrenia can be understood as an attempt by the patient to become an individual, rather than to fit into the stereotyped, rigid mold of the family.[8]

Wynne and Singer have been able to identify disturbed styles of parental thinking by comparing Rorschach test protocols and interviews of families of schizophrenic children with tests and interviews of control families.[9, 10] A more recent study, however, could not replicate this finding.[11] Bateson and his co-workers also recognized disturbed styles of parental thinking in a kind of communication pattern called the *double bind*.[12,13] Five conditions are necessary for the double bind:

1. There must be two people who are significantly emotionally involved with each other.
2. There must be repetition of the behavior.
3. There must be a primary injunction.
4. There must by a secondary injunction, which contradicts the primary injunction.
5. There must be a tertiary injunction, which does not permit escape.

The classic example of the double bind is the mother who walks over to her son (two people), says to him over and over again (repetition), "kiss me" (primary injunction) then, if he attempts to do this, moves away from him (secondary injunction), and berates him for not being a good son (tertiary injunction). The identified patient is asked to respond to a communication that has an overt and covert message requiring mutually exclusive or incongruent responses.

This kind of family communication was hypothesized to be causal in the etiology of schizophrenia. More recent work has indicated it is not present in all families in which the identified patient has schizophrenia; it also occurs in relation to other psychiatric illnesses and it can even occur in "normal" families.[14] On the other hand a study of the double bind situation comparing parents of schizophrenics to parents of normal children, delinquents, and children with ulcerative colitis found that the parents of schizophrenics gave the most invalid interpretations of the test situation and disaffirmed their own or their spouse's interpretations most frequently.[15]

The siblings of schizophrenics seem to avoid becoming symptomatic either by constricting their personalities and family interactions or by openly rebelling and physically leaving the family.[16] Other observers have noted that the siblings of a schizophrenic are more independent, less troubled with decisions, and less involved with his or her parents.

Schizophrenic families have greater difficulty than normal ones in acknowledging conflict and are much less flexible in problem solving.[17-20] They are less adequate in communicating instructions and are more ambiguous.[21] They have more difficulty in making plans.[22] Problem solving, moreover, is further handicapped because such families appear to utilize idiosyncratic views from within the family to the exclusion of those from without. Feelings are acted on as though they were facts. Parents distort reality in the service of their own emotional needs and infantilize their children to make themselves feel more mature. Laing and others feel that the signs and symptoms of an individual's schizophrenia may be a logical adaptive response to an illogical family.[8] Laing has used the term *mystification* to describe the family's negation and denial of the patient's schizophrenic experience.

What about the role of genetic factors in the etiology of schizophrenia? The incidence of schizophrenia among the general population is 1 percent. The incidence of schizophrenia among the siblings of a schizophrenic is 9 percent—a ninefold increase. The incidence of schizophrenia among those siblings of a schizophrenic who are also children of a schizophrenic parent goes up 12 percent, and the incidence of schizophrenia in children whose parents are both schizophrenic is about 35 percent. These figures on incidence raise the question of the role of the family in schizophrenia.

All studies confirm the existence of some genetic element in the etiology of schizophrenia, but there are several additional points that should be mentioned. In recent studies of children of schizophrenic parents who were adopted by another family, the incidence of typical schizophrenia in the *biological* offspring of schizophrenics—although higher than in the *adoptive* offspring—did not, by itself, account for the statistically significant differences. It is only when additional forms of psychopathology were considered that the difference between these two groups became statistically significant. Others feel that the illness is the outcome of some combination of genetic predisposition and psychological stress.

Where it can be clearly demonstrated that families with schizophrenic offspring have evidence of thought disturbances or are prone to give double bind messages, one possible interpretation is that these families predispose a member toward schizophrenia. There remain two additional possibilities, however, that are at least equally plausible. One is that the families, in accordance with the genetic evidence just cited, may harbor a nascent form of schizophrenia. The other is that having a schizophrenic offspring causes families to react in the apparently pathological manner. In any case, abnormalities have been demonstrated in the interactions of families in which the identified patient has schizophrenia.[23] These abnormalities clearly precede the onset of the disorder.

We do not imply that in the treatment of schizophrenic patients the family should be ignored. Obviously it is necessary to help the patient deal with the psychologically important persons in his life and to help these people deal with the patient. What is unfortunate is the tendency of some psychiatrists to regard the families of schizophrenic patients as villains responsible for the illness. Genes alone probably do not cause schizophrenia—although studies of adoptive twins clearly indicate a strong genetic factor. It probably is neither genes *nor* environment but both—differently weighted in different individuals.

These studies have been provocative in opening the door to the study of the family's role in the etiology of schizophrenia. The entire issue of interactional process and schizophrenia is discussed in detail in an extensive monograph by Mishler and Waxler[24] and more recently by Wynne and associates.[25]

Treatment

A general consensus favors the treatment of schizophrenic patients, both in the acute stages and for later follow-up care, with a combination of appropriate antipsychotic medication and psychosocial therapies.[26] Among the latter family treatment is often useful.

Treatment of the acute stage of the illness will be described in Chapter 16. In the follow-up phase, with the nationwide trend of treating schizophrenic patients in the community (rather than in remote state hospitals), a large number of patients now live with their families or significant others.[27] This arrangement involves two problems—the patient's illness and also the family's problem in living with one member who has a chronic illness that may markedly interfere with his ability to interact with others, to work, or to socialize.[28-31] It has been found that in certain families, relatives have significant influence on the course of a schizophrenic illness.[32, 33] Such influence centers on the quality of the emotional relationship between a schizophrenic patient and the relative with whom he lives. Those patients living in highly critical, hostile, emotionally over-involved homes relapsed significantly more often than those living in more benign homes. Patients would be less likely to relapse, however, if they received regular phenothiazine medication or managed to avoid close contact with the family.

It may be necessary for the family therapist to find ways for the identified patient to reduce hostile face-to-face contact with his family or ways for the entire family to develop new, more positive patterns of interaction instead. It is not always possible to have such a patient move out of the house, find employment, or enroll in a day center.

One of the tasks of the family therapist is to assess the family unit's ability to allow and encourage differentiation and separation. Often a late adolescent schizophrenic is "stuck" in his attempt to separate from his family. The treatment goals may then revolve around these issues, thus either enabling the separation to take place eventually or allowing the patient to function better within the family.

Another task in treatment is related to the well-documented difficulty with communication in schizophrenic families.[34] Family members other than the identified patient, who are not schizophrenic, seem to exhibit many communication peculiarities, which are especially noticeable when the family group (even without the schizophrenic member present) attempts to communicate. The family as a whole will often seem to have a subtle thought disorder.[9, 10] There often is difficulty in focusing attention and in goal directedness. There can be a pervasive sense of meaninglessness and extensive use of "mind reading." The therapist frequently hears of what others "really mean." There will also be much silence.

The therapist must take some of the focus off the identified patient and place it on the family and its dysfunctional patterns. The therapist has to be active and organized (to counter family disorganization); he must be able to encourage verbal (rather than nonverbal) communication, make clear who is communicating to whom, and must indicate goals and test reality. The therapist, in a sense, lends his or her own ego to the family members, teaching them how to communicate effectively. The therapist helps family members disagree with what is bizarre or helps them to ask about something that they do not understand.

As simple as these techniques may seem to the beginner, it is necessary for the therapist to repeat them over and over while treating these families. It is just as important to straighten out the disturbed communication *process* as it is to straighten out the communication *content*.

The nature of schizophrenia and the secondary reaction of family members to the identified patient may need to be explored, as may the importance of rehabilitative processes. The therapist must be sensitive to the family's denial of the identified patient's illness or (equally unfortunate) the family's treatment of the patient as a complete incompetent. Groups composed of other families with a schizophrenic member are thought to be useful.

Whether or not the identified patient takes medication often depends, in part, on his relatives' belief in the efficacy of the medication.

Mrs. S was a 35-year-old white female with a 39-year-old husband, a lawyer, and two teenagers. She had developed schizophrenia at the age of 22 and had been progressively nonfunctional as a wife and mother over the previous 13 years. Prior to a consultation with a family therapist and based on the husband's belief that medication was wrong for his wife, the husband made sure that she was treated with psychoanalysis 4 times per week over an 8-year period. Medication was suggested by her psychoanalyst but rejected by the patient and her family. The rest of the family tolerated her in the home and had hired a housekeeper who essentially functioned as the mother. When the husband developed an ulcer (which he felt was caused by his wife) he consulted a family therapist. Family therapy was oriented around helping the family and Mrs. S deal with her realistic difficulties in functioning as a wife and mother. A condition of the family therapy was that the patient would have to take medication.

An extremely difficult problem exists when one member of the family is paranoid, with such symptoms as suspiciousness, jealousy, evasiveness, religiosity, irritability, and grandiosity. Appropriate medication may be refused by the patient. This is unfortunate, because some therapists will refuse to treat families if the patient will not take medications. Whatever approach is used in working with paranoid patients, the therapist must be as open and honest as possible, must avoid power struggles, and must try to maintain a professional, nonintrusive stance, especially since the paranoid patient may be frightened, belligerent, or assaultive. This factor must be taken into account, as usually little or no beneficial therapeutic work can take place in an atmosphere in which people are concerned about their physical safety.

A case example is presented to illustrate the use of the family model in the treatment of schizophrenia.

In the B family the identified patient was the 18-year-old son. He came to treatment because he refused to leave his room or eat. The family consisted of the parents, both in their sixties, and two older daughters. The family evaluation revealed that the patient had always been a somewhat unusual child, shy and isolated from his peers. He had managed to do all right until his junior year in high school when he complained of dizziness and stomachaches and refused to go to school. He said that he did not want to leave his room because he heard a variety of voices telling him that there were devils outside. His parents conceded to this request.

The parents were hard-working and were emotionally well until the birth of their third child—the identified patient. At that point they stopped having sexual relations because they didn't want another child, and many years had passed since there had been any kind of intimacy between them. The mother quit her job as a cashier to take care of that child. The father was a factory worker. The evaluation of the identified patient was compatible with the diagnosis of catatonic schizophrenia.

Family treatment was oriented around two primary treatment interventions. First, it was decided to use a family system model with the goals of involving the entire family in rehabilitating the identified patient and in changing the family's functioning. Mother and father were instructed not to let the patient boss them around. Techniques for improving their communication were worked on. The older sisters were useful as mediators in helping the parents work with the patient. Later on in treatment, mother and father began sexual therapy. Second, the patient began taking, and was maintained on, a phenothiazine.

The identified patient returned to school and was graduated. He made friends with other boys, but was not able to date. He was able to do his homework, but was not an "A" student. The mother and father began having regular sexual relations. The oldest sister finished her master's degree and the younger one was able to move out of the house.

This case illustrates how in schizophrenic families the entire family system sometimes has to change in order for one family member to change.

AFFECTIVE DISORDERS*

Genes are a large contributing factor in major affective disorders, such as in schizophrenia, and, as in schizophrenia, somatic and psychosocial treatments are often indicated. In acute stages of mania, for example, it is often mandatory to treat the patient with lithium and to see the family together in order to manage the patient's inappropriate behavior. With the seriously depressed person who may be actively planning suicide, the family may believe that the patient is faking and thus feel angry and fed up. They often covertly wish the patient would commit suicide because of their protracted frustration in trying to cope with the situation.

The most troubling symptoms of depression for the family have been found to be suicide attempts, hopelessness, lowered self-esteem, and increased dependency.[35] For mania, the most troubling symptoms are violent behavior, anger, impulsive spending, and a decreased need for sleep. The spouse is often in the position of being the caretaker–provider.

Studies that have been done on the family patterns of manic-depressive disease indicate the possibility that both the identified patient and spouse feel weak and dependent.[36] Both have a wish for the other to be strong.[37] The identified patient often marries someone who will control him or her. It has also been postulated that in families with a manic-depressive member, there may be a transmitted family difficulty in dealing with depressive affect, with the patient representing this disability in its extreme form. (This is analogous to the theories of the transmission of irrational modes of *thinking* in the families of schizophrenic patients.)

Psychotherapy in addition to medication decreases recurrence of bipolar affective illness.[38] Family therapy helps by using the family to monitor the patient's mood and to continue medications, to ease the patient's and family members' fears of an exacerbation, and to help develop new family patterns.[39] Through therapy the family can be helped to see that the identified patient is not "bad" but has an "illness." It is important to help the family recognize the earliest symptoms of recurrence of either depression or mania and get them to seek help.[40] Family members may not like the changes that treatment brings

*This category includes the disorder formerly called manic-depressive psychosis.

about; for example, they may have preferred having the patient feel a little high (i.e., feeling "good") or moderately depressed.[41]

The M family consisted of Mr. M, a farmer who was 50 years old, and his 48-year-old wife. Mr. M had had one or two episodes of mania each year over the last decade. Between episodes he was cheerful, ebullient, and a hard worker. When he became manic, he had to be hospitalized at the local state hospital until his episodes subsided. After lithium treatment he no longer had manic episodes. Unfortunately he also became less cheerful and there was a decrease in the frequency of sexual relations between him and his wife. Mrs M. wanted him to stop taking medication.

The task of the family therapist was to clarify their options when Mr. M had two manic episodes a year or when he had no manic episodes but was less attractive to Mrs. M. If they chose the former, they would go back to their previous pattern of emotional instability, which had been unsatisfactory. If they chose the latter, various adaptations would be needed. Mr. M might hire an assistant to work the farm and the couple would have to find other common interests to replace the decreased enjoyment of their sexual activities.

Some patients with affective illness may have less need for marital and family therapy than patients with schizophrenia because, by definition, in remission they return to baseline personality functioning. Before marital therapy is initiated, the identified patient should be treated with appropriate medication and then reevaluated for psychotherapy.

Depressed patients are often unable to meet the needs of their children and their spouses. This may result in depression in the child.[42] Combined treatment with psychotherapy and medication is probably "more effective than either component alone,"[43] based on the rationale that: "diathesis for depression is well established; antecedent psychosocial stresses are frequently found; and coexisting problems in interpersonal relationships are the rule in depressed patients."[44]

ANXIETY DISORDER: AGORAPHOBIA

The syndrome of agoraphobia consists of a generalized fear of leaving home.[2] There are a variety of theories to explain this disorder. For the family therapist, this condition represents an interpersonal problem. There may be a mutually reinforcing system in which the dependent person is kept dependent by the significant other, usually the spouse, to cover up that individual's anger and dependence. The symptom bearer finds a symbolic, dysfunctional way of communicating with and controlling the spouse (e.g., a wife who refuses to leave the house and thus forces her husband to stay home and take care of her). Marital therapy or behavior therapy in combination with medication is a useful intervention.[45] Individual behavior modification is not nearly as effective as family behavior modification, because it tends to overlook the reinforcing nature of the interpersonal interaction.[46]

PERSONALITY DISORDER

A common situation arises when a marital couple enters therapy with complaints about one or both person's basic character structure. Only later may the problem come to be seen as arising from a change in the family phase or from an acute crisis in the family, such as the loss of a job. Restructuring personality is extremely difficult by any method, but it may be possible to help the family system master its life-cycle tasks or to live with the character styles of the marital partners.

Patients with hysterical personality (called "histrionic personality disorder" in DSM-III) are often excitable, unstable, overly reactive, self-dramatizing, seductive, and attention seeking. Such patients may marry obsessive–compulsive spouses, seeing in them strength, reliability, and firmness, whereas, at times, the spouses' real characteristics are those of rigidity and coldness. There are usually marked sexual problems between such couples.

Obsessive–compulsive marital partners are often attracted by what they take to be the other partner's sociability and spontaneity, only to later perceive that this same behavior is childish and nongoal directed. The obsessive–compulsive husband increasingly withdraws at the same time that the hysterical wife becomes more flamboyant in her actions. Drug or alcohol abuse is often found in this relationship.*

SUBSTANCE USE DISORDERS

Alcohol Dependence and Abuse

"Alcoholism isn't a spectator sport. Eventually the whole family gets to play."[47]

Alcohol abuse may be a way of dealing with conflicts that cannot be expressed directly with family members, and it allows the alcoholic to express feelings (for example, anger) that cannot be expressed to family members without drinking. When the family member is drinking, a position of one-upmanship or control over the nonaffected family members is assumed. It is thus a way of sending a relationship-defining message while at the same time denying the message.[48]

It has not been demonstrated that family therapy alone is effective in chang-

*See Chapter 5, page 94, under "Classification 4."

ing the long-term course of the chronic, fixed alcoholic, but it may be useful in helping the family to adjust to the identified patient's alcohol abuse.

A family approach to alcoholism consists of attaining sobriety and changing the family dynamics and structure.[49] The main and first task is to cool off the high degree of reactivity to the alcoholic and to increase the emotional distance in the family system. To attain sobriety, Antabuse or Al-Anon may be utilized. Family therapy is not possible while there is frequent disruptive drunkenness. The next phase of therapy is helping the nonalcoholic spouse to become detached from his or her emotional reactivity to the drinking. At this stage the spouse's distance may exacerbate the identified patient's emotional communication; thus there is a need for both AA (or Al-Anon) and conjoint family sessions to establish a new homeostasis or initiate sex therapy.

Not all patients with alcoholism follow a chronic course. An intermittent increase in drinking is often a response to a problem within the family. In these cases alcoholism can be appropriately treated with family therapy.

Care must be taken that the nonaffected spouse does not promote the alcoholic patient's drinking.[50, 51] The spouse is the supplier and the victim simultaneously. For example, in the D family the wife was the identified patient with an alcohol problem. Husband and wife came to treatment complaining that they never went out together. After months of therapy the husband took his wife to a wine-testing festival. The script involves a continual reenactment of provocation, misbehavior, remorse, and atonement.

Are women alcoholics different from alcoholic men? There have been very few systematic studies of family treatment for the woman alcoholic. A recent review by Dinaburg and associates has pointed out that among the studies that have reported some success for family therapy for alcoholic women, none were controlled, and there were no post-treatment follow-ups.[52] That group reported a case with a 9-year follow-up. The data suggested that marital therapy, as the only intervention is not efficacious for treating women alcoholics and their families.

In contrast to the generally accepted speculation that alcoholism may result from cultural, environmental, and psychological influences, new epidemiologic evidence suggests that in addition to environmental factors, there is probably a strong genetic component to this disease.[53]

Drug Abuse

There is a difference between chronic use of drugs that cause physical dependence, such as barbiturates and heroin, and casual use of nonaddicting agents, such as marijuana and LSD. The former category is often extremely resistive to family therapy intervention, although currently it is being tried on an experimental basis. Such drug users are sometimes removed from their sociocultural milieu, and family therapy is often not possible. Some facilities are treating the nonaddicted drug user (even those, for example, with occasional mixed use of alcohol, marijuana, amphetamines, and psychedelics) by using family therapy as a primary form of treatment. This is based on the rationale that the drug use is a symptom of disturbed functioning and communication within the family.[54, 55]

There are excellent critical of reviews studies related to the use of family therapy for treating drug abuse[56-59] and of studies of family treatment applied to drug problems.[60]

ORGANIC MENTAL DISORDERS

Organic mental disorders that are especially common are those associated with presenile or senile brain disease or with chronic atherosclerotic brain disease. In addition, there are a variety of other chronic brain syndromes—for example, cerebral vascular accidents—that incapacitate patients and create problems for their spouses and children.

Chronic dementias may create a great deal of havoc in the family. There is often much guilt (if the identified patient is hospitalized) and anger (if he is kept at home) felt by relatives. A family therapist in such situations must help the family face reality in coping with change and in making the necessary alterations in its structure and function. There may need to be greater contact with the extended family, relatives, or other members of the kinship system. A common problem is that guilt and anger are displaced. For example, when a father has a stroke, a lot of old feelings of anger and resentment may be stirred up in the son. The suggested intervention might be to transfer the father to a nursing home. The son may then say, "It's not that I don't want to spend the money; it's my wife who doesn't want to spend it." Alternatively the decision to bring an impaired parent into a nuclear family stirs up a great deal of feelings. When the disabled parent comes into the home and changes the family homeostasis, the task of the family therapist is to help the family to cope with these changes; in this situation the family should attempt change and not try to even up old scores.

As a last caveat, it should be noted that not all problems that appear to be due to family causes actually are. The family therapist should constantly be aware of the potential of organic disorders causing behavioral symptoms that at first glance seem to be causally related to change in the family.

The L family consisted of father, age 40, mother, age 36, and son, age 7. After 10 years of reasonably happy married life, the mother became disenchanted and decided she wanted a divorce. A bitter struggle ensued between the parents. Several months following this struggle the son began to have difficulty in school and developed temper tantrums. He became more and more of a problem to handle.

Based on the family difficulties, family therapy was suggested. Six months of family therapy resulted in worsening symptoms in the son, although the parents' separation became smoother. At this point the son became disoriented and had greater difficulty with schoolwork. A neurological consultant discovered signs of organic change. A full diagnostic evaluation revealed that the son had a brain tumor.

DISORDERS THAT USUALLY FIRST MANIFEST THEMSELVES IN INFANCY, CHILDHOOD, OR ADOLESCENCE

Although the field of child psychiatry recognizes the importance of the family, both theoretically and practically, it often does so on the basis of concepts first worked out for individual dynamics and therapy. Child psychiatry often uses an individual psychotherapeutic model, with collateral therapy for the parents, in which family members are seen individually by one or more therapists. Usually only several key family members are seen, instead of all family members together. In the last few years, however, there has been a change in that pattern, and now some children's clinics are using the concepts and techniques of conjoint family therapy.[61]

When the identified patient is a mid-to-late adolescent, family therapy is relevant as part of an overall treatment program if the adolescent is still living at home or is still strongly bound, financially or emotionally, to his family of origin. For the adolescent who has become more autonomous, emphasis should be placed on either individual or group psychotherapy.

Pervasive Developmental Disorder: Infantile Autism

There is a heterogeneous group of disorders that includes infantile autism, previously called childhood schizophrenia. When the disorder is severe and the child has few communicative skills, interactional therapies yield poor results. Some writers have noted a symmetry between the mother–grandmother interaction and the mother–child interaction. Controlled studies of family therapy with this group are scant. There has been very little evidence supporting the notion that the family may be the causal agent for this disorder. Having an autistic child makes it difficult for a family to function effectively.

Family therapy by itself has not been shown to be effective treatment for this disorder.

Attention Deficit Disorder

Attention deficit syndrome is characterized by hyperactivity, short attention span, restlessness, distractibility, and impulsiveness. Treatment is centered on medication for the identified patient as well as family therapy to help with the problems of childrearing and adapting to the identified patient.

Mental Retardation

The term "mental retardation" comprises a variety of etiological possibilities, but in most instances there are inevitably secondary family problems.

In addition to the real problem of social development and functioning of the identified patient due to his possibly damaged biological equipment, there are the associated, often maladaptive, family reactions. The family feels a sense of antipathy, a sense of guilt, often social isolation, and actual anxiety about caring for the child's usual health needs.[62] Family members may make the mentally retarded child a scapegoat to cover up unresolved conflicts between mother and father or between parents and children.[63] Help must be focused on both the identified patient's specific needs and on the family's attitudes and behavior.

A high percentage of youngsters who originally are diagnosed as mentally retarded turn out on closer examination to have interpersonal, familial, or cultural deprivation as the etiologic factor for their "mental retardation," rather than any specific organic or constitutional factors. This suggests some obvious family involvements both in the precipitation of this "disorder" and in its amelioration.

Conduct Disorders

The problem of delinquency appears to be an extremely complex one involving social and cultural factors that have to be taken into account in any overall evaluation.

The parent of the same sex as the identified patient may be absent or inadequate. Parental limit setting is either too lenient, too harsh, or extremely inconsistent. A "negative identity" and "bad-me" self-image may exist in many of these individuals.

The delinquent behavior is thought to be conditioned by parental covert expectations or overt approval. The child may get implicit cues to act in antisocial ways, together with explicit prohibitions against such activity. The unspoken message is, "Do it, but don't get caught!" The identified patient acts out the unconscious needs of the parents, who cannot tolerate such actions in their own behavior.[64]

Criminal behavior in adults may be residues of such earlier factors. In either juvenile delinquency or adult criminality, careful evaluation must be made to ascertain the extent to which patterns are acute or chronic, associated with stress or not, and acceptable to the individual or not. With respect to the possible use of family therapy, the involvement and interest of the family members in the antisocial individual need to be ascertained. Such evaluation should aim to differentiate those instances in which family therapy would be helpful from those in which it might be fruitless.

In the area of juvenile delinquency, family therapists have attempted to direct their intervention toward ameliorating the defects mentioned above. Analogous attempts would be instituted in the case of adult criminality.

Minuchin views delinquency as a symptom of family disturbance.[65] The focus is on helping the family to delay gratification by discussing their decisions before acting on them. The therapist attempts to define and strengthen the role structure of the family. Environmental manipulation is a major technique. The therapist must be extremely active in the therapy, especially in helping to reduce blaming. The identified patient often resists the work of family therapy and the therapist must counter his self-destructive maneuvers.[66]

Family therapy is the treatment of choice for some conduct disorders of adolescence. Acting-out adolescents are less likely to form therapeutic alliances in individual therapy. With family therapy, blame may not be as focused on the offending adolescent, and it often shifts the responsibility for change onto all members of the family.

Separation Anxiety Disorder

School phobias are ideal situations for family therapy. Most commonly, when mother and child find it difficult to separate, there is an underlying marital problem. With all types of phobias, treatment of the individual by behavior modification should be considered. If that does not work, consideration should be given to family treatment and possibly family behavior therapy.

EPISODIC DYSCONTROL

In families in which the identified patient has episodic violent behavior, the members have great difficulty in transmitting values regarding the control of aggression.[67] Often the family is afraid of the identified patient's aggression. One or more family members may have overly close alliances with the identified patient because of difficulties they are having with a third family member. Treatment includes focusing on ways of handling dyscontrol episodes, emphasizing that the patient is responsible for his own actions and altering the family structure so that the identified patient does not have to act out the problems he observes in other family members.

REFERENCES

1. Diagnostic and Statistical Manual of Mental Disorder (DSM–III), (3rd ed). Prepared by the Task Force on Nomenclature and Statistics of the American Psychiatric Association, Washington, D.C., January, 1978

2. Micro-D, Revisions in the Diagnostic Criteria of the DSM–III, 1/15/78 draft. Prepared by the Task Force on Nomenclature and Statistics of the American Psychiatric Association, Washington, D.C., January 2, 1979

3. Rabkin J: Public attitudes toward mental illness: A review of the literature. Schizophrenia Bull 10:9–33, 1974
4. Fleck S: Family dynamics and origin of schizophrenia. Psychosomatic Med 22: 333–344, 1960
5. Alanen Y: The families of schizophrenic patients. Proc Roy Soc Med 63:227–231, 1970
6. Lidz T, Fleck S, Alanen YO, et al: Schizophrenic patients and their siblings. Psychiatry 26:1–18, 1963
7. Wynne LC, Ryckoff I, Day J, et al: Pseudo-mutuality in the family relations of schizophrenics, in Bell NW, Vogel EF (eds): A Modern Introduction to the Family. Glencoe, Illinois, Free Press, 1960, pp 573–594
8. Laing RD, Esterson S: Families and schizophrenia. Int J Psychiatry 4:65–71, 1967
9. Wynne LC, Singer MT: Thought disorder and family relations of schizophrenics. I. A research strategy. II. A classification of forms of thinking. Arch Gen Psychiatry 9:191–206, 1963
10. Singer MT, Wynne LC: Thought disorder and family relations of schizophrenics. III. Methodology using projective techniques. IV. Results and implications. Arch Gen Psychiatry 12:187–212, 1965
11. Hersch S, Leff J: Parental abnormalities of verbal communication in transmission of schizophrenia. Psychol Med 1:118–127, 1971
12. Bateson G, Jackson DD, Haley J, et al: Towards a theory of schizophrenia. Behav Sci 1:251–264, 1956
13. Bateson G, Jackson DD, Haley J, et al: A note on the double bind—1962. Fam Process 2:154–161, 1963
14. Sluzki CE, Ransom DC (eds): Double Bind: The Foundation of the Communicational Approach to the Family. New York, Grune & Stratton, 1976
15. Sojit C: The double-bind hypothesis and the parents of schizophrenics. Fam Process 110:53–74, 1971
16. Lidz T, Fleck S, Cornelison A: Schizophrenia and the Family. New York, International Universities Press, 1965
17. Lerner P: Resolution of intrafamilial role conflict in families of schizophrenic patients. I. Thought disturbance. J Nerv Ment Dis 141:342–351, 1966
18. Lerner P: Resolution of intrafamilial role conflict in families of schizophrenic patients. II. Social maturity. J Nerv Ment Dis 145:336–341, 1967
19. Reiss D: Individual thinking and family interaction. III. An experimental study of categorization performance in families of normals, those with character disorders, and schizophrenics. J Nerv Ment Dis 146:384–404, 1968
20. Reiss D: Individual thinking and family interaction. IV. A Study of information exchange in families of normals, those with character disorders, and schizophrenics. J Nerv Ment Dis 149:473–490, 1969
21. Levin G: Communicator-communicant approach to family interaction research. Fam Process 5:105–116, 1966
22. Haley J: Research on family patterns: An instrument measurement. Fam Process 3:41–65, 1964
23. Reiss D: The family and schizophrenia. Am J Psychiatry 133:181–184, 1976
24. Mishler E, Waxler N: Fam Process and Schizophrenia. New York, Science House, 1968

25. Wynne LC: Toohey ML, Doane J: Family studies, in Bellak L (ed): The Schizophrenic Syndrome. New York, Grune & Stratton (in press)
26. Goldstein MJ, Rodnick EH, Evans JR, et al: Drug and family therapy in the aftercare of acute schizophrenics. Arch Gen Psychiatry 35:1169–1177, 1978
27. Segal SP: Community care and deinstitutionalization implications for family policy. Social Work (in press)
28. Cohen M, Freedman N, Englehardt D, et al: Family interaction patterns, drug treatment, and change in social aggression. Arch Gen Psychiatry 19:50–56, 1968
29. Brown G, Birley J, Wing J: Influence of family life on the course of schizophrenic disorders: A replication. Br J Psychiatry 121:241–258, 1972
30. Strauss J, Carpenter W: The prediction of outcome in schizophrenia. Arch Gen Psychiatry 27:739–746, 1972
31. Vaillant G: The natural history of the remitting schizophrenias. Am J Psychiatry 120:367–375, 1963
32. Brown GW, Birley JLT, Wing JK: Influence of family life on the course of schizophrenic disorders: A replication. Br J Psychiatry 121:241–258, 1972
33. Vaughn CE, Leff JP: The influence of family and social factors on the course of psychiatric illness: A comparison of schizophrenic and depressed neurotic patients. Br J Psychiatry 129:125–137, 1976
34. Feinsilver D: Communication in families with schizophrenic patients. Arch Gen Psychiatry 22:143–148, 1970
35. Dibble E, Targum SD, Gershon ES, et al: Family Perceptions of Mania and Depression. Presented at the Annual Meeting of the American Psychiatric Association, Atlanta, Georgia, May, 1978
36. Ruestow P, Dunner DL: Bleecker B, et al: Marital adjustment in primary affective disorder. Compr Psychiatry 19:565–571, 1978
37. Wadeson H, Fitzgerald R: Marital relationship in manic-depressive illness. J Nerv Ment Dis 153:180–196, 1971
38. Benson R: The forgotten treatment modality in bipolar illness: Psychotherapy. Dis Nerv Syst 36:634–638, 1975
39. Ilfeld FW: Current social stressors and symptoms of depression. Am J Psychiatry 134:161–166, 1977
40. Feldman L: Depression and marital interaction. Fam Process 15:388–395, 1976, p 391
41. Demers R, Davis C: Influences of prophylactic lithium treatment on marital adjustment of manic-depressives and their spouses. Compr Psychiatry 12:348–353, 1971
42. Philips I: Childhood depression: Interpersonal interactions and depressive phenomena. Am J Psychiatry 136:511–515, 1979
43. Weissman MM, Prusoff BA, DiMascio A, et al: The efficacy of drugs and psychotherapy in the treatment of acute depressive episodes. Am J Psychiatry 136:555–558, 1979
44. Lipton MA: Diverse research strategies for depression and alcoholism (editorial). Am J Psychiatry 136:497–501, 1979
45. Zitrin CM, Klein DF, Woerner MG: Behavior therapy, supportive psychotherapy, imipramine, and phobias. Arch Gen Psychiatry 35:307–316, 1978
46. Hafner RJ: The husband of agoraphobic women and their influence on treatment outcome. Br J Psychiatry 131:289–294, 1977

47. Rebeta-Burditt J: The Cracker Factory. New York, MacMillan, 1970
48. Gorad S, McCourt W, Cobb J: The communications approach in alcoholism. Q J Studies on Alcohol 32:651–668, 1971
49. Berenson D: A family approach to alcoholism. Psychiatric Opinion 13:33–38, 1976
50. Deniker P, De Saugy D, Ropert M: The alcoholic and his wife. Compr Psychiatry 5:374–384, 1964
51. Rae J: The influence of the wives on the treatment outcome of alcoholics: A followup study at two years. Br J Psychiatry 120:601–613, 1972
52. Dinaburg D, Glick ID, Feigenbaum E: Marital therapy of woman alcoholics. J Studies on Alcohol 38:1247–1258, 1977
53. Rutstein D, Beech R: Genetics and addiction to alcohol (editorial). N Engl J Med 298:1140–1141, 1978
54. Ganger R, Shugart G: The heroin addict's pseudoassertive behavior and family dynamics. Social Casework 57:643–649, 1966
55. Rosenberg C: The young addict and his family. Br J Psychiatry 118:469–470, 1971
56. Harbin HT, Maziar HM: The families of drug abusers: A literature review. Fam Process 14:411–431, 1975
57. Klagsbrun M, Davis DI: Substance abuse and family interaction. Fam Process 16:149–173, 1977
58. Seldin NE: The family of the addict: A review of the literature. Int J Addict 7:97–107, 1972
59. Stanton MD: Drugs and the family: A review of the literature. Marriage Family Rev 2(2), 1979 (in press)
60. Stanton MD: Family treatment of drug problems: A review, in DuPont RI, Goldstein A, O'Donnell J (eds): Handbook on Drug Abuse. Washington, D.C., National Institute on Alcohol, Drug Abuse and Mental Health Administration, Department of Health, Education and Welfare: and Office of Drug Abuse Policy, Executive Office of the President, 1979
61. Mandelbaum A: Family process in diagnosis and treatment of children and adolescents. Bull of the Menninger Clinic 35:153–166, 1971
62. Adams M: Social aspects of the medical care for the mentally retarded. N Engl J Med 286:635–638, 1972
63. Vogel EF, Bell NW: The emotionally disturbed child as the family scapegoat, in Bell NW, Vogel EF (eds): A Modern Introduction to the Family. Glencoe, Illinois, Free Press, 1960, pp 382–397
64. Szurek S: Some lessons from efforts at psychotherapy with parents. Am J Psychiatry 109:291–295, 1952
65. Minuchin S, Auerswald E, King C, et al: The study and treatment of families that produce multiple acting-out boys. Am J Orthopsychiatry 34:125–134, 1964
66. Minuchin S, Montalvo B: Techniques for working with disorganized low socioeconomic families. Am J Orthopsychiatry 37:880–887, 1967
67. Harbin HT: Episodic dyscontrol and family dynamics. Am J Psychiatry 134:1113–1116, 1977

The Family of Charles IV Detail by Goya, 1800. Courtesy of the Prado Museum, Madrid.

13

Family Treatment and Social, Cultural, Ethnic, and Economic Issues

OBJECTIVE

- To understand and effectively treat families of differing cultures, ethnic origins, socioeconomic status, and life-styles.

WORKING WITH FAMILIES OF DIFFERENT CULTURES AND ETHNIC ORIGINS

In the course of their teaching efforts, the authors are often asked how one works with a German family, a wealthy family, a black family, a single-parent family, and so on. In each of these situations, there may be differences in marital patterns and childrearing roles, and different ways of coping with each life stage. All families, however, have the same basic framework, the same general life course, and the same essential need to establish some structured ways of coping with their tasks.

The Therapist-Family Fit

Should the therapist be of the same race and culture as the family in treatment? It is probably true that the closer the therapist is to the family in terms of race, ethnic background, social class, and value system, the greater the potential for mutual understanding and sensitivity. The fact that the therapist comes from a background similar to a specific family does not guarantee, however, the therapist's successful treatment of that family. The therapist will still need to check all presumptions with the family. It would be ill advised for the therapist to imagine that he or she can avoid the process of getting to know the family because of similar backgrounds. For one thing families of a particular culture or race should not be stereotyped. Families that require treatment have often been found to function aberrantly for their particular cultural or racial group; while the therapist may have particular blind spots that are related to sociocultural factors. The therapist must be aware of these attitudes since they may impede rather than facilitate working with families with similar characteristics (see Chapter 10, "Therapist Reactions to the Family"). Also it would not be unusual for families to have negative attitudes toward working with a therapist of a similar background. Some individuals seem to prefer therapists from a different background. There is never a perfect fit between family and therapist, but racial and cultural differences should not be an absolute contraindication to their working together.

In different cultures the role of therapist means different things. In some cultures the therapist is often a stranger to the family, an outsider whom the family members are suspicious of. They may feel sensitive about their failure in taking care of a family member within their own extended family organization. This is to be contrasted with families in other cultures who at the first sign of family trouble go for help.

Guidelines for Understanding Various Family Patterns Within Different Cultures

The following is a brief itemization and summation of ways in which families of different cultures can vary.[1]

1. *Role*. How are family members perceived in terms of their roles? The role of father, teacher, or doctor may be quite different in one culture from that of another in terms of power and authority.
2. *Interpersonal Relationship and Reciprocity*. How does the family handle interpersonal relationships and reciprocity? In some cultures there may be a strong sense of interpersonal reliance and mutual obligation within the family unit, whereas in other cultures the trend may be toward independence with each person doing "his own thing."
3. *Propriety*. Cultural standards of right and wrong are important components of family functioning. Families of some cultures have a defined set of acceptable behavior, while families of other cultures may rely on a more pragmatic and flexible style of behavior. Overt public shaming of "wrongdoers," together with internalized guilt, is not an unusual form of chastisement in some cultures.
4. *Time and Relationships*. In traditional cultures there are extended family clans, organizations, and records that institutionally reinforce the feeling of family continuity over a period of centuries; in more modern cultures it is

not uncommon to find that lower-class families are more present oriented than the future oriented middle- and upper-class families of the same culture.

5. *Symptoms.* The identified patient's culture, race, and class may have an influence on his symptoms. In some middle-socioeconomic class families feelings are supposed to be controlled whereas in many upper-class families feelings can be expressed at will. In lower socioeconomic class families physical symptoms may be more acceptable than psychological ones.

6. *Models of Mental Illness.* In different cultures families will conceptualize mental problems in differing ways. In some cultures psychological problems and symptoms are more stigmatizing.

There may be differences that create strains between generations in the same family. These are accentuated when families migrate, as when black families move from the rural South to the urban North. These families are often more comfortable in discussing their difficulties in their own style than they are in the manner of the predominant culture. Even though cultural issues play an important role, they may not be the sole cause of problems.

The therapist does not have to become an expert in every culture in order to be effective, but should understand and respect cultural norms. Many treatment principles cut across different cultures. The therapist should remember that what is therapeutic in his or her culture may not be appropriate for the family in its own culture. A good example of this is sex therapy, in which many therapists have extremely liberal values and feel fairly comfortable dealing with sexual matters. But they may encounter great difficulty when they try to translate their values into concepts and techniques and try to apply them to a conservative family. The therapist must be sensitive to the values of other cultures and not impose the values of his or her culture on the therapy.

The K family consisted of a mother, father, son, and younger daughter. The identified patient was the daughter, a 23-year-old Japanese sophomore college student who had lost 40 pounds. Her diagnosis was anorexia nervosa.

The parents (as typical of their culture) favored the older son. The father worked as a food inspector and the mother prided herself on being an excellent cook. The therapist speculated that the area in which the daughter could have some leverage on the family was by starving herself to death. This caused the family great concern because everyone noticed the daughter's weight loss, which caused the family to lose face. The parents' relationship had deteriorated over the years, with a lessening of intimacy.

Treatment strategy was oriented around bringing father and mother closer in a manner that would enable them to feel comfortable as individuals and also be compatible with their culture. The eldest son was used as an ally to change some of the parents' behavior in order to decrease the identified patient's symptoms. He would suggest to the parents that they give his sister more freedom. But on the other hand, he was fearful of yielding his favored position, for he believed that if his sister got more power, he would have a more difficult time with his parents.

The family believed that the cause of her not eating was physical. The therapist never directly challenged this belief but suggested that if its cause was physical and if they wanted their daughter to eat more, the husband should work with his wife in preparing the meals. The aim was to increase parental intimacy and at the same time decrease the emotional distance between parents and children. Differentness in the family was also attended to—the daughter continued to attend Buddhist services with the parents once a week, but for the remainder of the time the parents were encouraged to allow her to pursue her own type of life-style at the liberal university she was attending.

WORKING WITH WEALTHY FAMILIES

In upper-class families, marital coalitions may be less well structured than in middle-class families. There may be a considerable lack of emotional cohesiveness that is oddly reminiscent of the lower-socioeconomic-class family. Parenting may be intermittent, inconsistent, and largely managed by people other than the parents. This, again, is similar to the pattern of some low-income families. Offspring in these families may evidence an inability to formulate life goals and may seem to drift aimlessly. A family therapist for such families must be sensitive to their particular patterns, which include their tendency to escape difficulties through the use of money and their ability to bribe the therapist with high fees and then to treat him like a servant.

WORKING WITH POVERTY FAMILIES

Special modifications of family therapy have been suggested for the needs of poor families. A meaningful balance must be struck between dealing with reality issues (food, clothing, housing, interacting with public agencies) and internal family issues. Too often the former areas have been neglected, based on the assumption that the family was capable of coping with its basic survival needs or that such matters did not properly belong in the province of family therapy.[2-4]

Many such families cannot come in for treatment during regular working hours, and the routine schedules of therapists and agencies should be more flexible to accommodate their needs. Emphasis should be directed to concrete problem-solving activities and behavioral rehearsals (rather than insight and intellectual understanding), current issues (rather than past history), and day-to-day realities (rather than fantasies) from session to session. The therapist often will have to go to the family rather than the family going to the therapist. (In this way family psychiatry can serve as a basis for community psychiatry.)

WORKING WITH SEPARATED, DIVORCED, OR SINGLE-PARENT FAMILIES[5-8]

With separated, divorced, or single-parent families, the therapist needs to evaluate the relationship between parent(s), other caretakers, and the children. The deficits noted in family functioning should be altered, based on the needs of the family. One immediate resource is the psychosocial kinship system.

When a couple is *separated,* the family therapist can help uncover the problems that prevent some people from living together successfully on a sustained basis. Maintaining a lasting relationship is often more difficult than forming a new one, although some people hold onto a relationship in order to avoid change. For this reason the family therapist can, quite reasonably, err on attempting to hold a marriage together rather than breaking it up. Not everything can be changed, and the therapist needs to be realistic in helping the husband and wife to accept parts of themselves that cannot be changed. When emotions are high, separate individual therapy for one or both partners, or group therapy, may be indicated.

If children are involved, no matter what their ages, the reasons for separation or divorce should be discussed openly, honestly, and in a way that the children are able to understand, given their age level. Parents need to make clear that the separation or divorce is taking place because they cannot get along with each other and not because of any primary problems with the children. The children should be aware that both parents are still interested in them and love them.

Parents should not use children as hostages or as ammunition to support their arguments. They should not denigrate each other to the children. Unfortunately one parent often accuses the children of growing up just like his or her spouse and even blames them for the divorce. What constitutes good parenting varies with the developmental needs of children and each parent does not necessarily provide the optimal degree at each stage of his or her child's life. The family is not a static system; therefore, its needs, expectations, desires, and abilities do change over time.[9]

Once *divorce* (see Chapter 3) has taken place and reconstituted families are established, the focus is on enabling the exspouses to assume their responsibilities to each other and on attempting to find resolutions that do not necessarily place them in adversarial positions. Both parents may need to focus on being as constructive as possible in regard to the needs of the children. Other goals include ensuring that: (1) children have access and ongoing relationships (rather than mere visitation) with both their parents and their families, in order to define their own identity and identifications; (2) parents and children remain emotionally attached and responsible to each other; (3) guilt and anger are reduced for parents and children; and (4) the noncustodial parent's participation is increased. (Legal and judicial aspects of the separation and divorce processes are discussed in Chapter 17.)

Reconstituted families (see Chapter 3) have another set of problems, potentials, and options, which may need professional help.[10] There are special concerns of reconstituted families that need to be addressed—for example, roles of stepparents vis-à-vis the children, relationships with exspouses, and so on. In general, the principles of working with reconstituted families are similar to those used with other families.

REFERENCES

1. Shon S: Material presented at Grand Rounds, Langley Porter Neuropsychiatric Institute, October 25, 1977
2. McKinney J: Adapting family therapy to multideficit families. Social Casework 51:237–333, 1970
3. Mannino F, Shore M: Ecologically oriented family interaction. Fam Process 11:499–504, 1972
4. Adams P: Functions of the lower-class partial family. Am J Psychiatry 130:200–203, 1973
5. Bernstein NR, Robley J: The detection and management of pediatric difficulties created by divorce. Pediatrics 30:950–956, 1962
6. Derdyn AP: Children in divorce. Intervention in the phase of separation. Pediatrics 60:20–27, 1977
7. Wallerstein JS, Kelly JB: The effects of parental divorce: Experiences of the preschool child. J Am Acad Child Psyhiatry 14:600–616, 1975
8. Gardner RA: The Boys and Girls Book about Divorce. New York, Aronson, 1970
9. Nadelson C: The impact of divorce on families. Presented at the Annual Meeting of the American Psychiatric Association, Chicago, 1979
10. Visher EB, Visher JS: Common problems of stepparents and their spouses. Am J Orthopsychiatry 48:252–262, 1978

Study for "Dance in the Country" by Pierre Auguste Renoir (1841-1919), France.
Courtesy of the Honolulu Academy of Arts, purchase, 1937.

14

The Family: Marital and Sex Therapy

OBJECTIVES

- To point out the connections between sexual problems and other family problems
- To make clear the relationship between marital therapy and sex therapy
- To describe techniques of combining family and sex therapy

INTRODUCTION

It has been estimated that 50 percent of American marriages are beset with sexual difficulties. According to Masters and Johnson, there is no uninvolved partner when one member of a couple presents with sexual inadequacy, which Masters and Johnson define as problems with potency or ejaculation in the male and with orgasm or intercourse in the female.[1] In 44 percent of the couples referred to them, both partners had a sexual dysfunction. The majority of marital units with sexual dysfunction seen by Masters and Johnson had no evidence of a primary relationship problem other than the specific symptoms of sexual dysfunction. The sexual dysfunction, therefore, may not be a symptom of a disturbed marriage but the core issue itself. Sexual dysfunction need not be a symptom of psychiatric disorder; rather it is often caused by ignorance of sexual anatomy and physiology or by negative attitudes and self-defeating behavior. Although sexual functioning is not the sum total of any marital relationship, it is thought that few marriages can exist as effective, complete, and ongoing entities without a comfortable component of sexual exchange.

There has been a marked shift in the general attitude toward female sexuality in recent years. Women are increasingly expecting not only to receive pleasure from sexual activities but more specifically to achieve orgasm. They also expect to participate in a more assertive way, since they have had their sexual interests and activities legitimized. Men have become disturbed and sometimes dysfunctional because of the changing and increasingly assertive sexual role of women. Men at times feel that they have failed if their partner has not reached orgasm. Each partner should decide how much they are responsible for the other's pleasure and how much for their own.

Sex therapists have to assess the capabilities of each partner in giving and receiving sensual and sexual pleasure. The notion of sex as recreation, rather than as a marital obligation or an exclusively procreative function, is receiving increasing attention. It has long been obvious that sexual activity is mixed with a variety of motives such as power, hostility, dependence, and submission. The traditional equation of sex and love has come into question. The blurring of stereotyped gender roles has led to additional complexities in sexual relationships. Hostility and mystery may be more important components of sexual attraction than many are willing to admit.[2]

A recent study of sexual complaints from couples who believe that their marriages are working reasonably well has revealed that, although 80 percent of the couples reported their marital and sexual relations were happy and satisfying, 40 percent of the men reported erectile or ejaculatory dysfunction, and 63 percent of the women reported arousal or orgasmic dysfunction.[3] In addition 50 percent of the men and 77 percent of the women reported difficulty that was not dysfunctional in nature (for example, lack of interest or inability to relax). The women were not only probably experiencing greater dysfunction but were more willing to admit their dysfunction. It was learned that husbands underestimated their wives' dysfunction. The therapists noted that the partners' actual sexual performance seemed less important to them than the feelings they had for each other.

RELATIONSHIP BETWEEN SEX THERAPY AND MARITAL THERAPY

For a majority of couples seen in marital therapy, there will probably be a more complex relationship between their marital and sexual problems than there will be in patients who are treated by sex therapy. A careful evaluation of their total interactions needs to be done by the therapist. When it appears that the basic marriage is a sound one, but that the couple suffers from specific sexual difficulties (which may also lead to various secondary marital consequences), the primary focus might be sex therapy per se. In many cases, however, specific sex therapy cannot be carried out until the relationship between the two partners has been improved in other respects; indeed the sexual problems may clearly be an outgrowth of the marital difficulties. When marital problems are taken care of, the sexual problems may readily be resolved. It may be difficult to disentangle marital from sexual problems or to decide which came first. The priorities for therapy may not always be clear.

Healthy sexual functioning can be throught of as resulting from relatively nonconflicted and self-confident attitudes about sex and the belief that the partner is pleased by one's performance. In this type of situation, a reinforcing positive cycle can be activated. One of the fundamental principles of the new sex therapies is to reduce performance anxiety, while at the same time building communication, relieving guilt and other restrictive attitudes, and utilizing specific sexual techniques in a learning and training atmosphere.

When either partner has doubts about his or her sexual abilities or the ability to please the other, his or her sexual performance may suffer. This morbid self-absorption and anxiety will characteristically produce a decrease in sexual performance and enjoyment and can lead to impotency and orgastic difficulties. Marital and individual difficulties of various sorts might then follow. A vicious cycle may be activated with worries being increased, leading to increasingly poor sexual performance.

Couples who continue in marital or individual treatment for long periods of time can resolve some of their marital problems, but can still suffer from specific sexual difficulties in their marriage. It is also true that specific sexual problems may be dramatically reversed after relatively brief periods of sex therapy, which utilizes some of the newer techniques, even though such problems may have proven intractable following long periods of more customary psychotherapy.

Usually when a marital couple has a generally satisfactory relationship, any minor sexual problems may be only temporary. Resolution of sexual problems in a relationship, however, will not inevitably produce positive effects in other facets of a relationship as well.

Marital and sexual problems interact in various ways:[4]

1. Sexual dysfunction produces secondary marital discord. Sex therapy would usually be considered the treatment of choice in these situations, especially if the sexual dysfunction occurred in relationships other than the current one.
2. Sexual dysfunction is secondary to marital discord. In such situations conjoint marital treatment might be considered the treatment of choice. If the marital relationship is not too severely disrupted, however, a trial of sex therapy might be attempted, because a relatively rapid relief of symptoms, possible with sex therapy, could produce beneficial, motivational effects on the couple's interest in pursuing other marital issues.
3. Severe marital discord would usually produce sexual problems but probably would not be amenable to sex therapy because of the partners' hostility to each other. Marital therapy would usually be attempted first, with later attention given to sexual dysfunction.

Mr. and Mrs. L had both been raised in traditional backgrounds. Mrs. L had been taught that sex is dirty and should not really be discussed. Having fantasies about other men was strictly taboo.

Mrs. L had problems during adolescence dating "men who my mom didn't like." Through twice-a-week individual psychotherapy, she had worked through these problems and married Mr. L and had a child. Two years after the marriage, marital problems developed, focused around sex. Frequency and enjoyment of sex for both partners was markedly decreased. Mrs. L refused to have sex, saying that she was too upset.

Whereas at one time individual psychotherapy might have been the treatment of choice, the therapist decided to use both marital therapy and sex therapy. Marital therapy helped to open communication between the couple. It was discovered that Mrs. L was using the tactic of sex refusal because she was angry at her husband for not helping with childrearing responsibilities. In addition Mrs. L felt that sex was wrong and was upset by her fantasies of having sex with other men.

The couple was encouraged to deal more directly with their differences and with the disappointments underlying their anger. Issues related to each partner's family of origin were brought up. Roles were restructured—Mr. L took over more of the childrearing responsibilities. As the marital relationship improved, their sexual problems were addressed.

Because of the interrelatedness of these two problem areas, therapists who undertake to treat couples should become competent in *both* marital and sex therapy. Therapists should be in a position to move freely from one of these areas to the other (also see Chapter 21 on training). If they are not they should refer such a couple for either the marital or the sex therapy that they themselves may not feel able to offer.

TAKING A PSYCHOSEXUAL HISTORY

What type of vocabulary should be used when discussing sexual topics? Some authorities advise against the use of terms that would be offensive or uncomfortable for either the therapist or the couple. Care must be taken, however, to avoid using bland generalities and ending up with no specific sexual information at all.

In questions and discussions about sex, the therapist should assume that everyone has done everything. Rather than phrasing the question, "Have you ever had any homosexual experiences?" the therapist should ask, "What kinds of homosexual experience have you had?"

Euphemisms should be discouraged and frankness encouraged. When there is vagueness, the therapist should feel free to use follow-up questions.

The therapist should use simple language or use the simplest technical sexual term that the patient is comfortable with. Some patients will misunderstand technical terms. For others the use of the vernacular by the therapist may be inappropriate. The problem faced in the choice of language is itself an indication of our general cultural discomfort with sexuality. The therapist's own use of a particular sexual vocabulary can be a model to help the marital partners feel comfortable in communicating with each other more openly.

Adolescents, racial and ethnic subgroups, gays and lesbians, and others may have specialized sexual argots that they use. The therapist's ability to use this language in a comfortable and knowing manner may serve to enhance rapport and reduce communicational barriers.

Specific methods have been devised for eliciting a sexual history and for evaluating sexual functioning. Descriptions of techniques in sex therapy have been thoroughly described in the literature.[1, 5] The marital therapist should become familiar with these ideas and obtain experience in their utilization. Some marital therapists still are not well informed about their clients' sexual histories. This presumably arises from their own discomfort about such material and from their lack of a conceptual frame of reference to help them utilize the sexual data they might obtain.

PSYCHOSEXUAL DISORDERS AND THEIR TREATMENT

The types of sexual problems that have lent themselves to the new sex therapy techniques have been those that fit into a task-oriented, symptom-removal model. These problems include:

1. Inhibited sexual desire
2. Inhibited sexual excitement
3. Inhibited female orgasm
4. Inhibited male orgasm
5. Premature ejaculation
6. Functional dyspareunia
7. Functional vaginismus

General techniques for these problems may involve joint sexual history taking and discussion, joint "sexological" examination, educational and desensitization techniques, and encouraging improvement of verbal and nonverbal communicational techniques between the couple. In addition to these general aspects of sex therapy, more specific techniques involving the assignment of behavioral tasks, homework, and use of mechanical equipment have been developed to deal with each of the problem areas. A gratifyingly high proportion of couples with uncomplicated sex problems have been helped rapidly by these methods. These techniques can be tried with the expectation that a fairly short-term course will show dramatic improvement.

In those couples who did not do well, three factors were found, either singly or in combination, when they returned for additional treatment after a standard two-week sex therapy program.[6] These were categorized as difficulties in the areas of pleasure, intimacy, and cooperation. A variety of additional therapeutic interventions may be required to deal with these issues, supplementing the standard sex therapy techniques. With such couples treatment using behavioral-experiential techniques and family therapy techniques are needed.

Other factors that have been cited as relative contraindications to successful sex therapy include situations in which the marital problems outweigh the sexual problems and certain psychiatric disorders, such as antisocial behavior, schizophrenic disorder, paranoid disorder, and severe personality disorder.

Sexual ennui, another type of psychosexual disorder, may actually be "marital ennui" and may not lend itself to specific sex therapy. Some of the more general techniques used in the sex therapies, however, such as sensate focus, mutual massage, and permission for sexual fantasies of various kinds, may serve to improve this situation. More often a general examination of the state of the marriage is indicated.

For treating *general sexual inhibition,* techniques similar to those utilized in the preliminary aspect of the therapy of sexual disorders may be useful, as outlined in the previous paragraph.

OTHER SEXUAL CONCERNS

Homosexuality or Bisexuality in Either Partner or Offspring

The fear of or actual presence of homosexual behavior in either partner may present various types of marital difficulty, although marriages can work successfully even with overt homosexuality in one partner. When such issues emerge in marital treatment, the therapist needs to discover in what specific ways they are a problem, and to whom. If the homosexual orientation has been a "secret" or has only recently come into the affected partner's awareness, there may be questions as to whether the marriage should continue, whether "conversion" or "reversion" treatment should be undertaken, or whether some current marital or other dissatisfactions have temporarily produced a "pseudohomosexuality."[7]

If the situation has progressed to actual sexual dysfunction in the marriage, the couple may present themselves for therapy with one partner being unaware of the other's underlying agenda. For some couples the bisexuality of one partner has been an established and agreed on part of the covert marital arrangement, but questions may emerge when children are born or the affected partner becomes more flagrant in his or her homosexual behavior. Concerns may arise about the effects on the children or whether the marriage has become untenable. Marital therapy might then be indicated.

Many parents worry about the possibility of one of their children growing up to be homosexual. Such concerns are often unrealistic, and even if they are based on good evidence, dispute exists as to what course to pursue with an adamantly homosexual offspring. Books have been written to help parents try to forestall homosexual tendencies in their children on the premise that they are undesirable.[8] Such thwarting actions, however, are highly questionable and may cause more harm than good. Some recent work dealing with the life history of homosexual patients has implicated the family system as contributing to the individual's homosexual development.[9] There is reason to believe, however, that the causes of homosexuality are much more complex and variable.[10]

Similarly *transvestism, transsexualism,* and other sexual variants have been ascribed to particular patterns in the family of origin. Whether they are amenable to one or another type of preventive family intervention is an open question.

Family treatment may be important in helping to deal with these often extremely difficult issues once they have surfaced into the family's awareness. Some families may be aided in understanding and accepting life-styles that cannot be changed without disrupting positive and important relationships.

Sexual Problems After Medical Illness

Couples often raise the question of sexual intercourse after a myocardial infarction in one of the spouses. "Coitus is *infrequently* associated with sudden cardiac death."[11] Usually the spouse's coronary is used as a weapon in the family interaction to prevent emotional closeness.

Total abstinence is unjustified. Sexual intercourse, with some limitation of the amount of activity, might be justified on psychological (rather than physiological) grounds. For those couples who feel that they are informed as to the risks versus the benefits, there is no reason medically to prohibit such activity.

Sexual Problems in the Elderly

With the rapid growth in the number of elderly people, there has been an increased interest in their psychiatric and sexual problems. In couples over 60, many of the primary problems that exist are sexual, which may be one reason why fewer couples are staying together. Contrary to popular belief, however, sexual activity does not have to decrease once couples pass their forties. The family therapist can help couples realize the following.[12]

1. Advancing years are not a contraindication to sexuality and sensuality.
2. It is perfectly acceptable for the couple to have less frequent intercourse.
3. Older men may achieve erection and orgasm more slowly and may not necessarily ejaculate each time they have intercourse, and older women may have a shorter excitement phase, and their orgasms may be less intense with

slower vaginal contractions. Both partners, however, can still have a regular ongoing sexual life.

Even after an elderly patient has had a severe disability, such as a stroke, his or her sexual life can still be maintained. The couple can be aided in adjusting to changes of sexual functioning by using a variety of sexually stimulating techniques available to them.

Incest and Child Molesting[13]

In many cases of frank incest, the study of the family interactions involved reveals a covert or an overt acceptance by the uninvolved spouse of the sexual relationship between parent and child. The mechanisms involved often are relatively complex, but they seem to permit the uninvolved spouse to avoid sexual relations.[14,15] The incestuous behavior can also serve to maintain the homeostasis of the family unit.

The I family sought help following discovery of an incestuous relationship between the father and the 14-year-old daughter. The mother sought help for the family to find out "whether Max is a sex maniac and ought to be put away or whether he's just plain rotten and ought to be put in jail and divorced."

Evaluation revealed that the wife and husband had not been getting along for many years. Recently, the wife had begun to leave home after supper, telling her husband and daughter that she might be working all night, and cautioning them not to "get in trouble." The husband and daughter had then begun mutual petting prior to bedtime, which had progressed to intercourse.

Rape

With the recent emergence of the Women's Movement, there has been a new understanding of rape. No longer is the woman seen as a provocateur and the rapist as an emotionally frustrated, psychologically intact male. In fact the rapist has been found to be a psychologically damaged individual, and rape is viewed as aggression, rather than a sexual process. The term "rape" is more accurately a legal one with different implications for the lawyer than for the family therapist and the family.

"An important aspect in response to rape, to be considered by those caring for the victim, is that it may affect relations with the family and among friends."[16] In contrast to most personal crises in which sharing is usually beneficial, there is a real possibility that rape will alter the marital and family relationship in a disruptive way. Families often prefer to avoid discussion because of their own anxiety and because of the difficult feelings they may stir up. This avoidance reinforces the victim's guilt and prevents successful coping with the experience. The family therapist must cope with his own feelings and biases toward rape and help the victim and family to deal effectively with the event in reestablishing the marital and family homeostasis.

REFERENCES

1. Masters W, Johnson V: Human Sexual Response. Boston, Little, Brown, 1966
2. Stoller RJ: Sexual excitement. Arch Gen Psychiatry 33:899, 1976
3. Frank E, Anderson C, Rubinstein D: Frequency of sexual dysfunction in "normal" couples. N Engl J Med 299:111–115, 1978
4. Sager CJ: The role of sex therapy in marital therapy. Am J Psychiatry 133:555–559, 1976
5. Kaplan HS: The New Sex Therapy. New York, Brunner/Mazel, 1974
6. Levay AN, Kagle A: A study of treatment needs following sex therapy. Am J Psychiatry 134:970–973, 1977
7. Masters W, Johnson V: Homosexuality in perspective. Boston, Little, Brown, 1979
8. Wyden P: Growing Up Straight. New York, Stein and Day, 1968
9. Brown D: Homosexuality and family dynamics. Bull of the Menninger Clinic 27:227–232, 1963
10. Tripp CA: The Homosexual Matrix. New York, McGraw-Hill, 1975.
11. Cobb LA, Schaffer WE: Letter to the editor. N Engl J Med 293:1100, 1975
12. Feigenbaum EF: Geriatric psychopathology—Internal or external? J Am Geriatric Soc 22:49–55, 1974
13. Meiselman KC: Incest: A Psychological Study of Causes and Effects. San Francisco, Jossey-Bass, 1978
14. Lustig N, Dressen J, Spellman S, Murray T: Incest. Arch Gen Psychiatry 14:31–41, 1966
15. Machotka P, Pittman FS, Flomenhaft K: Incest as a family affair. Fam Process 6:98–116, 1967
16. Nadelson CC: Rapist and victim. N Engl J Med 297:784–785, 1977

Death in the Sick Chamber by Edvard Munch, 1893. Courtesy of Nasjonalgalleriet, Oslo.

15
Brief Family Therapy*

INTRODUCTION AND GUIDELINES

Traditional marital and family organization seems increasingly vulnerable to rapidly changing sociocultural conditions. When viewed positively, this situation is one in which it is more possible than ever before for families and their members to experiment and to build the kinds of lives more nearly suited to their wishes and potentials. Gender roles, structural stability, and task assignment are more a matter of individualized negotiation within each family setting.

What is the role of family therapy in such a social climate? One view would be that the family therapist should avoid being the "expert" and the bearer of cultural norms regarding family life and would be well advised to convey the notion that families need to learn the techniques of dealing not only with change but also with the uncertainties inherent in working out their own answers. Rather than offering definitive end points consisting of family pseudostability, the therapist must be able to help families continue to grow and develop without outside aid.

This attitude would allow the therapist to concentrate on important long-range family processes, such as clarity of communication, the ability to negotiate differences and to cope with ambiguity, change, and loss—tools that the family will need in an ongoing way indefinitely. Teaching families these skills, rather than helping them solve specific problems, may be more realistic and valuable, given the social changes impinging on families today. This type of process goal can fit a brief therapy model, perhaps with family readjustments and "tune-ups" from time to time.

The frequency and availability of help may be the key element in a successful outcome, even when the overall duration of therapy is brief. In crisis situa-

*This chapter has been adapted from: Kessler DR, Glick ID: Brief family therapy. Psychiatric Clinics of North America 2:75–84, 1979. Reprinted with permission of W. B. Saunders Co.

tions, for example, daily contacts with the therapist and a provision for backup services for the family on nights and weekends may be essential.

Although brief therapy can be thought of as being short term and intensive, it may at times also take place over a widely spaced, extended period. There are situations that lend themselves to an initial evaluation and intervention, followed by a period of "homework" and "therapeutic vacation," with only intermittent contact with the therapist thereafter.

Brief family therapy can include two to six crisis-intervention sessions, sector treatment of a particular aspect of family interactions for up to several months, or weekend marathon "growth" groups. The goals in these various formats would be somewhat different.

With crisis intervention the goal might be to keep an identified patient from having to enter a psychiatric hospital or it might be to return the family to its preexisting equilibrium following an unexpected, overwhelming traumatic event. In sector therapy a specific, crucial segment of a family's pattern might be selected for intensive, time-limited attention—for example, its way of dealing with separation and loss. The ramifications of dealing with an especially central family theme might be far reaching in scope and may also be carried forward long after the formal therapy sessions had terminated. In a relationship-enrichment experience, for example, marital couples might be actively encouraged to prac- tice new behaviors with other members of a large group.

The format chosen will depend, to a large extent, on the nature of the problem (e.g. its urgency) and by the therapist's stylistic preferences and flexibil- ity.

COURSE OF TREATMENT

The initial referral contact and evaluation interview can be used to set the stage for brief family treatment. The therapist can clarify the goals and expecta- tions and channel the interactions in ways suited to short-term work. For exam- ple, if the family situation fits one of the types discussed above, then the evaluation data gathering will focus on material and processes relevant to that category and its goals, and other types of data will be given less attention.

The evaluation process can be made more efficient and revealing by utiliz- ing various structured family tasks that are designed to elicit one or another important aspect of family functioning. Such assignments and "games" can include asking family members in various combinations to plan something they would enjoy doing together; requesting that family members discuss their own and others' good and bad characteristics; and having the marital couple play a game designed so that if they compete, they both lose, whereas if they cooperate, success is possible (see Appendix A).

Before the end of the first session, the therapist will have made a contract with the family outlining the goals and duration of treatment. There may also be an agreement as to what goals will *not* be sought. Anything else that is made explicit to the family about the process of treatment may vary, but the therapist should have a blueprint in mind.

As the therapy proceeds the therapist will actively keep the family on the track and discourage derailments of various sorts. Depending on the type of treatment involved, the family will be rewarded for continuing in the necessary stepwise sequence or for gaining mastery in a more adaptive way of dealing with an old pattern. The therapist will be conductor, traffic cop, referee, mentor, and model, utilizing a knowledge of individual and group dynamics, as well as family processes.

The family will be reminded of the limited nature of the treatment. The therapist will be aware of the possibility of termination anxiety, with reemergence of distress as the end of treatment approaches, even when positive gains have been made during the earlier phase of treatment. The therapist will resist attempts to prolong therapy beyond the agreed time and will deal with the family's fear of being unable to cope and its pull toward dependence, instead. The family members will be helped to summarize the gains they have made during treatment and to rehearse their future problem-solving efforts.

TECHNIQUES

In this section specific techniques are discussed that have been established as especially useful in brief family evaluation and treatment. Although the list is by no means exhaustive, it is meant to be extensive enough to give an adequate idea of the variety of therapeutic options available. There is no necessary and absolute connection between any one technique and the three general strategies outlined in earlier chapters, although some techniques obviously lend themselves more easily to one strategy than to another.

Experienced therapists are most likely to be flexible in what they do, from case to case and from minute to minute. The following categories, then, should be thought of as freeing the therapeutic imagination rather than restricting it into a straitjacket.

Limited Goals and a Definite End Point

It is especially important in brief therapy that the therapist be clear as to the goals of treatment. When brevity is not part of the agreed-on contract, the reasons for therapy often remain vague and ambiguous. Sessions are likely to continue with no fixed termination agreed to in advance and with changing goals and directions as treatment proceeds. Symptomatic and behavioral progress is not taken as a sign of the possibility of ending treatment, but rather as a confirmation of the positive effects of treatment and the desirability of continuing it.

In brief therapy the therapist has to keep clearly in mind that the amount of contact with the family will be limited and will have a definite end point, either in terms of the number of hours or in the achievement of a specific goal. The therapist's concept may be centered on the *least* that needs to be done to help the family to continue on its own, rather than on more ambitious, if not grandiose, notions of what the family's potential might be.

If the evaluation indicates that the family has been functioning satisfactorily until a recent crisis, efforts will be made to restore the preexisting equilibrium as quickly as possible. For example, crisis intervention techniques (q.v.) may be utilized in a family in which the 22-year-old son, living with his parents, has had a behavioral exacerbation of his chronic schizophrenic condition. The parents panic, demand hospitalization of their son, as well as his permanent removal from the home. With ventilation, attention to what triggered the upset, support, symptomatic relief for all concerned, and a setting that allows for daily visits to the therapist, brief but intensive therapy may avoid hospitalization and quickly restore the family's ability to cope.

If the family's distress seems more related to long-lasting patterns of interaction, some attempt can be made to intervene in one or two crucial areas in a way that will open up new possibilities for the family to grow and develop on its own, without further reliance on the therapist. For example, when a wife's suicide attempt seems related to chronic unspoken doubts about the viability of the marriage, the therapist will work toward getting the husband and wife to express more openly to each other the extent of their current needs, disappointments, and frustrations. As soon as they are able to engage satisfactorily in these transactions, the couple may be ready to carry on without the therapist's presence.

The family gets the message that time is limited, that goals must be realistic and achievable, and that all problems cannot be solved once and for all. They will not "live happily ever after" but will have to continue to grow and develop, utilizing the communicational, interactional, problem-solving, or other skills imparted or catalyzed by the therapist.

Setting a fixed number of sessions with the family is often desirable, and it is essential that this commitment to terminate be adhered to, in spite of various attempts the family may make to undermine it. The essence of such treatment may actually consist of helping families begin to understand how they do not keep agreements and how they sabotage attempts at changing dysfunctional patterns.

Active Focus; Reinforcement of Family Strengths; Reconceptualization

The therapist will be alert to the need of staying on target during the course of the treatment and will continually help the family to stick to the one or two primary goals that have been agreed on. Other issues that emerge can be conceptualized as relating to the core issues in some important ways or as resistances to dealing with those issues. Alternatively "extraneous" matters can be noted as important but not germane to the current focus, and perhaps they can be left for the family to deal with later on its own.

Whatever treatment focus has been selected will benefit from underlining and positive reinforcement from the therapist whenever possible. Because an important family pattern will have been selected for therapeutic attention, there should be no lack of examples of this pattern for the therapist to point out and utilize to encourage change.

Family therapy requires the active contribution of the therapist, more so than in some other forms of psychotherapy. In brief family therapy, even more therapist participation is usually needed. Passivity and indecisiveness only tend to activate the family's dysfunctional repetitive patterns.

Existing and emerging family strengths should be reinforced and supported, as should the concept that all members of the family are doing the best they can. Especially in brief therapy, in which there is little opportunity for the gradual development of rapport, the therapist must be nonblaming and encouraging and must indicate that an attempt is being made to understand the situation from each member's, as well as the whole family's, vantage point. Especially for effective brief therapy, each family member needs to feel understood and accepted by the therapist. Informal moments before, during, and after sessions are invaluable for the therapist to add a personal touch of contact with each family member.

When addressing a family unit, it is difficult to use language that will be meaningful to an elderly grandmother, an uninvolved father, or a 6-year-old child. The therapist must often alter the language content and direction to keep these individuals motivated and involved.

Successes in substituting more functional patterns during the course of the therapy should be rewarded. Indications that the family can change should be highlighted, and the important idea that the therapist is there to catalyze the changes and help the family learn how to carry on this process alone should be emphasized. The therapist may temporarily be extremely active and directive but always with the end in mind that the family needs to learn how to monitor and direct itself. The therapist discourages any long-term reliance on outside "experts" and challenges and educates the family to take charge of itself in more gratifying ways. Some families may use the therapist's active and directive approach to resist change; therefore, a paradoxical strategy may be needed.

Ms. E, age 21, and her brother, age 16, were angry at their mother's insistence on continuing family evaluation. The therapist, at the end of the evaluation, "agreed" with Ms. E that change was perhaps not possible *now* and that she *may* go on having her symptoms. Ms. E was so surprised at the therapist's "dismissal" of the family and at the "permission" that she called the next day to set up another appointment for the family.

The strategy of shifting the areas of responsibility for change from the therapist to the family worked in this case, but judgment and skill are needed for such a maneuver to be successful; otherwise it can easily backfire.

Crisis Intervention

In an acute situation family "first aid" may be indicated. This would be analogous to a serious medical emergency in which primary efforts would be directed toward maintaining vital body functions, stopping any loss of blood, and providing for supportive conditions until the system stabilizes. At such a time, no definitive reconstructive or elective procedures can be undertaken.

For family emergencies attention must be given to the carrying out of necessary family tasks, including the basic provision of food, clothing, and shelter. Physiological needs, such as sleep, may require professional intervention, and outside sources of help (relatives, friends, other agencies) may need to be utilized. Behavioral controls and at least a modicum of emotional stability should be sought while an evaluation is made of the "last straw" that resulted in the acute family disequilibrium. Every effort should be made to eliminate, contain, buffer, understand, or reconceptualize this factor, so as to allow the family to return quickly to its former level.

After the acute crisis has passed, further intervention may not be needed or desired. Often, however, a new contract (or referral) can be made for ongoing treatment with new goals.

Active Exploration of Alternatives; Behavioral and Emotional Rehearsal

Sometimes families need to be given permission to consider alternative patterns to those they have been living with or feel they will be facing in the future. The mere raising of such an issue can be a liberating experience. A middle-aged couple, facing the oncoming empty-nest syndrome in which their parental role will be sharply curtailed, may find it exhilarating to consider the idea of rethinking their marital contract and marital roles. Once such a door has been opened by the therapist, the couple may quickly find that they are able to proceed on their own.

Couples who have secretly thought about separating but have never dared to make such ideas explicit may at first feel threatened by a therapist who openly suggests this as one way out of their situation. With a skillful therapist such a couple can come to face ideas and feelings they have been too afraid or guilty to express before.

During the therapy sessions family members should be given the strength to express themselves more openly to one another than before. The therapist should make it safe for them to do so but then should also explore with the family the subsequent consequences of such openness. Repeated rehearsals of possible consequences may be required before more open communication can be established as being safe.

When a child is the "problem," rehearsals aimed at strengthening the *parental* coalition may be essential. The parents may be undermining each other's authority, and this is often related to weaknesses in their *marital* relationship.

Homework and Family Tasks

For therapy to be effective, changes must be noted outside the treatment sessions. To speed up this process and to maximize the effect of the limited number of available sessions, family members can be asked to carry out "homework" assignments. These should be relatively simple and achievable and should bear on those crucial patterns that are the focus of treatment. They may involve, for example, various types of communication exercises. Husband and wife may be requested to practice the negotiating of differences at home. They can be told to make explicit to one another their position on a given issue, with the expectation that the partners repeat to one another their understanding of each other's position.

Interactional and behavioral exercises are often helpful. For example, two estranged family members can be asked to jointly plan and carry out a dyadic activity that they would enjoy and to report about it at the next treatment session. Negative injunctions, such as the prohibition of recriminatory dredging up of the past, should also be kept in mind.

Sometimes a family member can be aided to clarify or modify an important outside relationship, such as with that member's family of origin. A wife who has felt squeezed between her love for her husband and her mother's disapproval of him can be asked to start talking to her mother about this in an attempt to resolve the issue.

Videotape and One-Way Mirror

Videotape playback during sessions can help families come to a rapid realization of interactional sequences and responses. Gaining mastery over new processes can be speeded up, and, eventually, with training, the family learns to be its own therapist, especially if this technique is available as homework.

Observation of family transactions through a one-way mirror can aid family members to quickly recognize and alter unwanted patterns.

Both of these techniques allow family members to take distance from the family system and can be especially worthwhile in giving them a sense of a growing mastery over their lives.

Making Contracts

To encourage rapid transactional changes, explicit contracts between family members can be negotiated by the therapist. The mother may be asked to agree to let her teenage daughter stay out until midnight on weekends in return for the daughter's having all her homework completed by then. Such contracts can bring a temporary halt to bickering, can offer a model for mutually satisfying negotiations, and can allow the family sessions to get on with other issues.

CONCLUSION

Family therapy has proven clinically to be an effective modality for helping troubled families and their members. We can infer from outcome studies on individual psychotherapy that there is reason to believe that brief family therapy may be as useful as long-term therapy. The challenge for the future lies in investigating this belief and in more clearly elucidating those situations and those strategies that fit most appropriately with the brief family therapy model.

Work and Rest by Jean Charlot, private collection.

16

Family Treatment and the Psychiatric Hospital

OBJECTIVES

- To understand the role of the family in the psychiatric hospitalization of one of its members
- To be able to treat such a family with the goal of preventing rehospitalization and of reaching the highest functional level for the identified patient
- To contrast inpatient with outpatient family therapy
- To become aware of family approaches and alternatives to hospitalization

INTRODUCTION

The traditional view of a family with one person in a psychiatric hospital showed its members as, at best, purveyors of historical information to the social worker and as payers of the bills. At worst they were seen as malignant, pathogenic individuals who had played a major role in causing the patient's symptoms and who tended to make nuisances of themselves by interfering with the patient's treatment by the hospital staff.

The staff acted in *loco parentis* and often inappropriately blamed the family for the patient's symptoms. The family was frequently not allowed to visit during the early part of the hospitalization. The psychiatric hospital was associated with much fear and stigma, and in many cases families were only too happy to stay away. Prior to the availability of effective somatic treatments, hospital stays were much longer and already fragile family ties were broken.

At the time of discharge, the hospital staff members would tend to attempt to remove the patient from the family setting because they viewed the family as an adversary. In the authors' experience, such efforts are ill advised and usually backfire. The emotional bonds that tie the patient to his family are not easily overcome by family therapists in the hospital. Until considerable change has taken place, such efforts are often doomed to failure.

In other cultures families are sometimes considered a vital part of the psychiatric hospitalization of any of their members. Because of a scarcity of trained professionals, families are needed in the hospital to care for the needs of the identified patient. They, in fact, often stay with the patient in or near the hospital. The assumption in other cultures is that the patient is an integral part of the family network, and it is unthinkable that the patient would return anywhere else but to the family.[1]

Over the last ten years there has been an increasing use of the family model in inpatient settings, but not without problems:[2]

Regrettably, however, the family therapy literature is not particularly helpful to those working on inpatient units; such concepts as "defining the family as the patient" tend to alienate both the medical staff of an institution and the already overwhelmingly guilt-ridden families. The polarized approaches of family therapists, who generally operate on a "system" model, which overemphasizes interactional variables, and of psychiatrists, who generally operate on a "medical" model, which overemphasizes individual variables, disregard the complex and complementary interplay, biological, psychodynamic, and interactional factors. . . . A collaborative relationship between families and the hospital staff could be developed by the establishment of treatment contracts and by combining these two models, thus accepting the patient's illness as the focus *while* recognizing the importance of family variables.[3]

FUNCTION OF THE PSYCHIATRIC HOSPITAL VIS-A-VIS THE FAMILY

A modern function of the hospital in relation to the families of psychiatric patients includes temporarily removing the identified patient from a family environment—when it seems no longer possible to contain the situation by other means. In acute individual and family crises, and in emergency situations, hospitalization may be a means of decreasing behavioral eruptions. This may offer substantial relief to a desperate family that is headed for serious deterioration. This enforced separation is undertaken with the goal of evaluating and changing the conditions so as to improve the family's patterns of interaction.[4]

Hospitalization can also be used to involve the family members in a controlled, structured setting that allows for continual observation and discussion of relevant family patterns. This permits establishment of a motivation for seeking marital and family treatment after the patient's return to a better functioning family setting. It may also set the stage for consideration of separation, where appropriate, in deadlocked marital or parent–child interactions.

Involvement of the family also makes possible the avoidance of staff over-identification with the patient against the family, the reduction of the stigma of psychiatric hospitalization, and the establishment of motivation for aftercare following hospitalization. It allows family members to stay together when one member has to be hospitalized, as in postpartum psychosis, when mother and child are housed on the same ward.

FAMILY INFLUENCES ON THE HOSPITALIZATION PROCESS

The process leading to hospitalization and the family's role in it have been understood in a variety of ways.

1. The family is in a crisis and the hospitalization is an attempt to solve the crisis.[5-7] In this connection some couples have described the outcome of a psychotic episode and their attempts to cope with it as a strongly positive experience for them.[8]
2. The family extrudes the identified patient from the family in an attempt to solve the crisis.[9]

The M family consisted of mother, boyfriend, and two teenage daughters. The eldest daughter had anorexia nervosa. The other sibling was functioning well in high school. The mother had long-standing chronic paranoid schizophrenia and was extremely dependent on her own mother. She had been divorced about ten years previously and had finally found a boyfriend.

After the mother formed a relationship with her boyfriend and was seriously considering marriage, she began to argue with the elder daughter more frequently. The daughter began eating less and became paranoid. The mother then contacted a pediatrician, stating that the daughter was seriously ill and needed hospitalization. The mother reported she was unable to take care of the identified patient's demands because she was fearful of losing her boyfriend since doing so would prevent her from spending time with him. The pediatrician hospitalized the daughter.

This case illustrates how one family member can extrude another member from the family in order to take care of his or her own needs. The mother was afraid of losing her boyfriend and therefore restructured the family by having the identified patient hospitalized.

3. The family uses the hospital to get treatment for a member other than the identified patient. The hospitalized member is not necessarily the only "sick" one (or at times, not even the "sickest" one) in the family. A family approach allows for the observation and evaluation of all significant others, with appropriate treatment (including medication) for the group and for the

nonpatient individuals who may require it. Therapists concentrating on the treatment of one individual may entirely overlook even gross, florid psychological disturbance in a close relative. When therapists views their role as that of therapists to a family unit, this sort of blind spot is less likely to occur.

4.   The family uses the hospital as a resource to regain a "lost" member. For example, a father who drinks and is never home is finally convinced to go into a hospital because of his drinking. The family's motivation is to have him back as a functioning father and spouse; but the family may also need to keep him "sick" for its own needs.

5.   The hospital is used as a neutral arena to change long-standing maladaptive patterns of family functioning.

If these assumptions about the influences of hospitalization are valid, then it follows that in such cases the treatment program is inadequate unless it includes the family.

GUIDELINES FOR RECOMMENDING FAMILY THERAPY IN A HOSPITAL SETTING

The guidelines for recommending family therapy in a hospital setting are similar to those described in Chapter 19. If the family is present and available, it is more efficacious to utilize family therapy than to withold it.[10] In most cases the identified patient's illness is so severe that, by necessity, the patient is dependent on the family; furthermore, it may be difficult to change the identified patient's hospital and posthospital functioning without involving the family.[11]

THE PROCESS OF FAMILY TREATMENT BY THE HOSPITAL TEAM[12-15]

The process of family treatment by the hospital team involves the following steps (not all are necessary in each case). Treatment should be individualized and fitted to the needs of the particular family.

Involving the Family

Work with the family should start very early, preferably prior to hospitalization, when the family is trying to arrange admission, or certainly by the time of actual admission. Many hospital personnel have had the experience of beginning discharge planning late in the course of hospitalization, only to discover at that time that the family, implicitly or explicitly, resists having the patient at home. It usually has to be pointed out to the family that hospital treatment of the identified patient involves (or requires) treatment of all family members. This also may be made a condition of admission. A family representative may be appointed to be the central communicating link with the primary therapist in the hospital.

Evaluating the Family

Evaluations of such families may indicate the following:

1. In some families the family system is contributing to the symptoms of the identified patient, and treatment of the family may "cure" the problems of the identified patient.
2. In some families treatment of the family unit will *not* help the identified patient's symptoms, although the family is an important factor in producing the symptoms of the identified patient.
3. In those families that are *not* thought to be directly related to causing the symptoms, treatment of the family unit may nevertheless result in more effective treatment of the identified patient. For example, a schizophrenic patient who requires medication may not take it without the cooperation of the family (see Chapter 12).

Redefining the Problem

After family evaluation the therapist may next help to redefine the problem with the family. Previously family members have clung to the view that "this is all Junior's problem" or "Junior has no problem, he needs a rest." The family therapist can point out the structural and functional problems of the family in terms of role, communication, and so forth.

Setting Goals

In defining the crucial short-term goals, it is emphasized that the family therapist will not attempt to solve all the problems that the family has ever had but will focus *only* (or primarily) on the core problems, such as

1. Problems that brought the patient into the hospital
2. Problems that are crucial in the maintenance of the identified patient's problems or the family disequilibrium
3. Problems that are important for the posthospital period.

When the identified patient has a psychosis, short-term goals may include the following:[16]

1. The patient and the family are able to accept the fact that the patient has had a psychosis.

2. The family is willing to identify some of the probable precipitating stresses in the patient's life at the time the psychosis occurred.
3. The family will attempt to generalize from the specific past stresses to the identification of future stresses to which the patient and the family are likely to be vulnerable.
4. The family will attempt to do some planning on how to minimize or avoid these future stresses.

In such therapy the patient and significant others can be helped to use the events of the psychosis, rather than sealing them over and deflecting attention away from the psychotic episode.

Increasing Communication

Increased communication between the family members is almost always valuable. How amazing it is that impaired families rarely sit down together to discuss their problems. The hospital is one place where this can and should be done.

Changing the Family

The family therapist should begin to help the family make the needed changes in terms of role, function, and separations. Focus should be on the issues that will allow the identified patient to return home to the family and community. For example, a family therapist may or may not suggest that the identified patient live with someone else. Changes in roles, may be suggested; for example, the father should begin managing the money rather than the mother. The therapist may suggest the restructuring of family relationships. The degree and extent of the changes will be limited by the amount of time available for hospitalization.

Connecting to Aftercare

Finally after evaluating the family, redefining the problems, increasing communication, suggesting family changes, and working on the precipitants and crucial issues, the therapist will attempt to connect the family to posthospital family therapy resources. It cannot be over emphasized that the purpose of hospitalization is to help the patient and the family feel and function better *in the community, not only in the hospital*. The hospital staff often loses sight of the crucial issue of helping the family with posthospital treatment. Planning for this should start early in the hospitalization.

Because one of the goals of hospitalization is to improve the functioning of the identified patient and the family, family therapy sets the stage for such a change after completion of the hospital stay. It allows for unadaptive family patterns to be changed in the hospital and to be tried out prior to discharge.[17] It prevents family resistance to having the identified patient at home. Most importantly, it enables families who might ordinarily resist therapy to start treatment. Thus when the identified patient leaves the hospital, family treatment should continue. Clinical impressions indicate that such family treatment may decrease the risk of subsequent hospitalization.

After the chronic patient's symptoms decrease, a choice has to be made as to whether to (1) keep the patient in a hospital or move him to a day hospital; (2) suggest that the patient return to live with the family; or (3) refer the patient to a foster home, residential setting, or halfway house.

Foster homes, compared to the milieu of state hospitals for chronic patients, may not be a panacea.[18] Both hospital patients and foster home patients may have reduction in symptoms. Foster home residents may shift toward "passivity, characterized by loss of vigor, determination, inner drive, and interests." The day hospital patients often have greater socialization opportunities than those in foster homes. Working with the family, although difficult, time-consuming, and painfully slow, in the long run will often be the best way for increasing functional improvement for the hospital patient.

A case illustrating the family treatment process in a psychiatric hospital is the following:

In the L family the father was a 40-year-old lawyer married to a 40-year-old housewife. They had met while he was in law school. Mr. L was described as a self-made man who had left home after the death of his mother and father in his early teens and put himself through high school, college, and law school. The patient's mother had escaped Nazi persecution with a few members of her family. She felt that she was lucky to be alive. The predominant credo in her family was that "if you work hard enough, anything can happen."

When they met Mr. L was not entirely sure that he wanted to be married but believed he would like the stability that marriage offered. Mrs. L felt that she could finally stop running and achieve the security that she always wanted. Shortly after marriage Mrs. L became pregnant. Although they were both contraceptively informed, Mrs. L decided to let the pregnancy happen, because that would solidify the marriage.

Unfortunately their son, the identified patient, was from the start shy, withdrawn, clinging, demanding, and unable to achieve the developmental milestones of either his peers or his subsequent siblings.

This caused Mr. L, who was disappointed in his son, to intensify further his life-long pattern of working hard and leaving the childrearing to Mrs. L. Mrs. L responded by making her son "the focus of my life." She felt that if she worked hard enough, he could catch up to his peers. The boy later developed hallucinations, delusions, and a variety of school problems.

The identified patient, now 16 years old, was presented at the hospital with an intensification of symptoms to the point that Mr. L was having trouble in his law practice. The treatment process included helping to redefine the problem for the family. Some of the symptoms of the identified patient were related to the problems his mother and father were having. (Previously mother and father had not acknowledged that there were any difficulties.) It was emphasized to them that the therapist would not attempt to treat all the problems of their marriage or of their families of origin but would focus on the problems that brought their son into the hospital.

In this case the crucial issue was the widening emotional and functional distance between the parents. The treatment goal was to help the parents find ways to tolerate spending more time together. At the same time the patient was treated for his symptoms, using a combination of individual and group psychotherapy as well as medication. Communication between the family members was increased.

Mother and father were encouraged to share the parenting of their son. In order for the mother to do this, a plan was designed for her, involving working and "trying harder" to find ways for the father to spend more time at home.

After two months of hospitalization, arrangements were made for continuing family therapy. Signs of impending exacerbation of illness were then pointed out to the family, such as, increased withdrawal or paranoia.

TECHNIQUES OF FAMILY TREATMENT BY THE HOSPITAL TEAM

Timing

Family therapy should start in the decision-making process leading to hospitalization. The family will often refuse to be involved in conjoint family therapy in the hospital until the symptoms of the identified patient have totally cleared. Some family therapists, however, believe that family therapy should begin immediately, even if the patient is very symptomatic, or absent altogether. Other therapists choose to start therapy once the acute symptoms start to diminish.[19]

Family therapy should usually last throughout the entire hospitalization. The nature of the sessions will depend on the goals and the length of hospitalization. There are some families that need to be seen 3 times a week for 2 hours, others once a month for 15 minutes. Progress can be gauged by noting the process of family therapy sessions, their consequences, and the effects of any home visits by the patient.

Staffing

Who should do the family therapy? The primary hospital therapist is the one in the best position to do the family therapy, because he or she has the best overall grasp of the case. The advantages of one therapist doing both the individual and the family therapy far outweigh the disadvantages. Time constraints may not always make this possible, however, and alternative solutions may have to be devised.

How can the need for maximal communication among staff members be reconciled with the need for confidentiality of the patient and the therapist?

Communication between staff seems crucial for effective treatment. The family should be told that the therapist will use all the material that is available in both the individual and family contacts to help the family function better. (This issue has been discussed in greater detail in other parts of this book.)

How about a cotherapist? Some therapists believe that family therapy in a hospital setting is the most difficult kind of psychotherapy. They recommend that every family therapist have a cotherapist to share the emotional strains of such therapy. Cotherapy in a hospital setting may be more practical than in a private office practice. One member of the ward staff can be assigned as liaison to the family and should be available to the family at times mututally convenient, such as on nights and weekends.

Family Techniques and
Their Hospital Utilization

A variety of family therapy techniques are available for use in the hospital setting. These include:

1.   Individual family therapy
2.   Multiple family-group therapy
3.   Family psychodrama
4.   Family sculpture

As discussed in Chapter 9, both psychodrama and family sculpture are nonverbal techniques that are often more helpful than cognitive techniques when treating a hospitalized (i.e. often nonverbal) sample of patients.

It is rare for family treatment to be the primary therapy for hospitalized patients. Usually for psychotic patients it is prescribed along with medication and other rehabilitative therapies. For nonpsychotic patients it is usually part of a treatment package consisting of individual therapy, rehabilitation therapy, and other interventions.

Family therapy has been carried out by all members of the hospital treatment team. Nurses, at visiting or other scheduled times, can meet with the patient and family. Occupational and recreational therapists can utilize family treatment. They can prescribe activities for the family, such as preparing a meal together or going on a picnic together. These professionals have crucial roles in changing long-standing behavior patterns in the family system.

The hospital milieu is especially advantageous for observing and pointing out family interaction patterns. For example, if an adolescent child is paranoid about the nursing staff, it may be demonstrated to him that this is similar to the way he reacts to his mother. Accurate, on-the-spot observation of the family may reveal that the patient has some good reasons for his symptoms.*

---

*Family diagnosis and therapy in the context of rehabilitation therapy, psychology, social work, and psychiatric nursing are described in Chapter 17.

OTHER TYPES OF FAMILY INVOLVEMENT AS AN ALTERNATIVE TO PSYCHIATRIC HOSPITALIZATION

At times of family crisis, psychiatric hospitalization of a family member is one solution. With the gradual shift of psychiatric services out of the hospital and into the community, other alternatives have emerged. Schizophrenic patients, in some cases, can be kept out of hospitals altogether by sending the treatment team to see them in their homes.[20, 21] Day hospitalization with a focus on family treatment is another alternative to psychiatric hospital admission.[22] Day hospitals also have moved toward utilizing family therapy as a primary method of treatment. The population of such settings is chronic, and difficulties with family relationships are a major problem. Individual psychotherapy has been replaced by a shift to family interventions to stabilize the patient or prevent deterioration in his level of functioning.

In the L family there were two brothers, A and M. The father had died and the mother was the grieving widow. One son lived by himself, managing marginally, while the other son came to a day hospital for management of his schizophrenia.

Treatment at the day hospital was oriented around helping him to obtain volunteer work. Whenever the volunteer counselor and his therapist at the day hospital came close to finding a job placement for him, they noticed that the patient would start screaming, become paranoid, and collapse on the street. Further investigation of these symptoms revealed that on the nights before the patient was to go to his appointments, his mother would, in painstakingly minute detail, describe her anxiety about not knowing his whereabouts, and how her heart would not pump as a result. She told him that she would not want to stop him from leaving but at the same time needed to know that he was safe in the day hospital, rather than at some volunteer job where she could not call him.

This case is typical of many chronic patients whose level of function is marginal. Any change in that level is often perceived as a threat by the family.

Often a change in the balance of family forces precipitates the request for hospitalization, and understanding the shift can result in strategies to prevent extrusion of the identified patient.[7] Although hospitalization can be avoided, continued family work is needed to change behavior patterns that prevent the identified patient from functioning.

REFERENCES

1. Bell J, Bell E: Family participation in hospital care for children. Children 17: 154– 157, 1970
2. Harbin HT: Families and hospitals: Collusion or cooperation? Am J Psychiatry 135:1496– 1499,1978

3. Anderson CM: Family intervention with severely disturbed inpatients. Arch Gen Psychiatry 34:697–702, 1977

4. Rabiner E, Malminski H, Gralnick A: Conjoint family therapy in the inpatient setting, in Gralnick A (ed): The Psychiatric Hospital as a Therapeutic Instrument. New York, Brunner/Mazel, 1969, pp 160–177

5. Sampson H, Messinger S, Towne RD: Family processes and becoming a mental patient. Am J Sociol 68:88–96, 1962

6. Sampson H, Messinger S, Towne RD: The mental hospital and family adaptations. Psychiatric Q 36:704–719, 1962

7. Langsley D, Kaplan D: The Treatment of Families in Crisis. New York, Grune & Stratton, 1968

8. Dupont R, Ryder R, Grunebaum H: Unexpected results of psychosis in marriage. Am J Psychiatry 128:735–739, 1971

9. Bursten B: Family dynamics, the sick role, and medical hospital admissions. Fam Process 4:206–216, 1965

10. Gould E, Glick ID: The effects of family presence and family therapy on outcome of hospitalized schizophrenic patients. Fam Process 16:503–510, 1977

11. Vaughn CE, Leff JP: The influence of family and social factors on the course of psychiatric illness: A comparison of schizophrenic and depressed neurotic patients. Br J Psychiatry 129:125–137, 1976

12. Burks H, Serrano A: The use of family therapy and brief hospitalization. Dis Nerv Syst 26:804–806, 1965

13. Fleck S: Psychotherapy of families of hospitalized patients, in Masserman J (ed): Current Psychiatric Therapies, vol III. New York, Grune & Stratton, 1963, pp 211–218

14. Laquer HP, La Burt HA: Family organization on a modern state hospital ward. Mental Hygiene 48:544–551, 1964

15. Lennard H, Epstein LJ: Effects of psychoactive drugs on family behavior. Am J Orthopsychiatry 38:236 (abstr) 1968

16. Goldstein MJ, Rodnick EH, Evans JR, et al: Drug and family therapy in the aftercare of acute schizophrenics. Arch Gen Psychiatry 35:1169–1177, 1978

17. Tauber G: Prevention of posthospital relapse through treatment of relatives. J of Hillside Hospital 13:158–169, 1964

18. Murphy H: (Reported by Trainor D) No clinical advantages found in foster home care. Psychiatric News, August 6, 1975

19. Guttman H: A contraindication for family therapy: The prepsychotic or postpsychotic young adult and his parents. Arch Gen Psychiatry 29:352–355, 1973

20. Pasamanick B, Scarpitti F, Dinitz S: Schizophrenics in the Community. New York, Appleton-Century-Crofts, 1967

21. Davis A, Dinitz S, Pasamanick B: The prevention of hospitalization in schizophrenia: Five years after an experimental program. Am J Orthopsychiatry 42:375–388, 1972

22. Zwerling I, Mendelsohn M: Initial family reactions to day hospitalization. Fam Process 4:50–63, 1965

Family, by Rachel Glick.

17
The Family Model and Other Fields

OBJECTIVES

- To enable the professionals in related fields to adapt the family model to their particular needs
- To enable the family therapist to understand the needs of other fields and work collaboratively in using the family model

INTRODUCTION

The 1974 Nathan B. Ackerman Memorial Conference held in Venezuela had as its theme "The Growing Edge of Family Therapy." The theme was selected because, during the last decade, there had been an increasing adaptation of the family model in a variety of fields, seemingly unrelated to the family. These fields included (but were not limited to) medicine and its subspecialties, the legal profession, and various mental-health disciplines. The authors present here a summary of recent material concerning the adaptation of the family model as utilized in other disciplines.

THE FAMILY MODEL AND FAMILY MEDICINE
With Robert S. Hoffman, M.D. and Sanford R. Weimer, M.D.

Introduction: The Role of the Family in Family Medicine

In caring for the whole family the physician not only gains in knowledge, but also enlarges his scope of action. Whenever the situation requires it, he can change his focus from individual to family and back again. In the many situations in which the illness of an individual is accompanied by family dysfunction, he can quite readily direct his actions to the family as a whole. The family doctor not only knows about the family—he knows them. This personal knowledge can be put to good use.[1]

Related to the increasing interest in family practice among medical students, there has been a rediscovery of the family's role in family medicine and in primary care.[2,3] Several studies of service patterns in family medicine have revealed that only 15 percent of all patients who come for help have a problem that fits the medical model—for example, otitis media. In contrast the remaining 85 percent have problems that relate to complicated psychosocial factors instead— for example, the patient who complains of "tiredness," when the problem is actually a marital problem. Similarly exacerbations of chronic physical illnesses may be initiated or maintained by family disturbance. To manage this large group of patients effectively, it is important to understand the principle that a presenting somatic complaint may reflect a problem in the family system. The following case should make this point clear.

In the D family Mrs. D was the identified patient by virtue of the fact that she had had seven episodes of diabetic acidosis in the last six months. Medication and dietary control had not decreased the frequency of these episodes. After the seventh episode the physician, prompted by an offhand remark of Mrs. D's unmarried daughter who lived at home that "these episodes always seem to occur after a weekend when the family is all together," called in the entire family.

It was discovered that Sunday was feast day in this Italian family and that the mother prepared a large meal, sampling all the dishes. An important part of the disintegrating relationship with her husband was preparing and eating large meals, and he felt this maintained his shaky status within his family. The diabetic acidosis seemed directly related to the mother's going off her diet on Sundays.

Management included a preliminary meeting with the entire family to clarify the situation. Separate meetings with the couple were then arranged. The physician encouraged the family to work out its own solutions. Mrs. D's married daughter began to prepare meals in her home rather than in the mother's. The elder son moved out of the house. An eight-month follow-up revealed no subsequent episodes of acidosis, and Mr. and Mrs. D's relationship improved.

This case illustrates how important it is for the family physician to see the entire family in order to make a correct diagnosis and delineate an appropriate treatment plan. Evaluation in this case would have been inadequate had only the identified patient been seen. The identified patient would have continued to go into diabetic acidosis had not a management and treatment plan been worked out that involved the entire family.

Family Interaction Patterns
and Medical Consultation

A number of recent studies have suggested that certain patterns of family interaction influence a family member's decision to seek medical help, using symptoms such as colds or urinary frequency as the "ticket of admission."[4] In one-third of these families, both patients and their relatives in "neurotic" families have been found to have higher attendance rates and a higher incidence of physical illness than patients and relatives from "nonneurotic" families. Illness of whatever kind in one family member affects other members and in turn affects their physical and emotional well being.

With the growth of liaison and consultation psychiatry, it has become evident that an important part of such consultations should be evaluation and management of the family and their input into the problem of the identified patient.

In the X family Mr. X was a diamond merchant; his wife was a stockbroker. They were both in their sixties and had been married 20 years or so. Mr. X had long-standing hypertension. As the wife's career developed and their children moved out of the house, the couple became distant and communication markedly decreased. Mr. X became more and more despondent, finding that his business no longer interested him the way it had when he was younger.

Just prior to hospitalization he called his wife to talk about how "blue" he was feeling; she told him she could not talk to him because she had a conference. Soon afterwards he swallowed 100 antihypertensive pills, then again called his wife and the police. He was brought into the intensive care unit of a general hospital. The psychiatric consultant focused on the hypertension and the acute episodes but did not involve the identified patient's wife. Mrs. X was "too busy" with her job to come to the hospital. He was discharged after three days only to make another suicide attempt two months later.

At this time the family therapist, working with the staff of the consultation service, had the wife come in for a joint interview. During this session Mr. and Mrs. X were able to lay out their difficulties for the first time and decided to enter marital therapy in which they could pursue a realistic plan to bring them closer.

Relationships between the Family System
And Somatic Illness

EFFECT OF THE FAMILY SYSTEM ON
SOMATIC ILLNESS[5]

Family researchers have observed that the initiation or maintenance of some somatic illnesses (e.g., ulcerative colitis) can be correlated with certain problems in family functioning (e.g., symbiosis between the mother and the identified patient). It has further been demonstrated that the onset of somatic illness is correlated with life changes directly related to family functioning—for example, death of a spouse or close relative, divorce or separation, jail term, personal illness or injury, or even marriage itself.[6] It is hypothesized that a breakdown in family homeostasis causes development of somatic symptoms in the member of the family who is most vulnerable at that time. The exact causal mechanisms are not well understood.

The N family, in which the maternal grandmother was dominant, experienced major changes when the maternal grandfather died (he was the primary support for his wife). The married daughter, mother of two, developed tuberculosis and became depressed. Her husband then developed an ulcer. Later, when a son rejoined the family, the mother got better; when he left again the mother developed arthritis. The mother, in this case, seemed peculiarly susceptible to somatic illness when important men in her life left the family. This seemed to be connected with her inability to deal with these separations in a more straightforward way, such as a grieving reaction.

There are many physical disorders in which psychological factors are believed to play an important contributing role (e.g., peptic ulcer). In contrast to conversion disorders, these disorders are characterized by objective signs of physical dysfunction, usually a single-organ system (e.g., gastrointestinal) that is under autonomic innervation. The physiological changes involved are those that normally accompany certain emotional states (e.g., increased gastric acid secretion during excitement); but changes are more intense and sustained, eventually resulting in structural changes or demonstrable and persistent alterations of physiological function.

It has been suggested that such families are rigid, that the illness occurs after family stress events, that the illness stabilizes the family system, and that the mothers "label" the illness while the fathers collude in the process.[7] It is thought that, in fact, the profound emotional ties within the family determine the degree of impact on the individual's autonomic nervous system. Often the illness seems to serve as a mechanism to avoid looking at problems that exist within the family. For example, in the W family, whenever Mr. W wanted to talk about the budget, Mrs. W experienced a recurrence of migraine. Whenever she wanted to talk about his long business hours, he developed an asthmatic attack.

As an illustration of these mechanisms, one study found a correlation between asthmatic children and their mothers.[8] Asthmatic children were divided into two groups—those with strongly allergic features and those with weakly allergic features. The mothers also fell into two groups. The children with strongly allergic features had relatively "nonneurotic" mothers, whereas the children with nonallergic features had highly "neurotic" mothers. Such studies suggest that a combination of constitutional and family factors may be necessary for the development of some somatic illnesses.

A family-oriented treatment approach has been developed to treat intractable asthma that can serve as a model for family interventions in other illnesses (e.g., brittle diabetes) thought to have important psychological determinants. Liebman and coworkers have organized this plan into three phases.[9]

Phase One is concerned with the alleviation of the symptoms of asthma to prevent its use by the patient as a means of detouring family conflicts. Once the symptoms are reduced, there is more freedom and flexibility available to promote change within the family.

Phase Two consists of identifying and changing those patterns in the family and extrafamilial environment that tend to exacerbate and perpetuate the symptoms.

Phase Three consists of interventions to change the structure and functioning of the family system to promote lasting disengagement of the patient in order to prevent a recurrence of the symptoms or the development of a new symptoms barrier.

Treatment is oriented around an operant-conditioning paradigm as well as family therapy interventions. Although the numbers of cases are small (14), follow-up was anywhere from 1 to 5 years and showed "good results." Further controlled research is needed to evaluate the effectiveness of this technique.

Several case reports have suggested that anorexia nervosa is also a reaction of the identified patient to problems in the family.[10-12] Family therapy is used in the service of changing those patterns in the family that prevent the identified patient's regaining lost weight and becoming more independent. As in treatment of the asthmatic patient, Liebman, Minuchin, and others have worked out a treatment program that uses family therapy in conjunction with other treatments to deal with the symptoms of the identified patient.[13] To give an idea of how this model works for somatic illness, the authors have listed here some principles of the treatment program.[14]

1. A complete medical evaluation to rule out organic causes for the anorexia and weight loss
2. Informal lunch sessions involving the patient and the family psychiatrist to assess the degree of negativism and anorexia
3. Application of an operant-reinforcement paradigm to initiate weight gain in the hospital
4. Family therapy lunch sessions to accelerate weight gain
5. Discharge from the hospital
6. Application of an outpatient operant-reinforcement paradigm as a family task to prevent weight loss
7. Outpatient family therapy to change the structure and functioning of the family to prevent relapses

EFFECT OF SOMATIC ILLNESS ON THE FAMILY SYSTEM

Primary care physicians have long recognized that any illness in an individual family member, especially when chronic or severe, will profoundly affect the family system. Changes in an individual's role function, ambulation, earning power, sex drive, or independence inevitably will evoke more or less adaptive coping mechanisms on the part of the rest of the family. The following statement, given by the wife of a dialysis patient with chronic renal disease, is an example of the above:

> There is always tension between us because when he is not feeling well, which is very often. He is very irritable and takes out all his frustrations on me. I try to understand him, but it is very difficult. I'm a very sensitive person. When he gets extremely irritable, he sometimes wants to kill me. . . . Sometimes I really don't think I can make it with him, but I'm trying to make the best of what we have because I love him so much.[15]

Such situations may produce significant emotional difficulties, exacerbations of physical illness, or new functional complaints in the patient's family. They may even lead to frank disruption of the family itself.

In the B family, the father, who was in his forties, had long-standing rheumatoid arthritis. The mother, also in her forties, had long-standing ulcerative colitis. Both parents had these diseases for over 20 years. The illnesses became more severe, and family homeostasis began to change. When the mother was found to have a precancerous lesion and the father's arthritis began not to respond to medication, the following events occurred: The father became hopelessly depressed, and he felt that nothing could change. The mother believed she would die soon and felt unable to do anything for the family. The oldest daughter, in graduate school, became despondent and felt incapable of helping her parents, since she had always leaned on them for support and direction. A younger son escaped the situation by dropping out of college for an extended trip around the world. The youngest son became the "identified patient" when he started using drugs and was caught shoplifting. Prior to this he had been a "model child." The entire family agreed that there was now a pervasive sense of withdrawal, noncommunication, and "giving up." It was at this point that they sought help for the youngest son, and an alert family physician was able to discern the serious family difficulties.

In most medical practices there are many patients who are suffering from cancer, arthritis, migraines, low-back syndromes, and end-stage vital organ disease. These unfortunate people often function poorly despite the best medical efforts available. In many cases the family believes that if the patient only tried harder, he or she could do better. As a result the patient is scapegoated. The family physician, using family resources, can aid such patients to function significantly better. The family not only can be reeducated but can be helped in finding ways of assisting the patient to cope better with his or her illness.

What the family physician can be alert to is a shift in family homeostasis arising from the physical illness of one member. For example, when a grandmother, recently confined to the house by increasing arthritis, begins helping around the kitchen, the mother may feel intruded on and begin yelling at the children or spouse. The family physician can be sensitive to these kinds of changes and, using the family systems model, help the family to cope with the changes.

Use of Family Systems Concepts and Techniques by the Family Physician

The initial approach to any patient with significant somatic illness should include a preliminary exploration of the family situation. In some cases this may be brief and a few questions posed to the patient may suffice. In other cases, interviews with other family members may be required. Relevant data would include:

1. The "illness onset situation" (i.e., changes in family interactions or stresses among family members that may be contributing to the initiation or exacerbation of the illness)
2. Effects of the patient's illness on other family members
3. How the illness affects the daily routines of family life (e.g., the assignment of household responsibilities, the family financial situation, and so on)
4. The ability of family members to respond to the patient's illness in a helpful manner

The last item should be of special concern to the physician when noncompliance with the treatment plan is suspected. An example of noncompliance would be failure to take prescribed medications or to keep medical appointments, which in some cases is traceable to a family member "sabotaging" treatment because of a need to deny or minimize the patient's illness.

Using systems concepts the physician is no longer caught in the bind of having to think in terms of cause and effect. It is not either the family using one member's illness to avoid conflict *or* the family reacting to a member's illness. Rather there is a system with multiple vectors operating, of which one member's illness is a part. The linear thinking of "cause and effect" is too simplistic for families and often leads to incorrect conclusions and treatments.

In most cases difficulties in these areas can be effectively managed by a concerned family physician utilizing a few basic principles of family treatment. The authors suggest the following:

1. See the entire family together, rather than relying on the patient as the intermediary.
2. Encourage the family members to discuss their reactions to the patient's illness and its effect on family life. This sounds simplistic but can exert tremendous influence, expecially in families whose members are unaccustomed to sharing family concerns openly with one another. Even if no further psychological techniques are employed, such discussions may exert beneficial effects.
3. Provide information about the illness to all family members. Such information, if presented only to the patient, may often be distorted (whether intentionally or not) in transmission to the rest of the family, permitting their misconceptions about diagnosis, prognosis, or treatment plan to persist to a

detrimental degree. It is important for the physician to elicit the beliefs, hopes, and fears of each family member and to respond fully to them.

4. Interview the family so that a serious inability to cope with the patient's illness may be revealed in one or more members, either because the stress is too much to bear or because of a coexisting emotional disorder such as depression, schizophrenia, or alcoholism. At times additional supportive interviews with these family members may remedy the situation; at other times referral for psychiatric treatment may be indicated. Family interviews may further reveal the existence of a shared family "myth" revolving around the patient's illness, which is producing a serious degree of distress in the family. For example:

A 45-year-old man with hypertension suffered a mild cerebral vascular accident. By the time of his discharge from the hospital, his focal neurological deficits had cleared and his blood pressure was under good control. On follow-up visits the patient mentioned to his physician that his wife had become cool toward him and that his 14-year-old son had begun exhibiting deliquent behavior. A family interview revealed that the patient's wife and son were extremely afraid that if they irritated or angered the patient in any way he would suffer an immediate rise of blood pressure and a second stroke. The patient himself, previously somewhat submissive toward his wife, seemed to encourage this belief. Due to the myth that "if father gets angry he will die," the power relationships in the family shifted abruptly and communication was sharply diminished. The mother's pent-up and unexpressed resentment increased, which the patient noted with dismay. None of these events was discussed. At this point the 14-year-old son provided a focus of attention (his delinquent behavior) that served to displace his parents concern away from their own difficulties and onto him—that is, he became the newly identified patient.

The family physician requested additional family meetings and encouraged an open discussion of the patient's illness, the fears that it aroused, and its effects on the family life. In the process the physician managed to demythologize the family's belief that disagreement was physically dangerous to the patient and promoted the idea that pent-up negative feelings were actually producing some significant difficulties. After three meetings, in which the above issues were aired, a measure of family homeostasis was restored, the marital relationship improved, and the son's delinquent behavior ceased.

5. Offer practical advice, which is sometimes more effective than attempting to interpret family dynamics, even though an understanding of the latter may be helpful in formulating this advice. If, for example, a temporarily disabled father is becoming despondent over not being the breadwinner and is irritable at being confined to the house all day, the suggestion might be made that he informally tutor his son, who is having difficulties in his high school algebra course. If the father's physical condition permits, he might undertake a long-postponed home improvement project such as constructing a set of bookshelves or a coffee table. Providing this sort of advice requires some improvising on the part of the physician; this is an important facet in the art of family practice.

6. Utilize community agencies in certain situations. For example, the American Heart Association provides a wealth of resources for families of persons who have suffered heart attacks or undergone cardiac surgery, including informal counseling by expatients and discussion groups for patients and their families. Similar organizations exist for patients and families who are learning to deal with pulmonary disorders, diabetes, renal disease, mastectomies, ileostomies, and so on. Sometimes the support and practical advice provided by expatients who have successfully coped with such illnesses or procedures is of equal or greater effectiveness than that which a physician can provide.

7. Realize that if the above measures fail to remedy family difficulties, this may indicate a serious degree of family pathology that may have antedated the physical illness and is, under the current stresses, reaching crisis proportions. In such cases referral to a family therapist may become necessary. Some families may accept such a referral with relief and gratitude. Other families will be highly resistant to such a suggestion, in which case the family physician may find it useful to request a consultation from a family therapist on how to best manage the situation without an actual referral.

The family physician must understand that taking time with patients and their families is equally as important as taking their blood pressure or ordering an expensive battery of laboratory tests. The time the family physician spends with the family can be paid for in the same way as families pay for other services of the family physician, such as a cardiogram. The talk between family and physician is a kind of "medicine" designed to change the family in the same way that digitalis changes heart function. Not every physician will feel comfortable in talking with families, and certainly no physician should be forced into such a situation.

THE FAMILY MODEL
AND PHYSICAL MEDICINE

The Effect of Illness on the Family

When one member of the family has had a cerebrovascular accident, loses a limb, or has another severe injury, there is a corresponding ripple effect on the rest of the family.[16] This loss of function in the one member must be compensated for by other members. This creates changes in structure and roles. Common dysfunctional patterns include:

1. The family does not pick up the function of the ill member.
2. The family withdraws from the ill member. This is especially true if the identified patient is the mother or wife (rather than husband) for reasons we discussed earlier in Chapter 12, regarding the relative's response to illness.

3. The other family members do not allow the ill member to return to previous levels of function. Reasons vary but may relate to family dynamics that existed prior to illness—for example, the member was too dominant, as in the "overpowering mother." The other family members may take revenge at this point by taking over the patient's role, just keeping the patient around, or getting rid of the patient—leaving him or her to "gather dust."

The Effect of the Rehabilitation on the Family [17]

After the identified patient has suffered the illness and there have been changes in the family that resulted from that illness, it is at this point that the interventions of the physical medicine team must involve the family in the rehabilitation of the identified patient.

Mrs. A, a 50-year-old black female, was the dominant member of her family. Husband and children cowered when she raged. She developed a cerebrovascular accident with a right hemiplegia. Husband and children threw themselves into filling her role and her function. They felt closer than they had been in years. Although Mrs. A's rehabilitation went well in the hospital, at home it went badly. Mrs. A was not allowed to do the things she learned to do in the hospital (activities of daily living), nor was she found to be as motivated by the team to do her exercises. Family members were continually losing her crutches, canes, and other adjunct rehabilitative devices. It was only after her physical therapist brought the family together to discuss the situation and had a preliminary 10-minute meeting in her home prior to her home visit that Mrs. A was able to continue her recovery. The physical therapist's tactic was to maintain some of the new power with the father and children and to encourage a closer relationship between Mrs. A. and her husband.

An ingenious technique for anticipating the difficulty of family patterns as a result of disability has been worked out by one group.[18] A special unit has been built at the hospital in which the family can actually live. The family lives here for two or three days prior to the patient's leaving the hospital. At this point the problem areas are identified and family interventions are made. Follow-up contacts are made at periodic intervals to make sure that the rehabilitation as well as the family therapy continues.

THE FAMILY MODEL
AND GENETIC COUNSELING

With Helen M. Blau, Ph.D.

With the rapid explosion of knowledge about genetic diseases, there has been an increased need for genetic counseling. This increase is directly related to the development of amniocentesis, a procedure that makes it possible to obtain cells of fetal origin and determine whether a fetus believed to be at risk actually has certain disorders.[19-21] Genetic counseling involves communication between counselor and family concerning problems associated with the occurrence of a genetic disease in the family. The genetic counselor provides a diagnosis if possible, information concerning the disorder, an understanding of choices and options available to the family, and support in the form of referrals and scheduled revisits. Contrary to popular notions, genetic counseling attempts to be largely nondirective, offering families information about alternatives rather than advice. What makes genetic counseling different from other types of medical care is that the information provided often leads to unique problems for families.

The family who comes in for genetic counseling often has a member with a hereditary disease that is of a chronic nature. Such chronic disease can be a tremendous burden to all family members. The discovery of a genetic disease in a family member creates very real financial and emotional burdens that compound preexisting family problems. Parents often feel guilty because of the nature of genetic disease—that is, that it is inherited—*even when* they had no previous knowledge of their carrier status. Such guilt and blame can greatly affect parental interactions. In the experience of genetic counselors, parents with good relationships can withstand such chronic stress, but already strained marriages may suffer further. The genetic information may be denied, distorted, or magnified to suit the family's emotional needs; the genetic data become ammunition in the ongoing conflict. Mourning the loss of a normal child is a healthy grief response and often precedes acceptance of the handicapped child. Overconcern with genetic facts, however, or lack of emotion or silence on the part of one member of a couple are symptomatic of deeper problems within the marriage and signal the need for family therapy.

In addition to parental problems, the family therapist or counselor should be aware of the special plight of healthy siblings. They may be affected by financial deprivation, since caring for a family member with a chronic illness is expensive. They often suffer from emotional neglect, since the family focus may rest with the handicapped child. Even if a severely handicapped child is placed in an institution outside of the home (an option that is often not available), healthy siblings may be plagued with guilt, feeling that they caused the disease in this sibling by the normal competitive desire to get rid of him or her—a feeling that is not uncommon from time to time in children of normal families. Furthermore siblings may experience a fear that if they fall short of perfection they, too, will be disposed of.

Family therapy is indicated for many families who experience genetic counseling. In therapy, attempts to reduce guilt and blame should be made and better means of coping explored. Genetic counselors should be encouraged to continue working with these troubled families to the extent they feel it appropriate; if further family therapy is indicated, the genetic counselor should feel free to make a referral (see Chapter 19).

THE FAMILY MODEL AND CHILD ABUSE

With Harvey S. Kaplan, M.D.

Parent-induced child abuse is a major clinical problem of childhood. The various forms of this syndrome appear in families representative of all social classes and ethnic and religious groups, although there is a bias toward the identification and reporting of child abuse in lower socioeconomic families. Neglect can rival poverty in its harmful effect on children's health and developmental potential.

The spectrum of child abuse includes physical abuse in the form of the battered-child syndrome of infancy and early childhood, maternal deprivation during infancy resulting in the failure-to-thrive, child sexual abuse including incest, and in the form of the unworthy or scapegoated child who is the end product of psychological and emotional rejection. Physical abuse of children under three years of age results in the highest morbidity and mortality rate among abused children. Death is usually the result of major head or abdominal injury. Physical survival is associated with many sequelae of nervous system injuries from direct trauma or severe shaking (whiplash-shaken-infant syndrome). Neglect itself produces physical harm due to starvation from underfeeding, developmental retardation (sensory-deprivation syndrome), or from "accidental" injury due to lack of parental protection and supervision. Recurrent accidents and poisonings from ingestions usually occur in severely chaotic families.

A nonnurturing or physically dangerous and threatening family environment focuses the child's energies on survival strategies and may leave little margin for emotional and psychosocial development. Personality and behavioral traits seen in abused children include lack of self-esteem, fear of failure, pseudomaturity, and indiscriminate and shallow relationships with peers and adults. Reflecting the violence of their childhood, abused children themselves develop aggressive and violent tendencies and become problems for society, both as adolescents and adults. School problems related to speech, language, and learning disorders are also seen.

Factors that may identify parents as high risk for being abusive include history of abuse in their own childhood, a strong belief in the value of harsh physical punishment, social isolation, low self-esteem, and inability to experience pleasure. In 10 to 20 percent of the child abuse cases, serious psychosis in one or both parents may preclude adequate child care, as may serious drug abuse or an extremely deviant life-style. Abusive parents expect performance or behavior control from their children that is totally inconsistent with their child's age ability. Severe punishment follows the failure of the child to meet these unrealistic expectations. There may be emotional role reversal of the normal parent–child relationship, where the young child seeks to pacify or interpret and meet the needs of the parent. Although the parenting style may be abusive and emotionally destructive, such parents are acutely sensitive to criticism of their abilities and often resent or reject outside efforts to change them. This reflects their own childhood experience of having been treated as "no good and worthless."

In the G family, following a stormy marriage, the couple were divorced, with the mother being granted custody of their young son. Over the next few years, the battles between the exspouses continued with the boy being shuttled between them physically and emotionally. Ultimately the mother started living with a new boyfriend and the husband remarried. The battles continued over alimony and child-support payments, and the mother began indicating that the boy was resembling her exhusband in terms of personality characteristics. She came to feel, increasingly, that the son was in need of stringent "discipline," and she and her boyfriend undertook to carry this out, especially by means of allocation of food. The boy entered into this situation by at times refusing to eat, and by at other times becoming so enraged that he would threaten to kill his mother.

This cycle led to the boy's being chained up in the bathroom at times and ultimately to his being admitted to a hospital where, at age 11, he weighed 60 pounds and on admission was comatose. He subsequently expired during the hospitalization on the basis of chronic starvation. The mother stood trial with her boyfriend for murder. She maintained steadfastly that she had been unaware of her son's deteriorating physical condition, had never had any intention of causing the boy any harm, and did not consider the regimen the boy had been placed under as punishment.

Harlow and coworkers have demonstrated pathology in mother monkeys who never had consistent caring experiences with a mother themselves and who never played with peers at an early age. These monkeys show two characteristic behaviors toward their own offspring.[22] They may either totally ignore them or become extremely aggressive with them. Attempts to "treat" these experimentally induced disorders are extremely complicated and involve using "junior therapists" in a graded series of stepwise procedures and self-paced therapy over a long period of time. The application of these therapeutic techniques to humans, although unknown, appears consistent with clinical family techniques now being employed.

Treatment of child abuse requires a multidisciplinary team approach to be effective. The coordinated efforts of physician, social worker, therapist, and others must focus on the needs of the entire family who often are confronted with medical, psychological, and legal problems related to the abuse or neglect. The juvenile or family court often must decide if the child should stay with the family or if the foster care should be terminated and the child returned home. Support services for the family to assist in childrearing include in-home friends to parents, homemakers, day care for the child, respite care for the parent, visiting public health nurses, and 24-hour telephone parental stress hotlines.

Recent pediatric attention has focused on the events of the perinatal and postpartum period in order to identify those parents who may be high risk for possible abuse or neglect. Similarly so-called high-risk infants, such as premature babies or infants with birth defects or infants who are simply seen as different and unattractive to their parents, may require special follow-up in order to strengthen maternal– infant bonding and prevent the more serious forms of abuse and neglect.

The family therapist who treats an abusive parent should be aware that the primary step is to allow the parent to develop a trusting relationship with someone before a specific behavioral change can be expected. This is called the "reparenting process" and is a nurturing phase that must precede any form of psychotherapy. Similarly admonitions, accusations, and confrontations may drive such parents away from help. A physician or a therapist, however, must also guard against overidentification with problems and needs of the abusive parent to the point where the need of the child for protection from harm is overlooked.

A crucial step is to restructure the family so as to relieve the stresses that upset the delicate balance between parents and child, which causes the parent to act against the child.

One community mental health clinic with a large population of child abusers has set up a program called "parent-performance training program for child abusers."[23] The objective is to educate these parents in more effective childrearing practices. The first step is to assign a programmed text for the parents to read. (Five texts, consisting of a total of 161 fill-in-the-blank statements are given.) The second step is to assign a "home project," using the behavioral principles that the parents learned from the text. Finally the home project is evaluated in conjunction with marital therapy. The technique appears to work best with the less-disturbed parent or family or the "worried" parent who has not actually hurt his or her child. Many abusive parents are hard to reach, resisting and rejecting everyone, and thus making it hard to "teach" them anything. They are the ones whom social workers and probation officers see, and they usually do not stay in mental health clinics very long, if at all.

It is often felt by professionals that reporting suspected child abuse to the appropriate agencies may be seen as a betrayal of the parents when, in fact, it is the first important step toward interrupting an abusive cycle and providing the family with the type of intervention, via the team concept, that is most likely to be successful. In approximately 70 percent of the cases, early identification and intervention may make it possible for the child either to remain in the home with supportive help or to be eventually returned to the home after a period of foster care and improvement of the home situation. Although it may be difficult to improve the psychological environment for the children who remain in their homes, physical reinjury can be significantly reduced with intervention. Termination of parental rights is indicated when the parent is extremely psychotic or sadistic, or totally rejects the child.

It must be stressed that repeated visits to the emergency room, pediatrician, or internist by the mother with the battered child is a cry for family intervention. In such early stages seeking to provide the battering parent with insight into the family dynamics may be too psychologically threatening and lead to guilt in the parent and termination of the treatment contact.[24, 25]

THE FAMILY MODEL AND THE REHABILITATION THERAPIST

With Susan Williams, O.T.R. and Susanne Currie, O.T.R.

The field of rehabilitation therapy has been gradually expanding from a primary focus on rehabilitation within an inpatient setting to include rehabilitation in the community. The rehabilitation therapist's function in both settings is to return the identified patient to a maximum level of functioning within the community.

Currently rehabilitation therapists work in a variety of settings including traditional inpatient settings, as well as day treatment centers, community mental health centers, and, to an increasing extent, private practices where rehabilitation therapists provide therapy or consultation (or both) to various therapists doing psychotherapy, to extended care facilities, and to various private therapeutic facilities.

Although rehabilitation therapy has traditionally been practiced with the focus on both the individual and that individual's role in a group setting, there has been little emphasis on the family as one specific group configuration. Concurrent with the emergence of the family therapy movement, rehabilitation therapists have placed greater emphasis on the functioning of the identified patient *in the context of* the family. It is becoming patently clear that the identified patient is dysfunctional not only because of a psychiatric disability but also because of forces in the family.

The Family and the Rehabilitation Process

When the identified patient has a disturbance in functional capacity (for example, vocational or avocational impairment), an assumption is made that the functional capacity of the identified patient depends, in part, on the emotional climate of the family. For example, in the empty-nest syndrome, the mother may not want the children to go out and get jobs, because that would mean she is left alone with the father. She may, therefore, prevent their functioning. It is the initial task of the rehabilitation therapist to uncover the problems of the identified patient as they are understood within the family constellation.

Rehabilitation Assessment

No matter what the setting, the immediate task of the therapist is assessment of the family. There are a variety of rehabilitation-oriented assessment procedures in which the task is to determine how the identified patient functions within the family context.

For some families it is useful to interview the patient and the family with an emphasis on past functioning in relationship to family dynamics, interactional patterns among members, and family methods of coping with stress. For many families, however, an interview reflects the established "persona" of the family and may not accurately convey family roles and lines of authority. Task-oriented and projective family interactional techniques may be more revealing and ultimately more useful to the family. For example, the family may be asked to cook a meal together. In a situation like this, the therapist can observe interactional patterns in a "hands-on" way and eliminate the discrepancies of verbal reporting. The therapist notes both how the individual functions and how this functioning is influenced by the family.

For some families more projective-expressive techniques may be useful in the initial assessment. Art therapy has been extremely helpful in encouraging nonverbal communication and expression. The family members may be asked to respond to one another nonverbally through making lines and symbols on the same piece of paper. It is not difficult to see how this task might also clarify interactional patterns and lines of authority in the family. In another assessment procedure family members may be asked to cut shapes out of construction paper to represent themselves and each family member. These are then placed on another piece of paper to reflect the closeness/distance dimension in the family. From this exercise, both the therapist and the family gain a fairly clear graphic depiction of the family dynamics from the point of view of each family member.

Techniques and Effect of Rehabilitation on the Family

Once the family problems are identified, tasks can be set up under the guidance of the rehabilitation therapist to correct the deficiencies. Problems can be corrected on the spot. For example, a father who does every task for his son can be helped to allow his son to do more for himself. If the identified patient is in a hospital setting, the notion of family "visits" can be changed to make the family's participation in various activities mandatory.

Often the family can more accurately assess its own problems through tasks rather than through verbal interventions. Many families are performance, rather than verbally, oriented (perhaps because of limitation in verbal comprehension and concept formation). The idea of tasks makes more sense to them. A family-activity planning session can focus around various tasks in which the whole family might be involved and should include both leisure-time and house-maintenance activities. Other tasks for a family planning session might include:

1. Planning the family vacation: what will each member pack; who will be responsible for the packing; who will share in what preparatory task; and so on
2. Planning a family picnic or household festivity

3.   Delegating weekly chores for various family members
4.   Preparing and participating in a family meal

One therapeutic setting has a "family activity night" as part of the clinic's adolescent program. These activities have been found to be useful in assessing family dynamics, pointing out "here and now" behavior, assessing the power within the family system, and evaluating each individual member's capacities for decision making and reality testing in relation to activities of daily living. These activities are especially useful for motivating the family members to do things together and for getting them to listen to, and communicate with, one another. Other treatment techniques involve more psychotherapeutically oriented interventions. An art project involving the drawing of a family situation may lead to understanding how the father, for example, may be handling a situation in ways similar to his own father. Often the graphic portrayal, or acting out, of situations may reinforce associations that verbal discussion may not.

The increasing involvement of rehabilitation therapists in day treatment settings provides an opportunity for the fostering of closer community ties and close monitoring of family functioning. Rehabilitation therapists can work with patients daily around tasks geared to return the patient to full community functioning. Rehabilitation therapists in private practice are also focusing more on work with families and the often important role played by the identified patient within the family setting. Regardless of setting, the rehabilitation therapist is able to provide assessment, treatment, and consultation regarding the functional status of clients in relation to the family.

THE FAMILY MODEL
AND CLINICAL PSYCHOLOGY

With Edward Gould, Ph.D.

Clinical psychology, like the field of psychiatry, has been in a state of flux. Multiple models are being utilized. Unlike psychiatry, however, the medical model has not been found to be a useful perspective or approach for dealing with many clinical problems.

Hence the family or systems view has attracted many adherents. Psychological assessment, traditionally a major function of clinical psychologists, has been extended from the individual to the family context. (Discussion of this issue can be found in Chapter 5, where the clinical issues are discussed, and in Chapter 18, where research and methodological issues are detailed.) Clinical psychologists in organizational or institutional work settings other than hospitals have been moving increasingly from individual-centered to group- or system (family)-centered approaches.

Indeed clinical psychologists have used the family model, perhaps to a greater extent than other professionals, both in their assessment and psychotherapeutic work.

FAMILY THERAPY AND SOCIAL WORK

With George Johnson, M.S.W.

The centrality of the family has been a cornerstone of social work philosophy and practice since the establishment of charity societies in the late 1800s. Although these societies have all but disappeared, their legacy is still apparent in hundreds of existing family service agencies in the United States.

The Family Service Association of America (FSAA) is the national body to which most voluntary family agencies are affiliated. A variety of services are provided, including family, conjoint, and individual counseling; family advocacy; homemaking services; legal assistance; day care programs; dental and health programs; vocational guidance; mental health clinics; and other programs. Social workers have carried this family focus to many other agencies and settings—that is, probation departments, medical hospitals, schools, private industry, and so forth.

Despite this long historical family orientation, the family systems model is relatively new in social work. The individual model dominated the social work profession prior to the development of family therapy. Family members were frequently seen one at a time, or individual family members were seen by more than one social worker. Families with multiproblems were often seen by more than one agency or by more than one social worker in the same agency. The therapists involved met only sporadically with each other to review the progress of the family. In one study six percent of the families used more than half of all the available agency time.[26] Since each agency saw only part of the family's problems, it was suggested that a focus on the whole family, rather than just the particular individuals involved, was needed for effective help.

The development of family therapy and the family model has provided a new perspective for social workers, who currently use a variety of methods and techniques in their work with families. There are few well-designed studies, however, of the effectiveness of the methods and techniques. Two exceptions are the multiple impact therapy approach[27] (see Chapter 7) and the Chemung County study,[28] the latter demonstrating that casework methods with multiproblem families are not effective.

THE FAMILY MODEL AND PSYCHIATRIC NURSING

With Sheila Greenberg, R.N. and Patricia R. Underwood, R.N., D.N.S.

Schools of nursing in the United States are now including as part of their curriculum courses in family dynamics. The nurse has an opportunity to learn to handle the complexities of family functioning as they affect a patient's illness.

Psychiatric Nursing with Families: An Overview

Psychiatric nurses work in a variety of settings, ranging from community mental health centers to inpatient psychiatric units in both psychiatric and general hospitals. With advanced training and experience, nurses may assume, as part of their overall responsibility, the role of family therapist or cotherapist. When the nursing means working with the family as a nurse rather than as a therapist, the relationship with the family takes a different focus and involves different interaction and interventions. The following discussion concerns the nurse involved in family work, performing as a nurse and not as a family therapist.

In working with the family, the first task is assessment. Analysis of the patient and family in their daily living is the foundation of such assessment. The nurse focuses on assisting the patient and the family to develop a more realistic view of the patient's skills and potential for providing for self-care. The focus of the work with the patient and family is to enable the patient to assume responsibility for daily living. A common pattern in families with psychiatric patients is that the family treats the member as one totally incapable of assuming even minimal self-responsibility.

Effects of Nursing Intervention on Patients and Family

As the nurse–patient relationship develops, the nurse is better able to assess the patient's ability to assume responsibilities. The attempt to assist the family and the patient to change often results in reactions from the family because the change will most likely affect the family system homeostasis, role, and structure. The family may be resistive to fuller participation by the patient in the family system if such change means more problems for the family.

When the nurse does not understand the identified patient's role in the family or has had little or no contact with the family, reaction to the family resistance may be to project blame for the patient's condition onto the family. Nursing contact with the patient over a 24-hour (three 8-hour shifts) period provides the opportunity to see the patient function in a variety of day-to-day activites. As the patient's functioning improves, the nurse who does not understand the patient and family interactions often believes that the family is the "cause" of the patient's not functioning maximally. As understanding of family dynamics and interactions develops, the patient's level of functioning becomes apparent. The nurse can then use the relationship with patient and family to improve the patient's functioning within the family and to stop placing blame on either the family or the patient.

Techniques of Psychiatric Nursing Intervention with Patient and Family in Problems of Day-to-Day Living

The nurse develops a daily care plan for patients and families that is congruent with the medical treatment plan, but its focus is also on the goal of returning the patient to the community. The individual patient care plan will include those areas in day-to-day living that seem most troublesome to the patient and the family, as well as the health teaching that is necessary for the family members to understand the patient's condition and the care and treatment following discharge.

The major role of the nurse with the family and the patient is to work with daily living problems. The nurse identifies the problem areas and works on them with the patient. Family visits are used for on-the-spot, here-and-now work with these problems, as well as for discussions to help both the family and the patient identify alternative behavior that will encourage and allow the patient to realize his full potential.

The nurse begins work with the first family visit and at this time starts working on the patient's daily functioning with the family. The family is not viewed by the nursing staff as visiting a "sick" family member in the hospital because of their own guilt, but rather to be actively involved with the patient and staff in working on the daily living problems that occurred in the home and are often repeated during family visits. For example, many psychiatrically ill patients will withdraw to bed to avoid facing family problems. Often families, not knowing what else to do, will allow or even encourage this maneuver. The psychiatric nurse, using the relationship that has been established with the patient, works with the family and patient when this occurs. An attempt is made to provide them with alternatives for facing problems. It is pointed out that both the family and the patient allow the withdrawal and then attempt to find more productive solutions—that is, (1) the patient may go to bed for a limited time but then must return to the situation; (2) the patient may take a walk to get away for a while but must come back; (3) the family may agree to stop talking about the problem for a limited time while they think about how the patient feels before beginning the discussion; and (4) the nurse, seeing that the dysfunctional behavior results from unresolved arguments, may act as a facilitator to help the family and patient discuss the situation calmly.

Another common family problem revolves around eating. Often families allow disturbed members to set up bizarre eating routines and make little or no effort to interrupt them. Patients may eat only certain foods or eat only in their rooms or eat only if the house is empty. Again this is neither the fault of the patient nor of the family but may be the result of interaction of the family members. While hospitalized or in day treatment, the patient may be introduced to regular meal times and, after initial resistance, eats as expected with firm, consistent encouragement from the nursing staff. The nurse discusses, with the family and patient together, the expected meal routine and assists the family in providing firm, consistent encouragement to help the patient accept the mealtime routine. This may be the topic of many family visits before the patient is ready for passes or discharge.

Two other major issues are often part of the nurse–patient–family interaction. These are medication and discharge to some facility (halfway house, board and care), other than home. The nurse, as the dispenser of medication, is often viewed by the patient and family as making the patient sick with medication. Many families and patients tend to blame psychiatric symptoms on the "pills" or "shots" rather than on the illness. Family members are often heard to say, "He was better before medication." They may mean he was less trouble because he was withdrawn. As medications work to relieve symptoms, the patient's improvement may be resisted by the family. The nurse, as the identified "pill pusher," can use visiting time with families and patients to teach and explain the use and expected results of medication. By working with families and patients together when questions, problems, or concerns arise about medications, the nurse can increase understanding and acceptance of them. This is particularly important because 30 to 50 percent of inpatients do not comply with a medication regimen. The nurse can help to ensure that members of the family will assume some responsiblity for the patient's medications and be less likely to undermine treatment by allowing, or even encouraging, the patient to stop taking prescribed medication. When the nurse deals honestly with the patient about medication and includes the family in the process, the family is helped to learn ways of coping with the patient.

What about discharge planning? Nurses working daily with patients have an opportunity to observe and assess their patients' ability to care for themselves. In some situations a patient may be unable to return home due to illness or inability to function, and in other cases the family may no longer be able to provide all the care, time, and treatment needed by the patient. In either instance it is often hard for the patient and the family to accept this even when they all know it is true. Although the primary therapist works with the family and the patient together and individually in therapy, the nurse can be supportive to both patient and family. In this way the family members are helped to view the patient more realistically and helped to see that they may need assistance with the patient that they are unable to give. Nurses can encourage patients' potential and also help them recognize that families are not always able to provide all the care required on a day-to-day basis. By focusing on the here and now, support and encouragement are provided that may help alleviate guilt ·or feelings of abandonment. The nurse can point out reality for both a patient and family in order to facilitate discharge planning and actual discharge.

THE FAMILY MODEL AND
ARCHITECTURE AND DESIGN
With Earl Pope, Architect

According to some architects the field of architecture has been overly dominated by technical, aesthetic, and economic considerations, rather than by the needs of the families.

How can the architect quickly and effectively become aware of and understand family needs so that optimal design can be achieved despite the above limitations? It is obvious that each architect will have to develop a method for doing fairly rapid family evaluation, based not only on the principles that we discussed earlier (Chapters 3, 4, and 5) but also on principles especially adapted to architectural needs. The architect would need to go through a series of steps including:

1. Meeting the whole family, rather than only one member
2. Attempting to understand the family needs and how the family functions
3. Delineating objectives for the design, but only after understanding the problem

An example of such a procedure would be the following:

The family consisted of Mrs. S and her two teenage sons who lived in a low-income apartment with very limited space. Mrs. S told the architect, who was conducting a program on family space planning and furnishing for the neighborhood community center, that her older son never brought his friends home. Furthermore he never wanted to stay around the house, thereby hindering all communication with her. The architect met with the family and discovered that the son was an excellent athlete who had won many trophies for his achievements in sports. The apartment they were housed in was designed in such a way that the son was living in a small room, shared by a younger brother, where he had very little space for himself. The architect sensed the need for the son to feel better about his room and home to make it more his place and so that he would feel comfortable in bringing his friends there and would spend more time there himself. One small part of the solution was to provide a shelf in the son's small room that would run around the entire room at door height and that would have enough space for him to display his trophies. His change in the relation to his home was startling.

This is obviously an oversimplification of a complex set of events. It does highlight, however, the points that we discussed above.

Family patterns of dining (Chapter 5), become an important area for architects to consider. Dining space might be set up not only for eating but also to maximize family communication.

When low- and moderate-income housing standards are used, minimum spatial requirements (such as HUD Minimum Property Standards) often become the maximum, leaving little opportunity for families to adapt their living space to their members' needs. Also many housing programs are designed for small families (two children at the most), rather than for a variety of family sizes. The result is that larger families with problems specific to their needs are not dealt with, such as needs for multiple study areas and privacy for parents as well as children.

Middle-income families have a similar problem. Most speculative housing (the most common type of middle-income housing by far) is stereotyped in form—three bedrooms and a family room, with the living room and the dining room reserved for ceremonial use only. The middle-income family often, by convention or by design of the developer, lives in a large square foot area theoretically, but its living pattern is confined to a small square foot area not unlike a low-to-moderate-income family (the family room and three bedrooms).

Finally there are issues beyond personal space. The family must also relate to the community. If the family's personal environment is satisfactory but it feels alienated from its community and neighbors, all parties will suffer. Does our environment suggest communications other than a casual nod in the elevator? Are there places to meet, to talk, to exchange ideas, or to develop an identity with a neighborhood? Are we threatened and vulnerable, or do we look forward to seeing our neighbors during a casual communal encounter?

In a like vein, in designing multiple-occupancy dwellings, the needs of the families should not get lost in the overriding needs of the community. For example, a principle that many architects follow is to house families without children on the upper floors, whereas families with children (who need to be close to other children in playgrounds) are housed on the lower floors.

These are only a few of many examples that can be cited. For a full discussion of the subject see references.[29-32]

THE FAMILY MODEL AND THE LEGAL AND JUDICIAL SYSTEM

With Carl Burak, M.D., J.D., and Gail Saliterman, Ph.D., J.D.

The family therapist must recognize that the legal system is an adversarial system. Thus, although it is designed to resolve conflicts, it frequently cannot do so without touching on, and affecting, the prior relationships of all the parties involved—that is, a husband and wife, their children, and the therapist. As a result the law may well be used and even abused by one member in order to hurt the other. The therapist must be aware of its potentiality to generate either conflict or cooperation.

The Family Evaluation

A family therapist may commonly be asked by an attorney or judge for an evaluation of the family, or a particular family member. The attorney for one spouse in a custody fight may, for example, want the family therapist to testify in the hope of showing that his or her client is the better parent. The family therapist should decline. The family therapist should not divulge confidential information, even if all parties consent. *Family therapy* should be kept separate from *family evaluation*. Any family therapist confronted by a request from an attorney to testify should advise the attorney to seek an independent therapist to conduct an evaluation of the family.

The therapist should also point out to the attorney that family therapy does not lend itself to evaluating the independent worth or the disabilities of a particular family member. The family therapist considers not only the identified patient but the capacity of the entire system to deal with the needs of each member, particularly the children. This very advantage of family therapy forcefully establishes a treatment that is best for all concerned, rather than one that is suitable for only one of the family members. Attorneys, in contrast, usually want individually oriented reports that favor their client's interest. Thus even if a family system report is ordered by the court, the family therapist could well find one or both parties objecting to the admission of the family evaluation. Again, however, even if none of the members object, the therapeutic advantages of the family sessions might well be lost if any party harbors the slightest concern that what is being said in therapy could end up being revealed to others.

In many states either party can ask the court to strike the family system evaluation from the record if it is not favorable. Other states require that if such a report is made, both parties have a right to see it; and if the report is unfavorable to one client, that client's attorney is free to seek another, possibly more favorable report. If this occurs the family therapist as evaluator is almost certain to be caught in the adversarial legal system. The therapist is likely to be asked to testify in a court hearing that is likely to involve heated cross-examination on the part of the opposing counsel. Thus in drafting a family evaluation report, the therapist should be certain that the report is clear and meaningful, and that it outlines the options available for the court and gives the reasons behind any proposals.[33]

Confidentiality and Privilege

A situation may arise in which one spouse wants to compel the other to testify in order to gain a personal advantage about material that came up during family therapy. The rules of evidence specifically prohibit testimony regarding "interspousal communications" without the consent of the nontestifying spouse. For example, the wife wants custody of the children and the husband had admitted during therapy that he consumed large quantities of alcohol in secret. The husband could object to the information about his drinking being received by the court as evidence for the custody hearing. This objection would be valid, even if the couple were already divorced, as long as the information came up in treatment while they were married.

The information would not be privileged, however, if it came to light once the spouses were formally separated or divorced, even if they were together with the therapist because they hoped to reconcile. The therapist working with a separated, but not yet divorced couple should be aware of this reality and make sure the patients are also aware of it.

There is one major exception to these confidentiality rules. The family therapist can and is encouraged to take the best interest of a child into account. Some family therapists use this power as a way to force the parents to decide an issue. Specifically in cases in which the spouses cannot agree on a custody issue, an experienced therapist can inform the family that he or she will go to court and testify to the facts that suggest that the child should be placed in foster care. The therapist does this out of a conviction that when one spouse "wins" on the custody issue, as inevitably happens, the child ends up feeling so torn by conflict and guilt that the custody decision may prove detrimental to his or her future growth and development.

On the other hand many are critical of the therapist who assumes this role because it is aggressive and seems to threaten the therapeutic process. However resolved, the example demonstrates the power that the therapist has in the ajudication of custody disputes.

Separation and Divorce Counseling

Even attorneys who are unusually sensitive to family situations must suppress their broader concerns in the interest of obtaining the outcome that is best for their particular client. The competent attorney will utilize any tactical device that best serves his purpose. Given this adversarial context, the family therapist should be prepared for an escalation of differences between the parties. This escalation may well be counterproductive to some of the goals of family therapy. The wealthier spouse, frequently the husband, is likely to be advised by his attorney in the divorce action to make the wife feel that he will give her as little as possible. He may even lead her to believe that he is willing to abandon all visitation and custody rights regarding the children. This, of course, is not what he intends to do. He wants to share custody and wants to provide adequately for the children, but he will use the threat of abandonment in order to force his wife to compromise. She, of course, is worried that he might actually intend not to support her and the children. She may feel threatened. At the very least, her smaller income puts her at a disadvantage in negotiations. The family therapist must understand that the role of most attorneys in separation or divorce proceedings comes from a different frame of reference and is played by different rules for different goals.

There is a trend, probably healthy, to encourage family law specialists to be more conciliatory, more psychologically sensitive, and more intent on securing the best outcome for *all* members of the family unit. Whether the courts will encourage this trend remains to be seen.

The family therapist who has been working with a family therapeutically might be able to diminish the impact of the adversarial context as a legal scenario begins to unfold by focusing one of the sessions on the process of change in family inter-action. Another focus, consistent with the goals of family therapy, would be to ask the family members what they each feel would be in the best interest of the child or children. Most parents and children will find that these sessions are an extremely useful way to cope with the adversarial posture in the divorce situation. Obvious-ly the "best interests of the child" depend on who is conceiving that interest. This, however, is the point the therapist wants the family to recognize.

It may also be the responsibility of the therapist, acting in the best interests of the family, to minimize the excessive beneficence of one of the spouses. Fre-quently a spouse under the influence of an exaggerated sense of guilt will make a decision about the disposition of a child or of family assets that is too generous. In the long run this generosity could be counterproductive to the best interests of the family as that spouse's guilt turns to anger.

A guilty husband with a new lover wants a divorce and is willing to offer $2000 a month in alimony and child support, although he only makes $3000 a month. His wife, also a professional earning a substantial salary, should fairly receive $1000 a month. Both attorneys want to call in a family therapist to help the husband understand that the generosity is based on guilt feelings. The attorneys will desire this simply to avoid the future legal hassles that the overreaching settlement of $2000 a month will generate.

Another major question is the extent to which the family therapist discussses the allocation of income available to the family while the couples are separated, pending divorce, as well as the access to whatever community property the family has—that is, bank account, house, car, and so on. Community property becomes an issue as soon as a couple begins to think about divorce. Frequently the first one to claim the joint monies gets them. This issue is particularly important since women, with the repeal of special alimony laws, often end up with little capital or means of support. Any unemployed woman thinking about divorce must consider what means of income will be available to her until she can support herself. The community property assets may be her only resource.

A marital therapist may recommend a trial separation. The couple involved needs to be aware that should this separation come about, the spouse who relinquishes custody of the children, even during this trial period, may be at a disadvantage in any future legal action with respect to more permanent custody arrangements. Similarly whatever financial arrangements are instituted may well serve as a precedent for the postdivorce arrangements.

As a result the therapist might suggest that the couple also meet with an attorney. This suggestion is in contrast to the idea that each spouse must go to a separate attorney. Of course the attorney who sees the couple together cannot act as attorney for either partner without running the risk of professional negligence due to the conflict of interests. Once the conflict is understood and the couple agrees in writing to waive any cause of action against the attorney, the joint visit can serve to instruct the couple in the realities of divorce; furthermore, the visit will stimulate the emotions that will be involved in the actual divorce proceeding.

The therapist should also advise both parties that each may need a separate attorney for any concrete advice on individual rights. The joint visit, however, like the visits with the marital therapist, may facilitate the development of mutually equitable arrangements.

It may be important for the marital therapist to establish relationships in advance with a number of attorneys who are willing to provide such information and counseling to the couple. Communication between the medical and legal world needs to be fostered. The therapist might even have the attorney join a particular family session to help resolve some of the issues in that context. The attorney will not be serving in an adversarial role but will be free to utilize his or her professional confidence in the consultative capacity, which would be more congruent with therapeutic goals. Alternatively the family therapist might work with an attorney directly, so that the couple can be provided with basic information about the legal implications of divorce.[34]

Children's Rights

Perhaps the single most important area of concern for the family therapist is new trends in children's rights.[35] Whenever the state is involved in the action involving families, it can be assumed that the children's interests and the parents' interests are not identical. Ideally family therapists can work for the good of the total family unit at the same time that they are protecting the expectations of the individual members, including the children. Inevitably, however, if a therapist tries to take the whole family's interest into account and acts in its best interest, irreconcilable differences may appear.

The family therapist should be aware that there are other interested parties in society, such as the advocates of children's rights, who believe that the therapist, when confronted with the choice between helping the children or the family unity, should be concerned mainly with the children. Specifically these advocates argue that children must have their own attorney. In such cases the family therapist may be caught in the middle of a number of conflicting views.

Adoption and Foster Home Placement

The areas of adoption and foster home placement are closely related. A common situation in marital therapy is the couple's belief that the solution to their problem is to adopt a child. (This myth is discussed in Chapter 4.) Even if this is an appropriate move, the therapist may be asked by the placement agency to evaluate the parents' suitability for adoption. To repeat, the authors believe that family therapy is different from family evaluation. The separate functions should be done by different therapists. Furthermore family therapists can only provide information on a couple's functioning; so the evaluation must be left for others to make.

To the extent possible, children should remain with their natural parents.[36] This principle is largely derived from a comparison with the existing alternatives of child care. There have been some cases reported in which couples (or their parents or other agencies) who are having difficulty with one or more children believe that the solution to their problem may be to give the child (or children) up for adoption. This view is the opposite of the myth that "everything will be all right if we have a child." In these instances the therapist should first carefully evaluate the family situation and, if possible, engage in a trial period of family therapy before coming to the conclusion that placement outside of the home offers the best alternative. The following case should make this clear.

In the M case the identified patient was Mrs. M, 31 years old. Her husband was 35 years old. They had a 5-year-old daughter and a 3-year-old son. The patient gave a 10-year history of periodic depressions and inability to function. While in these episodes, the patient was unable to take care of the children. During the course of the marriage, the husband became more and more involved in his work and spent less time with both the wife and children. When Mrs. M was symptomatic, neither parent cared for or disciplined the children. Because of school problems with one of the children, the parents were brought to the attention of legal authorities, who suggested that the children would need foster care placement.

The problem for the family therapist was whether to have the children placed in a foster home or to try to pull the family together. An evaluation was made of each spouse's functional capacities as a parent and his or her *willingness* to carry on this role.

Even when it appears reasonable for the child to be placed, and even after the parents agree on adoption after dealing with their ambivalent feelings, it is not uncommon for the natural parents to later want to have the child back. In this situation experience indicates that it is better for the child that the placement decision be irrevocable.

Foster home placement may be only a temporary solution. The family therapist and the lawyer should realize that once a child is placed in foster care, it is usually temporary. Perhaps the best interest of the child is served when there is permanent placement in a foster situation and the rights of the natural parents are terminated. The foster family should adopt the child rather than serve as a temporary way station.

In summary there are three options of child care available to the parents. The first is to have the child stay with them. The second is to separate the child from the home (permanently and irrevocably) and move toward adoption on the grounds that the couple is not functional. The third is the middle-ground position of foster care with the notion that this is temporary and the child will return to the natural parents once they are more functional. The role of the family therapist would be to encourage and facilitate the discussion of these issues with recognition of the strongly ambivalent feelings that will inevitably be present, so as to help the family move toward a decision.

Custody

Historically it was mandated by Western tradition that the father had the exclusive right to custody of the children. This doctrine has gradually changed in the last 100 years, so that by the early 1900s the mother became the custodial parent in about 90 percent of the cases. A recent New York State study has recommended a "no fault" custody order to give parents joint child custody. The rationale behind this is that present patterns unfairly exclude fathers—making them exfathers as well as exhusbands. In such cases the father must barter for rights to visit his children, the "trade" perhaps being a redistribution of the inherent unequal power structure between the parents. Clearly as society and roles change, so do custody practices. The family therapist can help to emphasize for the children the importance of the spouses coming to an agreement regarding their *parental* roles, even though they may not be able to resolve all their disagreements regarding their *marital* roles.

The family therapist should be aware that at times he will be encouraged by representatives of the legal and judicial systems to become the "expert" on various family issues. Many of the questions involved are very ambiguous, thorny, and crucial. At times it may appear that lawyers, judges, and case workers would be only too happy to shift the burden of decision making in regard to these questions to the presumed "family expert." The family therapist would be well advised to be cautious in accepting this assignment, because it may confuse and contaminate the basic role of helping a family and its members to arrive at decisions that are best for them. Also, empirical data on which to base "expert" pronouncements may not be available. What may be substituted instead, unfortunately, may be the personal opinions and prejudices of the family therapist, which may then be all too readily accepted by other social systems dealing with the family.

For example, a recent text asserts that emphasis should be placed on "the child's right to the best psychological parent, regardless of competing adult claims."[37] This publication adheres to the traditional bias of giving greater emphasis to the mother–child relationship than to the father–child relationship. Unfortunately, as we mentioned earlier, empirical data on this question are not available. The personal predilection of many family therapists seems to be that both parents should have input in the raising of the child. They further believe that if both parents can reasonably agree on parental decisions, then joint custody should be recommended—that is, both parents should share equally in decision making.[38] On the other hand if the two parents are continually fighting and using the children as a battleground, then the therapists should recommend custody to the "better" parent.

References and Legal Citations

For legal citations supporting the arguments advanced in this section, the reader is referred to the textbooks by Foote, Levy, and Sander[39] and Kaslow and Abroms.[40]

FAMILY THEORY AND INSTITUTIONS

Some writers see many similarities in the structure and functioning of institutions and families. Because all members of any corporation come from and usually have families, many of their own interactional patterns, rules, and multibelief constellations may be translated into their work situation. Sometimes it is easy to see the "father," "mother," "grandfather," "youngest-child" equivalents operating in the board room and daily life of an institution.

Family theory may in the future provide some fascinating insights into how these structures operate adaptively or nonadaptively. Collaboration between sociologists, management consultants, and family therapists may provide an even broader foundation in helping to understand our cultural environment and institutions.

REFERENCES

1. McWhinney IR: Family medicine in perspective. N Engl J Med 293:176–181, 1975
2. Kraft AM: Psychiatry: A Concise Textbook for Primary Care Practice. New York, Arco Publishing, 1977
3. Ransom DC, Vandervoort HE: The development of family medicine: Problematic trends. JAMA 225:1098–1102, 1973
4. Kellner R: Family Ill Health: An Investigation in General Practice. Springfield, Ill, Charles C. Thomas, 1963, p 79

5. Meissner WW: Family process and psychosomatic disease. Int J Psychiatry in Med 5:411–430, 1974

6. Holmes TS, Holmes TH: Short-term intrusion into the life-style routine. J Psychosomatic Res 14:121–132, 1970

7. Grolnick L: A family perspective of psychosomatic factors in illness: A review of the literature. Fam Process 11:457–486, 1972

8. Block J: Parents of schizophrenic, neurotic, asthmatic, and congenitally ill children. Arch Gen Psychiatry 20:659–674, 1969

9. Liebman R, Minuchin S, Baker L: The use of structural family therapy in the treatment of intractable asthma. Am J Psychiatry 131:535–540, 1974

10. Barcai A: Family therapy and treatment of anorexia nervosa. Am J Psychiatry 128:286–290, 1971

11. Bruch H: Family transaction and eating disorders. Compr Psychiatry 12:238–248, 1971

12. Crisp A, Toms D: Primary anorexia nervosa, or a weight phobia in the male: Report of 13 cases. Br Med J 1:334–337, 1972

13. Liebman R, Minuchin S, Baker L, et al: Chronic asthma: A new approach to treatment in McMillan MF, Henao S (eds): Child Psychiatry. Treatment and Research. New York, Brunner/Mazel, 1977, pp 153–171

14. Liebman R, Minuchin S, Baker L, et al: The treatment of anorexia nervosa. Current Psychiatric Therapies, 15:51–57, 1975

15. Steele TE, Finkelstein SH, Finkelstein FO: Hemodialysis patients and spouses, marital discord, sexual problems and depression. J Nerv Ment Dis 162:225–237, 1976

16. Sasano EM, Shepard KF, Bell JE, et al: The family in physical therapy. Physical Ther 57:153–159, 1977

17. Peck RB: Physical medicine and family dynamics: The dialectics of rehabilitation. Fam Process 13:469–480, 1974

18. Davies NH, Hansen E: Family focus: A transitional cottage in an acute-care hospital. Fam Process 13:481–488, 1974

19. Globus MS, Loughman WD, Epstein CJ, et al: Prenatal genetic diagnosis in 3000 amniocenteses. N Engl J Med 300:157–163, 1979

20. Tsuang MT: Genetic counseling for psychiatric patients and their families. Am J Psychiatry 135:1465–1475, 1978

21. Fraser FC: Genetic counseling. Hospital Practice 6:49–56, 1971

22. Harlow duplicates battered child syndrome in monkey experiments. Psychiatric News, XI: 2, January 21, 1976

23. Hughes RC: A clinic's parent-performance training program for child abusers. Hosp & Comm Psychiatry 25:779–782, 1974

24. Helfer RE, Kempe CH: Child Abuse and Neglect—The Family and the Community. Cambridge, Mass, Ballinger, 1976

25. Martin HP (ed): The Abused Child—A Multidisciplinary Approach to Developmental Issues and Treatment. Cambridge, Mass, Ballinger, 1976

26. Buell B: Community Planning for Human Services. New York, Columbia University Press, 1952, p 9

27. MacGregor R, et al: Multiple Impact Therapy with Families. New York, McGraw-Hill, 1964

28. Brown GE (ed): The Multiproblem Dilemma. Metuchen, N.J., Scarecrow Press, 1968

29. Hall ET: The Hidden Dimension. New York, Doubleday/Anchor, 1969

30. Neutra R: Survival Through Design. New York, Oxford University Press, 1969

31. Newman O: Defensible Space: Crime Prevention Through Urban Design. New York, Macmillan, 1972

32. Sommer R: Tight Spaces: Hard Architecture and How to Humanize It. Englewood Cliffs, N.J., Prentice-Hall, 1974

33. Vague psychiatric reports can be harmful. JAMA 229:1156, 1974

34. White SL: Providing family-centered consultation to a juvenile court in Massachusetts. Hosp & Comm Psychiatry 27:692–693, 1976

35. Wittenberg CK: Children's rights issues debated at annual meeting. Psychiatric News, XI:25–26, July 2, 1976

36. Boszormenyi-Nagy I, Spark G: Invisible Loyalties. New York, Harper & Row, 1973

37. Beyond any discipline's competence. Yale Law Journal 83:1304–1313, 1974, in Goldstein J, Freud A, Solnit AJ: Beyond the Best Interests of the Child. New York, Free Press, 1973

38. Greif JB: Fathers, children and joint custody. Am J Orthopsychiatry 49:311–319, 1979

39. Foote C, Levy RJ, Sander FEA: Cases and Materials on Family Law (ed #2). Boston, Little, Brown, 1976

40. Kaslow F, Abroms G. Family Therapy, Law and Values. San Francisco, Jossey-Bass (in press)

Family Meal by Johann-Mongels Culverhouse. Courtesy of Hammer Gallery, New York.

18

Results of Family Therapy

OBJECTIVES

- To become familiar with the positive and negative results of family therapy
- To be able to compare the outcomes of family therapy, other psychotherapies, and nontreatment
- To appreciate the limitations of family therapy
- To appreciate the current "state of the art" of evaluation of outcome in marital and family therapy
- To help the reader formulate clinical generalizations from the outcome data

INTRODUCTION

Family therapy is a relatively new approach; it has been on the scene for about 20 years. As with most new psychiatric treatments, workers became overenthusiastic about their results.[1] Fifteen years ago the first reports on the outcome of family therapy appeared, which sometimes contained small notes reporting "outstanding results." These reports were useful in helping to advance the cause but were of relatively little value in evaluating the effects of therapy. At most they seemed to suggest that the treatment was not making the problem worse.

Later, the results from larger series of families in therapy were reported.[2-4] Most of these studies indicated that family therapy was a "good" form of treatment. By 1973, however, there still were only a few carefully controlled studies.[5,6] By "controlled" we mean a study that includes randomization procedures and comparison with control groups receiving no treatment or other forms of treatment, for example, group therapy.

Over the last five years, a number of controlled studies have begun to compare the outcomes of family treatment with those of both individual and group therapy. The objectives of this chapter are to review those data and integrate them with other aspects of the family treatment model.

OVERVIEW OF PSYCHOTHERAPY OUTCOME RESEARCH

Before trying to decide whether or not family therapy is effective, one has to place that question in context. The following is a summary of the field of psychotherapy evaluation:[7]

Approximately half the studies of psychosocial treatment have been concerned with treatment outcome. Although the studies have failed to specify in comparable terms such variables as patient characteristics, nature of the intervention, environmental influences, and indices of change, some findings have been remarkably consistent. Among them are the following:

Most forms of psychotherapy are effective with about two-thirds of nonpsychotic patients. About 10 percent of treated patients become worse.

Controlled research has successfully demonstrated that treated patients show significantly more behavioral and attitudinal changes than untreated patients.

Any seemingly differential effectiveness of various forms of psychotherapy gradually disappears with the passage of time. It has yet to be convincingly demonstrated that one form of psychotherapy is superior to another.

Patients who benefit from psychotherapy are those who experience acute discomfort because of their condition and are highly motivated to receive treatment and expect to be helped by it. They show a higher degree of personal integration, are intelligent and reasonably well educated, have achieved some social success, are reflective, and can experience and express emotion.

The characteristics of the effective therapist remain unclear. The popular belief that he or she need only be genuine, empathic, and warm is not supported by recent research.

OVERVIEW OF FAMILY THERAPY OUTCOME RESEARCH

"What kinds of change are produced in what kinds of problems, by what kinds of therapists, using what kinds of techniques, under what kinds of conditions?"[8] Furthermore, because each family and each family member are unique, how can the family therapist generally respond to the particular family in treatment from studies of many families? The data to answer these questions are simply not available at this time. Nevertheless we pose the questions so that the reader will be able to appreciate the complexity of the studies that must be done.

Such studies should meet criteria that are scientifically adequate for evaluating family therapy outcome. The most important issues are:[9]

1. Controlled assignment to treatment conditions (random assignment, matching of total groups, or matching in pairs).
2. Pre- and postmeasurement of change. (This is in contrast to postevaluation only.)
3. No contamination of major independent variables (e.g. therapist experience level, number of therapists per treatment condition, and *relevant* therapeutic competence—such as, a psychoanalyst using behavioral therapy for the first time offers a poor test of the power of the behavioral method).
4. Appropriate statistical analysis.
5. Follow-up. As J. P. Scott has written, "The follow-up is the great exposure of truth, the rock on which many fine theories are wrecked and upon which better ones can be built. It is to the psychiatrist what postmortem is to the physician."[10]

Other, less important criteria, include the following:

1. The treatment should be equally valued. (Biases are often engendered for both patients and therapist when this criterion is not met.)
2. Treatment carried out as described or expected.
3. The use of multiple change indices.
4. The use of multiple vantage points in assessing outcome.
5. Outcome not limited to change in the "identified patient." (This criterion is perhaps uniquely required in marital and family therapy).
6. Data on other concurrent treatment (evidence of none or, if present, of its equivalence across groups).
7. Equal treatment length in comparative studies.
8. Outcome assessment allowance for both positive and negative change.
9. Therapist–investigator nonequivalence. (Early reviews found the two to be the same person in about 75 percent of the studies examined.)

IMPROVEMENT RATES OF MARITAL AND FAMILY THERAPY

The data on results of both marital therapy and family therapy have recently been reviewed.[9-12] The results as summarized in Table 18-1 show some 75 studies of marital ($n = 36$) and family ($n = 39$) therapy that reported gross improvement rates. Most of these studies were from outpatient settings. Most of the marital studies dealt with individual family member's outcomes, dyadic marital relationship changes, or family system changes; a variety of diagnoses

Table 18-1

Summary of Gross Improvement Rates in Nonbehavioral
Marital and Family Therapy[11]

Treatment Type and Setting	Number Studies Reviewed	Total N	Improved (percent)	Little or No Change (percent)	Worse (percent)
		Marital Therapy			
Individual	7	406	48	45	7
Conjoint (marital Rx)	8	261	70	29	1
Conjoint group	15	397	66	30	4
Concurrent	6	464	63	35	2
Total	36	1528	61	35	4
		Family Therapy			
Outpatient	26	897	76	23	1
Day hospital	3	194	59	37	4
Inpatient	10	341	78	22	0
Total	39	1414	75	24	1
Grand total	75	2942	68 (1988/2942)	30 (883/2942)	2 (71/2942)

(Reprinted with permission of Family Process, Inc.)

were represented. Outcome was based on measures varying from highly objective (e.g., weight gain) to highly subjective (e.g., satisfaction with treatment) and included a full range of rating scores. The modal study usually used only one evaluative perspective—that of the therapist's—and used global outcome as the only measure, rather than including outcomes from multiple perspectives and multiple evaluative measures. Marital therapy was found to produce a positive change for about two-thirds of the patients who came for help for a marital problem.*

Are the results the same when a child or an adolescent is the identified patient and the treatment is family therapy? In general the answer to that question appears to be yes. When the identified patient is a child or adolescent, improvement occurs in about two-thirds of the cases. The remaining one-third will show no improvement or a worsening of their present condition. Long-range effects on the child or adolescent who is *not* the identified patient are unknown.

In summary both conjoint marital and conjoint family treatment are superior to no treatment at all.[12] Both achieve results at least equal to those obtained with other kinds of psychotherapies—that is, there is an improvement in about two-

*This includes nonbehaviorally oriented marital therapy, specifically conjoint therapy, conjoint group therapy, and collaborative–concurrent marital therapy.

thirds of the cases. By "improvement," we mean positive change in the marital relationship (in marital therapy), in the identified patient (either in the adult or child), or in the family (in family therapy).

COMPARISONS OF OUTCOME OF FAMILY THERAPY WITH OTHER PSYCHOTHERAPIES

Evidence is accumulating that would indicate that individual therapy for a marital problem results in positive change in about 50 percent of the cases.[9, 13] This compares to the figure of about 66 percent positive change resulting from marital therapy. For the first time marital therapists are now in a good position to assert that marital therapy may be not only as efficacious as individual therapy but rather may be even *better*. (Further research is necessary to clarify this finding, but at least the question of the comparative efficacy of those two kinds of psychotherapy has at last been raised.) Marital therapy also appears to have approximately one-half the deterioration rate (5 to 6 percent unimproved or worse) as compared with individual therapy (about 11 percent).

Tables 18-2 and 18-3 suggest that family therapy appears to be superior to individual psychotherapy "when one member of a family unit or dyadic relationship asks for treatment with problems involving family living."[9] Although these data are preliminary and must be taken with caution, in every study that has compared family therapy with other types of treatment, the former has been shown to be equal or superior to the other therapy.

Controlled Studies of Outcome

Only within the 1970s have there been controlled studies of family therapy. Are they consistent with the trends suggested in the preceding two sections? Tables 18-4 and 18-5 indicate that family therapy is better than other treatment options (usually no treatment) in 10 out of 15 comparisons.

There have been three controlled, comparative studies of family therapy in schizophrenia.[14, 16] All three showed family therapy to have an advantage over the treatment with which it was being compared.

Therapist Factors in Outcome

There seems to be some validity to the notion that the more experienced the therapist, the better the outcome. In addition, not only knowledge and special technical competence but warmth and empathy on the part of the therapist will help the family members to *stay* in treatment. (This, of course, leaves unanswered the issue of efficacy of treatment.)

PREDICTION OF PROCESS AND OUTCOME

Predictions of treatment process and outcome are still extremely difficult to make. This has not, however, deterred some senior clinicians from making them. The normative responses of the family to conjoint family therapy have been described: "Most families who accept conjoint family therapy when it is offered, and even families who might be considered unsuitable for therapy for various reasons, will enter into and participate in treatment."[17] Most family members will not initiate a move to drop out of therapy. It is difficult to predict in advance which families will be easy to treat and which will be difficult and what resistance will occur during treatment. It appears that an experienced therapist has a good chance of anticipating the members' common resistance that "only others in the family have troubles."

It was also found that "one can conclude that conjoint family therapy is rarely harmful to members of the treated family." Predictions of the effectiveness of family therapy made to the family were uniformly underestimated by the therapist. (The same thing is done in clinical medical practice when the therapist tells the family that he may not be able to help them or help them only to a limited degree.)[18]

LIMITATIONS OF FAMILY THERAPY

It is obvious that not all problems are due to defects in the family. There are many families in which overall family structure and function are relatively healthy but, nevertheless, one member has a problem.

Mrs. B, a 46-year old, came with her husband and four children seeking therapy. She told the story of both parents dying in a plane crash when she was a year old. Throughout her life she was raised by a series of adoptive parents and relatives. At each point of the comings and goings in the family—for example, an adoptive father being drafted into the army—she would become very depressed, tearful, and angry, blaming other family members for their various deficiencies.

Family therapy was sought at this time because the family was having trouble living with Mrs. B in her depressed state—a problem that had been present for 30 years. The task of the family therapist was to see what could be changed. It turned out that the precipitant was the oldest daughter going away to college. So the family therapist helped the identified patient and the rest of the family cope with the derivatives of the mother's classical separation experience (loss of the parents at an early age as it now affected the family structure). The family therapist could *not* change the fact that the identified patient would have a strong and dysfunctional reaction to loss.

The family therapist commonly assumes that when a family comes for help with a specific problem, the cause is generally found in system problems of more serious nature. Therefore it follows that the treatment strategy is to treat the system. The assumption is that treating the system will cause the symptom to change. Treating the system and even changing the system to function better does *not* necessarily mean that all symptoms in the family will show improvement. In practice there are symptoms that will be left untreated.

What are the variables that limit change in families? To the extent that families or couples have not been able to cope with and master previous stages of development, they may have limitations in coping with a current phase. Other limiting factors include the degree of rigidity of chronic character traits and styles of couples, as well as biological, physical, and social variables.

NEGATIVE EFFECTS OF FAMILY THERAPY

If a treatment—any treatment—induces beneficial results, it must also be capable of producing harmful effects.[19] Although not a great deal has been written about this subject in family therapy literature, most experienced clinicans would agree that family therapy can, to an unknown extent, induce negative effects.

Table 18-6 points out five categories of negative effects, as follows. First, exacerbation of presenting symptoms: In most cases there is a phase of family therapy in which problems may worsen. Second, appearance of new symptoms: This is common (but not universal) in family therapy. What usually happens is that a new symptom occurs in a family member other than the identified patient. Third, patient abuse or misuse of therapy: Most commonly one family member tries to use the family therapy for "one-upmanship." Father might say, "Dr. So-and-So said that I seemed to have the best judgment in the family," and then proceed to blast his spouse and children. Other times families refuse to terminate therapy even though the therapist believes they are capable of functioning without it. Fourth, the family's overreaching itself: Some therapists believe that "anything is possible" and encourage families to attempt tasks and try for goals that clearly are beyond their reach. Such attempts are destructive and should be avoided. Fifth, disillusionment with the therapy or the therapist, or both: The family may try family therapy as a last resort. When therapy does not produce beneficial change (at least in the family's terms), the family may be worse than at the start, since the members have lost their last hope.

The precise incidence of negative effects resulting from family therapy is not known, but it probably occurs in 5 to 10 percent of all cases (see Table 18-7).

What happens if the outcome of marital treatment is separation or divorce? One might automatically assume that such an outcome is deleterious and that marital and family therapy should be designed to hold the families together. On reflection, experience seems to indicate otherwise. Marital therapy allows the partners to examine whether or not it is to their advantage to stay together, and it gives them permission to separate if that is what they need to do.

In the A family the couple were in their thirties. He was a dentist, she a housewife who had previously been a teacher. She came from a family in which her father had been a chronic "runaround," and she married her husband because he appeared to be reliable and stable. He came from a family in which the mother was dull and masochistic, and he married his wife because she seemed exciting and interesting.

The couple came to therapy after 5 years of marriage when it was "discovered that the husband was having extramarital affairs." (He had left several notes from girl friends around.) Exploration of the situation revealed that soon after marriage Mrs. A had become slowly and almost imperceptibly disillusioned with her husband when she found that he was very insecure about himself, was very unreliable, and characteristically "lied and cheated." Dr. A perceived after several years that his wife was not as exciting as he had thought and would not fulfill the role that he had envisioned for her—that is, being the "slave" to a professional husband.

The therapy allowed the couple to examine some of the original premises on which they had gotten together and they found them faulty. The process of therapy, and not the therapist's values, gave them the necessary permission to separate.

DEFECTION AND PREMATURE TERMINATION OF FAMILY TREATMENT

In one study about 30 percent of all the families referred for family treatment failed to appear for the first session (defected) and another 30 percent terminated in the first three sessions, leaving about 40 percent who continued.[20] The main reason families gave for termination was a lack of activity on the part of the therapist, whereas defectors in general had a "change of heart" and denied that a problem existed. The motivation of the husband appeared to play a crucial role—the more motivated he was, the more likely the family was to continue treatment. (See Chapter 10, "The Course of Treatment.")

PATIENT AND FAMILY SATISFACTION

There is a major difference between patient satisfaction, family and "significant other" satisfaction, and outcome of treatment as judged by the therapist. Sometimes all three correlate. In many cases, however, they do not. Often what the patient feels is an improvement is actually considered a regression by the family. Similarly what the therapist considers an improvement is considered by both family and patient as a change for the worse. The following case vignette will serve to illustrate these points:

The K family, consisting of mother, father, and three children ranging between 15 and 25 years, had come for treatment following the death of one of the teenage siblings due to leukemia. Some of the problems included the father's drinking and difficulties in communication between the mother and father and between the children and father. A long course of family therapy resulted in marked improvement in all of these areas. The mother and the children considered it a very successful outcome. The father consistently maintained that nothing had been accomplished: he could not remember changes made in the family as a result of the therapy and therefore felt that nothing had been done in therapy.

CLINICAL IMPLICATIONS OF DATA FROM FAMILY THERAPY OUTCOME STUDIES

Using conclusions from the Gurman and Kniskern review, important implications for family therapists can be formulated.[9] The following is a list of their conclusions with the authors' appended implications:

1. Individual therapy for marital problems is a very ineffective treatment strategy and one that appears to produce more negative effects than alternative approaches.

    Implication: Traditional clinical lore has always been that individual therapy was the treatment of choice in marital problems. For the first time recent research has questioned this assumption. It may be that marital therapy is not only as good as individual therapy for marital problems, but it may even be better. We recommend that the family therapist use the option of individual or marital therapy depending on his understanding of the needs of the case (see Chapter 19).

2. Couples benefit most from treatment when both spouses are involved in the therapy, especially when they are seen conjointly.

    Implication: Both partners should be involved in conjoint therapy.

3. Family therapy appears to be at least as effective and possibly more effective than individual therapy for a wide variety of problems, including both "individual" difficulties as well as more obvious family conflicts.

    Implication: For some problems individual therapy might be the treatment of choice, whereas for others family therapy would be preferable. In the absence of research data to use as guidelines for treatment, the choice between these approaches probably should "continue to reflect the biases and training of the individual practitioners."

4. For certain clinical goals and problems—for example, decreasing hospitalization rates for some chronic and acute inpatients, treating anorexia nervosa, many childhood behavior problems, some forms of juvenile delinquency and sexual dysfunction—systems therapies offer the treatments of choice. Specific effective treatment programs and strategies exist for some of these

problems and should be taught in any training program in marital and family therapy.

Implication: Since the results of family treatment for these conditions are encouraging, such strategies should be taught in any training program pending further definitive outcome results.

5.   Short-term and time-limited therapies appear to be at least as effective as treatment of longer duration; moreover, most of the positive results of open-ended therapy were achieved in less than five months.

Implication: Family therapy appears to move more rapidly than individual psychotherapy. This may be due to the fact that it is more action oriented, more geared to the present than the past, more geared to problem solving than to "insight," deals more with transactional issues with all family members present, and is based on more direct observations of behavior and interaction, than a report from only one member of the family. Some of the changes, however, take considerably longer than five months to manifest themselves. (The transcript in Chapter 22 illustrates such a case.)

6.   Several marital and family "enrichment" programs appear to have promise as useful preventative strategies in family living.

Implication: Although the data are not yet in, the range of family therapy is rapidly expanding. Family therapists should probably remain cautious about claims of efficacy at this point.

7.   The more members of the family involved in the family therapy, the better the outcome seems to be. This is especially true when the child is the identified patient.

Implication: For the symptom to change, the situation should change.[21] Evaluative measures should include not only the presence or absence of "better behavior" but also evaluation of whether or not the *system* in which the behavior took place also was changed. The more family members involved, the better the outcome seems to be. This may require some major changes in clinical practices—for example, inpatient services, child psychiatry services, and so on. Family therapy is the most economical treatment in time and money for multiproblem families.

8.   Therapist relationship skills have major impact on the outcome of marital family treatment regardless of the "school" or orientation of the clinician. Training programs must focus on both conceptual–technical skills and relationships skills for beginning family therapists.

Implication: Family therapy relies on the therapist's cognitive and technical skills, but there should also be an emphasis in any training program on what kind of person the family therapist is. The kind of experience the family has with the therapist as a person will affect outcome.

Table 18-2*

Outcomes of Comparative Studies of Marital Therapy[9]

Author	Treatments Compared (Setting)[a]	Outcome Criteria (Source)[b]	Outcome (Design Quality)
Beck and Jones (1973)	Short-term; open-ended; conjoint; individual (FSC)	Overall change (P,T); overall change (P,T)	No difference; conjoint superior[c]
Burton and Kaplan (1968)	Group; individual individual; concurrent (OPC)	Global self-change (P); global self-change (P)	Group superior; concurrent superior (poor)
Cookerly (1973)	Group and "interview" con-current, conjoint, and Individual (OPC)	Marital status (O); quality of outcome status (J)	Conjoint and conjoint group superior (poor)
Cookerly (1974, 1976)[d]	Concurrent, conjoint, and group (OPC)	Individual, personal– social, and marital adjustment (P)	Concurrent superior on individual pathology; conjoint and conjoint group superior on marital; no difference in social (good)
Cookerly (1976)[e]	Group and "interview" con-current, conjoint, and Individual (OPC)	Marital, social, and personal adjustment (P)	Conjoint and conjoint group superior in marital adjustment (poor)
Cookerly (1976)[f]	Group and "interview" con-current, conjoint, and individual (OPC)	Divorce rate 1 to 3 years post-therapy (O); marital status satisfaction (P)	Lowest divorce rates and most satisfaction in conjoint (37%) and conjoint group (40%) (poor)
Corder et al. (1972)	Conjoint group; individual group (IP)	Alcoholic spouse's drinking (6-month follow-up)	Conjoint group superior (fair)
Davenport et al. (1975)	Group; individual; community care (MF)	Rehospitalization (O); marital status (O); social functioning (P)	Group superior (fair)

276

Study	Treatment modalities	Outcome measures	Results
Freeman et al. (1969)	Conjoint; group; individual[g] (OPC)	Marital relationship; division of responsibility (P,T)	No differences (poor)
Friedman (1975)	Conjoint; drug therapy (OPC)	Depression of identification point (P,J); family role performance and marital relationship (P)	Marital therapy superior for marital relationship; drug superior for depressive symptoms (good)
Graham (1968)	Conjoint; conjoint and individual (CC)	Positive references to spouse (J); reconciliation (O); interpersonal dominance and affiliation (P)	Conjoint superior (good)
Hepworth and Smith (1972)	Individual; conjoint and individual[h] (FSC)	Achievements of goals (J)	No difference (poor)
Hickman and Baldwin (1970)	Conjoint; programmed communication training (CC)	Reconciliation (O); marital relationship (P)	Conjoint superior (very good)
Macon (1975)	Conjoint; conjoint group (FSC)	Communication (P); self-esteem (P); problem-solving skill (P); spouse-image (P)	No difference (fair)
Matanovich (1970)	Encounter group tapes; Individual and conjoint (CC)	Reconciliation (O); interpersonal dominance and affiliation (P); rating of helpfulness (P)	No difference on any criteria (very good)
Mayadas and Duehn (1977)	Communication modeling (CM); CM plus video feedback (CMV); verbal counseling (VC) (OPC)	Five problematic communication behaviors (O)	CMV>CM>VC (very good)

*Tables 18-2 through 18-5 and Table 18-7 are reprinted with permission from Gurman AS, Kniskern DP: Research on marital and family therapy: Progress, perpsective and prospect in Garfield SL, Bergin AE (Eds): Handbook of Psychotherapy and Behavior Change: An Empirical Analysis (2nd ed), New York, John Wiley & Sons, Inc., 1978.

Table 18-2 (continued)
Outcomes of Comparative Studies of Marital Therapy[9]

Author	Treatments Compared (Setting)[a]	Outcome Criteria (Source)[b]	Outcome (Design Quality)
Mezydlo et al. (1973)	Parish pastoral counseling; "office," priests; lay therapists (all conjoint) (catholic FSC)	Target complaints (P)	Office outcome>lay>parish (poor)
Pierce (1973)	Communication training; group (OPC)	Communication skill and self-exploration (J)	Communication training superior (fair)
Reid and Shyne (1969)	Conjoint; individual brief; open-ended (FSC)	Presenting problem (T,J) Presenting problem (T,J)	No difference; brief superior on some dimensions (good)
Smith (1967)	Conjoint group; individual group (IP)	Alcoholic spouse's drinking (H,W,T)	Conjoint group superior (fair)
Swan (1972)	Communication training; eclectic conjoint (CC)	Level of conflict (J)	No differences (good)
Valle and Marinelli (1975)	Communication training; group (PP)	Facilitative skill (J); marital relationship (P); individual functioning (P)	Communication training superior (fair)
Wattie (1973)	Short-term; open-ended (FSC)	Marital congruence (P); global change (P,T,J)	Short-term superior on husband change only (good)
Wells et al. (1975b)	Communication training; conjoint[l] (FSC)	Marital adjustment (P); dyadic empathy and warmth (P)	No difference at termination; conjoint superior at 3-month follow-up (fair)
Ziegler (1973)	Long group; intensive group (OPC)	CPI and omnibus personality inventory (P)	No clear difference; long had more intense change, intensive, wider range of changes (good)

Summary

Conjoint		Individual		Group	
Conjoint superior	16	Individual superior	2	Group superior	15
Tie	10	Tie	5	Tie	8
Others superior	0	Others superior	12	Others superior	2
Conjoint superior	4	Individual superior	1	Group superior	0
Tie	2	Tie	1	Tie	6
Individual superior	0	Group superior	9	Conjoint superior	0
		Conjoint and group (combined) superior	31		
		Tie	11		
		All others superior	2		

Note: Comparative studies of behavior therapy are reported elsewhere in this chapter.

a FSC = family service center or family counseling centers; CC = conciliation court; PP = private practice; MF = medical facilities; IP = inpatient.

b P = patient; T = therapist; J = judge or trained observer; O = objective indices not based on behavioral observation.

c This major national census study examined comparative treatment modalities as at most a secondary (and probably a tertiary) goal; thus the standards of experimental research are probably not appropriately applied here; hence, we have omitted a design quality rating.

d The author's 1974 report included data only on MMPI changes; his 1976 report included these data plus the other criteria noted. Both reports used the same sample and are therefore combined here.

e "Outcome" was actually based on client's "immediate attitudes" toward the helpfulness of sessions and was based on postsession responses for each therapy session over a 4-month period.

f All of Cookerly's studies, two of which (1973, 1974) had been previously reported, were reported in his 1976 paper.

g Although these were the predominant treatment forms, an indeterminable number of study patients were involved in an indeterminable mixture of treatments.

h Although the authors describe this study as one comparing individual and conjoint therapy, it is in fact one of individual versus conjoint *plus* individual therapy; in the "conjoint" condition, averaging 26 sessions per case, 41 percent (11 sessions) were held with wives alone, 31 percent (eight sessions) with husbands alone, and only 28 percent (seven sessions) conjointly.

i Actually, due to clinical necessity, several of the conjoint couples also receive some communication training, although not in groups; although the initial intent was for the conjoint condition to be "behaviorally oriented" (Wells et al., 1975b, p. 1), this treatment clearly emerged as quite eclectic.

Table 18-3
Comparative Studies of Family Therapy Outcome[9]

Author	Treatments Compared (Setting)[a]	Outcome Criteria (Source)[b]	Outcome (Design Quality)
Abroms et al. (1971)	Family;[c] individual (IP)	Identified patient symptoms at discharge (S)	Family improved 86%; individual improved 81% (poor)
Alexander and Parsons (1973)	Family behavioral-system; client-centered family; eclectic-dynamic family (OPC)	Identified patient recidivism at 18 months (O)	Behavioral systems = 26% recidivism; client-centered = 47%; eclectic-dynamic = 73% (good)
Bernal and Margolin (1976)	Behavioral parent counseling (BT) Client-centered parent counseling (CG) (OPC)	1. Child's verbal abuse (O) 2. Deviant child behavior (O) 3. Targeted child behavior (Par) 4. Parental attitudes toward child (Par) 5. Satisfaction with therapy (Par)	No differences within or between groups on criteria L and 2; no difference between groups on 3; but both showed change; partial superiority for CC on 4; BT superior on 5 (good)
Budman and Shapiro (1976)	Individual;[d] family[d] Individual terminators;[e] Family terminators[e] (OPC)	Identified patient functioning at 4½-month follow-up (Par,P) Identified patient functioning at 4½-month follow-up (Par, P)	No difference in reported functioning Individual terminators were more positive in reports of patient functioning[f] (poor)
Dezen and Borstein (1975)	E_1 = probation with family therapy E_2 = probation services as usual (OPC)	Identified patient recidivism at 6 months (O) Identified patient symptomatology (Par) Parental overinvolvement (Par) Report of parental behavior (C)	Family probation superior on symptom measure only (fair)
Evans et al. (1971)	Conjoint;[g] individual (IP)	Identified patient symptomatology (S) Return to work (O)	Conjoint superior to individual on both measures (poor)

Ewing (1975)	Crisis intervention; psychodynamic child guidance (OPC)	Patient functioning (M)	Crisis equal to child guidance in one-tenth treatment time (poor)
Finol (1973)	Guided videotaped feedback; guided audiotaped feedback;	Positive and negative comments toward patient (O)	Videotape superior to audiotape on one measure and to discussion on one measure (good)
Gould and Glick (1976)	Conjoint family; conjoint and multiple family; no family therapy (family unavailable); no family therapy (family available) (IP)	Severity of illness (S); psychiatric function (S); role function (IP, Family); employment (S.O.)	On all measures, conjoint>conjoint and multiple>no family therapy (family unavailable)>no family therapy (family unavailable) (fair)
Hendricks (1971)	Multifamily group counseling (MFG) Standard inpatient treatment (IP Addiction Treatment Center)	Continued discharge (out-patient) status at 1-year follow-up (O)	41% of MFG patients remained outpts. versus 21% for standard addiction treatment (fair)
Jansma (1971)	Conjoint family; multiple family (OPC)	Family adjustment (Family); family congruence (Family); family satisfaction (Family); marital satisfaction (Par)	Multiple superior to conjoint on 7 out of 9 measures (good)

Table 18-3 (continued)
Comparative Studies of Family Therapy Outcome[9]

Author	Treatments Compared (Setting)[a]	Outcome Criteria (Source)[b]	Outcome (Design Quality)
Johnson (1971)	Conjoint family; nonfamily treatment (OPC)	Patterns of communication (O)	Conjoint superior to individual on 8 out of 9 measures (good)
Klein et al.[h] (1975)	E_1 = family behavioral-system; E_2 = client-centered family groups; E_3 = eclectic-dynamic family (OPC)	Sibling court contracts in 3 years (O)	Behavioral-systems = 20%; client-centered = 59%; eclectic-dynamic = 63% (good)
Langsley et al. (1969)	E_1 = family crisis intervention (Home); E_2 = hospital treatment as usual	Rates of rehospitalization (O) Social adjustment inventory (Family)	Family superior to hospital in length and frequency of readmissions; no difference on adjustment (good)
Love et al.[j] (1972)	Family-oriented videotape feedback of interaction; individual child psychotherapy; parent counseling (OPC)	Identified patient school interaction ratings (J); grades (O)	Feedback = parent counseling individual therapy on grades; all treatments improved interaction (good)
Pittman et al. (1968)	E_1 = conjoint family crisis intervention E_2 = individual long term (OPC)	Return to work (O)	Conjoint superior to individual (poor)

Study	Treatment	Outcome measures	Results
Rittenhouse (1970)	Family therapy (home); hospital treatment (IP)	Overall improvement (P); identified patient readmissions (O); family pathology (F); community functioning (S.O.)	Family superior to hospital on patient improvement and readmissions; no difference on family or community (good)
Sigal et al. (1976)	Psychodynamically oriented conjoint; early terminators from conjoint treatment (OPC)	Identified patient presenting symptomatology at 4 years from termination (Family); Identified patient new problems (Family); level of family functioning (Family)	Early terminator had fewer new problems; no differences on other measures[k] (fair)
Stanton and Todd (1976)	Structural family therapy; standard methadone treatment (OPC)	IP heroin use (O); IP work and school adjustment (F)	Family therapy superior to usual heroin addiction treatment (very good)
Trankina (1975)	Traditional child guidance; crisis family therapy (OPC)	Family satisfaction and adjustment (Par); family life quality (Par); child behavior (Par); overall improvement (S, Par)	Crisis therapy superior on criteria 4, with fewer dropouts and in less time (fair)

Table 18-3 (continued)
Comparative Studies of Family Therapy Outcome[9]

Author	Treatments Compared (Setting)[a]	Outcome Criteria (Source)[b]	Outcome (Design Quality)
Wellisch et al. (1976)	Conjoint family; individual problem oriented (IP)	Rehospitalization (Family); Identified patient return to work or school (Family); Family interaction (J)	Conjoint superior on all measures except family interaction (good)

a OPC = outpatient clinic; IP = inpatient.

b S = staff; Fam = family; O = objective indices; J = judge or trained observer; Par = Parents; P = patient; S.O. = significant other; C = children; M = mother.

c Inpatient families were treated with a variety of individual, group and conjoint family therapy.

d Patients or families attending four or more sessions of therapy.

e Terminators are those patients or families who attended from 1 to 3 sessions.

f Family terminators reported two identified patients had deteriorated; no reports of deterioration in individual terminators.

g Treatment as usual in this setting included individual sessions in all cases and often included medication and ECT.

h Data is based on follow-up of siblings of identified patients reported on in previous study (Alexander & Parsons, 1973).

i Treatment as usual included individual and group psychotherapy, milieu therapy, and medication.

j Some of these subjects reported in Kaswan and Love (1969).

k There was a strong trend for long-term treatment families to report better family functioning.

Table 18-4
Controlled Studies of Marital Therapy Outcome[9]

Author	Treatment(s); (Treatment Length);[a] Setting[b]	Outcome Criteria (Source)[c]	Results (Design Quality)
Alkire and Brunse (1974)	Videotape feedback in ongoing groups (short); VA-OPC	Self-concept (P); marital casualties (divorce, separation separation, suicide) (P)	More casualties and more *decreased* self-concept in treated groupe (good)
Cadogan (1973)	Conjoint group (moderate); OPC	1. Drinking behavior (P) 2. Marital communication (P) 3. Acceptance and trust (P)	Treatment>control on criterion 1, not on 2 and 3 (very good)
Cardillo (1971)	Conjoint communication training (short); OPC	1. Self-concept (P) 2. Interpersonal perception method (P) 3. Helpfulness of therapy (P)	Treatment>control on all measures (very good)
Cassidy (1973)	Conjoint communication training (short); PP	1. Communication (P) 2. Target behaviors (P) 3. Attitude toward spouse (P)	Treatment>control on all measures (very good)
Christensen (1974)	Conjoint communication training (short); OPC	1. Self-esteem (P) 2. Decision making (J) 3. Choice fulfillment (P)	Treatment>control on some measures of criterion 1, and on 2; no difference on 3 (very good)

Table 18-4 (continued)
Controlled Studies of Marital Therapy Outcome[9]

Author	Treatment(s); (Treatment Length);[a] Setting[b]	Outcome Criteria (Source)[c]	Results (Design Quality)
Friedman (1975)	Conjoint (moderate); OPC	1. Two psychiatric rating scales (J) 2. Global change (J) 3. Symptom ratings (P) 4. Family role performance (P) 5. Marital relationship (P)	Treatment>control on most measures (very good)
Graham (1968)	Conjoint; conjoint plus individual (short); CC	1. Reconciliations (O) 2. Positive references to spouse (O) 3. Dominance and affiliation (P)	Conjoint>control on criterion 1 only; conjoint plus individual = control on all criteria (good)
Griffin (1967)	Individual (short); FSC (wives)	1. Perception of self (P) 2. Perception of spouse (P)	Treatment>control on both measures (good)
Hickman and Baldwin	Conjoint; programmed communication training (short) CC	1. Reconciliation (O) 2. Attitude toward marriage (P)	Conjoint>control on both criteria; programmed = control (very good)
Matanovich (1970)	Encounter tapes[d] (moderate); conjoint plus individual (short); CC	1. Reconciliation (O) 2. Dominance and affiliation (P)	Encounter tapes>control on criterion 1; conjoint plus individual = control on both criteria (very good)

Pierce (1973) — Communication training; conjoint group (long): OPC

1. Communication skill (J)
2. Self-exploration (J)

Treatment I>control on both criteria; treatment II = control on both criteria (fair)

Summary

Conjoint>control	3	
No difference	0	
Conjoint<control	0	
Group>control	1	
No difference	1	
Group<control	1	
Individual>control	1	
No difference	0	
Individual<control	0	
Communication training >control	5	
No difference	1	
Communication training. <control	0	
Conjoint plus individual >control	0	
No difference	2	
Conjoint plus individual <control	0	
Total		
Treatment>control	10	
No difference	4	
Treatment<control	1	

[a] Short = 1 to 10 sessions; moderate = 11 to 20 sessions; long = 21 or more sessions.

[b] CC = conciliation court; FSC = family service or counseling center; OPC = outpatient clinic; PP = private practice; VA = veterans administration.

[c] J = trained judge or interviewer; O = objective records; P = patient.

[d] Although this treatment was carried out in a group setting, the report emphasizes within-dyad encounteres instead of group process; so that in the summary the study is classified as communication training, not group therapy.

Table 18-5
Controlled Studies of Family Therapy Outcome[9]

Author	Treatment(s); (Treatment Length);[a] Setting[b]	Outcome Criteria (Source)[c]	Results (Design Quality)
Alexander and Parsons (1973)	Behavioral-systems; (short); client-centered (short); eclectic-dynamic (moderate); OPC	Identified patient recidivism at 18 months (O)	Behavioral system superior to control; client-centered and eclectic-dynamic = control (good)
Beal and Duckro (1977)	Conjoint (short); juvenile court	Termination of court hearing or referral to noncourt agencies versus appearance before court (O)	17% of treated IPs appeared in court versus; 35% of untreated cases ($p < .05$) (fair)
Garrigan and Bambrick (1975)	Conjoint (short); school	1. Family adjustment (P) 2. Behavior symptoms (teach) 3. IP self-concept (P) 4. Family relationships (P)	Treatment superior to control on family adjustment only (good)
Garrigan and Bambrick (1977)	Conjoint (short); school for emotionally disturbed children and adolescents	1. Family adjustment (Par) 2. Marital facilitative conditions (F) 3. IP self-concept (P) 4. Family members' state-trait anxiety (F) 5. IP symptoms (Par)	Treatment superior to control on Par rating of family adjustment, on two out of four facilitative conditions and on IP symptoms; no difference on criteria 3 and 4 (very good)

Study	Treatment	Measures	Results
Jansma (1971)	Multiple (?); conjoint (?); OPC	1. Family adjustment (F,T) 2. Family congruence (F,T) 3. Family satisfaction (F,T) 4. Marital adjustment (F,T)	Multiple superior to control on eight out of nine measures; conjoint family superior to control on one out of nine measures (?)
Katz et al. (1975)	Conjoint (short); OPC	Family interaction (J)	Treatment superior to control on appropriate topic changes; no difference in speech clarity or humor (very good)
Klein et al.[d] (1975)	Behavioral-system (short); client-centered (short); eclectic-dynamic (moderate); OPC	Sibling recidivism at 3 years (O)	Behavioral-systems superior to control; client-centered and eclectic-dynamic = control (good)
Knight (1974)	Parent effectiveness training (short); OPC	1. Frequency of enuresis (Par) 2. Anxiety (Par) 3. Interpersonal distance (F)	No significant positive effects, some deterioration in female identified patients and parents (?)
Reiter and Kilmann (1975)	Mothers' groups (short); OPC	1. Marital integration (Par) 2. Verbal interchanges (J) 3. Child symptoms (Par) 4. Family congruence (Par)	Treatment superior to control on measures 1 to 3 (very good)

Table 18-5 (continued)
Controlled Studies of Family Therapy Outcome[9]

Author	Treatment(s); (Treatment Length);[a] Setting[b]	Outcome Criteria (Source)[c]	Results (Design Quality)
Stanton and Todd (1976)	Conjoint (moderate); OPC	Identified patient heroin use (O); identified patient work and school adjustment (F)	Therapy superior to attention placebo and no treatment group on both measures (very good)
Stover and Guerney (1967)	Filial therapy (mothers' groups) (short); OPC	1. Mothers' reflective and directive statements (J) 2. Child's playroom behavior (J)	Treatment superior to control on measure 1; no difference on measure 2 (very good)

Summary

Adult/family IP>control		2
No difference		1
Adult/family IP<control		0
Child/adolescent IP therapy>control	6	
No difference	6	
Child/adolescent IP therapy<control	1	
Total		
Family therapy>control	8	
No difference	7	
Family therapy<control	1	

a Short = 1 to 10 sessions; moderate = 11 to 20 sessions; long = 21 or more sessions.
b OPC = outpatient clinic.
c O = objective records; P = patient; Par = parents; F = family; Teach = teachers; J = trained judge; T = therapist.
d Same families as reported on in Alexander and Parsons (1973).

Table 18-6
What Constitutes a Negative Effect?[19]

Exacerbation of Presenting Symptoms	Appearance of New Symptoms	Patient's Abuse or Misuse of Therapy	Patient "Overreaching" Self	Disillusionment with Therapy or Therapist
1. *"Worsening,"* increase in severity, pathology, etc.	1. *Generally,* may be observed when (a) psychic disturbance is manifested in a less socially acceptable form than previously; (b) symptom substitution occurs when a symptom that had fulfilled an imperative need is blocked	1. Substitution of intellectualized insights for other obsessional thoughts	1. Two forms: (a) undertaking taking life tasks (marriage, graduate school, etc.) that require resources beyond those of patient; (b) undertaking life tasks prematurely	1. May appear variously as (a) wasting of patient's resources (time, skill, money) that might have been better expended elsewhere; (b) hardening of attitudes toward other sources of help; (c) loss of confidence in therapist, possibly extending to any human relationship; (d) general loss of hope (all the more severe for initial raising of hopes that may have occured at onset of therapy.
2. *Generally,* may take form of or be accompanied by (a) exacerbation of suffering; (b) decompensation; (c) harsher superego or more rigid personality structure		2. Utilization of therapy to rationalize feelings of superiority or expressions of hostility toward other people	2. May be related to (a) intense wishes to please therapist; (b) inculcation of inachievable middle-class "ideals"; (c) increased "irrational" ideas	
3. *Specific* examples of symptom exacerbation: (a) depressive breakdown; (b) severe regression; (c) des-	2. *Specific* examples: (a) erosion of solid interpersonal relationships; (b) decreased ability to experience pleasure; (c) severe or fatal	3. Therapy becomes an end in itself; a substitute for action		

Table 18-6 (continued)
What Constitutes a Negative Effect?[19]

Exacerbation of Presenting Symptoms	Appearance of New Symptoms	Patient's Abuse or Misuse of Therapy	Patient "Overreaching" Self	Disillusionment with Therapy or Therapist
tructive acting-out; (d) increased anxiety; (e) increased hostility; (f) increased self-downing; (g) increased behavioral shirking; (h) increased inhibition; (i) paranoia, (j) fixing of obsessional symptoms; (k) exaggeration of somatic difficulties; (l) extension of phobias; (m) increased guilt, (n) increased confusion; (o) lowered self-confidence; (p) lowered self-esteem; (q) diminished capacity for delay and impulse control	psychosomatic reactions; (d) withdrawal; (e) rage; (f) dissociation; (g) drug/alcohol abuse; (h) criminal behavior, (i) suicide; (j) psychotic breaks	4. Fear of "intellectualization" prevents patients from examining their ethical and philosophical commitments 5. Participation in more radical therapies encourages belief in irrational in order to avoid painful confrontation with realities of life 6. Sustained dependency on therapy or therapist	3. May result in any or all of the following (a) excessive strain on patient's psychological resources; (b) failure at task; (c) guilt; (d) self-contempt	

Reprinted with permission from the Archives of General Psychiatry Copyright 1976, American Medical Association, 33:1291–1302, 1976

Table 18-7

Summary of Reported Deterioration Rates in Studies of Nonbehavioral Marital and Family Therapy[9]

Therapy Type or Setting	Number Studies Reporting Improvement Rates	Number Studies with "worse" Category	Number Studies Reporting Deterioration	Percent Studies with "worse" Category Reporting Deterioration	Deterioration Rate Across Studies with "worse" Category (percent)
Marital Therapy					
Conjoint	8	3(37%)	1	22	2.7 (2/72)
Individual	7	5(71%)	4	80	11.6 (27/233)
Group	15	7(47%)	4	57	16.6 (17/102)
Concurrent/Collaborative	6	4(67%)	1	25	3.3 (11/332)
Total	36	19(53%)	10	53	7.7 (57/739)

Table 18-7 (continued)
Summary of Reported Deterioration Rates in Studies of Nonbehavioral Marital and Family Therapy[9]

Therapy Type or Setting	Number Studies Reporting Improvement Rates	Number Studies with "worse" Category	Number Studies Reporting Deterioration	Percent Studies with "worse" Category Reporting Deterioration	Deterioration Rate Across Studies with "worse" Category (percent)
Family Therapy					
Inpatient	10	2(20%)	0	0	0 (0/17)
Outpatient	26	13(50%)	4	29	2.1 (10/477)
Day Hospital	3	2(67%)	1	50	7.3 (7/96)
Total	39	17(44%)	5	29	2.8 (17/580)
Grand Total	75	36(48%)	15	42	5.4 (74/1337)

REFERENCES

1. Group for the Advancement of Psychiatry. The Field of Family Psychiatry. Report No. 78. New York, Group for the Advancement of Psychiatry, 1970
2. MacGregor R, Ritchie A, Serrano A, et al: Multiple Impact Therapy With Families. New York, McGraw-Hill, 1964
3. Freeman V, Klein A, Richman L, et al: Allegheny general hospital study project, Final Report. Pittsburgh, PA, Mimeographed, 1964
4. Friedman A, Boszormenyi-Nagy I, Jungreis J, et al: Psychotherapy for the Whole Family: Case Histories, Techniques, and Concepts of Family Therapy of Schizophrenia in the Home and Clinic. New York, Springer, 1965
5. Langsley D, Kaplan D: The Treatment of Families in Crisis. New York, Grune & Stratton, 1968
6. Alexander J, Parsons B: Short-term behavioral intervention with deliquent families: Impact on family process and recidivism. J Abnorm Psychol 81:219–225, 1973
7. A 25-year review of mental health research: Highlights of a report from NIMH. Hosp & Comm Psychiatry 26:711–715, 1975
8. Parloff MB: Discussion: The narcissism of small differences—and some big ones. Int J Group Psychother 26:311–319, 1976
9. Gurman AS, Kniskern DP: Research on marital and family therapy: Progress, perspective and prospect, in Garfield SL, Bergin AE (eds): Handbook of Psychotherapy and Behavior Change: An Empirical Analysis (ed 2). New York, Wiley, 1978
10. Scott JP: Critical periods and behavioral development. Science 138:949–958, 1962
11. Gurman AS, Kniskern DP: Deterioration in marital and family therapy: Empirical, clinical, and conceptual issues. Fam Process 17:3–20, 1978, p 4
12. De Witt KN: The effectiveness of family therapy. Arch Gen Psychiatry 35:549–561, 1978
13. Gurman AS: Contemporary marital therapies: A critique and comparative analysis of psychoanalytic, behavioral and systems theory approaches, in Paolino T, McCrady B (eds): Marriage and Marital Therapy: Psychoanalytic, Behavioral and Systems Theory Perspectives. New York, Brunner/Mazel, 1978
14. Goldstein MJ, Rodnick EH, Evans JR, et al: Drug and family therapy in the aftercare of schizophrenics. Arch Gen Psychiatry 35:1169–1177, 1978
15. Langsley DG, Pittman F, Swank G: Family crisis in schizophrenics and other mental patients. J Nerv Ment Dis 149:270–276, 1969
16. Ro-Trock GK, Wellisch DK, Schoolar JC: A family therapy outcome study in an inpatient setting. Am J Orthopsychiatry 47:514–522, 1977
17. Rakoff VM, Sigal JJ, Epstein NB: Predictions of therapeutic process and progress in conjoint family therapy. Arch Gen Psychiatry 32:1013–1017, 1975
18. Siegler M: Pascal's wager and the hanging of the crepe. N Engl J Med 293:853–857, 1975
19. Hadley SW, Strupp HH: Contemporary views of negative effects in psychotherapy. Arch Gen Psychiatry 33:1291–1302, 1976
20. Shapiro R, Budman S: Defection, termination, and continuation in family and individual therapy. Fam Process 12:55–67, 1973
21. Haley J: Communication and therapy: Blocking metaphors. Am J Psychiatry 25:214–227, 1971

Family Group by Philip Levine, 1966. Courtesy of Julius and Florence Myers Collection.

19

Guidelines for Recommending Family Treatment

OBJECTIVES

- To understand the general and specific situations for which family treatment is usually recommended, including situations in which there is an identified patient
- To be aware of the changing criteria for recommending family treatment
- To outline situations in which family treatment is the treatment of choice

INTRODUCTION

Some family therapists believe that their field offers the best hope for many types of interpersonal distress. They tend to believe that it should be the exclusive method used and that it should never be used in combinations. Others, however, utilize family therapy as only one type among many and feel that it is "not a panacea, a substitute for all other approaches, or even appropriate in all cases as a totally self-contained service."[1]

Since the 1960s, as the family field has evolved, more therapists have shifted to the latter view. Enough well-controlled outcome studies, which might guide us, have not been carried out, however, nor is there the needed empirical evidence on the spontaneous rate of change for families and patients who come for treatment with family and marital problems.[2,3] In formulating guidelines for family therapy, research data are included where available, but otherwise the recommendations are based on clinical experience (see Chapter 18).

In the past decade there have been a number of major changes in the delivery of mental health services (e.g., shift from inpatient to outpatient and community work), new scientific discoveries (e.g., new psychopharmacologic agents, studies of effectiveness of family therapy compared to other therapies), and social changes (e.g., more one-parent families). The clinician needs an appreciation of those that affect the guidelines for family therapy.

SITUATIONS IN WHICH FAMILY THERAPY IS OFTEN RECOMMENDED

Family treatment is often advised when either the therapist conceptualizes or the family indicates that the family system is involved to a significant degree in some type of psychosocial problem. Family treatment is appropriate for those situations in which the family's ability to perform its basic functions is inadequate. (These functions have been discussed in Chapters 3 and 4.)

Family treatment has been recommended for problems at all stages of the family life cycle and for "identified patients" (or clients) with all types of difficulties (correctional,[4] medical, [5, 6, 7] and educational). For example, school psychologists have moved increasingly toward using family therapy for "behavior problems" and for "poor performance." It has also been used for situations in which there are obvious conflicts between a family member and the community.

Family treatment is currently (1979) an accepted part of the treatment regimens for affective disorder and for schizophrenia (see Chapter 12). The management of schizophrenia has, for some patients, shifted away from individual, psychoanalytic psychotherapy toward "psychotherapeutic management with a focus around the family."[8] Having an identified patient with schizophrenia has long-term effects on the family.[9] Somatic treatments by themselves do not cure problems of living. They can control specific psychophysiological symptoms and behaviors, but alone they will not improve or alter the preexisting family relationships, ways of coping with stress, and other preillness behavior. For these issues family therapy is indicated.

Marital conflict and dissatisfaction.   Marital conflict and dissatisfaction seem to lend themselves especially well to conjoint marital treatment. Yet it is surprising to see how often such problems are still dealt with by means of individual treatment for one of the marital partners, with relatively little attention paid to the impact of the individual treatment on the marital system as a whole. The field of marital counseling[10-12] some time ago accepted the need to see the marital couple together in such instances, and this trend toward marital therapy appears to be growing, as results from outcome studies are being reported.[2] It is believed to be more efficient in terms of time and cost to treat a couple or a whole family rather than only an individual member, especially since the role of the identified patient in multiproblem families often shifts from one member to another.

Sexual problems.   In recent years conjoint treatment for sexual problems has shown increasing promise[13, 14] (see Chapter 14). Common sexual problems have often proven intractable to individual treatment. When these same problems are viewed in an interactional framework and treated with both partners present, using a combination of sex therapy and marital therapy, surprisingly effective and rapid results have often been obtained.

The child as the identified patient.   When a child is the identified patient, it has long been the practice of child guidance clinics to involve at least one of the parents, usually in collateral treatment in which the patient and parent are both in individual treatment but with different therapists. This at least represents token recognition of the importance of the family, both in the difficulty and in its resolution.

A more thoroughgoing approach than this, however, seems indicated in these cases, with evaluation of the possible role of the child as the "symptom bearer" of more general family problems (often unresolved marital issues). Usually the marital partners are seen as a couple for a major part of the treatment. The "identified patient" may benefit from some individual attention addressed to the child's particular symptoms and psychosocial difficulties. A common sequence of events is for the entire family to start out in treatment together, and then for various individual dyads and triads to be separated out for special attention after an interval of time. Of these the marital dyad is unquestionably the most important. Some family therapists suggest that whenever there is a symptomatic child who is prepubescent, family treatment is indicated, unless there are specific contraindications.

Over the past five years, there have been marked changes in the field of child psychiatry. Many institutions are shifting from an individual psychoanalytic focus to a family systems approach.[15] An increasing range of childhood disorders is now being treated with family therapy.[16] For example, school phobias are now being treated with family therapy plus an antidepressant.

The cause of child psychopathology is an unresolved issue. "Historical and evolutionary studies reflect evidence to support familial as well as intrinsic factors within the child as responsible for child psychopathylogy."[17-19] Another issue centers on the concept of the relative importance of the completion of "developmental tasks." Child psychiatrists believe that successful completion of developmental tasks are crucial to the functioning of the individual and the family. Family therapists have taken the position that what is important is the here-and-now. By implication less attention is paid to the family's past history and the individual's growth and developmental patterns. (Concepts that are, of course, central to the individual psychotherapy model.) Most family therapists primarily see adult patients and work with children using the family therapy model. The family model suggests that even if one does explore past issues of "growth and development," it does not change family patterns and behavior and therefore is a "useless exercise." Child psychiatrists disagree and argue that only by exploring the past can such changes take place. Until controlled studies are done, the relative efficacy of either approach remains to be seen. The authors would recommend helping to change family behavior in such a way as to allow for, among other things, optimal growth and development of the children.

The adolescent as the identified patient. With the adolescent as the identified patient, focus on the family is still indicated, especially while the adolescent is living at home, not yet having established psychosocial autonomy. A good deal of attention must often be focused on the marital partnership. The adolescent will often benefit from individual attention, as well as from the encouragement of peer group relationships. Presumably the more emancipated (capable of independent living) the adolescent, the less need there is for conjoint family sessions and the more emphasis there is on individual and peer group sessions.

An adolescent girl might become pregnant as a way of expressing her feelings or solving her problems within the family. Specifically if the adolescent is rebelling against parental authority, one way to show that she is "her own person" is to become pregnant and refuse an abortion, thereby forming a single-parent family. Family therapy is helpful in increasing communication and resolving conflicts in such a family.

In treating a family with an adolescent "authority problem," inclusion of the entire family group can dilute the adolescent's feelings about the therapist. (These issues are also discussed in different contexts in Chapters 12 and 17.)

Other intimate interpersonal systems. Other intimate interpersonal systems, less formally organized and sanctioned than marriages and families, may lend themselves successfully to conjoint interventions. Partners who are involved significantly with each other, whether or not they are married or living together, or are heterosexual or homosexual, have been effectively treated. The goal is to help the partners explore relevant issues and—if the relationship is premarital— the doubts and anticipations prior to the marriage.[20]

Mr. K and Ms. L consulted a family therapist after they had been dating for about 6 months. The reason for referral was that although they both expressed the desire to get married, they had some doubts as to whether the relationship could work. Both had been married previously. It turned out that Mr. K was an orphan and had been raised by a series of family members. He had joined the army and retired at the age of 40. He had been out for about a year, and divorced for about 2 years, when he met Ms. L. He expressed a strong need to be with her all the time.

Ms. L had been raised by a smothering mother, and her first husband had depended on her a great deal. She expressed a strong need to "find myself." She wanted to get a better grasp on her identity. Although she wanted a relationship with a man like Mr. K (reliable, strong, and a good sexual partner), she also wanted time on her own.

The therapist provided the opportunity for the couple to explore these issues and the ramifications of their marrying. After ten sessions the couple decided not to get married but worked out an arrangement in which Mr. K would spend 3 days a week with Ms. L at her apartment. A 2-year follow-up of this arrangement showed that it had worked out "just fine," according to both of them.

There has also been an increased emphasis on family therapy for families without problems or psychopathology. Here the focus is on "personal growth" defined as helping a couple or family to realize maximum potential in terms of functioning and feelings.

All too often people get married during the infatuation phase, when love is indeed "blind." This is that rare example in which a couple was able to realistically explore its own needs and each partner's personality (rather than what appears to be in the other partner's fantasy). Then, based on past patterns, the couple anticipated the future and worked out a realistic solution.

Marital or family system therapy may be the treatment of choice in the following situations:

1. *When it is thought that the identified patient has symptomatology that is the manifestation of a disturbed family as a whole.* A basic premise of family therapy is that the individual in distress may be the symptom bearer for a disturbed family unit. (The reader is again referred to Chapters 3 and 4.)

2. *When there is no improvement with individual therapy.* Family evaluation often can explain why there has been no improvement in such cases. The therapist may come to recognize that marital or family factors have been overlooked. Bringing the family into the treatment session often helps to break therapy deadlocks.

   In one instance a mother and father were having trouble communicating and were unable to work effectively together in setting limits on the delinquent behavior of their son, who was the identified patient. In other examples the family environment may prevent the individual from benefiting in individual therapy because he is pulled in opposite directions by warring factions in the family[21] (e.g., a father wants the son to work but the mother wants to keep him home with her). For a chronically phobic or anxious individual, however, behavior therapy or medication might be simpler, quicker, and more effective than family therapy, and changing the symptom might secondarily change the relationship.

3. *When stress or symptoms develop in other family members as a result of therapy with one member.* On occasion there may be successful treatment of one family member, but concomitantly another person in the family becomes symptomatic. Upon examination the therapist sees that factors of family equilibrium and homeostasis may not have been taken fully into account, and at such times other family members should be brought into treatment.

For example, the secondary gain of illness may be great for one or more members of the family.[22] If a mother is unable to function and psychologically needs to take care of her young son who will not go to school, it will be difficult to get him back to school; were this effort successful without the mother's involvement, a major increase in her symptomatology would likely occur.

4. *When the individual patient seems unable or unwilling to utilize the intrapsychic, interpretive mode of some forms of individual treatment.* Individuals are often seen who are unequipped to deal with symbolic psychological processes and are not attuned to benefiting from insight-oriented individual modes of treatment. These people, however, seem to be more amenable to a family system, action-oriented modality, which for them seems to be more understandable and practical.

   Some patients refuse to participate in individual sessions, fearing that they will be stigmatized as suffering from some type of mental disorder or will be made to feel guilty personally and individually for what has happened in the family. These people may often be more readily involved if they are included as part of an entire family and if common areas of concern to everyone in the family are addressed.

5. *When the individual patient uses most of the individual psychotherapy sessions to talk about a family member.* A relatively common situation of this sort is that in which one marital partner enters individual treatment ostensibly to complain about the spouse or to get the spouse into treatment. The marital therapist is often able, by skillful rechanneling of the underlying concerns, to get both partners involved in a joint endeavor to examine their marital interaction. This may be done by a reconceptualization of the problem in which both parties are asked to participate, helping them clarify what they each stand to gain in therapy.

6. *When the identified patient is in a hospital or other institutional setting.* Improvement occurring during the course of an individual's hospitalization often fades on return to the family unless the family was involved in ongoing family treatment during the inpatient stay.

   Hospitalization may have been used as a help to remove a patient from a supposedly "psychonoxious" family environment. When the patient becomes asymptomatic, plans for discharge are undertaken. If continuing work has not gone on with the family, the recovered patient will return to the same family setting, only again to become symptomatic. The recovered patient may find that the family has "closed ranks" in his or her absence, and there no longer appears to be any psychological room for another member in the family. Plans may be made for the recovered patient to leave the hospital but live away from the family. Often within a short period of time, however, despite the best-laid plans of staff, the patient and the family become engaged in the same types of nongratifying interaction as before, even to the extent of again living together. This would seem to indicate that successful separation cannot be externally imposed but is a process that takes time and should involve all the relevant people.

7. *When the family is unable to cope with the loss of one of its members.* Family therapy can be an effective treatment for grief. It provides the opportunity for family members to grieve together and to be mutually supportive.

> In the R family (discussed in Chapter 3) family therapy was begun on a once-a-week basis over a 6-month period, after one member had died. The marital interaction was marked by decreased communication, the wife being quite angry with her husband's drinking. An objective of treatment was increasing family communication, including that of the parents and children.
> The family discussed the move of the daughter out of the house. The children turned out to be extremely supportive to both parents in helping them reestablish a more intimate relationship. When the father and mother began doing things together, the father's drinking gradually decreased and the mother's depression gradually disappeared. The father and the mother worked together on the mother's business to help make it more successful. All children continued to do well in graduate school.

When a difficulty clearly seems to be mainly intrapsychic with relatively less impact on a marital or family system—as, for example, when someone lives alone and is not in close contact with the original family—individual therapy would seem to be indicated. This is probably also the preferable treatment modality for those who have difficulty in establishing intimate, one-to-one relationships. There will be many situations that are not so clear-cut, as when problems occur in a first marriage. Then the best judgment of the therapist must be used.

> Miss R, a 28-year-old, white, single female, came to the outpatient clinic asking for individual psychotherapy. She gave a history of being involved in five successive relationships with men 20 to 25 years older, none of which lasted more than 3 to 6 months. These relationships were characterized by her as sadomasochistic. This patient requested treatment in order to understand better what she was doing. Neither she nor her current partner was interested in being involved in conjoint treatment, and the partner was not interested in individual psychotherapy. In this case individual psychotherapy appeared to be the treatment of choice.

Group therapy is probably indicated in those situations in which a major part of the difficulty lies in unsatisfactory peer group relationships. For problems that exist between family units and larger community systems, help from social agencies rather than family therapists might be most appropriate.[23]

MORE COMPLEX SITUATIONS IN WHICH FAMILY THERAPY IS SOMETIMES RECOMMENDED

Some situations require special sensitivity and experience, and not all family therapists will feel comfortable working with such cases. To date there are no outcome studies to document which types of situations are least responsive to family intervention, and many of these areas must still be considered experimental. The authors have modified items 1 through 6 from Ackerman, as follows:[24]

1. *Families in the Process of Breaking Up*. If the family is irrevocably committed to dissolution—for example, if the actual process of divorce is going on—family therapy can often be helpful in permitting the breakup to occur in the most positive manner possible, with the fewest "raw edges" of unresolved feelings. Divorce therapy can lead to a less painful experience for each family member.[25] If the family members do not care about one another, they usually will fail in any form of family therapy.

   Inexperienced therapists, however, may be overly pessimistic (or overly optimistic) about the changes that can be brought about in families. Marital couples or families may begin therapy by talking about breaking up and may appear more chaotic in the early sessions than they will later. Many families start treatment by emphasizing their worst aspects, and during a first interview the therapist may feel that the situation is hopeless.

   After the family is known better, the therapist usually can see positive assets that the family may have been minimizing initially and that the therapist may have been overlooking. The fact that the family members come for treatment should in itself be taken as an indication that they are potentially seeking help for their difficulties. If the marital partners were determined to break up or divorce and if this were not a conflicted or difficult issue for them, they would see a divorce lawyer, rather than seek family therapy.

   Many family therapists claim that they do not take sides on the issue of whether a marital couple should separate. They believe, rather, that their role is to help the couple clarify their own feelings about this question and also to give the couple an opportunity to think about other solutions to their marital difficulties. (Often, marital partners have separation and divorce as a hidden agenda and may delay facing it until the therapist opens up the topic for discussion.) It will often prove useful to clarify the fact that everyone in the couple's family may be hurting and has been struggling, although relatively unsuccessfully, to find ways to ease their pain and disappointment.

   Other therapists feel that divorce is not a solution to marital problems because the spouses often remarry partners much like the previous one and continue in the same patterns. A few marital partners divorce and remarry each other several times. Everyone is familiar with marriages in which the spouses can neither live stably together nor stay apart. In such instances therapists might take a stand against useless divorce and, instead, actively encourage attempts to improve the current marriage.

2. *Unavailability of Family Members.* The more forceful the therapist is in insisting that all family members come to the sessions, the more successful will be the chances of getting them together. But if, as an example, one member is away in college, conjoint therapy with the whole family will be less possible. Family resistance to change may be more of an obstacle to cooperation than such factors as distance, finances, and job hours. Family therapists should adopt the attitude that all family members are expected to attend sessions. They should underline the benefits for each family member, as well as for the family system as a whole, of attending family sessions. The absence or other resistance of family members to the sessions will be scrutinized by the experienced therapist for what it reveals about the important processes in the family.

   The presence of all family members is desirable but may not be essential, however, to successful outcomes of family therapy. Family therapy can be effective when one parent is absent through death, separation, divorce, or other reasons.

3. *Psychopathology in One Family Member Making Family Therapy Ineffective.* Dishonesty or manipulation of the therapy for secondary gain would constitute a serious handicap to effective treatment. A family member may have a history of chronic stealing or lying. If this occurs in a child or appears to be more of a symptomatic resonse to a family situation than an integral part of a chronic character pattern, family therapy would be indicated.

   If one family member is extremely paranoid, manic, or agitated, medication might be initiated for behavioral control, prior to the onset of family therapy. Once the identified patient's conduct becomes more appropriate, family therapy can proceed.[26] Another possibility is to work with all family members except the one whose behavior prevents therapy from succeeding—but this is clearly a second choice. Others (a minority) have argued that acute symptoms are often reflections of a family crisis, for which family therapy is particularly well suited.

4. *Denial of Family Difficulties by the Family as a Whole.* There are some families whose whole way of life is oriented around denial of difficulties. Such a family makes family therapy extremely problematic but not impossible given the situation in which some other motivation can be developed to allow therapy to continue.

5. *Organic Disease in One Member of the Family.* Although no amount of family therapy can change the course of an organic disease, the family may be helped to live more comfortably with the secondary consequences of the

illness. What might be changed are the reactions of the patient and family to the symptoms and dysfunction.

6. *Family Problems Presenting No Current Emotional or Behavioral Consequences.* In a small number of families, the past is dredged up at a time when there are no current crises. The purpose often seems to be to affix blame for past family failures or disappointments on another family member. This situation may be particularly challenging if the motivations are primarily those of assigning blame or gaining "insight," rather than of expressing a desire for interactional change.

7. *Risks (or Consequences) of Treatment Worse than Benefits.* Family members may be concerned that treatment will leave them in a worse state than when they began. These possibilities should be explored at the outset and at all other appropriate points in treatment. The therapist should involve the family members in considering possible consequences of therapy and whether they wish to continue or abandon treatment.

> In the T family the identified patient was the son, R, who had been stealing cars. Mr. and Mrs. T, both suburban, upper-middle-class parents, were bewildered by their son's behavior. In the first interview they presented themselves as having an ideal relationship and being deeply in love. Their son, R, however, suggested that the two of them were not getting along. Further inquiry revealed that whenever the mother and father had an argument, the son would divert attention from their problems by getting into trouble with the law. In this family the mother and father actually had serious problems in their relationship. Exploration during family therapy led to threats of divorce by both spouses. This and other possible outcomes were aired with the family members, and they decided to discontinue therapy.

Another situation that illustrates the need to clarify treatment goals is the "doll's house marriage," a type of marriage in which there is an extremely unequal relationship. One spouse's incompetence is required or encouraged by the other. These marriages are extremely fragile and crisis prone and often break down with changes in the family situation, for example, the birth of a child. Although family treatment is problematic and the results uncertain, the therapy has a greater chance of success if it basically respects the unequal framework and works to reestablish the equilibrium existing prior to the crisis.[27] This example highlights the need for clarifying the goals of treatment and for being satisfied with realistic and attainable objectives.

8. *Identified Patient with a Fixed Physical Dependence on Alcohol, Barbiturates, Heroin, or Other Drugs.* Family therapy may not be successful as the primary mode of treatment in preventing or treating physical dependence on drugs. It may be of help in the early stages, before the pattern becomes well fixed, when behavior is symptomatic of other concerns, or

even later in aiding the family members to understand the condition and avoid nonuseful interventions and responses.

In the abuse of drugs in which physical dependence is not found, family therapy may have a more important role to play. Family therapy may be necessary to induce the user to discontinue the drugs when their use is a result of family psychopathology. This may be especially true for the adolescent drug user.

9. *Existence of an Important, Valid Family Secret.* Valid family secrets may exist that cannot be brought out in the open and that preclude the possibility of the family's doing any constructive work. Infidelity, bigamy, incest, homosexuality, and criminality may be issues that one partner refuses to discuss in conjoint sessions, and these may, in certain instances, interfere with the session's achieving beneficial results. Often, though, the antici-pated consequences of revealing secrets is exaggerated, or the "secret" is already known to the other partner. The revealing of secrets may lead to major changes in the family organization, and these changes need to be anticipated.

10. *Cultural, Religious, or Economic Prejudices.* Unyielding, inflexible cul-tural, religious, or economic prejudices against any sort of outside inter-vention in the family system would certainly also make family therapy difficult. In these cases other alternatives can be offered, such as working with a clergyman or a community worker, with the family therapist acting as a consultant.

11. *Necessity of Other Modalities of Psychiatric Treatment.* Other modalities of treatment should also be considered. In some cases one would want to wait until the identified patient has established a relationship with the therapist; this is especially true of adolescents. A psychotic patient who is paranoid might not be able to tolerate family therapy until he or she has been reconstituted through the use of anti-psychotic drugs; such a patient before then would be too suspicious of the therapist to benefit from treat-ment.[26]

12. *The Availability and the Type of Therapist.* Many therapists find them-selves uncomfortable doing family work and should not force themselves to undertake it. If the therapist encounters significant "countertransference" problems in working with a particular family, this, too, would be a con-traindication. Therapists would be well advised to avoid treating families with whom they have strong emotional ties.

The age, sex, and race of the therapist in relation to the type of family are, in the authors' experiences, usually not crucial factors in treatment. Much more important are the therapist's other personal and therapeutic qualities.

The therapist must be active and directive and must set limits in order to practice family therapy.[24] Allowing the identified patient or other family members to control the therapy will usually doom it to failure.

In each of the above situations, the therapist and family should carefully consider the possibility of benefiting from treatment. In spite of one or more complicating issues, this would be the factor most important in deciding whether or not to utilize family therapy.

CONCLUSION

Family therapy is an approach rather than a single technique. It is a group of therapeutic interventions, all focusing on the family but directed toward a variety of specific therapeutic goals. Therefore the relative importance of the particular guideline depends in large part to what extent the therapist uses the family model; that is, if the therapist treats all problems with family therapy, then the guideline is not important. Conversely, if the therapist treats different problems in different ways, then the guideline is all important.

Until the last 5 to 10 years, indications and contraindications for family therapy have been based on ingenious hunches as to treatment efficacy in a specific situation and on clinical experience (a term defined by some as "making the same mistake for 30 years").

More recently there has been some controlled outcome data that defines situations in which family or marital therapy might be the treatment of choice (see Chapter 18). These situations include:[2]

1. Marital therapy for a marital problem
2. Marital therapy for sexual dysfunction
3. Family therapy for certain childhood and adolescent behavior problems
4. Family therapy for anorexia nervosa
5. Family therapy for the "chronic patient" (i.e., those in need of long-term continuing care and rehabilitation)

Any final authoritative pronouncement as to when to suggest family therapy should be withheld until more controlled data are available comparing family therapy with other types of treatment.

REFERENCES

1. Group for the Advancement of Psychiatry. The field of family therapy. Report No. 78. New York, Group for the Advancement of Psychiatry, 1970, p 543
2. Gurman AS, Kniskern DP: Research on marital and family therapy: Progress, perspective and prospect, in Garfield SL, Bergin AE (eds): Handbook of Psychotherapy and Behavior Change: An Empirical Analysis (2nd ed). New York, Wiley, 1978
3. DeWitt KN: The effectiveness of family therapy. Arch Gen Psychiatry 35:549–561, 1978

4. Bard M, Berkowitz B: A community psychology consultation program in police family crisis intervention: Preliminary impressions. Int J Social Psychiatry 15:209–215, 1969

5. Jackson DD: Family practice: A comprehensive medical approach. Compr Psychiatry 7:338–344, 1966

6. MacNamara M: Family stress before and after renal homotransplantation. Social Work 14:89–98, 1969

7. Kellner R: Family Ill Health: An Investigation in General Practice. Springfield, Ill, Charles C. Thomas, 1963

8. May PA: Schizophrenia: Overview of treatment methods, in Freedman AM, Kaplan HI, Sadock BJ (eds): Comprehensive Textbook of Psychiatry (2d ed). Baltimore, Williams & Wilkins, 1975, pp 923–938

9. Segal SP: Community care and deinstitutionalization: Implications for family policy. Social Work (in press)

10. Ard BN, Ard CC (eds): Handbook of Marriage Counseling. Palo Alto, Ca, Science and Behavior Books, 1969

11. Klemer RH: Counseling in Marital and Sexual Problems. Baltimore, Williams & Wilkins, 1965

12. Vincent CD (ed): Readings in Marriage Counseling. New York, Crowell, 1957

13. Masters W, Johnson V: Human Sexual Inadequacy. Boston, Little, Brown, 1970

14. Kaplan HS: The New Sex Therapy. New York, Brunner/Mazel, 1974

15. Hollander L: Rethinking child and family treatment, in Sankar DV (ed): Mental Health in Children. Westbury, N.Y., PJD Publications, 1975, pp 297–304

16. Schomer J: Family therapy, in Wolman B (ed): Handbook of Treatment of Mental Disorders in Childhood and Adolescence. Englewood Cliffs, N.J., Prentice-Hall, 1977

17. Brodie HKH: Comment, in Brady JP, Brodie HKH (eds): Controversy in Psychiatry. Philadelphia, Saunders, 1978

18. Sussex JN: An evolutionary perspective on child psychopathology, in Brady JP, Brodie HKH (eds): Controversy in Psychiatry. Philadelphia, Saunders, 1978

19. Anthony EJ: Yes, no, and neither: The views from Freud to Laing, in Brady JP, Brodie HKH (eds): Controversy in Psychiatry. Philadelphia, Saunders, 1978

20. Gross A: Marriage counseling for unwed couples. New York Times, Magazine Section, April 24, 1977, pp 52–68

21. Greenberg IM, Glick ID, Match S, et al: Family therapy: Indications and rationale. Arch Gen Psychiatry 10:7–25, 1964

22. Toomin M: Structured separation with counseling: A therapeutic approach for couples in conflict. Fam Process 11:299–310, 1972

23. Favazza AR, Oman M: Overview: Foundations of cultural psychiatry. Am J Psychiatry 135:293–303, 1978

24. Ackerman NW: Family therapy, in Arieti S (ed): American Handbook of Psychiatry (vol. III). New York, Basic Books, 1966, pp 201–212

25. Toomin M: Structured separation with counseling: A therapeutic approach for couples in conflict. Fam Process 11:299–310, 1972

26. Guttman H: A contraindication for family therapy: The prepsychotic or postpsychotic young adult and his parents. Arch Gen Psychiatry 29:352–355, 1973

27. Pittman F, Flomenhaft K: Treating the Doll's House marriage. Fam Process 9:143–155, 1970

Photograph by Ken Heyman. Courtesy Ken Heyman, private collection.

20
Research on Family Process

OBJECTIVES

- To help the student be aware of principles underlying scientific research
- To evaluate the methods, findings, and problems in the field of family process research
- To encourage further family research

INTRODUCTION

This chapter is designed to enable the student to critically evaluate the literature on family process. Well over half of this literature has been an anecdotal, nonsystematic, uncontrolled reporting of observations that, at best, may have some value for the formulation of research and clinical hypotheses. "Worse still, research hypotheses and methods drawn from clinical practice have tended to be superficial, imprecise, stereotyped and most troublesome, uninteresting."[1] In the last few years, fortunately, studies have been more rigorous.

Much "family" research in the past has, in fact, focused on the individual. Identified patients often reported their view of how the family was functioning, and the investigator then accepted this as factual. Such individuals were assumed to be reliable, accurate informants about their own family. Such studies might include screening questionnaires about individuals, interviewing individual family members, and giving individual members projective tests. Following this, correlations to the family were made from the individual reports. Much was learned about individual family members, but, more often than not, a well-rounded picture of the family unit did not emerge from such data.

The studies of family process to be mentioned in this chapter are those that focus mainly on the family system rather than on the individual.

Some of the topics discussed below deal with such issues as family interaction patterns, feedback systems, and rules. Others attempt to delineate factors that differentiate families with various types of disturbances from those with no evident disturbance.

GENERAL PRINCIPLES OF SCIENTIFIC RESEARCH

The following are scientific principles that help to distinguish between fact and speculation:[2]

1. *Assurance of a representative sample.* The population being tested should have some relationship to the population that the family therapist treats. The sample should be truly representative of the "universe" from which therapy patients and their families are drawn. There are a variety of selection factors to be used to insure that every family has an equal chance of being in the sample.

2. *Assurance of control group comparisons and testing.* In psychotherapy research the safest course is to use one sample and randomize subjects into an experimental treatment versus a control treatment. It is hard to have a pure, no-treatment control.

3. *Assurance of an independent evaluator.* Because the results in the experiment must be judged by human beings (rather than standardized measuring devices) and because humans can be "biased," an evaluator who is not part of the study must be used. It is even better if that evaluator is "blind"—that is, if he does not know which of the treatments the family received. It is often not possible, however, for the subjects to be "blind" in this kind of research.

Finally there are two other guiding attitudes that are most important once results are in. First, for facts to be accepted as scientifically valid, they should be *replicated.* The entire experiment should be repeated by a different group of investigators. Second, the attitude toward all research should be one of *skepticism* rather than optimism. The annals of medical and psychiatric research show more examples of clinicians' accepting worthless therapies based on inadequate data than of clinicians' rejecting effective therapies.

ASSESSMENT OF FAMILY INTERACTION

Bodin has carefully surveyed the field of family interaction assessment, and we have borrowed extensively from his outline.[3] He has divided assessment procedures into subjective techniques and objective techniques. In subjective testing reliance is placed on the ratings of judges who are not in the family system. Objective techniques are more rigorously quantifiable and do not rely so much on the ratings of judges.

Assessment can also be considered with respect to whether it assesses individual or interactional data. Some tests assess both, such as the Rorschach[4] and the Strodtbeck Revealed Differences Test.[5]

For interactional studies members of the family are brought together, and the ways in which they actually deal with one another are studied. Methods include conjoint interviews in which standardized questions are asked, family therapy sessions, and task-oriented procedures—for example, games or questionnaires in which families must reconcile differences.

Subjective Techniques

There are three subtypes of subjective techniques: family tasks, family strengths inventory, and family art. For family tasks the most efficacious approach is to set up tasks that can be quantifiably scored, such as asking the family to decide on the kind of car they would like to buy if they had a given amount of money.

Another approach is to "rig" the task so that it is made more difficult for the family to perform—for example, by asking them to distinguish different colors when the colors are made extremely difficult to distinguish, or by giving them different stimuli without their knowing it, so it becomes impossible for them to agree, the purpose being to see how they handle disagreement.

When pictorial apperception tests are used, the entire family can be given the test. For example, using the Thematic Apperception Test,[6] the family is given cards with visual stimuli and is asked to agree on a story. There have been specially developed tasks for different problems; for example, cards might be specifically fitted to delinquent families. The cards have been modified for family work in that they can portray family scenes that are clearly recognizable and interesting and will engage the family in working together to produce a story.

Finally Watzlawick has developed what he calls the "Structured Family Interview" (Appendix A) as part of a diagnostic process.[7] A series of formal questions assess family functioning and role structure in a stepwise fashion. This has the great advantage of being a formal, systematized way of obtaining a lot of information about the family, although at the cost of taking a moderate amount of time for gathering material that might gradually emerge in the course of therapy.

There have been several attempts to formulate a family-strengths inventory in much the same way as an individual ego-strength inventory is formulated. Some of the categories include developing creativity, relationships with relatives, giving encouragement, and so forth.[8]

There are also techniques that attempt to assess family functioning through the medium of art. Others have attempted to assess family dynamics using art as a shared activity for the family.[9, 10]

Objective Techniques

There are three subclassifications of objective techniques: techniques that rely on communication, techniques that rely on game theory, and techniques that require conflict resolution. Haley, using a computer, has conducted studies showing who speaks after whom and for how much time.[11, 12] This is an excellent method for objective measurement. Ravich has developed a technique called The Interpersonal Behavior Game Test (see Chapter 5).[13]

Other procedures are based on conflict resolution. The Strodtbeck Revealed Differences Technique,[5] one of the most commonly used measures, asks subjects to make individual evaluations of a stimulus and then to reconcile any differences in interpretation that occur. Problems are set up so that only one of two possible alternatives can be used. This precludes any possibility of compromise on any given question. This procedure was modified by Ferreira, who used an "unrevealed" differences technique in which the experimenter does not reveal to the family specific instances in which they had disagreed.[14] Ferreira also allowed more availability of alternatives, giving greater assessment of more idiosyncratic thinking in families.

ASSESSMENT OF DIFFERENCES BETWEEN NORMAL AND DISTURBED FAMILIES

Hollander and Karp have summarized the literature obtained from studies of more sophisticated design that contrast "normal" and "abnormal" families.[15]

As opposed to normal families, abnormal families distribute their statements more evenly among family members,[16] have fewer nonlexical within-family speech similarities,[17] require more time to perform a task, are more silent, exchange less information, agree less, and fulfill one another's needs less.[18 20] Contrasted with normal families, abnormal families exhibit significantly fewer cases of three-way alignment between father, mother, and offspring, and significantly fewer cases of two-way alignment between parents.[21] Differences between normal and abnormal families have been found on several indices of power.[22, 23] No clear-cut pattern of parental dominance was reported, however, in several other studies.[24, 25] Family perceptions of adjustment and satisfaction have been used to discriminate between normal and abnormal families.[26]

Delinquent versus normal comparisons indicated that in families with delinquent children there was more parental rejection and hostility,[27] less father–son agreement, less maternal influence,[28] and more stable patterns of differential parental dominance.[15]

ASSESSMENT OF DIFFERENT TYPES
OF DISTURBED FAMILIES

The assessment of different types of disturbed families has been dealt with extensively in Chapter 12.

OTHER TYPES OF FAMILY RESEARCH

Two of the many other types of research are categorized here. First, there are statistical correlation studies of demographic variables, which are compilations of information on families with regard to such factors as the number of children per family, the number of children that are delinquent, and so forth. These factors are then correlated with other factors such as "broken homes" and "absent parents." By implication these associations are assumed to be relevant.

Second, there are anthropological studies that are observations of families in various cultures as part of a general attempt to portray the culture and examine its influence on individuals and their family. There are major problems in this type of research, not the least of which is that the main informants usually are outside the family. These informants serve as liaisons between the investigator and the families being studied. Many studies have correlated individual personalities and childrearing customs.

PROBLEMS OF FAMILY PROCESS RESEARCH

Well-designed experiments are needed to make reliable measurements of typical family interactions. The ideal experiment would observe family events that can be reliably measured. Inference must be minimized. A good illustration of "hard data" is Haley's work with measuring the amount of time that family members talk. Variables such as size of family, sex, ordinal position of children, and racial and cultural factors must all be controlled. Longitudinal as well as cross-sectional studies are badly needed.

Finally it must be restated that behavior is multicausal. Allowances for this fact must be made when evaluating a problem; for example, which of the symptoms of manic-depressive disease can be explained by family dynamics? Can it be demonstrated that differences between normal and various types of disturbed families are significant in any causative sense? Controls must be introduced, because comparison is the essence of research. As yet, however, there are few data on how even normal families function. (One example of careful work is that of Lewis and associates[29] discussed in Chapters 3, 4, and 8.)

An excellent discussion of the methodological problems in family research can be found in the proceedings of a conference dealing with this topic,[30] and in

Riskin and Faunce's review of family interaction research.[31] The latter has an excellent glossary of research terms.

STATE OF THE FIELD AND SUGGESTIONS FOR FUTURE RESEARCH IN FAMILY THERAPY OUTCOME AND FAMILY PROCESS

The authors are more optimistic now (1980) about the field of family research. We have moved far beyond anecdotal studies to the beginnings of carefully controlled, long-term, in-depth studies of family process and family outcome. This is a welcome sign that will help to maintain the vigor and permanency of the field.

The authors would agree with Riskin and Faunce and with Gurman and Kniskern as to their recommendations for future research.[31-32] We, too, favor longitudinal studies. They should be conducted for at least two years and possibly up to five years. Studies longer than that are difficult to sustain, mostly because of investigator consistency and morale. Family interaction techniques need to be developed to measure the changes in the family as a unit and the individuals in a family. The Family Evaluation Form is a significant start.[33] Tasks such as the Straus and Talman SIMFAM can be used to measure differences in families.[34] Careful controls are, of course, essential. Research should not only be done on pathological marriages and families, but on normal marriages and families. Replication, despite its many problems, must be done. For outcome studies, the design quality rating of Gurman and Kniskern mentioned in Chapter 18 should also be used.[32]

REFERENCES

1. Steinglass P: Personal communication. 1978
2. Altman L: Certain safeguards used to minimize risk of error. New York Times, January 23, 1977
3. Bodin A: Conjoint family assessment: An evolving field, in McReynolds P (ed): Advances in Psychological Assessment (vol I). Palo Alto, Ca, Science and Behavior Books, 1968, pp 223–243
4. Wynne L: Consensus Rorschachs and related procedures for studying interpersonal patterns. J Projective Techniques and Personality Assessment 32:352–356, 1968
5. Strodtbeck F: Husband-wife interaction over revealed differences. Am Soc Rev 23: 468–473, 1951
6. Winter WD, Ferreira AJ, Olson JL: Story sequence analysis of family TATs. J Projective Techniques and Personality Assessment 29:392–397, 1965
7. Watzlawick P: A structured family interview. Fam Process 2:256–271, 1966

8. Otto H: The Otto family strength study. Graduate School of Social Work, University of Utah, Salt Lake City, Utah, 1962. Cited by Bodin A (Reference 3 this chapter)
9. Day J, Kwiatkowska H: The psychiatric patient and his well sibling: A comparison through their art productions. Bull Art Ther 2:51–66, 1962
10. Zierer E, Sternberg D, Finn R, et al: Family creative analysis: Its role in treatment. Bull Art Ther 5:47–65, 1966
11. Haley J: Research on family patterns: An instrument measurement. Fam Process 3:41–65, 1964
12. Haley J: Speech sequences on normal and abnormal families with two children present. Fam Process 6:81–97, 1967
13. Ravich R: Game-testing in conjoint marital psychotherapy. Am J Psychother 23:217–229, 1969
14. Ferreira AJ: Decision-making in normal and pathological families. Arch Gen Psychiatry 8:68–73, 1963
15. Hollander L, Karp E: Youth psychopathology and family process research. Am J Psychiatry 130:814–817, 1973. p 814
16. Murrell S, Stachowiak J: Consistency, rigidity, and power in the interaction of clinic and nonclinic families. J Abnormal Psychology 72:265–272, 1967
17. Becker J, McArdle J: Nonlexical speech similarities as an index of intrafamilial identification. J Abnormal Psychology 72:408–418, 1967
18. Ferreira A, Winter W: Family interaction and decision-making. Arch Gen Psychiatry 13:214–223, 1965
19. Ferreira A, Winter W: Stability of interactional variables in family decision-making. Arch Gen Psychiatry 14:352–355, 1966
20. Ferreira A, Winter W: Decision-making in normal and abnormal two-child families. Fam Process 7:17–36, 1968
21. Sackett A: Alignment patterns in normal and abnormal families. Unpublished study. Institute for Juvenile Research, Chicago, 1970
22. Hutchinson J: Family interaction patterns and the emotionally disturbed child (abstract), in Winter W, Ferreira A (eds): Research in Family Interaction: Readings and Commentary. Palo Alto, Ca, Science and Behavior Books, 1969, pp 187–191
23. Schuham A: Power relations in emotionally disturbed and normal family triads. J Abnorm Psychol 75:30–37, 1970
24. Farina A, Holzberg J: Interaction patterns of parents and hospitalized sons diagnosed as schizophrenic or non-schizophrenic. J Abnorm Psychol 73:114–118, 1968
25. Becker J, Iwakami E: Conflict and dominance within families of disturbed children. J Abnorm Psychol 74:330–335, 1970
26. Novak A, Van der Veen F: Family concepts and emotional disturbance in the famililes of disturbed adolescents with normal siblings. Fam Process 9:157–171, 1970
27. Schulman R, Shoemaker D, Moelis I: Laboratory measurement of parental behavior, J Consult Psychol 26:109–114, 1962
28. Bodin A: Family interaction: A social-clinical study of synthetic, normal, and problem family triads, in Winter W, Ferreira A (eds): Research in Family Interactions: Readings and Commentary. Palo Alto, Ca, Science and Behavior Books, 1969, pp 125–127

29. Lewis JM, Beavers WR, Gossett JT: No Single Thread: Psychological Health in the Family System. New York, Brunner/Mazel, 1976

30. Framo J (ed): Family Interaction. A Dialogue Between Family Researchers and Family Therapists. New York, Springer, 1972

31. Riskin J, Faunce E: An evaluative review of family interaction research. Fam Process 11:365–455, 1972

32. Gurman AS, Kniskern DP: Research on marital and family therapy: Progress, perspective and prospect, in Garfield SL, Bergin AE (eds): Handbook of Psychotherapy and Behavior Change: An Empirical Analysis (2nd ed). New York, Wiley, 1978

33. Spitzer RL, Gibbon M, Endicott J: Family Evaluation Form. New York, Biometrics Research, New York State Department of Mental Hygiene. 1971

34. Straus MA, Tallman I: SIMFAM: A technique for observational measurement and experimental study of families. Unpublished manuscript, 1970

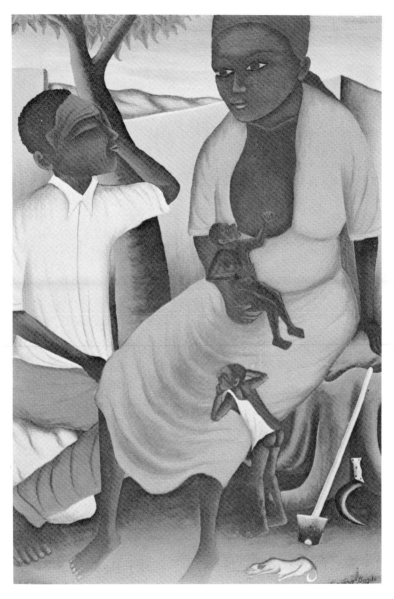

Haitian Family by Castera Bazile. Courtesy of Selden Rodman from *The Miracle of Haitian Art* by Selden Rodman.

21
Training for the Family Therapist

OBJECTIVES

- To provide the reader with an awareness of the elements of an optimum training program
- To identify the factors that advance or retard the learning of family therapy
- To describe a procedure for evaluating trainees
- To describe a continuing education program for the family therapist

INTRODUCTION

With growing interest and experience in the field of family therapy, questions arise as to the best training for family therapists. Many ideas have been promulgated and a wide range of training experiences, from the very informal to the highly structured,[1] have been established. In this chapter some of the relevant issues will be discussed.

WHO SHOULD BE TRAINED?

Before this question can be answered, the ultimate use of the training must be clarified. Most family therapists provide direct service to families in distress, along a traditional counseling or psychotherapy model. These therapists may be working privately or for any one of a number of different institutions. A variation would be the use of family therapy training for those engaged in psychiatric crisis or "triage" work. Such triage agents will require training in a variety of disciplines and will need to have considerable experience. In consultation work the family therapist does not provide direct clinical service but helps other care givers and agencies.

322

Family therapy training is being offered to mental health professionals, such as psychiatrists, psychologists, psychiatric social workers, marriage and family counselors, and psychiatric nurses. Professionals and trainees in other fields that involve working with families in distress have sought and been offered family therapy training courses (see Chapter 17). In this group are primary-care physicians, pediatricians, obstetricians and gynecologists, marriage and divorce counselors for the courts, ministers, probation officers, welfare case workers, teachers, and architects. The family model is now being taught in many law schools as a required part of family law courses.[2] With the spread of community psychiatry concepts and the increasing use of paraprofessional personnel[3, 4] in a variety of helping roles, family therapy training for housewives, college students, neighborhood leaders (or "ombudsmen") and "indigenous" persons is a reality.

What sort of person makes a good family therapist? The competent family therapist will be capable of thinking in family system terms. The family therapist will be able to empathize with the whole family's difficulties and deal actively with a complex interpersonal network. In family therapy, as in any form of treatment, the best results are obtained by those who have the best training and the most experience, knowledge, and sensitivity. Certain family therapists, however, without professional degrees or prolonged formal training, have been used effectively. Men and women from the community, who have already raised their own children, have been trained to act as therapists for families similar to their own.[5]

WHAT ABOUT TRAINING OBJECTIVES?

Training objectives should be defined prior to the onset of training and tailored to the objectives of a particular training program. There is a great difference between training those persons intending to become family therapists and those who come for family therapy experience as part of another professional training program. The training program described in this chapter fits the former category to a greater extent. For the latter a reasonable objective of training might be to provide basic understanding of the family systems model and a few general techniques of shifting family homeostasis.

WHAT SHOULD TRAINING IN
FAMILY THERAPY INCLUDE?

In an ideal world the family therapist would have all the requisite wisdom, knowledge, experience, compassion, and curiosity to do a competent job. More realistically one might hope that before embarking on training in family therapy a person would already have had experience with several prerequisites. It would be helpful if such people already knew about individual personality development, psychopathology, and psychotherapy, although family work will not often involve as minute a dissection of intrapsychic factors as is sometimes suggested for individual treatment. It would also be helpful if they understood group dynamics and had experience in group therapy. A knowledge of the family system itself—its development over time as well as its "disorders"—would obviously be germane, as would some knowledge of larger societal systems and the mutual interaction of these with family systems.

Many family therapy training programs offer essentially three types of experience: seminars, clinical work, and supervision. The following outline will indicate some of the elements of a fairly complete family therapy training program. Not all elements will be available in any one program, nor need they necessarily be available. The emphasis and priorities may be quite different from one program to another.

Basic Seminars

Some of these basic seminars would be discussion groups with assigned readings in relevant literature.[6] Others would make liberal use of videotapes or film (or both) to illustrate didactic points with case material.

THE FAMILY AS A SOCIAL INSTITUTION

   The history of the concept of marriage and the family
   Cross-cultural family studies
   Contemporary American marriage and family patterns
   Theories of family structure and function
   The family and other social institutions

THEORIES OF FAMILY PATHOLOGY

   History of the development of theories of family pathology
   Relevant variables in family pathology
   Models of family process and family pathology

TECHNIQUES OF FAMILY EVALUATION AND STUDY

   Family tests
   Interaction analysis
   Structured Interviews
   Obtaining family history and family process inventory
   Formulating the family problems
   Types of relevant settings and facilities

TECHNIQUES OF FAMILY THERAPY
AND FAMILY INTERVENTION

   Historical survey of family therapy and intervention techniques
   Levels of intervention
   Models of intervention: prevention, service, treatment, rehabilitation

Types of family therapy
Functions, values, and goals of the family therapist
Stages of family therapy

TRAINING AND TECHNIQUES OF SEX THERAPY*

Some of the subject areas of competence suggested for sex therapists include:

Sexual physiology and anatomy
Sexological examination
The social scripting of sexuality
Communicative skills
Stepwise progression toward sexual satisfaction
Overview of sex therapy
Taking a sex history (demonstration and practice)
Shared sensual experience
Theory and practice of home assignments
Solo sensual experience

Clinical Work

There is no substitute for actually sitting down with a live family and attempting to understand what is happening with them, although simulated families[9] and videotapes[10] may be quite helpful at times during the training experience.

One training center uses a stepwise series of increasingly graded exercises in responsibility for clinical work. Specifically the trainee first observes a supervisor working with a family, usually in a continuous case. The next step is for the trainee to work with an experienced cotherapist. Finally the trainee is allowed to work with a family alone.

The following types of experiences might be included:

Intake and evaluation
Brief and crisis treatment
Extended family treatment
Family consultation to community agencies
Training in family therapy supervision

Supervision

Supervision would be designed in a variety of formats to enable the trainee to have the benefit of examining clinical experience in some organized way and integrating it with theoretical concepts.[11] These formats might include the following:

---

*Every family therapy training program should provide training in sex therapy (see Chapter 14). More detail on training can be found in other excellent sources.[7, 8]

Individual supervision and supervision in groups (group supervision for family therapy trainees sometimes works more efficaciously than does individual supervision, because it may add the dimension of understanding group processes in families, and trainees may feel more comfortable in sharing what they are doing with other trainees than with a supervisor alone).

Intake conferences

Continuous case seminar

Treatment review

Family consultation seminar

Some training directors also include the experience of home visits and even living-in opportunities with families as essential parts of a family therapy training program. The use of videotape has opened up a helpful area, and family therapy training films are available.[12-16]

Some have suggested family therapy for the family therapist's own family, as well as an exploration of the therapist's own original family. "Mental health clinicians as a group are very likely to come from somewhat dysfunctional families. If this is so, they may have an unusually difficult time in conceptualizing realistic family treatment goals, both from the impact of their training and their own personal experience."[17] "A few institutions are now beginning to emphasize the need for trainees to study and understand *their* functioning in their own nuclear and extended families, as well as to develop a system orientation to life situations."[18] Others, more modestly, have suggested that close attention be paid in supervision to helping the family therapy trainee become aware of his or her own family attitudes and value systems.

Supervisors of family therapy have made extensive use of direct on-the-spot supervision. In this technique the supervisor observes the trainee through a one-way mirror, and there is direct communication via telephone or earphones. Either the supervisor or the trainee can interrupt the session at any time to ask questions or make suggestions. This technique offers the advantages of timeliness, reduction of trainee distortion of material, and immediate relevance. Its disadvantages include being more time-consuming, sacrificing the discussion that is essential to the learning process, and making some trainees feel unduly stressed.

Another technique frequently used is role playing. A trainee will take the part of a family member, and simulated families are set up using other trainees. Some important ground rules for this exercise have been delineated as follows:

First, the leader must establish trust in his ability to control the exercise. Second, warm-up procedures are necessary to diminish the group's anxiety about role play. Third, imposing rules regarding the actions of the group is important. The rules . . . relate to prohibiting the scapegoating of the therapist, encouraging audience participants to act as if they were the therapists, and analyzing family dynamics before analyzing clinical techniques and tactics. Out of this organized approach to the simulated situation emerges a vast array of learning opportunities for the participants.[19]

This experiential learning is greatly valued by some trainees, although others prefer more cognitive and didactic types of training, such as lectures and reading assignments.

Conferences of supervisors of family therapy training, although of uncertain value with respect to teaching effectiveness, are highly regarded by those engaged in supervision. A feeling of camaraderie is engendered, as well as an exchange of teaching techniques.

Students should be skeptical of predictions about process and outcome from their supervisors. Even experienced family clinicians cannot predict either process or outcome any better than chance, given the data available at this time.[20]

EVALUATION OF FAMILY THERAPY TRAINING

Evaluation is an important component of any training program. Since family therapy has only recently emerged from its infancy, evaluation of training in this field is still rudimentary. Periodic, systematic evaluation of the teachers and the program seems desirable, as do meetings of the faculty and student for the purposes of criticism and feedback.

A useful evaluation form has recently been published and modified for use in one training center (Fig. 21-1).[21]

NONDIDACTIC ASPECTS OF TRAINING

Since the first edition of this book, the family therapy model has continued its ascendancy from being a model rarely used in psychiatric training centers to one that plays a prominent part in training. The family therapy model is also being used in a variety of other nonpsychiatric training centers. Concurrent with this change in models, significant complications have arisen in the training process.

The family therapy model in training is often seen as competing with other models.[22] Some teachers believe that the family therapy model is incompatible with other models. Although this may be true in some cases, it is not nearly as true for the family model as it is for most other models. While it is true that the family model assumes that symptoms may be a result of problems between individuals, that does not exclude the assumption that symptoms can also arise from problems *inside* an individual. The task of the teacher is to help the student reconcile and integrate the different models. The trainee should be helped to see that in some illnesses the primary problem resides within the individual (e.g., schizophrenia) but that the successful management, in part, resides within the interpersonal system.

There are problems within and between disciplines. For example, for nurses to learn family therapy may mean disruption of their relationships with other health professionals on their team.[23] A nurse's becoming a cotherapist can be misconstrued as making her share in the ultimate responsibility for the patient. As things now stand that responsibility rests with the physicians. The teacher of family therapy must reconcile the new skill acquired by the nurse in a way that is most useful to the patient. What should be avoided is an either-or struggle between the doctor and the nurse to the patient's ultimate detriment.

Institutions must train or provide supervisors and teachers of family therapy without undercutting or devaluing the existing skills of teachers and other staff members who have not been trained in family therapy.

Integrating different approaches to family therapy *within* a family training program may also be difficult. There is a wide spectrum of family therapy training, ranging from experiential orientation at one end, to structural orientation at the other.[18, 24] The middle of the spectrum is a combination of these orientations. Probably the soundest recommendation is to take a pluralistic approach by combining the best of the various family therapy models and techniques.

Family therapy offers many models. Some therapists start by taking one of these models—for example, "structural family therapy" (after Minuchin)—and using its language concepts until they are thoroughly familiar with it. Also initially taking parts of various therapy models and applying them haphazardly will usually confuse both therapist and family about what is going on. That there is no generally agreed upon language, theory, and way of proceeding in family work can become upsetting to the trainee. In individual therapy there are at least some defined, established schools—for instance, behaviorist, psychoanalytical, Gestalt, and so on. In family therapy there are movements, but they are not yet sufficiently integrated or differentiated to have become established schools of thought.

Some critics feel that family therapy has no coherent theory. But, as in any new field, those who stay inquisitive and open-minded will find it more exciting to follow the shifting currents—where they will be able to contribute to defining what sort of family therapists they are—than to settle for an already existing model that provides security but perhaps limits growth. Family therapy may be the metaphor for change in the psychotherapeutic movement.

The days of cultism and dogma in psychotherapy, in general, and family therapy, in particular, are inappropriate for the training of a therapist. Human behavior is complex, multifaceted, and multidetermined. Therefore the teachers of family therapy should resist presenting either a one-sided model of family therapy or a single model of family therapy.

CONTINUING EDUCATION FOR THE STUDENT
OF MARITAL AND FAMILY THERAPY

Some trainees might find it particularly valuable to use source material for more extended study in the clinical application of family therapy principles. For such students the authors make the following recommendations to supplement the references already given in each chapter.

It is always useful to observe other therapists actually doing therapy, and a number of films are available. Ackerman's films are especially interesting for their historical importance and strong personal qualities, which do not always emerge so clearly in his writings.[13, 14] Haley and Hoffman[25] have put together an interesting book that contains transcripts with experienced family therapists. Included are discussions between the therapists and the authors of the book, in which the therapists are asked to explain what they are doing and why.

Some books that describe the family approach of a particular therapist or school are also recommended for comparison. Satir,[26] Ackerman,[27] and Minuchin[28] are three of the classic examples. Ferber, Mendelsohn, and Napier[29] and Bloch[30] have presented collections of individual papers for the student on a variety of topics concerning family therapy.

Papers of interest to family therapists appear in the journals *Family Process,* (which also includes book reviews) and the *International Journal of Family Therapy.* A more extensive and systematic annotated bibliography of the field can be found in the National Institute of Mental Health (NIMH) bibliography covering 1960–1964[31] and that of Glick and Haley covering 1950–1970.[32] There are articles in the journals of other fields, such as marriage and family counseling, sociology, psychiatry, nursing, and social work that are also of interest to the family therapist.

Part of the excitement as well as the potential confusion of this expanding field can be savored by being aware of and sampling current developments. In that sense we view this book as a beginning in bringing together some of the major currents and trends in the field.

POSTTRAINING EDUCATION

At the conclusion of a family therapy training program, the trainee's education is actually just beginning. In a rapidly changing field such as family therapy, an individual must begin a program of lifelong self-education based on a continual awareness of the literature and course work, and on the need to evaluate his or her own work: to entertain new ideas, and discard old ones. As obvious as this may seem, it is the inculcation of these principles that identifies the inspired and skillful clinician, teacher, or researcher.

TRAINEE EVALUATION FORM FOR FAMILY THERAPY

Trainee: _____

Supervisor: _____

Dates of
Supervising Period: _____

Type of therapy supervised:
(e.g. Individual Family Therapy, or Multifamily Therapy, etc.) _____

Frequency of Therapy: _____

Frequency of Supervision:
(e.g., each week for 1 hour in a group of 4, etc.) _____

The numbering system permits five choices. They can be defined as follows:
  (5) Far exceeds reasonable expectations. Only a few trainees will merit this.
  (4) Usually exceeds reasonable expectations, but is not really outstanding.
  (3) Always meets reasonable expectations, but occasionally exceeds them. Most will merit this rating.
  (2) In general meets reasonable expectations but occasionally falls short.
  (1) Often falls short of reasonable expectations.
  (0) Insufficient knowledge to make a judgment or not relevant.

Figure 21-1. Trainee Evaluation Form for Family Therapy Trainees. (Adapted from Payne Whitney Psychiatric Clinic's *Resident Evaluation Form* and from *Family Trainee Evaluation Form,* developed by Constantine.[21] Reprinted with permission of Family Process, Inc.)

330

I. *Overall Rating*

II. *Clinical Work*

These descriptions represent the current thinking on the criteria for successful completion of our (Cornell University Medical College) training program in each of five areas of competence. In each area the first description applies to completion of the first year and the second description to completion of the entire program.

A. Basic Knowledge _____

1. Has acquired a basic fund of knowledge about how family systems work and can demonstrate an ability to make conceptual links between his or her own experiences, the experiences of others, and this kind of knowledge. Understands and can make use of basic family-systems concepts: process and structure, psychopolitics, dimensional analysis of process, boundary and entry phenomena.

2. Has added to a basic fund of knowledge and integrated more elaborate and specialized concepts of how family systems function. Is familiar with more than one theoretical framework for understanding and affecting family systems. Can develop an idiographic (working) theory of a particular family and understands the uses of idiographic and nomothetic (general) theories of family.

B. Generation and Use of Information: _____

1. Has demonstrated an ability to take in, and make use of, information about the self and his or her professional behavior and performance, including openness to both approval and disapproval.

2. Has developed skill in selecting and delivering feedback to others; understands factors of style, modality, timing, and context that affect a person's ability to take in and utilize feedback. Can participate productively in mutual peer reviews and supervision of his or her family work.

C. Interpersonal Flexibility: _____

1. Can identify salient aspects of his or her interpersonal style, especially preferences for particular psychopolitical positions and maneuvers and is aware of his or her tendencies toward stuck arrangements.

2. Has taken specific steps to increase his or her interpersonal flexibility and has demonstrated increased psychopolitical flexibility in both therapy and peer group contexts.

Figure 21-1 (continued)

D. Self-Awareness and Use of Self: _____
   1. Has increased awareness of ways in which his or her self and personal family history are a part of present work as a therapist and other interpersonal process. Can relate seminar experiences and family-systems concepts to personal family experience. Has been able to share and make use of personal history in the learning process. Has revealed a capacity for change in some significant area.
   2. Has demonstrated increased awareness of his or her self and immediate experience of self and can use this information in the therapy situation. Has made use of personal experience and family history in therapy and learning processes. Is evolving an effective personal style of therapy that includes a presentation of self or style of entry compatible with being a therapist—that is, conducive to alliance formation, not excessively aggressive, critical, etc. Has gained insight into how his or her psychopolitical patterns originated and how these are played out in the present, especially family and interpersonal contexts that tend to lead to replay of old patterns.
E. Interviewing and Intervention: _____
   1. Has acquired a basic knowledge of the interview process and salient issues in initial interviews, including the interviewer's and family's anxiety, the entry process, the information of alliances, etc. Knows some of the strategic moves he or she *should be able* to make to gather information about the workings of a family system and to bring about change. Has developed skill as an observer of process and can organize his or her observations, in a meaningful and useful way.
   2. Has demonstrated an ability to conduct family interviews and to execute effectively therapeutic manipulations in live situations. Can evaluate a real family system and develop an idiographic theory or map of the family. Has shown an ability to plan evaluation and therapy strategically, making use of both idiographic and nomothetic theories to devise focused interventions. Has used a variety of tools and techniques of evaluation and intervention.

Figure 21-1 (continued)

III. *Supervisory Relationship*
      A. Ability to accept and utilize criticism   0 1 2 3 4 5
      B. Capacity to learn from supervisor   0 1 2 3 4 5
      C. Establishment of collaborative relationship   0 1 2 3 4 5

IV. Are there any questions about this trainee's integrity or emotional stability? This question is extremely important.   YES _____ NO _____

V. *Special Areas*
Comment on special talents, nature, and degree of character interference with learning or administration.

VI. *Additional Comments and Suggestions*

VIII. *Trainee's Response to Evaluation*
Include areas in which disagreement occured.

Trainee's Signature _____ Date _____
[This indicates that this evaluation was seen by the trainee and discussed with that person.]

Supervisor's Signature _____ Date _____

Figure 21-1 (continued)

REFERENCES

1. Sanders F, Beels C: A didactic course for family therapy trainees. Fam Process 9:411–423, 1970
2. Foote C, Levy RJ, Sander FEA: Cases and Materials on Family Law (2nd ed). Boston, Little, Brown, 1976
3. Umbarger C: The paraprofessional and family therapy. Fam Process 11:147–162, 1972
4. Hall R: A paraprofessional's view of supervision. Fam Process 11:163–169, 1972
5. Haley J: Problem Solving Therapy. San Francisco, Jossey-Bass, 1976
6. Bodin A: Family therapy training literature. A brief guide. Fam Process 8:727–779, 1969
7. Belliveau F, Richter L: Understanding Human Sexual Inadequacy. Boston, Little, Brown, 1970
8. Brecher E, Brecher R (eds): An Analysis of Human Sexual Response. New York, New American Library, 1974
9. Sager C, Brayboy T, Waxenberg B: Black Ghetto Family in Therapy: A Laboratory Experience. New York, Grove Press, 1970
10. Bodin A: Videotape applications to training family therapists. J Nerv Ment Dis 148:251–262, 1969
11. Ferber A, Mendelsohn M: Training for family therapy. Fam Process 8:25–34, 1969
12. Family Assessment Series. 16mm color sound film 240 min. (Psychological Cinema Register, Pennsylvania State University, University Park, Pa., 16802)
13. In and Out of Psychosis: A Family Study. 16mm black and white sound film 120 min., by Nathan Ackerman, MD. (The Family Institute, New York, N.Y. 10021)
14. The Enemy and Myself. 16mm black and white sound film 50 min., by Nathan Ackerman, M.D. (The FAmily Institute, New York, N.Y. 10021)
15. Family Therapy: An Introduction. 16mm black and white sound film 43 min., by Ira D. Glick, M.D. (Cornell University Medical College, Payne Whitney Clinic, New York, N.Y. 10021) and George J. Marshall, Sr. (Medical College of Georgia, Augusta, Ga 20904)
16. Family in Crisis. 16mm color sound film 48 min., by David R. Kessler, M.D. (Langley Porter Neuropsychiatric Institute, University of California, San Francisco Medical Center, San Francisco, Ca 94143)
17. Lewis JM, Beavers WR, Gossett, JT, et al: No Single Thread: Psychological Health in the Family System. New York, Brunner/Mazel, 1976, p 4
18. Beals EW: Current trends in the training of family therapists. Am J Psychiatry 133:137–142, 1976
19. Burdill DR: The simulated family as an aid to learning family group treatment. Child Welfare 55:703–709, 1976
20. Rakoff VM, Sigal JJ, Epstein NB: Predictions of therapeutic process and progress in conjoint family therapy. Arch Gen Psychiatry 32:1013–1017, 1975
21. Constantine LL: Designed experience: A multiple goal-directed training program in family therapy. Fam Process 15:373–387, 1976
22. Montalvo B, Haley J: In defense of child therapy. Fam Process 12:227–244, 1973
23. Shapiro RJ: Some implications of training psychiatric nurses in family therapy. J Marr Fam Counsel 1:323–330, 1975

24. Group for the Advancement of Psychiatry. The field of family therapy. Report No. 78. New York, Group for the Advancement of Psychiatry, 1970

25. Haley J, Hoffman L: Techniques of Family Therapy. New York, Basic Books, 1967

26. Satir V: Conjoint Family Therapy: A Guide to Theory and Technique. Palo Alto, Ca, Science and Behavior Books, 1964

27. Ackerman N: Psychodynamics of Family Life. Diagnosis and Treatment in Family Relationships. New York, Basic Books, 1958

28. Minuchin S: Families and Family Therapy. Cambridge, Mass, Harvard University Press, 1974

29. Ferber A. Mendelsohn M, Napier A: The Book of Family Therapy. New York, Aronson, 1972

30. Bloch D (ed): Techniques of Family Psychotherapy, A Primer. New York, Grune & Stratton, 1973

31. Family Therapy: A Selected Annotated Bibliography. Washington, D.C., National Clearinghouse for Mental Health Information, 1965

32. Glick I, Haley J: Family Therapy and Research. New York, Grune & Stratton, 1971

Family by Jonathan Glick.

22

A Case Transcript of a Family Treated Over a Sixteen-Month Period

OBJECTIVES

- To give examples of the types of processes that occur during the course of family treatment
- To give examples of the kinds of interventions that the therapist can make
- To discuss the rationales behind these interventions

INTRODUCTION

Many trainees find an actual case transcript useful in helping to bring to life the didactic concepts discussed earlier. In this chapter we present excerpts from actual family diagnostic and treatment sessions that lasted once a week for 16 months; also included is a 10-year follow-up.

An introduction to each segment, then the transcript, and finally comments will be presented. The transcript is from a movie made by one of the authors and is available for use in conjunction with this chapter.[1] It can also be compared to transcripts of parts of cases published by other family therapists.[2,3] Furthermore there is a book devoted to 11 excellent, full-length case studies of family therapy done by experienced therapists with a step-by-step account of their thoughts about the cases and their reasons for what they did.[4] In a like vein others have described their cases in depth, alternating transcript with explanation, session by session.[5]

BACKGROUND INFORMATION
ABOUT THE FAMILY

This transcript is based on treatment of a family over a 16-month period. It demonstrates family techniques (including videotape playbacks) and problems that arise during therapy and gives an overview of the course of a family treatment from beginning to end.

The family includes Mr. S, age 50, a minister; Mrs. S, age 48, a housewife who also plays the organ at her husband's church; a daughter, age 18, who is away attending college; and the identified patient, the 25-year-old son, Bill. Bill is an unemployed college dropout with a history of two prior acute schizophrenic episodes, the first one at age 16. Following his third decompensation, he was treated as an inpatient in a university hospital. After his discharge the primary treatment used was family therapy; antipsychotic medication was not used.*

These sessions demonstrate treatment techniques used in working with a family in which the identified patient has a psychotic illness. The treatment involves a family that is in the empty-nest phase of development, in which the offspring have reached chronological adulthood.

The transcript that follows highlights segments from certain sessions during the course of this therapy.

SEGMENT 1: ONSET OF TREATMENT

Segment 1: Introduction

In the initial session, communication from individual family members is directed mostly to the therapist, rather than among themselves. This may be related to the fact that the family often attempts to force the therapist to be the judge. The therapist goes along with this in the first session, using the rationale of the side-taking function (Chapter 9) and serving as a role model for the father and son in dealing with the mother. Other family therapists might use the style of encouraging members to talk to one another. This would be a matter of the therapist's choice.

Segment 1: Transcript

Therapist: In our initial consultation we ended up talking about what we would do for the future in terms of treatment for the family, Bill in particular. After reviewing the entire case and my discussion with all of you, it is my feeling

---

*In the early 1960s, the use of antipsychotic medication for the treatment of schizophrenia was more controversial than it is today.

that Bill's problems are very much related to the problems of the family, and, to best treat him, we should treat the entire family as a unit in family therapy. That is, we would meet every week for 50 minutes. I think from 3:40 to 4:30 every Wednesday, if that's okay with you.

Mr. S: Well, it is. It would suit us if we could meet a little earlier—we have engagements—she and I both on Wednesday nights; but *(pauses)* we're going to work with you at the time that you best feel.

Therapist: Okay. We've had a couple family sessions now, and the only rule I am going to set is that we all meet together. I'll be working with you— sometimes very much involved in one discussion, other times I'll let you carry it— you're the family and you have to make the decisions. And the main thing I'll be trying to do is to make sure that everybody gets a chance to talk. What we're working for is better understanding and communication, as well as the goals that you talked about last week. Do you recall them—what you wanted to get out of treatment?

Mr. S: Well I don't know if I recall just how we stated them, but I believe we said that, first of all, we wanted to help Bill to get into his problems and disturbances and then . . .

Therapist: Help Bill *into* his problems, did you say?

Mr. S: To get into his problems, I mean discover what the basic difficulties are, and I think probably we said something about helping him with the drinking problem, which may be due to these difficulties; and, if I remember right, we were going to try to improve the entire family situation.

Therapist: Uh-huh. And Bill, you also had some specific goals you wanted. Do you know what they were?

Bill: (looking down at the floor and not at the therapist) Well, I just wanted to relieve my mind a little bit somehow. During the last few days and all of today I've been thinking that's really the worst thing there is now that I'm getting all these meanings out of things and I just somehow know maybe that I don't read things right. I used to do this even in . . . just two or three years ago back at school; I'd just get off on some of these things, *(referring to his paranoid thoughts)* and . . . *(pauses)*

Therapist: One of the things, one of the goals you had, was to work on some of these thoughts and meanings. You also wanted to do something very concrete, as I recall.

Bill: Yeah, so I can get over this and maybe live.

Therapist: Live, meaning what? You said you wanted to get out . . .

Bill: Get out and go to work, and . . .

Therapist: Right, get out and work. Okay, that's what we decided and that's what we ought to aim toward: to get you out of the home and to get you working.

Mrs. S: (to therapist) We're willing to work with you to achieve these goals.

Segment 1: Comment

In Segment 1 we see that the therapist: (1) conveys the idea to the family that the problems of the identified patient have something to do with the entire family; (2) establishes rapport with the family; (3) explains the goals of treatment; (4) begins to point out the interaction processes involving the identified patient and the other members of the family (e.g., the comment about "helping" Bill, the identified patient, to get "into" his problems); and (5) begins to establish ground rules for treatment (such as, that the family members all meet together and that they all have a chance to talk).

In the initial session one observes both the family and the identified patient and notices that the patient is paranoid. He covers his face with his hands because he fears other people are talking about him and laughing at him. It is also revealed that he drinks when he begins to become delusional. At present, he is sleeping in the same bed with his parents, because they claim they are worried about his behavioral problems (when, in fact, they fear intimacy with each other).

SEGMENT 2: HISTORY TAKING (3 Weeks Later)

Segment 2: Introduction

Segment 2 illustrates techniques of obtaining a family history (Chapter 5). There are two main objectives: (1) to obtain factual historical material and (2) to clarify patterns of family interaction.

This segment also shows the effects of the interaction between the parents on the identified patient. While the parents fight, the patient holds his head and leans back in his chair. Mrs. S's role and the patterns of family interaction in general are beginning to change; the son is beginning to take a prominent role in the family's communication patterns.

Segment 2: Transcript

Therapist: All right, from Bill's comment earlier . . . he commented on a demand. Apparently there was some demand, though . . .

Mrs. S: Uh-huh. No, there was *not* a demand. In fact, I think I'm going to say this right now before Bill, although I don't want to worry him with it. We had tried to hold back from demanding, if you want to call it *demanding;* it wouldn't be *demanding,* ah . . . frankly, I think we've held back too much by trying to keep down any religious pressure that may be caused by his being a preacher's son. Sometimes I think we have held back too much and sometimes I think we've hurt Bill by holding back. . . . *(Family begins arguing and Bill holds his head and leans back against his chair)*

Therapist: This is a real . . . this is a real loaded. . . .

Mrs. S: If you wanted to go to Sunday school, you went. If you wanted to go to church, you went.

Bill: I never missed.

Mrs. S: No, you never missed but . . .

Bill: . . . except when I was going to college.

Therapist: Hold it a second. This sounds like a real loaded issue *(laughter),* something we're going to come to once we get a little more history—that of the question of your going into the ministry or even going to Sunday school. We'll get to that. (This issue is later discussed at another session.)
Now, let's see, you were talking about a problem in the marriage. How did you finally work it out?

Mrs. S: Well, now, doctor. There wasn't . . . really wasn't . . . a problem except naturally. . . . They were going to sort of complain, which is natural.

Therapist: Uh-huh.

Mrs. S: I know they expected me to be so-and-so, and I just wasn't going to do it.

Therapist: You say "they," who are you . . .

Mrs. S: Preacher's wife or no preacher's wife.

Therapist: . . . whom are you referring to?

Mrs. S: The people, church members, I wasn't going to do it.

Therapist (To Mr. S): How did you feel about that? It was your . . .

Mrs. S: You know. I mean, I wasn't desperate . . . I was . . .

Therapist: It was his congregation, right?

Mrs. S: . . . the little things that are asked of you behind the scenes. Frankly, if they bother you, I think you ought to say what you think.

Therapist: Well, how did you feel about that and what did you finally do about it?

Mr. S: Well, I don't know if I exactly get into what she's saying . . .

Mrs. S: Well, I mean that's a little . . . I mean it wasn't a problem. It was just that he was talking about us talking together about my role as a preacher's wife.

Mr. S: Oh, yes . . . I . . . I . . .

Mrs. S: You know, you come home and complain sometimes about your church.

Mr. S: .Well, actually . . .

Mrs. S: And he wouldn't dare complain to his members. . .

Mr. S: Ah, we didn't discuss it . . .

Therapist: Wait a minute. You're both talking at one time.

Mr. S: We didn't discuss her role as a minister's wife a great deal. I had told her from the very beginning (and have continued to do so through the years) that she should just do what she wants to do without feeling obligated to the congregation because they're not . . . they're not paying her salary; they only pay mine. I work, although she does play the organ at the church on a voluntary basis.

Therapist: I think I'd like to pause a minute to go back to get a little history, so we have some kind of foundation on which to talk. I'm kind of an outsider, and I'd like to go back a little bit since we're all here in a kind of family. Do you think you can tell me how it was that the two of you met?

Mr. S: Well, actually our families lived in the same community for a time when we were growing up. Of course, I'm nine years older than she is. My father was a Baptist minister in the community and her father was a Methodist minister, and, of course, I noticed her as a little girl, but not with any ideas that we'd ever meet. Some years later, however, we did meet when I went to the town where she and her family were then living. I started to court her, and then I went off to school in Texas but would come back occasionally to see her. Things kept moving along and in one form or another we became engaged.

Therapist: What was that form?

Mr. S: Well, I suppose when we were engaged there was some uncertainties about our relationship. Another man came into the picture and she was considerably undecided. I think . . . maybe she wasn't entirely settled when we married. Of course, I took the position that a plain heart never won a fair lady and pursued the thing until I got her.

Therapist (To Mrs. S): "Fair Lady," how did you feel about . . .

Mrs. S: Well, I taught with this other man, and, since we lived in the same boarding house, we were thrown together very closely. And if I had wanted to marry him, I—and this is not bragging, it's just facts—I could have married him several times, but I did not. I want that understood. I wasn't planning to marry him, although he certainly had a good personality and was a nice person. We were both teachers in the school, but I got together with him because my husband was going to school in another state and coming home very little. If you live in the same boarding house with a person, you will most likely be together some; you can't help it—even if it is only at meals. And it did cause some conflict, yes, in my relationship with my future husband. But, even if I had wanted to marry this other man, I would have held back. At that time, I didn't think it was right to break engagements . . . I feel very differently now. I am older now; and I have thought things over. I think about young people these days; if they are engaged and find that they are not in love enough to marry then they should break the engagement, rather than marry that person and not live congenially. But at that time . . .

Bill: So you feel like you should have broken the engagement?

Mrs. S: No, I am not saying that, I am not saying . . .

Therapist: Excuse me, if you don't mind my talking. You thought she was saying that . . .

Mrs. S: I'm not saying that . . .

Bill: . . . that she should have broken the engagement with Daddy.

Segment 2: Comment

In this segment we see some indication of the difficulties existing between the husband and wife. (See Chapters 3 and 4 for a discussion of these issues.) The mastering of certain family tasks (especially those of developing and maintaining a marital and parental coalition and those of rearing and enculturating the offspring) is a source of contention between the spouses that apparently has never before been discussed. Mrs. S's unresolved feelings about her own role as a minister's wife, as well as that of a parent, seem to be related to her statements that perhaps she and her husband did not provide enough religious grounding for the identified patient. The therapist senses that this is an important issue, but one that may be too explosive to discuss this early in the therapy.

A core problem is the relationship between the parents. There is a major disturbance in the marital coalition, which is being worked out through the son. The parents are using the son's problems as a means of holding their marriage together.

SEGMENT 3: EARLY-MIDDLE STAGE OF TREATMENT (2 Months Later)

Segment 3: Introduction

The family has been in treatment for 2 months. The inappropriateness of the son's sleeping in the parental bedroom has been discussed, and the son has now moved back to his own room. The next objective was to get the son out of the parents' home and into a work situation. Encouraging increased parental communication led to a major shift in the family system. Bill eventually moved 200 miles away from the family and began working.

In this segment Bill begins to see his symptoms as foreign rather than as part of him.

Segment 3: Transcript

Bill: I saw the vocational therapist today. . . . And I always had difficulty not being able to read into people what I think they're thinking and this and that . . . you know. In a way he has sort of a pensive look and I kinda read into him that he's thinking, you know, that, ah, "Heavens, he's really gonna have a hard time finding a job." *(Laughs)* You know, he had a . . ., but I have a tendency to read a great deal into what people are thinking, and this and that and the other thing. I mean, you know, just like I told you . . .

Therapist: What did he say?

Bill: Oh, he didn't say that, ah, but . . .

Therapist: I assumed that . . .

Bill: No, no I asked him—he looked, you know, rather pensive, ah, a little bit thoughtful and somber. He's very nice, very somber and all, and sort of kindly and I don't know; and I just got the impression that he might think, you know . . . but he said that . . . we talked in terms of short-range plans and long-range plans and the idea of having maybe a short-term job.

Segment 3: Comment

This short segment highlights the crucial shift in the family: that of the son moving out of the home and getting a job. The therapist lets the identified patient do the talking and is there only to support him in case he (or the family) backslides by trying to sabotage his job plans.

SEGMENT 4: MIDDLE STAGE OF TREATMENT (8 Months Later)

Segment 4: Introduction

It is now eight months into therapy. The family has accepted the central notion of family therapy; that is, the problems of the identified patient are related to the problems of the family. Bill's symptoms have decreased as other problems in the family have been brought to the fore. At this point core issues involving the intimate relationship between the couple can again be approached.

In this segment the marital couple are seen alone. The decision to do this was made only after a great deal of preliminary groundwork, the most important of which was separating the son from the parents and establishing rapport with the parents to reassure them that therapy would not make their relationship worse.

The couple, who have not been away in ten years, is talking about taking a vacation together. Mrs. S says that she does not want to be alone with her husband because it will mean that they may have to have sexual relations. It has taken eight months for this subject to be brought up, albeit in disguised form.

Segment 4: Transcript

Mrs. S: Disgusted, just disgusted! And I have felt that, just disgusted. And that's all there is to it, just absolutely disgusted with the whole thing. And I thought many times that he was positively acting childish, and I mean it, childish. Because we are plenty old enough not to get sexually frustrated and not to get all upset because of one point.

Mr. S: We're not into . . .

Mrs. S: Yes, it is important. I don't think it ought to *frustrate* people.

Therapist: I don't think frustration is the issue here; the issue is can the two of you . . .

Mrs. S: Well, he's said he's gotten frustrated.

Therapist: He also said that he wants to be close to you.

Mrs. S: Well, he's got to show up a little better himself, and I'm not blaming him.

Therapist: The two of you both have to make the effort.

Mrs. S: The two, yeah, I know it's the two.

Therapist: The two of you have to work at it. And if he's going to show some feeling toward you . . .

Bill, who has been outside, enters

Bill: Do you want to see me at all today?

Therapist: Yes, we do, and I'll be with you in just a second. You can wait outside.

Bill: Fine, I'll be right here. *(leaves)*

Therapist: It's got to work both ways, and I think this is very crucial to all three of you. And I think you have to try it. Even if you don't want to, you've got to.

Mrs. S: I'll just have to close my mind, and that's that.

Therapist: Well, I don't think you do because I think you have indicated in these sessions . . .

Mrs. S: I'll just have to close my mind.

Therapist: You have indicated that you have a great many positive feelings for him.

Mrs. S: Hmmm. I do have great concern for him. If I didn't, I'd have left him . . .

Therapist: Right.

Mrs. S: Yes.

Therapist: So I think you know that this can be tried. And you've got some time to think it over now. What did you decide about the vacation?

Mr. S: We'd decided to go but then she changed her mind. Later, with persuasion and consideration, she decided to go. We had planned to go Friday, but she was afraid that today's session would get her too upset and she would not want to go after all.

Therapist: Has everybody survived so far? Are you all . . .

Mrs. S: We're going to take you along.

Therapist (bantering): I could use a trip to Florida. *(Laughter)*

Mrs. S: Not because you're a doctor but just to have somebody else along. It might be good if we did have someone else along . . .

Therapist: I think it's a good decision for just you two to go.

Mrs. S: . . . and get our minds off of ourselves and our feelings.

Therapist (authoritatively): Look, go away, go to Florida, have a good time. As your doctor, I strongly recommend that you try this.

Mrs. S: Well, frankly, I'll have to close my mind to any sexual overtures; I mean that.

Therapist: Well, try to enjoy being with one another.

Mrs. S: All right, I'll just have to close my mind and be a . . .

Therapist: Let's have Bill come in and let's . . .

Mrs. S: . . . be a machine.

Therapist: Let's continue to discuss the same thing we've been talking about.

Mrs. S: Be a machine.

Therapist: I don't think you'll be such a machine if you truly love him. Allow for the intimacy to develop between you.

Bill enters

Bill: Well, have you said anything relevant about me?

Mrs. S: Have you seen Mr. Byron *(the vocational therapist)?*

Bill: No.

Therapist: Will anybody answer his question?

Bill: Has there been any discussion having to do with me?

Mr. S: Ah . . .

Mrs. S: Mainly with us.

Mr. S: The discussion was about us. We feel our relationship can be improved and that you have done a great deal on your part already. What we need to do is to . . .

Bill: As I came down the hall, I heard vaguely something about how I could slide back or something like that. Did you say that? I could just vaguely hear something. *(Puts his hands to his head)*

Mrs. S: We said that we wanted you to feel better, and that if we did better, you would feel better.

Therapist: Well, I also said the opposite, though.

Bill: What's that?

Mr. S: That if *we* didn't do better, you could slip back. That's what he said.

Bill: Is that what he said?

Mrs. S: And feel worse.

Bill: I thought I heard you say something like that.

Therapist: Well, I think you know that.

Bill: Yeah, yeah, I know, that's not surprising. Well, was anything else relevant said about me?

Therapist: What do *you* have to say about yourself that would be relevant. *(Laughter)*

Bill: I don't know. I just feel that somebody is always talking about me when I'm not around. I'm always, always . . .

Mr. S: Always what?

Bill: I'm just always suspicious toward people who are talking when I'm not around.

Mrs. S: You're not talked about as much as you used to be. You're not quite the center of the conversation as you used to be, because, for one thing, you're feeling better.

Bill: Well, I wasn't feeling good yesterday, nor do I today. I'm just really tired out. I worked 11½ hours yesterday and I am really exhausted. And I have been hyperventilating, too, a whole lot the last 2 days. Boy, that hyperventilation can really . . . *(Long pause)*

Mr. S: It's an out-of-condition body.

Bill: I have felt very dizzy all day and, yeah, just bad, just that I feel tired, that my face is hot and so on.

Therapist: Your complaints are the complaints of a hard-working man. . . .

Segment 4: Comment

At each point the therapist has to make critical decisions as to whether to intervene at all, and if so, in what way. The therapist must decide as best he can, during the onrush of the session, what the main themes and goals seem to be and how best to deal with them. Important issues recur continually. The experienced therapist does not worry that something important has been missed; there will always be another opportunity to deal with it later.

Since this was the first time in ten years that this couple was going away alone together, it was clearly an important item for them. Some therapists would have dealt with the vacation issue differently. Individual stylistic and attitudinal factors will specifically influence the manner in which the therapist intervenes and responds to a particular situation. Another therapist, for example, might have accepted the wife's offer to go with her on the couple's vacation in the hope of eliciting a reaction from the husband.

The other crucial intervention comes at the end of the segment when the therapist encourages the concept of Bill's working *in spite* of his symptoms. This is done in front of the parents, who in the past would have reinforced his dependency on them.

SEGMENT 5: VIDEOTAPE
PLAYBACK (10 Months Later)

Segment 5: Introduction

This segment illustrates how cognitive and verbal changes can occur as a result of behavioral changes. There has been a major shift in the family configuration. The family members are now able to talk about how "we weren't much of a family," the identified patient describes how he sent out "double messages," and they all talk about the ways in which their actions affect each other. The focus has also shifted from the identified patient to Mr. and Mrs. S, especially the latter. Bill is not absolutely quiet, as in the first segment, or hostile and negativistic, as in the second segment, but is showing more emotion, is better in touch with reality, and is experiencing more anxiety.

In this segment videotape playback is used with moderate success to try to break through the mother's denial and projection. Bill is commenting on what he observed during the playback of a previous session.

Segment 5: Transcript

Bill: What I want to do is to read out of it what is there.

Therapist: Well, what feeling was there?

Mrs. S: You've been suspicious for all these years, and if . . .

Therapist: Well, one other thing that was there was what Bill just said. . . . You said that your mother was what?

Bill: Oh, since the start she just sort of moved in and sort of took over; it seemed like she was protecting my . . .

Therapist: Right. We had said this about a month ago that she seemed to be. *(Turning to Mrs. S)* Remember I told you a month or two ago that I thought you looked like the center of the family and had taken over . . .

Mrs. S: I sure hope, I sure wish I hadn't been.

Therapist: You had said, "No, I'm not, I can't be." And here you are now as an independent observer looking up on the TV screen. Now watch the next session. See whether you can see who's running things.

Mrs. S: Okay, but wait. . . . You said something about me being the front of it. I didn't want to be the front.

Bill: Well, in the first one she wasn't so much as in that session.

Mrs. S: And I still mean it, too.

Therapist: Well, I think you are less now than you used to be, but let's see this videotape of the third session . . .

Mrs. S: Or, maybe if we had more participation . . . but I won't say on my husband's part . . . I wouldn't have talked in front of him.

Therapist: Right. I agree.

Mrs. S: Okay.

Therapist: Your husband agreed on that too. He said if he would have done more. . . . Let's see the third one.

Mrs. S: Okay.

Videotape of earlier session, focusing on history taking, begins.

Therapist: Well, there appears to have been a lack of communication concerning the decision to have a child.

Mrs. S: Well, frankly, I was just very happy during pregnancy, and I just took it a day at a time. I just never really thought about having a baby.

Therapist: Your pregnancy was very good as far as you saw it.

Mrs. S: Yes, I felt very good. I felt real good during pregnancy when maybe some other mothers were nauseated and sick and . . .

Mr. S: I'm not asking the questions, I guess, but I just wondered what she meant by the . . . what she meant when she felt physically good. I don't remember your feeling so good.

Tape is stopped.

Therapist (to Bill): Well, as you see from the videotape, I think it bothers you when your parents disagree. That's why you try to remove yourself by pushing your chair away from your parents and staring off in the other direction. Notice how you look away and frown when we discuss your mother's pregnancy.

Tape resumes:

Mr. S: Mentally happy, or what?

Mrs. S: Well, physically and mentally happy. I thought I was happy.

Therapist: (to Mr. S) Why do you ask that?

Mr. S: Well, I just wanted to know if by that time she had felt more settled and that our home was being established. I do recall that she had told me once or twice that she wanted to have a child because she felt it would help our relationship. *(Mr. S places his hand on his son's shoulder.)*

Therapist: Were you angry about being pregnant?

Mrs. S: Angry? Did I say angry? I may have been angry.

Therapist: I asked if you were angry.

Mrs. S: Naturally when you're pregnant, you're going to . . . you have to be more settled because certainly it makes . . . gives a marriage more seriousness.

Therapist: Can you be more specific on what you mean by *settled?*

Bill (interrupting): That she and Daddy were going to break up; that's what it sounds like.

Therapist: You think it sounds a little. . . . Was there some question of breaking up in those first two years?

Mr. S: Well, I don't know if there was any more doubt than there has been from the start.

Therapist: The beginning, in the beginning, what was the question?

Mr. S (hesitates): When we married she just didn't seem to be quite certain. She didn't even seem certain after we married.

Videotape ends

Therapist: I think that's it. That was an interesting segment.

Bill: Well, one thing, I did act quite differently. Like I said, I looked like I don't know . . . I acted like a four-year-old child.

Mr. S: Well, the discussion we were having could make you feel like that.

Therapist: Hmmm. Exactly.

Bill: Well, that's what the doctor said.

Therapist: Do you follow that point?

Mrs. S: You mean make Bill feel like a little child . . .

Therapist: Yes.

Bill: Oh, the discussion about the pregnancy and the relationship being unsettled. Once you get pregnant that kind of seals it, you know, that kind of settles it. That could have been . . . I can't . . . I don't remember what made me act like that. I didn't remember having been that childish, the way I was acting.

Therapist: Well, you see. I think that session pointed out what's been happening for a long time. That's what's bothering you about your relationship with your parents and you show it. And you're not even aware you're doing it.

Bill: Yeah, uh-huh.

Therapist (to Mr. S): Did you see that? You were talking. The discussion was on your breaking up, and Bill looked away horrified.

Mr. S: You know, he sure was.

Bill: I was not sure all that was going on. I really was, wasn't I? And that was very different from the other two. I mean, in the other two I was more fiddling with my eyebrow and so on, but I looked quite different in that one, very different. I was really, I was turning one way and the other and had my head covering my face and things like that, that I did not do in the first two.

Mr. S: Well, it would seem to me that probably his feelings there . . .

Bill: The topic of my mother's pregnancy was very difficult to discuss.

Mr. S: . . . were the feelings he had from, say way back, because he was able to observe that we weren't able to understand much about the relationship between us?

Bill: And from the time I knew how you felt about the pregnancy.

Mr. S: Well, I mean, beyond that, as you were growing . . .

Mrs. S: That may have had something to do with it, but the way Bill was looking was a carryover from the way he was looking the first time we ever came.

Bill: No. It's dramatically different. Very different.

Mrs. S: You say it was different. Okay, I'll let you off. I didn't notice it, and I'll just sit and listen.

Bill: Very different. The first time, yeah, I mean, both times were what the doctor would call strange behavior; but the third time that we just finished with was just all, I mean, it was just all so different. Very different. The other two I did at least sit up, but I kept fooling with my eyebrow and I was saying different things, too—the doctor says sending out different messages. The third time I wasn't really consciously sending out any message, I don't think, unless it was just all on the problem like I was in the other tape. But it was different behavior, and it had a different meaning to it. Evidently I still can't recall at the time thinking . . . yes, yes, I can. I think that way even now. It brings all sorts of ideas to mind about, I mean, just the way I was moving, the way I act even now.

Mr. S (laughs and hesitates): I acknowledge and confess to one thing. That looked like there wasn't much family relationship there, but I'm sure we don't act like that all the time. It is evident, however, that our behavior affected Bill.

Therapist: Well, it not only affected Bill, it affected all . . .

Mr. S: Yeah. Affected all of us.

Therapist (to Mrs. S): Did you see that? What did you see there? (Referring to her dominance and her husband's passivity)

Mrs. S: Ah, I want to comment first on one thing. *(To Mr. S)* You're looking so hard . . .

Mr. S: Looking so hard to?

Mrs. S: Looking so hard to be able to say what you just said.

Mr. S: You mean I'm looking hard to . . .

Mrs. S: And that's discouraging. You're looking so hard for what you just said.

Mr. S: Well, it is hard to say.

Mrs. S: I said you're looking for, ah, you're trying to be on the negative so much and to me it's disgusting. I don't like it.

Mr. S: Well, now, wait a minute.

Mrs. S: I mean, he's trying to see the negative points and he always has.

Bill: That's pretty negative saying that.

Therapist: It's the changes in your behavior that we're looking for.

Mrs. S: It's negative; trying to look for the negative. Everybody wasn't negative.

Therapist: If you all feel better about yourselves as individuals and as a family, then some positive changes have occurred as a result of these sessions.

Segment 5: Comment

In this segment the therapist tries to identify the patterns that have changed in order to maintain the gains after therapy has stopped. He is active in challenging the mother's denial of problems. Families often focus on the past in order to avoid changes. For this reason the therapist focuses on the present and the positive changes that have occurred.

SEGMENT 6: END STAGE
OF TREATMENT (16 Months Later)

Segment 6: Introduction

This is the last session, and it must be compared to earlier sessions. There is now a mood of tranquility in the whole family. Nobody is acutely ill at this point. A new equilibrium has been established. The couple is getting along reasonably well; they are more intimate and are having sexual relations regularly. The identified patient is adjusting well to his job and to living apart from his parents. There is considerable improvement from 16 months previously.

Segment 6: Transcript

Therapist (to family): You're doing pretty well, and *(to Bill)* you're doing pretty well.

Bill: Pretty good. I said, I'll tell you, it's really hard, I mean to imagine back when I was doing so darn much worse. I mean it's hard now, you know, to even imagine, so I am doing pretty good, I mean, compared to what I was doing, I'm doing just marvelously, I mean. I was just very . . . I don't know, the whole world just seems different altogether. But you're bound to run into a few snags if you are out of it as long as I was. And I pretty much was out of it. In fact I never, I don't know, I never really grew up at all, say like even when I was 14 or 15, and whether you just, whether you call it being extremely sheltered or what, it was that, and I don't know what else. I just was, I just don't know—shut in, maybe. I found out so many things just in the last eight months that I just didn't dream of, I mean, you know, that I just didn't have any idea that it was that way, you know, that things were that way. I just didn't get out in the world much, say from the time I was back in high school on, from the time I was maybe 14 or so.

Mr. S: I don't recall that we sheltered . . . tried to keep you from getting out or anything like that. In fact we've been wanting you to get out.

Long silence

Therapist (to Mr. S): I think we now realize that there was resistance on both sides over the issue of separating.

Segment 6: Comment

Although this segment is very brief, it does highlight the change in equilibrium. Whereas previously Mrs. S had been controlling, dominating, and hostile, now she is very quiet. Mr. S expresses his feelings and thoughts more readily. He also is able to tell his son that he wants him to get out from under the family's wings. Mr. and Mrs. S are now much better able to communicate and have a greater inner contentment as shown by the longer periods of comfortable silence. The identified patient also explains that things are working out for him. He does not have the same anxiety and somatic complaints that he demonstrated in the earlier sessions.

EPILOGUE (10 Years Later)

The family was contacted by telephone at 5 and at 10 years following onset of treatment.

The relationship between Mr. and Mrs. S had continued to get progressively better. They felt more comfortable with each other and were able to be more intimate. Mr. S continued to be more active, both as a husband and as a father. (This had been a problem prior to treatment.) Mrs. S was not as fearful or depressed about Bill's behavior or about her marital relations. She had worked for a year, stopped when they moved, and then did not go back to work. She described her role as "helping my husband," a family task she had previously resented. She described their relationship as "no two people could be closer." Husband confirmed this, as did the son (who had been quite critical of their relationship prior to his illness).

The identified patient had a 10-year history of working episodically for about three-quarters of the time. He had lost three of four jobs, probably related to his inability to do complex tasks. He had worked in his present job (as a teacher's aide) for 3 years and was receiving excellent evaluations. When he lived in a smaller town, he described his relationships with people "as more than adequate." Since moving to a larger city in order to get better employment, he had had fewer contacts with others, however, and described this as a "problem." He continued to be episodically symptomatic. He had minimal paranoid symptoms and mildly incapacitating obsessive–compulsive and phobic symptoms. He had two brief hospitalizations, one for 2 days and one for 7 days, and was treated with phenothiazines in low doses during this time. He has never regularly taken medication over a sustained period of time.

At the 10-year follow-up all three family members were very enthusiastic about the family treatment. They felt that the therapist had not put the blame on any one family member. Mrs. S said that the therapy was "a blessing." Bill said that therapy had helped him to improve greatly, and he felt as if it had "resurrected" him.

REFERENCES

1. Family Therapy: An Introduction. 16mm black and white sound film 43 min., by Ira D. Glick, M.D. (Cornell University Medical College, Payne Whitney Clinic, New York, N.Y., 10021) and George J. Marshall, Sr., M.D. (Medical College of Georgia, Augusta, Ga, 30904)
2. Minuchin S: Families and Family Therapy. Cambridge, Mass, Harvard University Press, 1974
3. Haley J, Hoffman L: Techniques of Family Therapy. New York, Basic Books, 1967
4. Papp P: Family Therapy. Full-Length Case Studies. New York, Gardner, 1977
5. Napier A Y, Whitaker C A: The Family Crucible. New York, Harper & Row, 1978

Siva and Parvati (?) Veined sandstone, Baphuon Style, Late 11th Century A.D., Khmer. Courtesy of Asian Art Museum of San Francisco, the Avery Brundage Collection.

APPENDIX A
The Structured Family Interview

One way of obtaining certain types of family information is to use a series of structured questions and tasks in family evaluation.[1, 2] These are used to probe certain specific variables and also to indicate to the family, by implication, some ways of thinking about families and some areas of family life that the family members themselves may have overlooked.

This procedure has been used as an initial evaluation and can be completed in 45 minutes to 1 hour. A one-way, vision–listening room may be desirable, since it allows the therapist to withdraw momentarily at appropriate points. This allows family members to work on the tasks, with the interviewer listening and observing but not actually present.

In one of its forms, this interview consists of seven parts. The interviewer meets with the entire family, and following normal introductions, questions the family or presents them with tasks as follows.

What is the central problem in this family at this time, in your opinion? The interviewer asks this of each family member, in turn, with all family members present. The interviewer attempts to maintain the focus on the *family problem at the present time* rather than on one or another individual, or on past difficulties. In this first task each family member receives an equal chance to speak, without interruption, and should get the impression that his or her opinions and views are worthwhile and important and will be listened to. Usually one of the parents will be called upon first, the other parent next, and then down the line of the offspring in descending chronological order. It may be useful to consider calling first on that parent who has been less involved in family matters or who seems more withdrawn, hesitant, passive, or weak.

The interviewer will begin to note the frames of reference that are delineated by the family members in discussing their difficulties, whether these are seen as family or individual problems, which individuals seem to be bearing the brunt of blaming, how the identified patient deals with his or her role, what the alliances are within the family, who seems to get interrupted by whom, who speaks for whom, and who seems fearful or troubled about expressing an opinion. The interviewer may offer some simple statement indicating an understanding of the family members' communications, but no extended discussion is necessary at this point. This, together with further elaboration of data gathered from the other parts of the structured interview, can be left for a separate, more extended discussion at the very end of the session or, if time is not available, it may form the basis for the second session, in which the therapist, after having had a chance to study and reflect on the data, discusses these with the family, with their implications for family difficulties and family therapy.

Plan something that family members can do together. The therapist first asks the entire family to spend a few minutes planning something that all of them would enjoy doing together. The therapist may step out of the room to observe and listen behind the one-way mirror and return to hear what they have planned in a few minutes. Next the children are asked to leave the room and the marital pair are asked to plan something together that just the two of them would enjoy doing together. The interviewer again leaves the room, to return in a few minutes to hear what they have planned. Then in similar fashion, depending on the size of the family, all other family dyads and triads might be called on in the same way. At the very least one would want to pair the marital couple, the identified patient with one parent, then with the other, and finally other combinations as appropriate.

This task, of course, is an implicit message to the family members that they should be able to interact with one another in all these combinations in mutually agreeable and satisfactory fashion. The interviewer–observer will often readily note from this section of the interview which family channels are open and which are blocked. The role appropriateness of the interaction can be ascertained, as well as the styles of decision making. In one instance a father and daughter working on this task came to realize that they had drifted apart, each thinking, erroneously, that the other was not interested in much mutual interaction, and neither checking this out verbally with the other over the years.

How did the marital partners meet and decide to get married? This is asked with just the husband and wife present, and they are encouraged to elaborate at some length on the implications of this question, first with the therapist on an individual basis and then together. Not only does this tend to focus on what was most often a happier time than the present—and so serve as a useful corrective to the discouragement and frustration that one often sees when families in crisis appear for treatment the first time—but it may also help to clarify the mutual illusions and expectations of the "infatuation phase" and shed light on later realizations, disappointments, and patterns. It is often valuable to note the reason for and nature of the early mutual attraction and to trace the relationship through the periods of engagement, marriage, and honeymoon. (Further elaboration on this period of the family's development is given in Chapters 3 and 4.)

There are often unresolved feelings of anger, bitterness, and guilt relevant to this phase. These have served to distort or at least strongly color subsequent family developments, and they may need to be aired as part of any other attempt at family therapy. One woman poured out in great detail strong feelings of bitterness at her husband's having abandoned her for long periods during their engagement and even subsequent to their marriage, forcing her for a time to return home to live with her mother, a circumstance which her mother used as further ammunition against her daughter. In addition the couple's sexual adjustment during the honeymoon period was very unsatisfactory. Both of these issues the wife had never discussed with her husband for fear that he would leave her altogether, since she was convinced of her basic unworthiness. The strong negative feelings were never resolved and only served to sour and cripple the marriage over the years.

The parents are asked to arrive at a mutually satisfactory interpretation of a proverb that they are given and then to call in their offspring and teach it to them. This process is, of course, particularly interesting to observe in the families of the schizophrenic patient. Their transmission of disordered thought processes—illogicality, general vagueness or meaninglessness—and the fact that no one has labeled this process as such may in such families be quite striking at times (see Chapter 12).

In one instance two parents were together able to decide on the meaning of the proverb "A rolling stone gathers no moss," although it was apparent that the mother had considerable difficulty making up her mind amongst a variety of possible meanings. When the two parents finally had agreed on a meaning and called in their daughter, a striking thing happened. The daughter, who had recently recovered after having been hospitalized for an acute schizophrenic episode, was asked by her parents what she thought the meaning of the proverb was. She responded with a variety of possible interpretations, one of which had to do with the possibility of a stone rolling uphill. The mother, at this point, instead of commenting on the unlikelihood or impossibility of such an event, commented on how interesting a possibility that was and how she herself had never thought of the meaning of the proverb in that sense, while the father kept silent.

Family members are handed cards on which they are asked to write down the outstanding fault of the family member seated immediately to their left. The interviewer indicates that several other cards have also been written based on the therapist's perceptions of some of the family members during the session so far. The cards are then collected and the therapist reads off some of the faults, one at a time, asking each family member in turn about whom in the family does the fault most apply. Through the addition of the extra cards, the therapist can make sure that certain concepts get discussed and can tailor the particular family traits to coincide appropriately with the particular family being dealt with. Thus for a rather low-energy, covered-over, pseudomutual type of family, some of the faults listed were "too good," "too weak," "no enthusiasm," "doesn't speak clearly," "too sensitive to criticism," and so forth.

In this section family members are obviously given permission to be critical of one another in a protected setting, with anonymity assured. The types of faults mentioned by them, as well as the degree of unanimity or lack of unanimity with respect to the family member matched with the fault, will be of considerable interest. The types of faults with which the therapist will "load" the discussion will often indicate to the family by implication that certain characteristics they may never have considered problematic or, in fact, may actually have considered positive attributes are here being thought of as carrying a negative connotation.

The second part of this section involves the therapist's asking each family member in turn to state what he or she considers their own outstanding fault to be. This is often strikingly helpful in making people more thoughtful about themselves and helps family members begin to understand one another much better. It may be the first time in their family history that they have carried out such a conversation together.

Family members are now asked to write down the most admirable quality of the family member seated immediately to their left, with the therapist again adding some cards of his own.

While the family members identify the positive qualities of one another, the therapist will add specific qualities to the discussion that may be particularly appropriate or provocative. Then the family members in turn will be asked to speak about what they consider their own outstanding quality.

In addition to being able to make the same sort of correlations noted above, this section also serves to give people permission to consider actively the positive features of other family members and explicitly encourages self-respect and healthy self-assertion by asking all family members to talk about their own best quality. This sort of interaction, too, may represent a distinct breakthrough for many families.

If the identified patient is an offspring, each family member in turn is asked which of the two parents the identified patient most resembles. This section can give valuable insight into family myths, alliances, projections, and displacements.

Obviously other specific questions will be found valuable in other circumstances, and not all of the above questions will always be equally appropriate.

This type of structured interview can be made to yield valuable data at the same time that it implicitly indicates to the family areas of interest and general attitudes that the therapist deems to be important. In addition the therapist's general manner and the specific sorts of family processes that are encouraged and discouraged during the interview will in themselves be seeds of therapeutic growth. The art of family therapy involves the therapist's making a series of judgments and disseminating information among family members in such a way that it leads to growth rather than destructive blaming, name calling, or needless suffering, which can lead to stagnation and fixation of patterns.

REFERENCES

1.   Watzlawick P: A structured family interview. Fam Process 5:256–271, 1966
2.   Family Interviews with Virginia Satir. Part 1. Structured Interview. 16mm black and white sound film 46 min., by Virginia Satir (School of Social Welfare, Educational Media Laboratory, University of California, Berkeley, Ca)

Holy Family with Saint John by Anthony Van Dyck. Courtesy of the Collection of the
Phoenix Art Museum.

APPENDIX B
The Family Case History

The family case history consists essentially of getting a detailed, narrative, longitudinal account of the family system through two or more generations (some family therapists strongly advise obtaining at least a three-generation family history), together with specific cross-sectional data relevant to the family's present characteristic modes of interaction and adaptation. This case history is in many ways analogous to the psychiatric case history (and its mental status examination) that is traditionally utilized in the individual treatment of psychiatric patients. As discussed in Chapter 5, the advantages of this sort of evaluation are that a great deal of information may be accumulated to help in trying to understand the family, that the history-gathering process itself may be quite therapeutic to the family, and that for the inexperienced therapist there is hardly any substitute for this technique as a means of becoming intimately familiar with what happens in a variety of families.

On the other hand this process may be slow and cumbersome, and the gathering of voluminous data may at times serve more to confuse than to clarify the nature of the important core issues. If the family is in crisis—as it often is when coming for therapy—and if the information gathering is conducted in a mechanical, inflexible manner with little or no attention to pressing, urgent cerns, the family may become impatient and turn elsewhere for help.

The comprehensive family data outline below was utilized by the Albert Einstein College of Medicine group.[1] This is a more conceptually complex outline than the one discussed in Chapter 5 and may be useful in helping the therapist consider various frames of reference, as well as in organizing the data to indicate where some key problem areas reside (see Table Appendix B-1).

SETTING

1. What is the nature of this situation in which you are learning about this family? What kinds of behavior do you expect to see in this social setting?

Table Appendix B-1
An Outline for Evaluating Families: Summary

	Content	Conceptual Framework
I.	Structure	Thinking as a demographer
	A. Internal	
	B. External	
II.	Individual Actors	Holistic and synthetic views: thinking as a novelist
III.	Family Themes (Content Issues)	
IV.	Values	Analytic cross sections: thinking as a social scientist
V.	Role	
VI.	Communications	
VII.	Emotions, feelings, moods	
VIII.	Object Relations	
IX.	Development	All of the above, with a time dimension

2. What is the overt, defined purpose of this interview in the mind of each participant?
3. What covert purposes emerge from the behavior of all participants during the interview? The interviewer–therapist has overt and covert purposes, too.

AN OUTLINE FOR EVALUATING FAMILIES (IN DETAIL)

I. Structure: Classifying the Family on "Public" Dimensions
    A. Internal
        1. What is the age, sex, and relationship of household members?
        2. Families of origin—who are they?
        3. Families of procreation—who are they?
        4. Who are the current "important" family members—that is who is emotionally relevant to the situation under scrutiny?
    B. In relation to total society
        1. What is the ethnic group—race, national origin?
        2. What is the class—occupation, education?
        3. What is the religion?
        4. What is the place of residence—that is, rural, urban?
II. Individual Actors: The Person in Center Stage
    A. How does each person feel about his relationship with each other person in the family? Each member's subjective experience of his family.
    B. What is that person like? An objective assessment of each individual as seen by a professional outsider.

III.   Family Themes (Shared Content Issues): The Family in Center Stage
   A.   Overt, what they talk about all the time—for example, money, moving to California, father's work failure, and so forth.
   B.   Covert, recurrent emotionally laden themes—for example, will we starve, can we trust one another?
IV.   Values: The Goals of Life
   A.   Family as a unit: are the family's values congruent with those of its community—that is, extended family, ethnic group, religion, social class?
   B.   Family as a system: are there value conflicts within the family—for example, between the couple, across the generations?
   C.   Family as a collection of individuals: within each individual are there value conflicts?
V.   Role: What People Do in Social Systems
   A.   Family as a unit
      1.   What is the family's relation to the economy—(give labor, get goods, have assets)?
      2.   What is the family's relation to polity—(give loyalty, get leadership)?
      3.   What is the family's relation to community—(give participation, get support)?
   B.   Family as a system
      1.   Major internal structures
         a.   Are there coalitions between the parents?
         b.   Is there a boundary between the sexes?
         c.   Is there a boundary between the generations?
      2.   Characteristic subgroups
         a.   Coalitions (working alliances)
         b.   Pairings (loving couples)
         c.   Splits (persistent hostilities)
   C.   Family as a collection of individuals
      1.   Husband as leader, lover, provider
           Father as nurturer, disciplinarian, companion
      2.   Wife as follower, lover, nurturer
           Mother as nurturer, disciplinarian, companion
      3.   Each child in age, sex-appropriate roles
VI.   Communication; The "How" of Meaningful Behavior
   Two basic kinds of information: what is new—the information about novel events: what is usual—the information about the static properties of the system, definition of constant relationships.
   A.   Family as a unit
      1.   Channel: how much of the two basic kinds of information in each channel?

         a.   Lexical
         b.   Paraverbal
         c.   Movement, gesture, posture, facial expression
         d.   Action—being present or absent, hitting, bribing

2. Clarity: does each message focus and become clear or does it become tangential (i.e., change into something else) or amorphous (i.e., dissolve into nothing)? A focus on the fate of a message through time.

3. Congruence: are the many messages about the same topic (there are always several congruent with one another)? This refers to the logical structure of the messages and their sequences (e.g., denial, double binds.)

B. Family as a system for each dyad

1. What is the relative degree to which that dyad is complementary or symmetrical?

2. What is the degree of overtness and covertness? How much do these people take responsibility for their messages to each other (Refers to A2 and A3)?

C. Family as a collection of individuals (each person may be assessed as a sender and receiver of information, utilizing the dimensions of A and B)

VII. Emotions, Feelings, Moods

A. Family as a unit

1. What are the family's typical moods, emotional climate?

2. What are the boundaries, the limits of feeling, in this family? What is *not* allowed or feared?

3. How much contagion of anxiety and depression? How dealt with?

B. Family as a system (examine each dyad in the family on the three polarities)

1. Accept–reject

2. Dominate–submit

3. Love–hate
Are there any concealed three-person systems as revealed by feelings of jealousy and envy?

C. Family as individuals
Refer back to II, Individual Actors

VIII. Object Relations
In an existential sense how are the family members related to the family and to one another? The following is a descending scale from mature to immature:

A. Mature: self-differentiated from other; other seen for his or her own qualities: relatedness present

B. Transference: self-differentiated from other; other seen as if he or she were someone else, usually a member of self's family of origin: relatedness present

C. Projection of "good me": self not differentiated from other; other seen as if he or she were someone else, the embodiment of self-valued qualities; self often feels a lack of these qualities and would like more of them; relatedness present

D. Projection of "bad me": self not differentiated from other; other seen as if he or she were someone else, the embodiment of self's hated qualities; self usually does not acknowledge that self possesses these qualities; relatedness present

E. Fusion–Merger: self and other not differentiated; contagion of affects with no "motive" for the feeling prominent; relatedness present

F. Self-relatedness: relatedness absent; self involved with self alone; other seen solely in terms of need gratifying or frustrating properties

All six modes of relatedness are seen in almost all families. It is the quantitative preponderance that is crucial.

IX. Developmental History through Time

A. Normative crises: the significant turning points each family must experience
1. First meeting of parents
2. Engagement
3. Marriage
4. Birth of children (especially first)
5. Children starting school
6. Children beginning adolescence
7. First child leaving the home
8. Last child leaving the home
9. Retirement of major wage earner
10. Death of spouse

B. Nonnormative crises
1. Internal: deaths, illnesses, separations, and additions of other members to family
2. External: major employment shifts, war, flood, moving

REFERENCES

1. Ferber A, Mendelsohn M: Personal communication

Author Index

Subject Index

a
b
c
d
e
f
g
0 h
1 i
8 2 j